COMMON GROUND

STUDIES OF THE WEATHERHEAD EAST ASIAN INSTITUTE,
COLUMBIA UNIVERSITY

STUDIES OF THE WEATHERHEAD EAST ASIAN INSTITUTE,
COLUMBIA UNIVERSITY

The Studies of the Weatherhead East Asian Institute of Columbia University were inaugurated in 1962 to bring to a wider public the results of significant new research on modern and contemporary East Asia.

For a complete list of books in the series, see page 231.

Common Ground

TIBETAN BUDDHIST EXPANSION AND
QING CHINA'S INNER ASIA

Lan Wu

Columbia University Press
New York

Columbia University Press
Publishers Since 1893
New York   Chichester, West Sussex
cup.columbia.edu
Copyright © 2022 Columbia University Press
All rights reserved

Library of Congress Cataloging-in-Publication Data
Names: Wu, Lan (Professor of history), author.
Title: Common ground : Tibetan Buddhist expansion and
Qing China's Inner Asia / Lan Wu.
Description: New York : Columbia University Press, [2022] | Series: Studies of the Weatherhead East Asian Institute, Columbia University | Includes bibliographical references and index.
Identifiers: LCCN 2021054367 (print) | LCCN 2021054368 (ebook) | ISBN 9780231206167 (hardback) | ISBN 9780231206174 (trade paperback) | ISBN 9780231556354 (ebook)
Subjects: LCSH: China—Foreign relations—1644-1912. | China—History—Qing dynasty, 1644-1912. | China—Politics and government—1644-1912. | Tibet Autonomous Region (China)—Foreign relations—17th century. | Tibet Autonomous Region (China)—History—17th century. | Tibet Autonomous Region (China)—Politics and government—17th century. | Dga'-ldan-pho-brang dynasty, 1642-1950—History. | China—Relations—China—Tibet Autonomous Region. | Tibet Autonomous Region (China)—Relations—China.
Classification: LCC DS754.18 .W85 2022 (print) | LCC DS754.18 (ebook) | DDC 327.51051/5—dc23/eng/20220217
LC record available at https://lccn.loc.gov/2021054367
LC ebook record available at https://lccn.loc.gov/2021054368

Cover design: Milenda Nan Ok Lee
Cover image: Detail of Mandala Gate, metalwork made in Tibet, 18th century, Rubin Museum of Art C2004.36.1

This book is dedicated to Inner Asian Buddhists in general—living or departed—and one in particular: Chen Guifang (1928–2017), my beloved grandmother. She lived her life to its fullest. I miss her, every day.

SONG [WHEN I AM DEAD, MY DEAREST]

When I am dead, my dearest,
Sing no sad songs for me;
Plant thou no roses at my head,
Nor shady cypress tree:
Be the green grass above me
With showers and dewdrops wet;
And if thou wilt, remember,
And if thou wilt, forget.
—CHRISTINA ROSSETTI, 1848

CONTENTS

ACKNOWLEDGMENTS ix

NOTE ON TRANSLITERATION AND TRANSLATION xv

Introduction: Buddhist Inner Asia 1

Chapter One
Campaigns 31

Chapter Two
Manufacturing 59

Chapter Three
Assemblies 86

Chapter Four
Governance 118

Epilogue: A Balancing Act 150

NOTES 157

BIBLIOGRAPHY 195

INDEX 221

ACKNOWLEDGMENTS

By any stretch of the imagination, writing a book in the English language had never crossed my mind as something I could or would ever do. Then, in the spring 2007, I stumbled across Gray Tuttle's seminar Ruling Inner Asia from Beijing. Even after that serendipitous semester, I continued to doubt whether I was equal to the task. Gray has always reassured me that it could be done and I could do it. As always, he is right. Now that I have my own students, I aspire to share the same support and empathy Gray extends to his students. Ever since I invited him to join my dissertation committee in 2010, Johan Elverskog of Southern Methodist University has always made time for my many questions and concerns about writing, research, career, and how to fit these puzzle pieces together. Madeleine Zelin has pushed me to think harder about how to tell a story of Qing history. Early on in my doctoral studies, I was pleasantly surprised to find inspiration in Pamela Smith's research seminar on knowledge production and circulation in the early modern world, her unfaltering support made my years at Columbia University much more memorable. Dorothy Ko has cultivated my appreciation of material culture through her research and her classes. Going to her class is a journey of discovering beautiful things and the history behind them.

Mentors outside of my dissertation committee have similarly shown their support in recent years. Lauran Hartley has expertly managed the

Tibetan collection at Columbia University. Mark Elliott of Harvard University taught me the Manchu language; his passion for history and his knowledge about Qing history made my summer in Cambridge delightful and fruitful. Mark also invited me to give a talk at Harvard University in February 2020. Little did I know back then that this would be the last time I joined a meeting in person—an experience that is now in the distant past, and many of us continue to long for its return. Isabelle Charleux has been so generous and kind in guiding me and sharing sources on Mongolian art production; after a chance encounter in the summer of 2021, who would have thought a Zoom conference call would be so helpful? Through an unexpected connection, Garret Olberding offered to read my manuscript when it was first completed in the summer of 2020. Garret returned it with thoughtful and constructive notes throughout. I don't know how to thank him enough for his kind offer, but I hope to express my gratitude to him in person in the valley in the near future.

Patricia Schiaffini-Vedani has inspired me to dream big, work hard, and live in the moment. Working with Pati since 2004 has fundamentally changed my outlook on life and taught me to embrace whatever life throws at me. Pati is my cornerstone. I would not be the person I am today without her.

I am not particularly good at maintaining contact, but a few friends have gone the extra mile to keep me in the loop. Daniel Barish has read chapters of my book and offered prompt and, more importantly, cheerful advice whenever I have reached out. Sujung Kim has saved this project, twice. Our daily writing accountability group in graduate school helped me finish a difficult chapter; during the COVID-19 pandemic, I was stuck with the same chapter once again. Sujung logged into Zoom each night with me for an hour—even though both of us were raising young children. If I could, I would put Sujung's name on the book cover as well. The amazing and inspiring Nicole Willock made sure to catch up whenever she was in town. Annebella Pitkin shares my challenges and my aspirations, and I will miss our writing dates. Sonam Tsering Ngulphu, Barton Qian, and Ling-Wei Kung have helped me locate sources and have offered support whenever I have reached out. Chelsea Zi Wang and Yijun Wang offered tips and advice on how to find time to write, or just write. Brenton Sullivan, Wen-Shing Chou, Benno Weiner, and Max Oidtmann have helped me with proposals for grants, with contacting presses, and finally with book revisions.

ACKNOWLEDGMENTS

It has been a long and costly process to produce this book, and I certainly could not have done it without financial support. I am indebted to Mount Holyoke College's Dean of the Faculty Office for its multiple grants and funds, and to the History Department for providing me with access to all the resources I needed to get this far. Prior to my time at Mount Holyoke College, I received institutional and financial support from Columbia University and from the University of New Mexico. In addition to conference presentations, Martin Fromm and Ling-Wei Kung have also invited me to deliver talks in recent years. All of these speaking engagements have helped me move the project forward. I thank them for these opportunities and thank those in the audience for their attention and questions. Librarians in Mount Holyoke College, the University of New Mexico, Columbia University, and many in East Asia have helped me obtain books or handle interlibrary loans beyond their call of duties. My heartfelt thanks to all of you.

Three anonymous readers provided constructive comments and helped me develop my narratives; I hope the final product here reflects many of their insights. Any errors are mine, of course. A superb editorial army has helped me in the last two years to bring this book to fruition. Ariana King of Columbia University's Weatherhead East Asian Institute and Caelyn Cobb, Monique Briones, and Leslie Kriesel at Columbia University Press have been patient, understanding, and, above all, professional in helping me cross the finish line. Robert Fuglei, Cynthia Col, and Adriana Cloud are three trustworthy editors who have helped me copyedit multiple drafts and have always asked the right questions to improve my prose.

The mandala gate that graces the cover deserves its own spot in the acknowledgments. I came across the image of the gate on one of these blah afternoons when I did not feel like working. Instead, I browsed the ever-growing selection of beautiful art on the Himalaya Art site. I was immediately drawn to this piece in the Rubin Museum of Art collection. Its intricate metalwork and its function as an architectural element are the reasons why I picked it for my book cover, because I discuss the topics in my chapters. I chose it long before I decided to use the mandalic concept to describe the fluidity and power gendered in Tibetan Buddhist expansion in the eighteenth century. It was a happy coincidence in the end. Thank you to Emily Nazarian of the Rubin Museum of Art for processing my request to use the image. People often say, don't judge a book by its cover; in this case, thanks to Milenda Nan Ok Lee's excellent work, please do.

I have had more than my fair share of good fortune to join two collegial history departments after my graduation. My brief stay in the University of New Mexico was truly humbling; it offered me the space to think hard about my research and learn from colleagues and students about what it meant to be a teacher. My more recent years in Mount Holyoke College have been equally enjoyable. I have learned so much from my interactions with all the bright young people, especially Karina Wu Fung, Cydney Hambrick, and Renee Russo. Colleagues in the History and Asian Studies departments have welcomed me and my family to the valley. It is not an overstatement to say that everyone in the two departments has offered tips on teaching and generously supported me as a junior faculty member. My colleagues on the third and second floor of Skinner have not only made me feel at home but have also invited me to their homes. I have emptied quite a few colleagues' fridges and have parked myself in their living rooms or on their decks. One of them got me back to running, and another one got me to go into the pool. Our office goddess, Holly Sharac, feeds me and shares my love for cooking and knitting. Last but not least, Lynda Morgan, what can I say? You are my sanctuary, regardless of your retirement.

It has been more than a decade since I first visited Amdo and got to know many scholars in Beijing, Inner Mongolia, and Mongolia. Life has changed, but challenges have persisted and difficulties have grown. My hesitation in naming my friends in all these places has unfortunately remained. You have fed me, hosted me, and taught me so much about history and life. It is my honor to have known you and to call you my friends.

My desire to leave my hometown and the subsequent long absence are, by all means, difficult for my parents, but they accepted them nonetheless. My in-laws have flown across the continent multiple times to fill in when I have needed to go to conferences or visit my parents. Abiel has put up with the grumpiness that overtakes me with each and every deadline. These moments have been numerous since we begun to build a life together—I don't think they will go away anytime soon, so good luck. As a working parent between a rock and a hard place, my answer to the perennial question of work-life balance is no, I don't have that balance, and I don't know how to find it. Oscillating between work and family, I have felt mostly unprepared and inadequate, and almost always tired. I must thank everyone who has helped me raise my son: babysitters, mom friends, all my child's teachers. It does indeed take a village to raise a child. Until I actually had a child, I thought I could be the village. No one has changed my life—literally or figuratively—more than Bayar. Each day he reminds me of what *joy* is in my life, and of course, it is him, not this book. Bayar decided he needed to step in to help me with the book when he was homebound during the pandemic. He highlighted page numbers, stapled pages, shot my portrait photo, organized my files, and never shied away from telling his friends that Mama was writing a book (Sorry, the book is not as interesting to you as *Big Nate*, I know). Bayar, please know that each time you ran to whisper your secret in my ear, I had the same secret to tell you: I love you.

Atkins Farm Country Market,
Massachusetts

NOTE ON TRANSLITERATION AND TRANSLATION

To render Tibetan names, I use the THL Phonetic System. For Tibetan Buddhist reincarnates, I provide generational order, title, and name; for example, the fifth Dalai Lama, Ngawang Lobzang Gyatso. For places, I use their commonly known names, such as Amdo (A mdo), Lhasa (Lha sa). I use Pinyin to romanize Chinese names, with Chinese characters provided on first mention. For Manchu terms, I use the Möllendorff transliteration system. I use the Library of Congress transliteration system to romanize Mongolian terms. All translations are mine unless otherwise noted. Cited publications are given in the original language, with English translations provided.

All official ranks and titles are translated in accordance with Charles O. Hucker, *A Dictionary of Official Titles in Imperial China* (Stanford, CA: Stanford University Press, 1985).

For research purposes, I have created a list of all figures and references included in the book on my website: HYPERLINK "https://commons.mtholyoke.edu/lwumhc/common-ground-whos-who/" https://commons.mtholyoke.edu/lwumhc/common-ground-whos-who/.

INTRODUCTION

Buddhist Inner Asia

> Revitalizing the Yellow-Hat Buddhists to propitiate the Mongols.
> —THE QIANLONG EMPEROR, *PROCLAMATION ON LAMAS*, 1792

The present book discusses the process by which the Qing imperial state and the Dalai Lama–led Tibetan Buddhist government came into close contact in the eighteenth century and developed strategies to grow symbiotically. The meaning of the book's title, *Common Ground*, is twofold. First and foremost, it underscores the process of finding common ground between the two powers. This fragile and contested process entailed both the Qing empire (1644–1911) and the Buddhist polity of the Himalayas relaying their respective standpoints, searching for areas where their concerns overlapped, and establishing a delicate balance when their paths crossed. Due to its precariousness, the process of finding common ground not only demanded negotiation and concession, but it also required acknowledgment that the balance was susceptible to changing power dynamics between the two sides and the specific context in which they interacted. One of the primary goals of the present book is to capture the changing dynamics in the space between the two political epicenters of Beijing and Lhasa. More importantly, the book also highlights the mutual interdependency upon which the two parties relied in their negotiations and how power flowed between the two. Broadly conceived, power in this project goes beyond political or social authority or control; instead, it was a "pliable substance" that moved among "different institutions and bodies of people."[1] Second, by deploying the term "common ground," the book also addresses how much this negotiated platform on which the Qing rulers drove home their vision of the empire owed to the cross-cultural Buddhist sphere in their Inner Asian border regions.

The introduction sets the scene for the study by providing historical context. It delineates how the Geluk School of Tibetan Buddhism rose to prominence in the Himalayas while the Manchus were gaining increasing authority in China—circumstances that led up to their more forceful encounter in 1723–1724, with the Lobzang Danjin Uprising in the eastern Tibetan region known as Amdo to the Tibetans. Against the backdrop of the expanding influence of these two overlapping polities, I proceed to introduce religious infrastructures that shaped the contours of a cross-cultural Buddhist knowledge network in the Qing empire's Inner Asia. This unique Buddhist space enabled both Tibetan Buddhists to extend their sphere of influence to the east and the Qing imperial rulers to craft their vision of empire.

BUDDHIST INNER ASIA BETWEEN BEIJING AND LHASA

What was Buddhist Inner Asia, and why is it important to use the space between Beijing and Lhasa to probe the process by which the two powers found common ground? The book's primary focus is space making, but it does not fixate space to a specific place or define a bordered legible administrative unit within an imperial framework. Instead, it destabilizes space and sets it in motion. The ultimate goal of this project is to consider how the process of making a Buddhist space within the Qing empire redefined power dynamics between two growing powers and how it was integral to imperial governance in the Qing, which inadvertently facilitated the eastward extension of the Tibetan Buddhist Geluk School's influence. Each of the sites under discussion was a nodal point that connected and stabilized yet restricted the cross-cultural Buddhist network; the making of each discursive site shows the contested nature of the interactions and negotiation of the two expanding powers. The interaction of the Qing imperial undertakings and the cross-cultural movements of Buddhist knowledge produced a sui generis space, which I call Buddhist Inner Asia. It has continued to influence the geopolitical relationships of modern-day China with its neighbors.

INTRODUCTION: BUDDHIST INNER ASIA

Where, then, was Buddhist Inner Asia? This spatially dispersed region stretched from Central Tibet in the Himalayas, crisscrossed mountain ranges and the upper reaches of the Yellow River, continued further east to Mongolian-speaking areas in present-day China's Inner Mongolian Autonomous Region, and finally to eastern Mongolia/southern Manchuria in present-day Liaoning Province. This narrow belt south of the Gobi Desert does not neatly fit Qing administrative divides, modern political configurations, or academic concentrations. This unusual spatial coverage of Buddhist Inner Asia calls for an explanation. I conceptualize its analytical framework with two aims in mind. First, Tibetan Buddhism had been a familiar religious force in these areas since the Mongol Yuan (1271–1368), and once again became a fixture after the sixteenth century, when Tibetan Buddhists devoted themselves to promoting the religion.[2] Buddhist literacy gained currency among increasing numbers of Buddhists living in this spatially expansive region. In the following pages, I explore how this writing-facilitated religious space emerged from both the Geluk School's efforts to produce Buddhist knowledge systematically on a large scale and the Qing's imperial patronage and appropriation of Tibetan Buddhism—especially in chapter 4, on Buddhist intellectuals in the Qing's capital city of Beijing. Second, Buddhist Inner Asia emphasizes the interconnectivity of regions, which current Qing historiography has categorically defined as the Qing's imperial frontiers, a term with the connotation of state power over and penetration of marginal regions. The Qing's annexations of Inner Asia reinforced the master narrative of military conquests, administrative shake-ups, and eventual absorption of the peoples living in the areas. This line of inquiry emphasizes the Qing's state policies and practices that strengthened vertical relationships between the state and each distinct region as well as thwarted lateral connections between these regions. However, this is only one side of the coin. By deploying the concept of Buddhist Inner Asia, this book intends to tell a story of lateral connections defined by Tibetan Buddhism under the Qing's imperial rule of these regions.

Tibetan Buddhism in Mongolia under the Qing in the eighteenth and nineteenth centuries was by no means simply a transplantation of Tibetan Buddhism from Tibet, nor was it independent from the political maneuvers of the Qing and the Geluk School's Buddhist government of Ganden Podrang, based in Lhasa.[3] In the chapters to follow, I will elucidate how the Buddhist space was not a static and empty canvas prior to the arrival of the Qing state; instead, it was full of vitality. Inevitably, the Geluk School's missionary endeavors realigned with the shifting geopolitical structure over the course of the Ming (1368–1644) and Qing.[4] However, this book views Inner Asia in the centuries leading up to the Qing imperial administration as a contested site where multiple systems of rule met, a dynamic space that was open to significant structural and social changes.

To open up new analytical space, I draw inspiration from research that has reshaped spatial boundaries in the transnational history and emergent histories of upland Southeast Asia, the Indian Ocean, the Mediterranean Sea, and the Atlantic world.[5] For example, a research forum on the Mediterranean and "the New Thalassology" has examined ocean-bound historical reconfiguration in studies of the Mediterranean, Atlantic, and the Pacific. This reconfiguration is not unique in rethinking space. Studies of trade and migrations across the Indian Ocean have similarly challenged the norm of the nation-state in historical narratives.[6] This new analytical paradigm defines the numerous—often flexible and permeable—spatial and temporal boundaries and uncovers new "frontiers" of the Indian Ocean world. Transnational history likewise highlights movement and interactions across space; for example, Engseng Ho has identified the term "Inter-Asia." This analytical framework draws our attention to mobile experience and artifacts in Asia and helps us to think more broadly about this mobile, spatially expansive, and interactive space that modern nation-states have tried to regulate and police.[7]

The space between states was a similarly useful analytical category in historical research before the dawn of the modern era. Thomas Barfield recommends considering the "mixed frontier zone" as a single historical system. This zone in Barfield's specific case not only stretched from Manchuria to the east to the Mongolian steppe to the west but also included north China.[8] Evelyn Rawski focuses on trade and interregional politics between 1550 and 1800—often called the "Ming-Qing transitional period" in North China and Northeast Asia, and shows that the nation-state or Chinese dynastic cycle should not be the only viable analytical scopes. Instead, state formation in China was influenced by how neighboring polities consolidated their power and thereby inched closer to China.[9] Indeed, accounts by and of diverse groups of mobile agents moved people, ideas, or practices across regions, and our historical inquiries must follow

INTRODUCTION: BUDDHIST INNER ASIA

them accordingly.[10] Moving beyond anthropocentric approaches, scholarly work on environmental history has studied patterns of human-nature interaction across space.[11] In *Common Ground*, I similarly adopt a spatial approach not defined by the Qing's administrative organization; in doing so, I seek to trace the movement of Buddhist knowledge assemblage in a highly mobile and spatially expansive Buddhist Inner Asia and stress the geopolitical changes and continuities caused by Buddhist expansion. Inner Asia as a Buddhist space helps undercut the assumption that lateral interactions between peripheral groups were either nonexistent or thwarted by the center.[12] Within Tibetan Buddhist texts, images, and ideas, Buddhist intellectuals formed an ever-expanding web of knowledge, which I heuristically call the religious knowledge network. Focusing on this network enables me to examine the movement of these Buddhist elements across regions and cultures. The Tibetan Buddhist knowledge network, as I approach it, is concerned with interpenetration between regions and sites, as well as with the power constructed in that transregional movement. Transregional studies of movement help eschew politically defined territory and complicate the binary metropole-periphery model.[13]

My proposal of the macroscopic framework of Buddhist Inner Asia is indebted to a number of recent works, all of which, in one way or another, depart from the binary model and study linguistically and administratively heterogeneous regions within Qing China. This book joins the growing effort to shift away from the imperial center in historical research. Two works that have been particularly helpful are Matthew King's *Ocean of Milk, Ocean of Blood* and Wen-Shing Chou's *Mount Wutai*. Chou's site-specific study of Buddhist sacred geography and how Mount Wutai was translated, represented, and interpreted in multimedia similarly addresses a Buddhist Inner Asia—even though Chou does not use the term—that was not defined by the Qing Qianlong emperor alone; instead, Mount Wutai was also a site "where the Buddhist Tibetans and Mongols could reinvent their own religious genealogies vis-à-vis the empire."[14] This discursive space traveled in and out of multiple media and helped shape both Mount Wutai and the Qing empire—an approach immensely helpful in my thinking about Buddhist Inner Asia. Similar in scope though different in content, Matthew King's study also explores Geluk monastic elites and demonstrates they were "active co-producers, mediators, and sometimes resistors of Qing imperial frameworks."[15] Accordingly, "networks of Inner

Asian scholastic institutions" (which I understand as Geluk's large Tibetan Buddhist monasteries that trained monk disciples) served as a constitutive element of the Buddhist world in Inner Asia.[16] In Qing historiography, the transregional approach has begun to overtake reliance on conventional culturally specific frontier studies. The growing literature on Xinjiang, Yunnan, Guizhou, Mongolia, Tibet, Taiwan, and, more recently, Manchuria has further challenged our understanding of how the Qing empire asserted its power and governed at the margins.

Many of the areas under discussion in this book fell into several administrative blocs within Qing territories from the eighteenth century. By the 1760s, the Qianlong emperor finally completed the territorial expansions that had kept his predecessors busy. For the preceding two reigns, a series of campaigns led the Qing troops to face many communities whose eventual defeats made them "frontier peoples" to the Qing empire. First, eastern and southern Mongolian groups formed an alliance with the Manchus. A quick administrative reconfiguration after the 1724 imperial campaign against the western Mongols managed to mask the always-contested political layout in the eastern Tibetan region known as Amdo. Central Tibet remained in the hands of the Geluk's Ganden Podrang government—which outlasted the Qing by a good four decades—until 1959, when the fourteenth Dalai Lama, Tenzin Gyatso (1940–), was forced to flee to India. The southwestern and southern parts of China were to experience the impact of a much more forceful Qing administrative presence, in which local chieftainships were transformed into district administrative positions (Ch.: *gaitu guiliu*), and the inflow of Han-Chinese migrants gradually changed the social life of these regions.[17] Areas to the far west beyond China proper came under Qing rule in the late eighteenth century, albeit with formidable challenges from a host of ruling elites.[18] If the Qing's administrative divisions are taken as an analytical foundation, research on the Qing's frontiers would more or less lead to distinctive units of fields: one on the Mongolian frontier, one on the Tibetan frontier, and one on the frontier with Xinjiang. These neatly demarcated socio-spatial categories run deep in research and have produced teleological historical concepts and narratives. This analytical approach considers the final stage of imperial consolidation as the default, which rendered the process static and altogether less relevant. Second, because the administrative divide was the point of departure for the construction of this analytical approach, focusing on state-engineered projects and issues associated with the center-peripheries divide made sense, but that is not enough, since imperial formation did not only occur in the court, in the metropolis, or at isolated frontiers. By reconsidering frontier zones as dynamic spaces interacting with the metropoles and other zones of contact, *Common Ground* argues that the Qing empire was not a state-engineered monolithic administration, but rather a flexible empire adaptive to shifting geopolitical landscapes, with a wide array of governing practices.

BEIJING: THE RHETORIC OF THE *PROCLAMATION ON LAMAS*, 1792

Imperial governance has been cemented as a central issue in Qing studies, and it is especially salient in research concerning Qing territorial expansions. The expansions and power consolidations were long undertakings that Qing rulers carried out until at least the 1760s.[19] The nearly six decades of the Qianlong reign (1736–1795) finally witnessed the completion of the prolonged expansion enterprise, which, unsurprisingly, has led to more concerted historical focus on the Qianlong emperor's visions of the empire. What made the process so lengthy and taxing was that Qing troops did not march onto "frontiers"—unclaimed lands where they could paint an empire on a blank page.[20] In fact, the Manchu Qing was not the only polity in the area looking to extend its influence in much of the eighteenth century.[21]

As his reign of almost six decades drew to a close in 1792, the Qianlong emperor (r. 1736–1795) decreed that a stela bearing his *Proclamation on Lamas* (Ch.: *Lama Shuo*) be erected at Yonghegong, the largest Tibetan Buddhist monastery in the Qing imperial capital, modern-day Beijing.[22] This quadrilingual statement in Chinese, Manchu, Mongolian, and Tibetan made two points. Firstly, it recounted how Tibetan Buddhists had been involved in the Mongol Yuan, Ming dynasty, and the Manchu Qing— the last three polities in the history of imperial China. The Qianlong emperor appeared to be critical of the institution of the imperial preceptor (Ch.: *dishi*) constituted in the Mongol Yuan because, he reasoned, these imperial preceptors "meddled in state affairs." He also refuted the allegation that he supported the Yellow Hat Buddhists imprudently (aka Geluk School–affiliated Tibetan Buddhists, whose yellow headwear set them apart from Tibetan Buddhists of other schools). He argued that only one imperial preceptor was recognized in the Qing by his grandfather, the Kangxi emperor (r. 1662–1722). He conceded that the institution of Buddhist reincarnation (Tib.: *trülku*) was problematic, because it had been compromised by Mongolian and Tibetan elites in preceding decades.[23] Indeed, the number of confirmed trülkus had skyrocketed since the 1740s, the early years of the Qianlong reign.[24] Many of the recognized trülkus intertwined with other lineages or local ruling elites both in Tibet and Mongolia. The religious concept of reincarnation is not a distinct Tibetan Buddhist one; an enlightened person is regarded as an emanation of a transcendent deity. But the trülku practice as an institution capable of mobilizing religious, political, and economic resources was unique to Tibetan Buddhism after the thirteenth century. The vast majority of trülku lines in Tibet have been male, and almost all the identified reincarnated Buddhists were recognized from a young age and grew up under the guidance of teachers and caregivers.[25]

How, then, to solve the problem? The Qianlong emperor's second point offered a solution: the practice of drawing lots, known as the "golden urn." Upon the passing of an influential line of trülkus, a name was to be drawn from one golden urn among several candidates, presided over by one of the two leaders of the Geluk School in Lhasa—the Dalai Lama or Panchen Lama—together with an imperial emissary; another golden urn was placed in Beijing's Yonghegong for the same purpose. The practice would essentially have been an intervention staged by a state power in managing important trülku lineages in Tibet and Mongolia, had it been implemented as intended.[26] Its actual implementation was far more complex and rested upon highly-placed Tibetan Buddhist trülkus, who saw in it something advantageous to themselves.[27]

The Qianlong emperor's statement in the *Proclamation on Lamas* recapitulated his long reign that had shaped much of Qing imperial geopolitical history, which in turn made him the very definition of a universalist emperor in early modern China.[28] Under his rule, the Qing imperial capital city became more cosmopolitan, and the empire prospered, with booming commerce and a tripled population. The proclamation was written at a time when his reign was winding down, and things were different from earlier decades, when he had seemed to embrace fully the practice of Buddhist trülku. To be sure, the Qianlong emperor's overtly critical remarks on the evolving institution of Buddhist trülkus were an important turning point.²⁹ However, as I will show in the following pages, to "propitiate the Mongols" in the proclamation was more a rhetorical device than an actual incentive for the Qing emperors to revitalize the Geluk School of Tibetan Buddhism. It would be misleading to take this afterthought for a blueprint for the Qing rulers, an approach that often portrays the Qing imperial imagination and management as a top-down scheme in a timeless fashion.

Common Ground seeks to understand how the Manchu imperial state developed strategies to consolidate its control in newly annexed territories in Inner Asia and how Tibetan Buddhists availed themselves of the state's imperial enterprise.³⁰ For that reason, it is imperative to look back beyond the final decades of the Qianlong reign, when the multiethnic empire was taking shape. It is vital to situate the Qianlong emperor's articulation of his imperial imagination within the changing geopolitical reality in Inner Asia that had started many decades prior to his reign. An exclusive focus on the magnitude of the Qianlong reign has three problems. First of all, it erases the imperial legacy that the Qianlong emperor inherited from his father and grandfather, who had dealt with their own geopolitical realities, before he was finally able to complete the imperial territorial expansions in the 1760s. Second, Inner Asia came to be seen as a timeless space, void of history and up for grabs. Owing to this perspective, current historiography is skewed toward paradigms focusing on state-driven Tibetan Buddhist patronage. It has reduced these Buddhists to mere silent recipients of imperial governance; even when some Buddhists command more substantial attention, they continue to be seen only in the shadow of the Qianlong emperor. A prime example is his religious teacher, the third Changkya, Rolpai Dorje (1717–1786).³¹ Finally, the focus on the endmost point of a variable process has produced a distorted story asserting that the Qing emperors supported Tibetan Buddhism to "propitiate the Mongols." To avoid these historiographical pitfalls, it is not enough to just recover the voices of the Mongols or Tibetans. Even if we accomplish that, we are still operating within the analytical structure that has positioned Manchu rulers at the top, Tibetans in Tibet, and Mongols in Mongolia, each of them apparently in an airtight compartment debarred from and policed against transgression. In contrast to this approach, *Common Ground* explores the movement of people, ideas, and practices, as well as the power generated by those movements. In doing so, the book calls into question the axiom of a stable, place-based narrative of Qing imperial encounters at the apex of its power. Each of the four chapters addresses the ever-evolving interdependency between Qing rulers and the communities they had labored to bring into their imperial and cultural orbit.

The period that *Common Ground* covers is bookended by two wars. This temporal scope overlapped more or less with two successive reigns—Yongzheng and Qianlong—within the epoch of the so-called long eighteenth century, or High Qing era.[32] This was a period of promise and prosperity that brought the Qing vast territorial and economic growth. First, in 1723, the Chuan-Shaan governor-general Nian Gengyao (1679–1726) led a military expedition to defeat the Qoshot, a strong subdivision of the western Mongol Oirat khanate, on the eastern edge of the Tibetan Plateau.[33] This conflict was a watershed moment in geopolitical realignment. At this time, the Qing empire was expanding into Inner Asia and the Himalayas; this expansion in turn gave rise to a cluster of Tibetan Buddhists from the region whose travels and writings formed the basis for this book. The timeline of the book ends with the war that prompted the Qianlong emperor to issue the *Proclamation on Lamas*. The proclamation's rhetoric was intended not only to curb Buddhist trülkus' influence over politics, but also to defend the more favorable approaches that he had taken in preceding decades. In 1790, General Fuk'anggan (1753–1796) drove a Gurkha army back to the Kathmandu valley in Nepal. The militant Nepali Gurkhas invaded Tibet due to an earlier dispute between Nepali authorities and the tenth Zhamarpa, Chodrub Gyatso (1741/2–1792). Significantly, the tenth Zhamarpa was a stepbrother of the sixth Panchen Lama, Pelden Yeshe (1738–1780), one of the most influential figures in the Buddhist Himalayas in the mid-eighteenth century.[34] The circumstances of this dispute may have changed the emperor's perspectives on the practice of reincarnation within Tibetan Buddhism across Tibet and Mongolia, or at least provided him with a pretext to make certain claims about it in his *Proclamation on Lamas*.

The Qing state's perspectives and practices have largely determined the framework for interpreting the imperial encounters between the Qing and whomever they later incorporated into the empire as borderland peoples. Seminal research has delved into wide-ranging topics, including the empire's careful safeguarding of imperial ideology, its military prowess, and its administrative rigor.³⁵ More recent work has complemented the state-focused approach by investigating local responses in specific cultural blocs.³⁶ Of the many distinct frontier zones, Tibet is no longer considered a self-explanatory description or a sufficient analytical category. Kham and Amdo merit their own histories, not just their respective inclusion within the entrenched power hierarchies of either Beijing or Lhasa.³⁷

LHASA: THE MANDALIC BUDDHIST GOVERNMENT OF GANDEN PODRANG

While the Qing's imperial practices have generated productive discussions, questions remain about Tibet, Tibetan Buddhists, the Geluk School, and the Geluk School's Ganden Podrang government around the same time. One persistent major issue is that Tibet came to be seen largely as a frontier zone that the Qing imperial state conquered and then governed. This approach has resulted in two trends in historical inquiry. First, the Qianlong emperor's long reign between 1735 and 1796 has attracted more attention, especially in terms of his Buddhist enterprise led by his religious teacher, the third Changkya, Rolpai Dorje. It reinforces the top-down view of the Qing's interaction with a community on its "frontier," which is true if and only if the Qing imperial perspective matters to its formation and governance. Second, within this framework, Tibet has mostly remained an internally homogenous and static entity in the studies of Qing-Tibet relations. This ahistorical outlook has conveniently—if unfortunately—reduced the Qing-Tibet relation to a legacy of the "lama-patron" (Tib.: *yönchö* or *chöyön*) relationship. This refers to a personal relationship forged between a lama and a ruler who mutually supported each other—a practice that had roots in Inner Asian traditions dating back to the Mongol Yuan ruler Kublai Khan (r. 1260–2294), when he appointed Pakpa Lodro Gyeltsen (1235–1280), the fifth patriarch of the Sakya School of Tibetan Buddhism as the imperial preceptor.³⁸ Even though recent studies have overturned the exclusive focus on this very paradigm and expanded the scope of research beyond the Qing imperial rulers, the lama-patron legacy has continued to influence current discussion of Tibet in the Qing empire.

Regardless, by the final year of the Qianlong's reign, the emperor, in his *Proclamation on Lamas*, clarified that the practice needed to be curbed due to Buddhism's influence in state affairs, a reference to the powerful

Sakya patriarch in Kublai Khan's court. The lama-patron heritage functioned as a sort of *translatio imperii* to evoke the long-established practice of the Mongol and the Sakya patriarchs, which the Qianlong emperor referred to when he envisaged a universal empire. However, the path to his crystallization of the Qing empire was complex and contested. To dislodge the Qing state as the only vector of historical investigations, it is imperative to understand and appreciate the complex sociopolitical history of Tibet between the fall of the Mongol Yuan and the comeback of the lama-patron reference in the Qianlong reign. The Geluk School is the youngest school of Tibetan Buddhism, posthumously recognizing Je Tsongkhapa (1357–1419) as its founder. Before its emergence as the dominant power, sociopolitical situations in Tibet had dramatically changed since 1260, when the Sakya patriarch Pakpa Lodro Gyeltsen received his title of "imperial preceptor" from Kublai Khan, the founding emperor of the Mongol Yuan dynasty and a grandson of Genghis Khan. By 1364, the Sakya estate had disintegrated into four parts, each of which was ruled by a member of the Khön family, also known as the Sakya clan, controlling the Sakya School of Tibetan Buddhism and the Sakya Monastery (f. 1073).[39] The division resulted in internal political and economic contests within Tibet that brought about new subsects and their respective monastic bases.[40] Even more consequentially, Sakya disunion contributed to the rise of the Pakmodru polity in 1350. The greatly weakened Sakya School did not have the resources to fend off the growing Geluk School, whose gradual dominance must be understood against this historically specific backdrop. The lack of aristocratic support and economic resources in general impelled Geluk Buddhists to diversify and expand their patron pool—Mongols and Manchus were all included later on. With the backing of the institutional and intellectual sources of Geluk power, these Buddhists' interactions with Qing emperors went well beyond the personal relationship of a religious teacher and patron. Qing-Geluk relations were fundamentally different from Yuan-Sakya relations, as the Geluk Buddhists commanded more resources at a much more volatile time.

Two years prior to the Manchu ruler crossing the Great Wall and relocating the capital in Beijing in 1644, the fifth Dalai Lama, Ngawang Lobzang Gyatso (1617–1682), seized political authority in Central Tibet. Like the Manchu rulers in these early decades, the founder of the Ganden Podrang government labored to consolidate his power. Assisted by his able regent (Tib.: *desi*) Sangye Gyatso (1653–1705), the fifth Dalai Lama established a strong presence in Lhasa, whereas other schools gravitated to other sites or reinvented their own monastic pratices in the changed political reality in and near the epicenter.[41] But his rise to power did not go unchallenged in the early years, even within the Geluk School.[42] The monastic establishments and the Dalai Lama's polity sometimes collaborated but at other times collided.[43] Even though the Dalai Lama trülku line is often considered synonymous with Geluk hegemony, the nominal head of the Geluk School is in fact the abbot of Ganden Monastery, one of three major Geluk monasteries in Central Tibet, founded in 1409 by Tsongkhapa. The Dalai Lama's Ganden Podrang government thus rested upon a complex power matrix both within his own school and also with other schools in Central Tibet. It had changed much of the sectarian and political landscape in Central Tibet and beyond since the mid-seventeenth century.[44] As Federica Venturi puts it, Tibet at the time was "a composite, nuanced and flexible structure in which power... fluctuated in one or another direction."[45] However, the fluidity in Tibetan politics rarely features in historical studies. The current binary paradigm of Beijing vis-à-vis Lhasa and the singular focus on the lama-patron dynamic leave little room to consider Tibet to be as multifaceted as it has always been, and, as a result, in studies of its interactions with the Qing empire, Tibet is oversimplified and deprived of its agency.

How did this governing body work and evolve over time? What implications did it have for the shifting geopolitical history of the region? Indeed, the operation of this particular polity has posed a challenge to understanding fully the dynamics between the two rising powers at the eastern terminus of the Eurasian continent. Recent reappraisals have identified the involvement of Tibet in cross-cultural and multidisciplinary projects; this identification reveals that Tibet has been integral to the unfolding of global history since the advent of modernity, with its own approaches to practices, technologies, and ideas that ultimately changed Tibetan society. If modernity is, in its most confined definition, a reference to "the West," then Tibet experienced "alternative modernities" at the very least.[46] But modernity has its own theoretical and empirical limits; as such, modernity creates its own set of issues for studies of Tibetan history—most notably, Tibetan modernity was adventitious, reactive, and circumstantial.[47] The harder we try to locate modernity in Tibetan history, the more disheartened we become, because it reminds us of Tibet's struggles to fit into the rigid and singular political framework of statehood in the modern era.

Tibet's Ganden Podrang Buddhist government was one such polity that lost its validity because it failed to achieve statehood in the twentieth century. Once again, the teleological historical approach has narrowed academic perspectives and distorted powerful regimes in the past. How did Tibet operate both within and without before modernity established the new world order? Was it possible for a power to be expansive without creating an empire? Could a polity create a structure without a centralized authority or clearly defined borders to be defended? More novel and positive responses to these salient questions reflect a changing current in studying empires across the world in recent decades. In his study of the Greater Comanchería, Pekka Hämäläinen delineates an extensive commercial network revolving around this Native American power whose "effective sphere of influence" extended south and west without "actual political boundaries." The expansive Comanche empire created a flourishing market and developed long-distance trading practices that stalled European expansions into these contested regions.[48] The Comanche people built "an interregional power with imperial presence" without a "rigid structure" or "clear-cut borders" that shaped the recent geopolitical history of the American Southwest and North America.[49] The Comanche people created an empire alongside those of the European powers in the eighteenth and nineteenth centuries. What enabled the Comanche people to successfully assert their power in the contested lands of the American Southwest, the southern Great Plains, and northern Mexico was their ability to forge flexible but highly organized systems to facilitate trade and alliances within Comanche society and with their allies and sometimes rivals. Inspired by this innovative approach to indigenous power, my book explores how religious infrastructures helped sustain a Buddhist presence even as the Qing grew more formidable in Inner Asia. It shows that Buddhist institutions helped shape relationships with other powers within and beyond Tibet.

Moreover, the workings of political structures have more norms than the prevalent hegemonic central state. This book takes inspiration from Stanley Tambiah's more holistic approach that he calls "the galactic polity"—a concept derived from the Indo-Tibetan Buddhist concept of the

INTRODUCTION: BUDDHIST INNER ASIA

mandala. In the mandalic model, a core (*manda*) anchors a surrounding element (*la*). Tambiah uses the galactic scheme to underscore the totality of Southeast Asian kingdoms and to emphasize the dynamics between the core and its surrounding polities.[50] As he explains, a galactic polity does not disaggregate the political, economic, religious, or cosmological dimensions of a polity; these kingdoms are "center-oriented but centrifugally fragmenting polities" that represent a fundamentally different political space.[51] These polities do not exhibit the prevalent bureaucratic hierarchy found in early modern empires or modern nation-states; rather, the center pulls together and holds in balance the surrounding polities.[52] To some, the concentric model of the mandala helps explain Tibet's unique legal cosmology or political ideology in pre-1950 Tibet. Rebecca French proposes that the entire legal system in Tibet resembles a mandalic structure: the sacred Buddhist core was encircled by secular administrative apparatus, and the central administration ultimately remains fundamental to all levels of legal administration.[53] Georges Dreyfus categorizes Tibet as a "semi-bureaucratic state" in which the political authority was in the hands of the charismatic Dalai Lama.[54] Both French and Dreyfus have focused on the centrality of powerful Buddhists in Tibet's secular political realms. In other words, the mode of the mandala in both of their studies firmly placed Tibetan Buddhism at the center, to which secular politics are moored.

My approach is different. I borrowed the concept loosely, finding Tambiah's galactic scheme to be useful in two ways. First, it helps to surmount the impasse of qualifying the Ganden Podrang government as a modern state. I hope to capture the ways in which Tibetan Buddhists exercised their power and extended their influence outside familiar political and administrative praxis. Buddhist practices and monastic institutions were operative in expanding Buddhism beyond Tibet in ways that were at once political, economic, religious, and spatial. Religious space, institutions, and practices have long been integral to political operations in the Buddhist Himalayas, including in Tibet. Seeing Tibetan Buddhism in light of political history does not reduce religion to a mechanism of political legitimacy; instead, it sees Buddhism as a social force that has shaped much of the geopolitical history of Inner Asia, northern China, and the Himalayas. Furthermore, this viewpoint emphasizes the flows of power caused by the center and its negotiation with varying levels of authority. Taken either as the original mandalic paradigm or as Tambiah's rebranded galactic scheme, the Ganden Podrang government is to be seen as situated within a discursive space, and its functionality as largely dependent upon other interrelated polities, all of which operated in a concentric fashion.[55]

THE OIRAT IN MAKING INNER ASIA

The Oirat people have been referred to as the Upper Mongols, the Oirat Mongols, the Western Mongols, or the Zunghar Khanate in Qing state narratives. The Zunghar state was a familiar fixture in Qing imperial history, and is centrally featured in Peter Perdue's rich monograph *China Marches West: The Qing Conquest of Central Eurasia*. In this extensive study, Perdue examines the Qing empire's westward expansion into Central Eurasia. Perdue focuses on the prolonged and taxing wars between the Qing and the Zunghar state roughly between 1670 and 1771, which spanned three reigns in the first half of Qing imperial rule.[56]

Prior to their final defeat at the hands of the Qing in the 1750s, the Oirat Zunghars claimed considerable influence over political, economic, and religious affairs along the eastern segments of the Silk Road, roughly the same area as modern-day Xinjiang and much of the eastern reaches of the Tibetan Plateau. Unfortunately, the perspectives of these important Inner Asian actors have not thus far featured sufficiently in Qing historiography, and when they have, they have often been seen as the historical backdrop against which the Qing empire succeeded in its expansion. This bias is in part due to the lack of attention to those who lost wars to the Qing. The Qing's long war against the Zunghar state was overwritten by the Qing's military triumph in historical accounts, as the victors write history. Recent reappraisal of the Zunghar Khanate and even the Oirat confederation shows promising new directions for reconsidering the regional history beyond the Qing's imperial perspectives.[57] Just how important was the Zunghar state in shaping early modern China? The Qianlong emperor counted the two campaigns between 1755 and 1757 to annihilate the Zunghar state among his "ten great campaigns" (Ch.: *shiquan wugong*) in his self-aggrandizing accounts of his achievements as an emperor. He was not the first emperor who loathed the elusive Zunghars, as his grandfather—the Kangxi emperor—led campaigns intended to capture Erdeniin Galdan (1644–1697), only to learn that he had already died years earlier. The

INTRODUCTION: BUDDHIST INNER ASIA

fearsome Zunghar leader's consolidated power had mounted pressure on the Qing's allies to the north and come face to face with the Qing in the 1680s, the start of the longest warfare that three Qing rulers were to engage in. The Kangxi emperor's several dozen letters to his crown prince while he was leading the faraway campaigns were saturated with agony and frustration about his failed campaigns to eliminate the resilient and powerful state in Inner Asia.[58] Perdue presents a detailed narrative of not only the Qing troops marching west and the tsarist Russian power moving east, but also the Zunghar state standing between the two powers as they closed in and signed treaties. In this volatile region and amidst increasing diplomatic negotiations between the Russian and the Qing empires, the Zunghar state collapsed and its people were nearly wiped out in the far northwestern corner of the soon-to-be enlarged Qing territory in the 1760s. What seemed to chiefly contribute to their downfall was, as Perdue argues, the economic vulnerability that pastoral nomadic powers have experienced throughout history. The environment did not work to the advantage of the Zunghars, and smallpox—a fatal epidemic for many Inner Asians—did not spare the Zunghars. What the Zunghars mastered in warfare simply did not make up for the odds against them off the battleground. The Zunghar state's ephemeral nature is often emphasized in order to explain the Qing's territorial expansions into its far northwestern reaches.

My intention here is neither to rewrite the Qing-Zunghar war that Perdue and a handful of others have pioneered nor to write a history of the Zunghar polity, whose nature is still up for debate and shows serious promise in terms of rethinking Qing imperial formation.[59] In fact, I have come to understand and appreciate the importance of the Oirat embarrassingly late, but better late than never. To me, to understand Inner Asia—whether as the Qing empire's Inner Asian frontier or part of the expansive Tibetan Buddhist world—one must keep in mind that the Oirat was a key variable in the historical development of this region. To that end, I will bring this important sociopolitical force into my discussion in three of the four chapters when specific historical events are crucial to rethinking how the Qing imperial rulers and Tibetan Buddhists found common ground.

For now, I will make two points with regard to the Oirat to shift the conversation away from an exclusive focus on the Qing's imperial perspectives. Firstly, I opened this section by using the term "Oirat" rather than

"Zunghars." The difference is central to this book. In scholarship, the Zunghar polity has been variously called a state, an empire, or a khanate. Its exact founding date has yet to be settled among scholars. This ongoing debate reflects our lack of understanding of how nomadic power organized its society when we do not insist on measuring it against state formation and politics in settled society. Moreover, there is no reason we should use the dynastic history of China as a yardstick to calibrate the social, economic, and political history of these nomadic regimes. Precisely for this reason, I use Oirat to situate the Oirat confederation as a driving force in shaping Inner Asian history in the seventeenth and eighteenth centuries, which covered but was not limited to the warfare between the Qing empire and the Zunghar state. My insistence on referring to the Oirat confederation is to extend my analysis both further back, to the era before the Zunghar formed a state in the 1670s, and farther south, from Zungharia in the northern half of present-day Xinjiang to the Buddhist world in the Himalayas. The Oirat expansion had a consequential impact on the Qing's negotiation with powers in both Central Tibet and eastern Tibet, which I will discuss in chapter 1.

RELIGIOUS INFRASTRUCTURES: MONASTERIES AND TRÜLKUS

This book argues that Buddhist infrastructural mechanisms enabled the Buddhist power to thrive. Some were mobile, like peripatetic Buddhists or portable Buddhist images; some were fixed, like monasteries and other built environments; still others moved across regions but not without elaborate planning, like Buddhist pilgrims and some truly enormous offerings. In the chapters to follow, I will address how composite religious infrastructures operated together to forge Buddhist Inner Asia. The working of the infrastructures not only helped define the shape of the transregional Buddhist knowledge network but also set it in motion. These physically grounded monasteries provided the friction necessary to stabilize the mandalic structure. Buddhists, texts, and artifacts mobilized knowledge in Buddhist Inner Asia; the act of writing and the dominant role of Tibetophone writings transcended multiple barriers and created a sense of religious belonging. In this sense, Tibetan Buddhist knowledge acquisition in the Qing empire's Inner Asia had a broad appeal to Tibetan Buddhists beyond Tibet. The interconnected formations of this Buddhist space under the Qing's imperial rule, as the book intends to show, were a product of the two powers' interaction, and in turn shaped their negotiation in that process. Buddhist Inner Asia, as I approach it, made the Qing empire's Inner Asia porous and full of vitality.

Both types of institutions—trülkus and monasteries—have engendered productive conversations and resulted in a range of new topics to define the current narratives of Tibetan history. Two recent studies on Tibetan Buddhist trülkus move beyond individual powerful trülkus or trülku lines, instead painting a fuller picture of the trülku institution in Tibet, especially since the seventeenth century. The trülku institution was a political innovation and a mode of transmitting religious authority. It provided an avenue for monastic groups to sever ties with the aristocratic families who had traditionally influenced monastic affairs. It emerged in the thirteenth century in Tibet and really took off in the fifteenth century.[60] Peter Schwieger meticulously charts the institutional history of Tibetan Buddhist trülku and situates the institution within the Tibetan Buddhist world across the Himalayas, and later on within the Qing empire.[61] Max Oidtmann discusses the history of selection of Tibetan Buddhist trülkus under the Qing in the eighteenth and nineteenth centuries and how Tibetan Buddhists negotiated their agency in that very process.[62] They both have gone beyond the individual trülkus and the Qing imperial rulers in thinking about Tibet vis-à-vis the Qing empire, but more needs to be done.

To be sure, it would be a major oversight to consider Tibetan Buddhist trülkus as the only type of Buddhist in the Qing empire's Inner Asia or within its imperial court. Isabella Charleux's thorough study of Mongol pilgrims to Mount Wutai on the border of China proper and Mongolia shows that not all Buddhist practitioners made the journey to one of the most important sacred mountains in the nineteenth century.[63] Wen-Shing Chou likewise attests to the financial and communal support that the Mongols poured into the monasteries on Mount Wutai when the Qing's imperial patronage waned in this century.[64] The sacred mountain similarly attracted Chinese-speaking Buddhists during the Qing. I, too, hope to expand the purview of Tibetan Buddhist world under the Qing beyond Tibetan Buddhist trülkus. As important as they were, they were not the only ones moving between Lhasa and Beijing, and, furthermore, the story of the Qing's interaction with Tibetan Buddhism needs to move out of the metropoles—both Beijing and Lhasa—and into the space in-between: Buddhist Inner Asia. This book does just that.

Even though my study primarily explores things and peoples in motion, it does not exclude immobility or the built environment, for they were essential to sustaining the network within which these mobile parts operated. The Qing and the Geluk Ganden Podrang government firmly placed their respective centers in Lhasa and Beijing; individually and together, they established Tibetan Buddhist monasteries in the Buddhist sphere of influence in Inner Asia. These monasteries were physically fixed in the landscape; they joined the two centers of Lhasa and Beijing to shape the contours of the Buddhist space, marked the shifting common ground in the negotiation of the two powers, and, most important of all, connected these nodes. Monasteries were the nodes of convergence in Qing Buddhist Inner Asia, also helping to transcend the spatial and administrative boundaries that have determined studies of the Qing frontiers. The major monasteries under examination here fell into different Qing administrative units, but shared mutual characteristics within the Buddhist world. This multimodal network provided the Buddhists with institutional mechanisms to reach far, and the Qing rulers with a place to materialize their vision of a cosmopolitan empire.

This book joins ongoing discussion of Tibetan Buddhist monasticism, a productive subfield of great energy in recent years. In his extensive study of monastic constitutions (Tib.: *chayik*), Brenton Sullivan showed how the Geluk lamas codified administrative practices within Geluk monasteries in the seventeenth and the first half of the eighteenth centuries. In his discussion, Geluk monks drafted, implemented, and abided by the monastic constitutions that defined a proper way of living as a Buddhist monk as the Geluk School expanded its power. Sullivan argues that those measures often found in state-building processes allowed Geluk monasteries to grow in a consistent and systematic manner. He challenges the prevailing narrative that the Geluk School's dominance in Tibetan politics and its geopolitical influence rested upon the power and money that the school received from its patrons, first the Oirats and the Mongols, and then mostly the Qing empire. Instead, his study argues that the rise of the Geluk School and its eventual ascendancy to power were fundamentally caused by making mega-monasteries: large monasteries with significant institutional complexity.[65] This institutional capacity of Tibetan Buddhist monasteries is the topic of another insightful book: in *The Monastery Rules*, Berthe Jansen illustrates how monasteries, especially those with established lines of trülku, brought in steadier incomes in the form of land or other material donations, including foodstuffs for designated rituals. Jansen likewise emphasizes that monastic constitutions clearly regulated the flows of wealth both within the monastic community (income distributions) and with the laity (stipulations of income distributions).[66]

Along with these discussions of monastic practices in general, in-depth studies of specific monasteries further elucidate how monasteries were indeed key to the growth of religious power.[67] Take Labrang Monastery, for example, which grew into one of the most influential Geluk monasteries in Amdo in the eighteenth century. Founded in 1709 by Jamyang Zhepai Dorje (1648–1721/2), the monastery became a vector of power negotiation among the Qoshot Mongols, Amdo Buddhist trülkus, and eventually the Manchu Qing court. This versatile Buddhist institution allowed all parties to find mutually satisfactory political common ground as geopolitical realities rapidly changed in the eighteenth century.[68]

Common Ground focuses on major monasteries in key nodal sites that connected Buddhists across Inner Asia. Many of these were built in the seventeenth and early eighteenth centuries, because of the eastward missionary activities out of Lhasa.[69] They predated the 1670s, when the Qianlong emperor entered his final years of territorial expansion. These monasteries speak to a different but equally vital issue concerning the Qing's Inner Asian undertakings. The choices made reflect a conviction I maintain regarding the Qianlong reign: it was the tail end of a long and contested process throughout which the Qing developed a versatile set of operations. The cluster of eight monasteries in the Qing's imperial summer resort in Jehol were by all means important to the Qing imperial enterprise, and they have received increasing attention from scholars. *Common Ground* complements this site-specific research and engages with those research projects centering on the Qing's imperial gaze.[70] By focusing on the network built upon Buddhists' shared schooling experience and the Buddhist network that stemmed from that experience, it calls into question the existing analytical privilege of Beijing and Lhasa. The geopolitical landscape looked quite different when the space between the two centers was contested and part of the process of finding common ground.

The lengthy negotiations between the two resulted in the Qing imposing restrictions on the size of monasteries and the number and selection process of Buddhist trülkus, and road passes for pilgrims. It also resulted in the Qing's patronage of selective monasteries, several of which will feature in this book, and support of Buddhist art production and recognitions of a handful of Buddhist trülkus.

Neither the Qing emperors nor Tibet's Ganden Podrang government accomplished their symbiotic growth alone. Instead, their pushes and pulls created a dynamic space for the Buddhists; in turn, the travels and writings of the Buddhists shaped the contours of the knowledge network in the Qing's Inner Asian Buddhist world. I refer to these followers of Tibetan Buddhism collectively as Inner Asian Buddhists. I choose the encompassing term to accentuate the gradual process of constructing imperial Buddhist subjects that transcended regional and ethnolinguistic boundaries. Taking such a broadened geopolitical scope may risk subverting Mongolian Buddhists' agency and undercutting their role in mediating a distinctly Mongolian Buddhist culture.[71] I am fully aware that Mongolian social life was not completely defined by Tibetan Buddhism in the centuries I discuss. Buddhism, like any religion, has adapted to host cultures, and Mongolian Buddhism was exercised in its own right. Mongolia itself was a discursive historical space that in no way remained uniform.[72] It is my hope that by highlighting linkages across the region and avoiding the loaded term "ethnicity," we will be able to see geopolitical power contests differently in these volatile areas. More importantly, we will reconsider the historical processes that produced these terms and rendered the region ahistorical and internally homogenous.

The Geluk monastic clusters, especially their connection established by the monks' schooling pipelines and highly structured and rigid curriculum, provided the necessary stability of the Buddhist network. Qing-Geluk interaction was imprinted with monastic practices unique to the Geluk and tied to the knowledge network that the two mutually produced. Melvyn Goldstein has summarized the Geluk way of organizing monastic lives as "mass monasticism"; this process emphasizes "recruiting and sustaining very large numbers of celibate monks for their entire lives."[73] The sheer size of the male monastic population, as Goldstein puts it, mattered to the individuals and the very position of Tibet in world civilizations.[74]

INTRODUCTION: BUDDHIST INNER ASIA

More recent case studies of individual monasteries reveal how the inner working of large monasteries carried great weight. The Geluk system focused on mass monasticism and the promotion of total dedication to scholarship.[75] Both of these features created new wealth and a new crop of people flowing between Lhasa and Tibet. Indeed, this resulted in a network shaped by the interaction between the Geluk Buddhist government and Qing imperial undertakings. Monastic regulatory frameworks and curricular designs demonstrate that monasteries were of paramount importance in Tibetan society.[76] Monasteries were more than a religious space in which only Buddhist practices were carried out; they functioned as crucial infrastructure elements to connect the concentric mandalic Buddhist power system.

Tsongkhapa, the founder of the Geluk School, underlined the importance of total dedication to study and meditation. This emphasis differed from other traditions of Tibetan Buddhism at the time. Nearly three hundred years later, the fifth Dalai Lama, Ngawang Lobzang Gyatso, and his able regent Sangye Gyatso institutionalized learning in the Geluk School. Ever since, Geluk Buddhists have excelled in many aspects of Buddhist learning. Lhasa's "three great seats" (Tib.: *gdan sa gsum*)—Sera, Ganden, and Drepung—became the ultimate dream institutes for Buddhist learning across Inner Asia, and their centrality established Lhasa as the epicenter of the Himalayan Buddhist world. Many of the Buddhists discussed in this book studied in these renowned Buddhist monasteries; that experience increased their intellectual capacities, lent them political capital, and forged lifelong friendships among them. Tsongkhapa's emphasis on total dedication to study and meditation was manifested in practices inculcated at an ever-growing number of Geluk monasteries, and his spiritual biography and writings were subject to translation and annotation in more than one language.[77] Young aspirant monks immersed themselves in the two fields of Buddhist knowledge, each of which consisted of five branches. The major and minor branches of learning encompassed a range of knowledge topics, gaining mastery of which required years of strenuous study. The Geluk's demanding monastic curriculum required monks to stay in these large monasteries for many years. Their extended stay offered monks an opportunity to cultivate friendships or mentorships within Buddhist circles. Many of the Amdo-associated Buddhists under discussion enrolled in Drepung's Gomang Monastic College (Tib.: Dratsang), such as the successive trülku of the Jamyang Zhepa line of Amdo's Labrang Tashikhyil, as well as many other Buddhists from Mongolia and Amdo. The centralized curriculum and extended residential clusters contributed to the rise of a slate of Buddhist intellectuals whose interests ranged beyond exclusively Buddhist scholastic subjects and included grammar, literature, and poetry. Amdo was the biggest beneficiary of these intellectual shifts, with many Amdo Buddhists honing their skills in Drepung Monastery.[78] Shared schooling experiences and subjects of study not only encouraged them to pursue a range of topics but also sustained their friendships after they returned home to manage their own monasteries. The intellectual knowledge network they forged across Inner Asia presents an overarching framework for the ensuing chapters, which focus on one or more aspects of the entangled geo-cultural history of Buddhist Inner Asia. Their connections were further reinforced through the moving elements of the Buddhist knowledge network, including Buddhists, texts, ideas, and artifacts, which collectively enabled the network to spread.

The network could not function without large monasteries that produced many Buddhist trülkus, who in turn continued to push for Buddhist dissemination. For instance, in mapping out a blueprint of a monastic network centering on Mingdröling Monastery near Lhasa, Dominique Townsend discovers the crucial institutional role played by this Nyingma Monastery in shaping a Buddhist sensibility at the turn of the eighteenth century.[79] Monasteries were not only a place for monks to advance their Buddhist knowledge, but also a hub to produce and circulate socially defined tastes and values. The monasteries were the joints upon which the Geluk mandalic components hinged. Religious institutions formed an alternative social geography that intersected with the state-regulated administrative structure. Indrani Chatterjee describes a "monastic geographicity" in the Brahmaputra valley in eastern India. Here, in the premodern time, the society was organized through a system of exchanges between interconnected groups based on marriage, trades, and political alliance.[80] Religious institutions were not the only institutional nodes that connected individuals within an expansive network; for instance, merchants from the Indian Ocean to the Mediterranean similarly relied upon structural nodes that facilitated the movement of people, goods, and wealth.[81] Various forms of structural connectivity nodes offer us an alternative avenue for studying how social forces shaped imperial experiences beyond official narratives.

Official accounts tend to deprive local ruling elites of their agency, even though they were crucial to the Qing's success in imperial governance. It was a power that other early modern empires also worked hard to establish. In the Ottoman Empire, nomads, merchants, Orthodox Christian elites, and translators proved indispensable to the Ottoman sultan's rule, although they also caused incessant concerns to the sultan. For the Ottoman state, governing mechanisms adapted different strategies to deflect or defuse tensions between local elites and the state, which largely helped buoy the Ottoman rule in a time of crisis.[82] Local intermediaries thus commanded the state's attention in finding ever-evolving common ground. *Common Ground* engages with scholars studying cultural brokers within a range of imperial settings. These intermediaries' unique linguistic, racial, or cultural plurality in imperial encounters enabled them to gain leverage in imperial encounters, but their alliances with the intruding power eventually absorbed them into the administrative apparatus.[83]

Power brokers within the Qing empire similarly had their own agenda. The intermediaries not only realigned the power hierarchy along Qing Inner Asia and western borders but also leveraged their role as emergent intermediaries. Their encounters mutually reinforced each one's growth on divergent paths and had an enduring impact on the cultural formation and struggles in the Qing and the modern Chinese nation-states.[84] By tracing the Qing's interactions with this transregional Buddhist world, I emphasize the connectivity between the two types of polity. This emphasis focuses on linkages across demarcated administrative units. It is imperative to challenge the dominant administrative and cultural divides. These Buddhists might be called in some sense the frontier elites, whom the Qing rulers courted arduously. The ensemble of diverse Buddhists in this book is different. Their distinctive positions as Buddhists in the Qing offered them leeway to transform their liabilities into assets and extend their influence without being fully incorporated into the Qing state.

The multifaceted Buddhist knowledge assemblage formed and transformed as the Buddhists exchanged perspectives, many of which are preserved in written form. I am fully aware of the promise and peril of using texts, especially enlightened Buddhist spiritual biographies, as historical sources.[85] I use the spiritual biographies precisely because of their selective nature. These accounts do more than simply document what happened; they also discuss why these events were important to the individual's spiritual journey to enlightenment, what equipped the individual with social capital, and ultimately what mattered most to the discussed person. Spiritual biographies restore a sense of social agency against a shifting historical backdrop. These texts present new modes of communal imagination, with the assistance of monastic printing enterprises, which vastly changed Buddhists' reading and writing experiences. A trove of multifarious documents forms the basis of this book.[86] These alternative narratives are not completely aligned with the Qing imperial vision, and as a result they present a rare opportunity to see how Buddhists appropriated state initiatives. Buddhist art also mediates a form of agency, as its production and circulation occupied a central place in Qing imperial practices.[87] Rather than limiting art to static and lifeless objects, in this book I insist on considering art as a dynamic process that consists of making, circulating, and viewing tangible things.[88] For this reason, I study artisanal manuals alongside art in circulation. In doing so, I delve into the very process through which the Qing's universalist vision was contested and constructed. My book shows how Qing imperial praxis was saturated with Tibetan Buddhism, and how the Qing emperors' investment in Buddhist operations helped drive home their imperial vision.

CHAPTER SYNOPSES

Common Ground consists of four chapters framed by an introduction and conclusion. It is organized thematically within a chronological framework. Each of the four chapters focuses on a specific site within the Qing empire's Buddhist Inner Asia. Collectively, these chapters trace how Tibetan Buddhists, Buddhist practices, materials, and ideas traversed the Qing empire's Buddhist Inner Asia, and examine the process through which this network was formed and sustained through its intersection with the Qing imperial enterprise. *Common Ground* joins the ongoing debate on the nature of Qing rule and argues that, since its inception, the Qing was an evolving entity rather than a cohesive and stable polity. However, my specific goal in writing this book is to focus on the interconnectivity across spatially bounded locations and the process through which places are defined through the "interaction between local particularity

INTRODUCTION: BUDDHIST INNER ASIA

and a wider web of connections."[89] Mobility and exchanges are key to illustrating the particularity of each site and their connections within Buddhist Inner Asia under Qing imperial governance.

Chapter 1: Campaigns

The first chapter introduces a group of Geluk Buddhist trülkus whose career trajectories were contingent upon two campaigns that brought their home region under Qing administration. The political reconfiguration took place after the Qing's military campaign defeating the Oirat Qoshot Mongols in the early months of 1724. This conquest transformed the border region into a zone of contact where conflicts, commerce, and communications persisted under Qing imperial governance. But this was not the only campaign that brought Qing imperial forces face to face with Tibetan Buddhists. Since the sixteenth century, a missionary campaign had been waged by the rising Geluk order of Tibetan Buddhism to win support outside Central Tibet. This sporadic yet persevering undertaking has so far remained underexplored by scholars. By juxtaposing these two campaigns, this chapter illustrates how the Geluk School's expansion and the Qing's desire to govern the region mutually produced Amdo as a distinct religious bloc. It was this interdependency that prompted Qing imperial rulers to develop versatile governing practices. The cooperation between Qing bureaucrats and local Buddhist establishments created favorable conditions for Buddhists to work on imperial governance. In that process, the Buddhist trülku practice functioned as a dialectic institution that redefined genealogical belonging amidst political reconfiguration. The shifting power hierarchy offered these Buddhists opportunities to reach beyond their home region and to play key roles outside the religious realm. The knowledge they embodied in Buddhist philosophy and practices rendered them indispensable to the Qing's imperial projects of constructing a multicentered Buddhist world, and it was this interdependency that prompted Qing imperial rulers to develop versatile governing practices.

Chapter 2: Manufacturing

The narrative of the second chapter follows the footsteps of the Tibetan Buddhists introduced in chapter 1. It examines the common ground

INTRODUCTION: BUDDHIST INNER ASIA

sought by the Qing rulers and Buddhists in their cooperative effort to manufacture a unique Qing Buddhist sphere in Inner Asia. The key to forming such a cross-cultural Buddhist space lay in the Qing's imperial capital of Beijing. This chapter focuses on the creation of Beijing's Yonghegong, vernacularly known as "Lama Temple," during the prosperous eighteenth century. Reading this religious site as a discursive space, I argue that the process of its construction reflected the crisscrossed and interdependent nature of creating a Buddhist Inner Asia in which Tibet, Qing China, and Mongolia were constitutive. In this Buddhist space, administrative and linguistic barriers posed challenges to be overcome. The very process of erecting a large Tibetan Buddhist monastery within the imperial grounds is indicative of how the Qing rulers drove home their vision of a universal empire. At the same time, the construction process itself offered Tibetan Buddhists an opportunity to reimagine the Qing capital city as an outpost of an expanding religious network where Mongol Buddhists connected with Tibetan Buddhists and brought Tibetan Buddhism to Mongolia. Mutual efforts served both sides of the encounter.

Chapter 3: Assemblies

The encounter between the two polities did not stop at Beijing. How did Buddhist praxis change in Mongolia, where the Qing state invested heavily in recrafting Buddhist Inner Asia? Building upon chapter 2, chapter 3 shows how the town of Dolonnuur grew to meet demands from many parties, and its evolving history illuminates the process through which the Qing rulers and Buddhists across Inner Asia found mutually beneficial common ground. Dolonnuur started as a small town on the southern edge of the Mongol steppe. In 1691, many Mongolian leaders assembled there to meet the Qing Kangxi emperor. Over the ensuing decades, two new monasteries were established there and became homes away from home for many Tibetan Buddhists. Dolonnuur was more than a monastic site, however; it also served as a bustling hub that attracted Buddhists, the laity, merchants, artisans, and displaced migrants.

Chapter 3 complements the preceding chapter in explaining how a network based on religious knowledge was essential for maintaining Buddhist Inner Asia under the Qing. In turn, this network helped propel the eastward extension of Buddhism into Mongolia. Focusing on the two imperially sponsored Buddhist monasteries, the chapter makes two points: First, within Buddhist Inner Asia, the spread of Buddhist knowledge was not always dictated either by the state or from Tibet to Mongolia. Rather, the multidirectional movement of Buddhists, objects, and practices reveals a much more holistic Buddhist space for which the Qing rulers were only partially responsible. By emphasizing lateral connections, this chapter further illustrates the multidirectional and complex engagement of the Qing imperial state with its margins, rather than considering it in a rigid power hierarchy with the Qing imperial governance atop it. Second, understanding the dynamics of cross-cultural Buddhist Inner Asia helps explain how Qing governance operated on the ground as the imperial center fine-tuned its vision of the empire.

Chapter 4: Governance

Imperial governance is the focus of this chapter. In deploying "governance" rather than the more common terms such as "state" or "administration," this chapter broadens the analytical scope of the term to embrace a range of governing practices and experiences. The chapter chiefly introduces two lay Tibetan Buddhists who were clansmen of the Qing's ruling Aisin Gioro family in the first half of the eighteenth century: Gombjab became a clansman by marriage, and Prince Guo Yunli was a clansman by birth. Both were polyglots who left behind voluminous writings in different genres and languages. Through a study of these individuals as well as the Buddhist knowledge network to which they both belonged, the chapter addresses two issues regarding the intersection of Buddhist Inner Asia and Qing imperial governance. To begin with, Tibetan Buddhism was far more integral to the Qing imperial vision than has been commonly understood. An exclusive focus on the Qianlong emperor and the Dalai Lama line of reincarnation misses the mark, reducing the intricate overlapping of two powers to the political strategizing of individual rulers. Instead, I look closely at how these two lay Buddhists ventured into Buddhist literary production, which sheds light on the fluidity of the religious network that had long been in the making. Secondly, *Common Ground* also hopes to show how these earlier historical connections, especially Buddhist intellectual exchanges and knowledge productions, were the prerequisite for the Qianlong emperor's articulation of his vision of the Qing empire at its apex. It helped the Qing to understand and produce territorial knowledge about the new space in Inner Asia, an imperative aspect of Qing imperial governance.

In conclusion, the terms of negotiation in the process were not dictated by the Qing rulers alone; rather, the Qing's real strength lay in its flexibility in adapting to fast-changing geopolitical reality. Its encounter with the mandalic Buddhist power rendered a Buddhist Inner Asia within the Qing empire, and their negotiation shaped the course of the imperial imagination and management of Qing China. Their mutual interdependency enabled them to grow symbiotically in a volatile time and place, and has continued to shape the course of history ever since.

Chapter One

CAMPAIGNS

Two campaigns of different natures were responsible for making the eastern Tibetan region of Amdo a part of the Qing's Buddhist Inner Asia. The chapter begins with the military campaign launched by the Qing army to annex Amdo in 1724. Even though this confrontation took place later in time, it is the better known of the two. The other campaign was the organized and tenacious enterprise that the Geluk School of Tibetan Buddhism built relentlessly to seek more patrons and extend its influence. This enterprise met with varied degrees of success over time and reached many places, but did not always align with the Ganden Podrang government's agenda. The rift between the Geluk's mandalic Buddhist government and regional strongholds inspired Amdo Buddhists to expand their patron pool to the east, especially in Inner and eastern Mongolian communities. As I will show in this chapter, Buddhist monasteries and a rapid growth of Buddhist trülku lines were essential for creating a Buddhist space that overlapped with the Qing empire's newly expanded Inner Asian frontiers in the eighteenth century.

The focus of this chapter is twofold. Firstly, it shows how the Qing state sought to close gaps in its knowledge of the border region in the aftermath of its triumphant military campaign led by the able governor-general Nian Gengyao (1679–1726). Secondly, it examines how local headmen availed

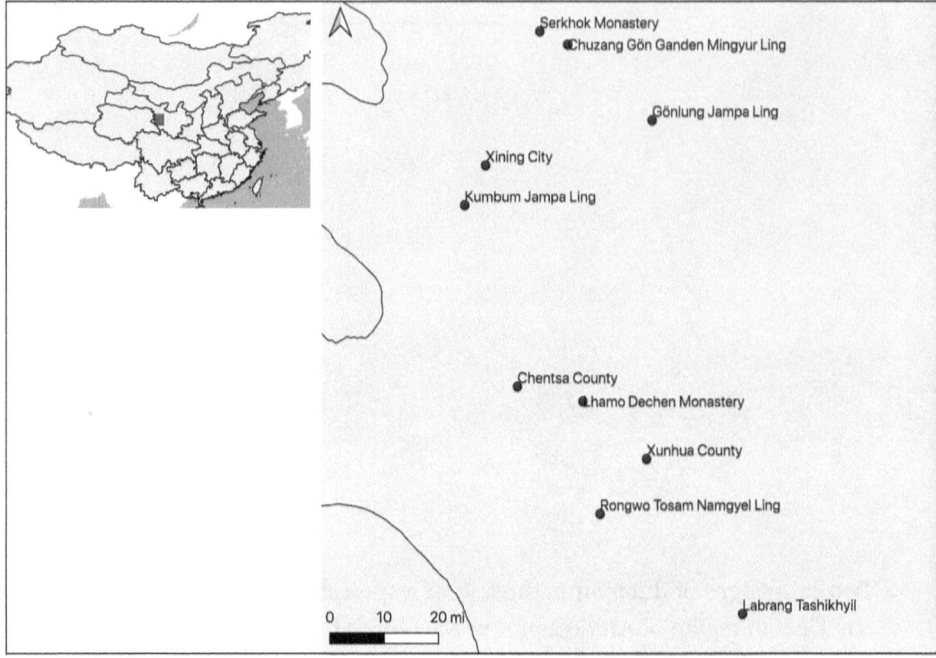

MAP 1. Sites discussed in chapter 1. Created by Lan Wu, adopting the shapefile of CHGIS, 2016, "1820 Layers GBK Encoding," https://doi.org/10.7910/DVN/2K4FHX, Harvard Dataverse, V1.

themselves of Qing imperial intervention to thereby transform themselves into imperial ruling elites. Their power and influence resulted from the negotiation between the Qing imperial state and Geluk School as their paths crossed and they extended their sphere of influence in multifarious ways beyond this contact zone. Their encounter, negotiation, and cooperation form the overarching theme of this chapter. The role of local ruling elites in imperial governance has been a recurring subject of inquiry in imperial settings around the world, and while these elites' eventual positions within the new political order varied, their standing gradually weakened overall.[1] These Tibetan Buddhists, however, managed to escape that fate. This chapter will explain their resilience.

The chapter introduces a cast of characters whose travels and writings form the foundation for the following chapters. Their emergence came out of the two campaigns that created Amdo and a new power dynamic that shaped much of the geopolitical history of China and Inner Asia. It is a story of how the Oirat Qoshot were dispossessed of this crucial region because of the Qing's triumphant military campaign. At the same time, it is also the story of how the Qing imperial enterprise remade the region within its own imperial vision. Two families stand at the center of my research, both of which were connected to the long-standing Mongolian powers in Amdo, and both produced several influential Buddhist trülkus. The stories of these two families encapsulate the very process through which local ruling elites seized upon the contact between two expanding powers—Lhasa's mandalic Ganden Podrang government and Beijing's Qing empire.

AMDO/KOKONUUR PRIOR TO THE 1724 CAMPAIGN

For Tibetans, the rise of Amdo was the result of intensified sectarian contests among Buddhists since the mid-seventeenth century. The region had been amplified by the Qing's subjugation of what was to become known as Qinghai in western China, which takes up most of Amdo.[2] But this administrative redesignation meant more to the Qing rulers than to the Tibetans and Mongolians living there. In geohistorical accounts of the region, Amdo registered persistently. The Tibetan presence in the area traces back to the seventh century, when the Tibetan emperor Songtsen Gampo (569/605?–649) seized the region as he expanded territory and demanded recognition from the Tang dynasty in China (618–906). The peace treaty between the Tibetan empire and Tang China brought the two contending powers to negotiation but failed to bring peace to the area. Both imperial powers diminished shortly thereafter and created a political void in Amdo that invited new contenders in the ensuing four centuries. After the Tibetan empire based in Central Tibet declined in the ninth century, Amdo became a hideout for Buddhists to sustain Tibetan Buddhism as the "keepers of the flames" in a time of uncertainty.[3]

The rise of the nomadic regime that came to be known as the Mongol Empire in the thirteenth and fourteenth centuries ushered in a new era. In this period, Tibetan Buddhism came to play a more significant and enduring role in geopolitical operations. Over the following centuries, regimes from east and north ingeniously legitimized their own rulership through a newly articulated universal sovereignty, and Tibetan Buddhism proved strategically indispensable in the articulation of the lama-patron relationship. This political innovation established a legacy that some scholars believe was perpetuated in successive regimes based in China proper, including the Ming (1368–1644) and Qing (1644–1911), to varying degrees of engagement and success.[4] The continuous Buddhist existence outside Central Tibet in tandem with the local aristocrats' declining political and economic resources led Buddhists to seek patronage beyond Lhasa. Their need to recoup strength became more urgent when the fifth Dalai Lama, Ngawang Lobzang Gyatso (1617–1682), gained support from the Oirat Qoshot with the assistance of his able regent, Sonam Choephel (1595–1658) in the 1640s. The Qoshot controlled much of the area between 1638 and 1723, then the Qing troops burned many monasteries to the ground. It was then incorporated into the Chuan-Shaan region, a Qing's administrative unit, as a prefecture under Gansu Province.[5] Two years later, the Qing began to experiment with a permanent post: the imperial commissioner in Xining (Ch.: *Xining banshi dachen*). The ad hoc office's transformation into a permanent post was indicative of the area's centrality and the Qing's efforts to incorporate it into the Qing's governmental framework, which required a more systematic approach to manage the region.

This brief historical overview does not do justice to the importance of Amdo as a crucial border region, which deserves a book of its own.[6] But a distinct regional history of Amdo was highly political; it only made sense in the eighteenth and nineteenth centuries, when such a regional identity was created and cemented in writing. By 1865, Drakgonpa Konchok Rapgye (1801–1865) traced the dissemination of the powerful Geluk School of Tibetan Buddhism in Amdo in his *Oceanic Book: The Elucidation of How the Buddhist Teachings Spread in the Valleys of the Mdo smad Country*, commonly known as *History of Dharma in Amdo*.[7] Even though his historical account was not the first text focusing on Amdo, and it might not have been the author's intention to write a regionally specific account of Amdo, the creation of the historical memory of Amdo as a distinct region still indicates that Amdo had evolved into a cultural identity deeply ingrained in the region and its history.[8]

The very fact that the region was known as Amdo, Kokonuur, or Qinghai underscores the multilayered social dynamics of the area and its complex past.[9] Here identities were in flux, and political structure overlapped; it was a contact zone fraught with encroachments and negotiations. The lack of a strong and persistent regional power gave rise to a host of contestants, with whom external forces had to form alliances to ensure relatively stable political operations in a region with a slightly larger territory than France. The local power agents provided the Mongol Yuan, Ming, and Qing administrations with many opportunities as well as challenges that each of the forces ventured to rely upon or regulate, and at times both. The area was a site of multiple and overlapping systems of rule, with a fluid and ambiguous sense of belonging politically and culturally.

For the intruding Qing empire, Amdo was a "gateway" to Tibet, as Zhuang Junyuan (1808–1879), a sub-prefect magistrate (Ch.: *fuyin*) put it.[10] It was part of the transregional Silk Road network that had facilitated movement across the heartland of the Eurasian continent for centuries. The new Qing prefecture was named Qinghai, after Blue Lake, which is located sixty-two miles west of the modern provincial capital city of Xining on the Tibetan Plateau. The same name rendered in Mongolian (Kokonuur) and Tibetan (tso ngön) had been registered for much longer in the region. The Oirat Qoshots and Tibetans were only two of the many distinct groups of people whose ethnic identities were defined by the modern Chinese state's ethnic classification project in the 1950s. These diverse ethnolinguistic compositions did not share a mutually intelligible language. Their multiplicity and heterogeneity made the region exceptionally volatile.

When the Qing struggled to develop feasible governing practices, local ruling elites stepped in, but not without a twist. Buddhist institutions such as monasteries and the trülku practice provided common ground for the Qing to close gaps in their knowledge of effective governing; this also presented a way for local power to renew its claims to privilege and agency. The latter had a broad impact on Qing imperial management as well as the geopolitical history of Inner Asia.

The 1723 confrontation between the Qing troops and the Oirat Qoshot Mongol leader Lobzang Danjin was the historical backdrop against which the two campaigns took place, and thus it warrants a brief introduction. In the final months of 1723, a swift military campaign defeated Lobzang Danjin, a Qoshot prince of the Oirat and leader of the Qoshot living in Amdo, in modern-day Qinghai Province in western China. The confrontation took place in the first year of the Yongzheng emperor's reign in 1723. Nian Gengyao, the governor-general (Ch.: *zongdu*) of Sichuan and Shaanxi in western China, led the pacification campaign; Lobzang Danjin fled to Zungharia after four months and remained elusive until the end of the

Zunghar state, approximately three decades later. In the aftermath, Nian Gengyao burned down major Tibetan Buddhist monasteries in the region, placed a cap on the number of monks residing in any given Tibetan Buddhist monastery there, and reconfigured the local administrative structure to prevent additional challenges to the Qing's imperial rule in this complex border region, where Mongols and Tibetans were only two of many communities living side by side for centuries. This military operation fundamentally shifted the political hierarchy in this region for centuries to come.[11]

The 1723 conflict certainly mattered to the regional history of Amdo and the Qing's eventual takeover and incorporation of Qinghai, but it was also a consequential event in the long and entangled history of Tibet, the Qing, and the Oirats, including both the Qoshot based in Amdo and the Zunghars farther north. If we trace further back to the founding years of the fifth Dalai Lama's Ganden Podrang government in the 1640s, it was clear that the Qoshot leader Güshri Khan (1582–1655) provided indispensable military backing. After his death in 1655, his successors did not have as much control over Tibet in the latter half of the seventeenth century. In 1717, the Zunghars invaded Lhasa and killed Lhasang Khan—the de facto ruler of Tibet and a grandson of Güshri Khan—and effectively ended Qoshot rule of Tibet. A joint force of Amdo-based Qoshot and Qing troops defeated the Zunghars and drove them out of Central Tibet, but around 1,700 Qing troops remained in Lhasa for more than two years. With the Zunghars retreated, the selection of the sixth Dalai Lama remained contentious, and Central Tibet was a political void. Should the Qoshots restore their control over Tibet, as it had been since the Güshri Khan's time many decades prior? To Lobzang Danjin, it seemed logical, and the Kangxi emperor did in fact make such a promise.[12] But the Kangxi emperor and his successor, the Yongzheng emperor, did not fulfill the promise; instead, the newly enthroned Yongzheng emperor conferred the title of "imperial prince" (*qinwang*) to Lobzang Danjin, along with two hundred taels of silver and five pieces of satin. Internal power struggles within the Qoshot also made matters more complicated, and the Qing's involvement certainly brought the tension to a boiling point. Frustrated and also perhaps alarmed, Lobzang Danjin moved to attack communities allied with the Qing and a garrison of the Qing's troops near Xining. He ultimately lost the fight a few months later and fled to Zungharia.

CAMPAIGNS

FROM BEIJING: QINGHAI PREFECTURE IN THE NORTHWESTERN QING EMPIRE

The military campaign and subsequent governing efforts transformed the region into an administrative prefecture of the Qing, but the reconfiguration was a long process that Tibetan Buddhist institutions also used to reinvent themselves in the new political order. When the expedition ended, Governor-General Nian Gengyao penned a secret palace memorial to the Qing Yongzheng emperor, who had ascended to the throne shortly before the conflict began. In his memorial, the governor-general expressed puzzlement as to why Buddhists and monasteries had joined forces with Lobzang Danjin and at how much power they wielded in the region. He reproached the monks for taking part in the uprising; moreover, he was frustrated that the monasteries seemed to be exempt from all state-dictated norms.

> Monasteries are supposedly built for religious practice, and practitioners' primary duties ought to be reciting sutras and seeking protection for people and the country. However, monks in Amdo's monasteries are from various ethnic groups, including Tibetans, Mongols, and Chinese. Some monasteries have as many as three thousand monks; the smaller ones even have five or six hundred monks. It is indeed difficult to keep them under control. Lawbreakers might have fled to monasteries and become monks. Local officials were not allowed to intervene in monastic affairs; as time passed by, monasteries became a shelter for wrongdoers. It is also unreasonable that local people pay taxes to the monasteries instead of to the government ... I [Nian Gengyao] ponder this: provided that monasteries do not pay tax, how is it that they collect taxes from the local people?[13]

Nian Gengyao then proposed to downsize the monasteries, remove their tax-exempt status, and place monks on rosters for official stipends.[14] All of his proposed injunctions were to materialize in two official statutes that defined the region within the Qing imperial governing apparatus: one was the *Thirteen Issues on the Restoration of Qinghai* (Ch.: *Qinghai shanhou shiyi shisan tiao*) and the other was the *Injunctions to Qinghai Mongols* (Ch.: *Jinyue Qinghai Menggu shi'er shi*). Between the two official decrees, the number of monks in any given monastery was capped at three hundred, and the number of rooms at two hundred. Monks were to be registered with local administrative offices; in turn, officials would inspect the monasteries biannually.[15]

Nian Gengyao's bewilderment and stern measures to curb monastic wealth and power were revealing. They reflected the Qing's struggle to understand the region and its urgent need to develop feasible governing practices, the latter relying upon the former. This chapter is thus an attempt to measure the gap between the Qing's imperial ambition and actual governing practices on the ground. The Qing's governing struggle also confirmed Nian Gengyao's anxiety over the power of Tibetan Buddhist monasteries. Much to his dismay, these regulatory proposals did not diminish the might of the monasteries or the monastic communities as intended.

What happened in subsequent decades, after the Qing established its presence in Qinghai? Nian Gengyao's proposed injunctions were the first step in incorporating the region into the Qing's administrative framework. The Yongzheng emperor assigned Danai (1691–1735), the commissioner at the time, to compile a set of legal codes excerpted from the Qing's Mongol legal codes. The codes more or less functioned as a transitional legal framework, and the state was meant to introduce something more permanent five years later, but in actuality, the state repeatedly declined to implement a Qing legal structure in Amdo.[16] As late as 1809, eighty years after the codes were first introduced, local officials were still unclear about what kinds of wrongdoing should receive a penalty and how to penalize the lawbreakers. The Qing state representatives felt increasingly anxious about compiling a complete set of legal codes, but this effort ultimately went nowhere. Certainly, it would be a mistake to assume that the Qing state intended to create a colonial infrastructure in Amdo.[17] Openly coercive colonial measures were a perfect recipe for more social upheavals, which commanded more administrative resources.

In 1808, Wenfu (1756?–1841) arrived at Xining, where he was to oversee the Qing's administrative arm as the highest-ranking official for the next three years.[18] Wenfu's career up to that point had not exactly prepared him for this assignment. His prior posts in the Qing administration in the central government in Beijing were mostly clerical and bureaucratic, but here he was the imperial commissioner in Xining (Ch.: *Xining banshi dachen*), with the title of vice commander-in-chief (Ch.: *fu dutong*).[19] His main tasks here were to manage the affairs of Mongols and Tibetans in Qinghai, a post created in 1724, shortly after the quick military operation that brought the region under the Qing. The title of vice commander-in-chief attested to the regionally specific administrative innovation that contributed to the long stability of Qing imperial governance.[20] For the northwestern region, including Gansu and Shaanxi, the most pressing issues were border security and defense of the North China Plain, where the capital was located. Qinghai Prefecture was established in the aftermath of the 1724 campaign and fell within the jurisdiction of Gansu Province, with the military-cum-administrative post as its highest office. Wenfu was one of the eighty-five appointees to the office between 1724 and 1911. During this period, the office navigated a complex social reality in Qinghai, and all but two of the appointees were Manchus or Mongols, who formed the bulk of the ruling elites of the Qing empire.[21] It may seem unremarkable to have established this prefecture within the Qing's vast territory, especially if seen from the state's perspective. But why did this region receive such priority in the Qing administrative apparatus?

Wenfu, in his own words, explained the geographical significance of the region: "The distant land connected Central Tibet and the Sichuan Province, and bound together the China heartland and outlaying peripheries."[22] To Qing-era officials, including Wenfu, the multifarious social practices on the ground made the job difficult, even more than eighty years after the region was officially incorporated into the Qing's administrative system. These eight decades set the parameters for this chapter. Even though I situate regional politics in terms of the Qing's imperial enterprise, Qing imperial governance was only one side of the story. What has often been missing are discussions of how and why local elites responded to state-engineered governing practices. One of the primary goals here is to address these issues by focusing on the two Buddhist infrastructural mechanisms of monasteries and the trülku practice. Both of these were powerful mechanisms to reclaim power and prestige, which the Qing state hoped to remove from Tibetan Buddhists of the region.

What made these Buddhists and their monasteries particularly powerful warrants an explanation. Territorial expansion and imperial governance were not unique challenges to the Qing rulers, and as in other contexts, local intermediaries played key roles. Land allocation did not change ownership in the Ottoman Türkmen and Kurdish tribes.[23] Historians of British India have argued that the British military's superiority over Indian armies was exaggerated in explaining British rule.[24] C. A. Bayly has insightfully pointed out that the East India Company was hard-pressed to produce knowledge about local society in Northern India; lacking this information, the British Empire was unable to penetrate the networks and effectively govern the region.[25] In tsarist Russia's steppe constituent polities, local Kazak intermediaries filled the gap in producing knowledge and forming state policies.[26] Within the Qing, local land-owning gentry and village elders bridged the gap between what the state needed in order to rule and what they could actually do.

Since Qinghai's military needs dominated the region, the intent initially was to rule the region as a garrison rather than as a prefecture under Gansu Province.[27] But this perspective does not explain why power brokers came to the aid of the intruding imperial state. The state-centric analytical approach is particularly noticeable in studies of the Qing's margins, and scholars have struggled to access source materials on this topic until recently. An unfortunate outcome of the limitations of this research approach is that antecedent social histories remained marginal, and frontiers appear to have been internally consistent and historically static in the face of a state presence.

TRANSFORMATIVE POWER OF BUDDHIST INSTITUTIONS

However, two dynamic Buddhist institutions—the Tibetan Buddhist trülku practice and monasteries—rendered the state's perspective incomplete. Trülku practice provided hereditary local rulers with a means to perpetuate their authority in a changed geopolitical landscape. Buddhist trülkus bolstered their power in the political vacuum created by the decline of Mongol leaders' political influence, by the Ming dynasty's laissez-faire approach to the border regions, and finally by the need of the Qing's field officials to penetrate the local nexus of power. As an institution, the practice of Tibetan Buddhist trülkus resembled family lineages in southern China in that they had impressive capacities to accumulate capital and increase investment, among other social and cultural functions.[28] The Buddhist trülkus operated with similar mechanisms to consolidate and perpetuate lineage wealth, including material resources such as land sharecropping, labor, and offerings, as well as social capital such as imperial titles and the trust of the community. Part of their institutional strength stemmed from the separation of wealth and familial affiliations.[29] This separation was especially important to the Geluk School, the youngest one compared to the more established schools in Tibet. It allowed the Geluk School to expand its patron pool and grow without the constraints of an aristocratic family's patronage.[30] The Geluk's emphasis on celibacy and strenuous scholastic training enabled it to concentrate power in monasteries. In these institutions, Buddhist knowledge was taught, and Buddhist trülkus redefined and circulated this knowledge. The flexibility of both institutions also made them susceptible to political currents and a process of constant historical flux. For those already in power in Amdo's local politics, trülku practice offered them space to negotiate their identity within a new imperial structure. It helped them avoid being completely removed from the political realms or being fully absorbed into the administrative apparatus, as had been the fate of their counterparts among other borderland peoples.[31] The Qianlong emperor's laments on the connection of powerful Mongolian families and the Buddhist trülku practice in the *Proclamation on Lamas* were not groundless, although clearly he could not extricate himself from muddling the institution, since the rise in recognized trülkus occurred in his reign.

The installation of the second Jamyang Zhepa, Konchok Jigme Wangpo (1728-1791), as the leading lama of Labrang Monastery exemplifies the practice. Konchok Jigme Wangpo was recognized and installed at the unusually mature age of twenty. Per convention, a young child was identified, to ensure a smooth transition between trülkus of the same lineage. Konchok Jigme Wangpo's succession to the Jamyang Zhepa title reveals the volatility of Labrang Tashikhyil's early institutional history. The first Jamyang Zhepa built Labrang Tashikhyil in 1709 and passed away in 1722, leaving the institution rife with internal conflicts. Ultimately, a nephew of the fifth Tongkhor, Ngawang Sonam Gyatso (1684-1752), was recognized and assumed the abbacy.[32] Konchok Jigme Wangpo's increasing power in turn brought more prestige to his already powerful family. When the second Jamyang Zhepa passed away in 1791, one of his nephews was among those selected to inherit the Jamyang Zhepa title. But this time around, the Qing official in Xining was said to have staged an intervention and to have removed him from the candidate pool under the newly instituted practice of the golden urn, as outlined in the Qianlong emperor's *Proclamation on Lamas*.[33] Despite the best efforts undertaken by the Qing state, the nature of the trülku institution had remained the same: the third Jamyang Zhepa turned out to be a son of a local chieftain and a nephew of the third Rongpo Drubchen, Gendun Trinle Rabgye (1740–1794), the abbot of Rongwo Tosam Namgyel Ling, which was in the vicinity.[34] As for the family of the second Jamyang Zhepa, Kongchok Jigme Wangpo, the selection did not end their influence in the monastery. One of his nephews returned to Labrang Tashikhyil upon the death of the second Jamyang Kongchok, Jigme Wangpo, in 1791 and served as the principal teacher to the third Jamyang Zhepa. Later, he initiated his own trülku lineage in Labrang Tashikhyil.[35] What was so special about the particular family that produced so many influential Buddhists in the eighteenth century?

The fifth Tongkhor, Ngawang Sonam Gyatso, was the oldest of eight brothers born to the chieftain family of the Nangra area of Chentsa in present-day Qinghai Province.[36] Chieftaincy (Ch.: *tusi*; Tib.: *dpon po*) was one of the several norms of local rules prior to the Qing's penetration of the region in 1724.[37] Local Tibetans were administered by many chieftains, whose territories and subjects often overlapped with individuals belonging to a nearby monastery. The Mongols formed their confederations to manage quotidian matters; some of these confederations grew strong and led the Manchu campaign in 1723. Several small ethnic groups fell into one or the other form of administration. The Qing reorganized the Mongols into thirty banners, whereas the chieftains remained the titular heads of existing Tibetan communities. However, the Nangra chieftain family of Chentsa offered a different perspective on how the Qing's imperial governance created advantageous conditions for local ruling elites. For them, Tibetan Buddhist institutions—both monasteries and the trülku practice—provided a less confrontational platform to craft new identities and perpetuated family prestige. After he assumed the abbacy of Amdo's Tongkhor Ganden Chokhor Ling, Ngawang Sonam Gyatso began to manage the monastery's associated communities; some of these were as far as 124 miles away and may have challenged the authority of Tongkhor Ganden Chokhor Ling.[38] These communities paid taxes or provided labor to the monastery. On one occasion, a member of the staff died inexplicably while on a business trip to an associated community, where the headmen began to disobey the Tongkhor Ganden Chokhor Ling. The situation worsened when Hor Namkha Gyeltsen Tongkhor, a *geshe* with *kazhi* (dka' dzhi, a learned-degree rank) status, decided to break away from the monastery.³⁹ This unfortunate man died mysteriously before he was able to organize a rebellion. The locals claimed that Tongkhor Ganden Chokhor Ling's protective deity had the rebellious headman killed to bring justice to him and the monastery. The cautionary tale was impressive enough that no other associated communities ever again dared to challenge the monastery.⁴⁰ Beyond the local level, this curious scenario also revealed a composite society within which an imperial justiciary-administrative system was powerful only in name, while the customary legal framework continued to settle disputes and challenge state-imposed justiciary practices. The twin system defined and continued to regulate social lives in the region.

Little is known about the institutional growth of the Tongkhor Ganden Chokhor Ling, but Paul Nietupski's meticulous study of Labrang Monastery may help illuminate the extent to which Tibetan Buddhist monasteries and Buddhist trülkus influenced local politics and socioeconomic norms in Amdo at the time. Labrang Monastery managed multiple socioeconomic groups that bounded eight "divine communities" (Tib.: *lha sde*). The ability of these monasteries to amass wealth and mobilize society greatly troubled Nian Gengyao and successive Qing field officials. In fact, Nian Gengyao's misunderstanding of monastic power was not unique to this time and place. Several decades later, Qing troops faced a similar situation in the city of Ili in a quest to defeat the Zunghar Mongols, whose ties with Buddhist monasteries posed challenges as well as opportunities.⁴¹

THE QING'S IMPERIAL GOVERNANCE AND TIBETAN BUDDHIST INSTITUTIONS

Upon the death of the fourth Zhabdrung Karpo, Lobzang Tubten Gelek Gyeltsen (1729–1796), in 1796, the Qing court decreed: "[Since] the Zhabdrung Karpo was responsible for day-to-day management of his Mongol banner, it would be better to find someone whom the deceased Zhabdrung Karpo's subordinates will support. The official (Wenfu) is in charge [of the selection]; there is no need to rigidly adhere to the golden urn practice."⁴² The Zhabdrung Karpo's trülku line was the only banner headed by a line of Tibetan Buddhist trülku.⁴³ The Qoshot Mongols were reorganized into twenty-nine banners, including the distinct banner led by the Zhabdrung Karpo trülku, who had established his seat in Lhamo Dechen Monastery in modern-day Chentsa County. Like the fourth Zhabdrung Karpo, Lobzang Tubten Gelek Gyeltsen, the succeeding fifth Zhabdrung Karpo skipped the golden urn lottery as well. In 1802, Kentsun Gyatso (1797–1831) was selected as the fifth Zhabdrung Karpo; his selection was confirmed by the Seventh Panchen Lama, Tenpai Nyima (1782–1853).[44] The reigning Jiaqing emperor reluctantly accepted the recommendation, and warned against such an approach in the future.[45] In fact, given the number of trülkus recognized and perpetuated in the Qing, few trülku lines were selected through the lottery practice; the rhetoric and actual practice of the golden urn illustrated the complexity of local politics as the Qing state attempted to assert its own power and realign the hierarchy as late as the first years of the nineteenth century. The deep-seated Buddhist institutions had proven resilient to imperial rule. Nayancheng (1764–1833), the commissioner between 1807–1808, offers us some bitter insights on this. He found that informants who understood the Chinese language did not possess any social capital:

> Previously, [field officials] had never gone deep into Tibetan communities and were unfamiliar with Tibetan customs when they handled cases related to Tibetans. Now, we have carefully observed, [and learned that] Tibetans, compared to Mongols, adhere more to lamas. Previous informants were nothing but the few Tibetans who understood Chinese language [speakers]; they were neither well respected in Tibetan communities nor reliable to us. It is consequently difficult to manage the region with [only] their assistance.[46]

As Nayancheng points out, it was not the linguistic barrier that prevented the Qing state from producing legible and knowable subjects; instead, the Qing state had a real challenge penetrating the social network built upon Tibetan Buddhism. Nayancheng's observation acutely reveals how Tibetan Buddhism was woven into the social fabric of this contact zone, and it was long in the making in this region. After the downfall of the Tibetan empire in the mid-ninth century, Amdo became a site for many Tibetan Buddhists to continue their practices, building monasteries and stupas.[47]

Instead, he proposed enlisting assistance from influential trülkus from major monasteries in the region. If they could indeed bring peace to the region, then the Qing state would confer titles on them and their monasteries.[48] Qing field officials had come to understand the power these

CAMPAIGNS

FIGURE 1.1. The main assembly hall, Kumbum Jampa Ling Amdo. Photo by Lan Wu, July 2011.

Buddhists wielded in their daily work only after years of struggling to govern the region. Nayancheng learned his lesson the hard way, describing an interrogation in an 1807 report involving members of a local Tibetan community in the Xunhua County. The Tibetans there often struggled with adjacent Hui people—the Chinese-speaking Muslims who also called the region home. Sometimes the Tibetans engaged in conflicts with Qing troops as well. When Qing troops defeated the Tibetans, several leaders surrendered, and Nayancheng rebuked them sharply for their wrongdoings. He proceeded to say, "I heard that [you] local Tibetans respect a lama [by the title of] Chahan nomonhan, why didn't he come with you? I cannot trust you unless he witnesses your confessing your wrongdoings and swearing not to rebel again."[49] These leaders tearfully reported that they in fact ignored the Chahan nomonhan's warning. They managed to escape the death penalty only after they convinced the trülkus to come to see the commissioner. The Chahan nomanhan line of trülku had been a vital power broker both in regional politics and in earlier Geluk missionary efforts in Mongolia.[50]

Nayancheng's account attests to the pressing issue that the Qing's imperial rule in Amdo had to confront in the eighty years after establishing the imperial post. Trülkus like the Chahan nomonhan upheld key social operations in the region. It also shows that the Buddhist trülkus' source of authority did not derive solely from Qing imperial support; instead, they had already mediated intracommunal conflicts before the Qing established its presence in the area and continued to play such a role until the late twentieth century.[51] However, their social capital made them more appealing than the informants whose multicultural or multilingual skills were first thought to be more practical to the Qing governance in the crucial border region.

Perhaps this also explains why Buddhist trülkus avoided being fully incorporated into the Qing's administrative apparatus. The full absorption of local chieftains was the fate that many in southwestern China were unable to escape. As in other early modern empires, intermediaries rarely had a chance to remain outside of the imperial bureaucracy.[52] Tibetan Buddhist trülkus were exceptional because they drew their authority from Buddhist practice. Their social capital originated from their religious authority, which allowed them to remain largely outside of the Qing's administration and continue to assert their power in multiple layers in the borderland.

Of course, the mutual acceptance of the central role played by these Buddhist trülkus was not a historical given, and Qing field officials learned about the trülkus' power the hard way. It was a contested process through which the Qing state and Amdo's existing local elites had located common ground in established Buddhist practices—namely, the institution of Buddhist trülkus and the monastic resources they commanded. It was historically contingent upon the struggle that Qing governance had faced for decades. Magistrate Zhuang Junyuan attributed the rise of Buddhist trülkus in local affairs to the military campaign in the winter of 1723 that removed the Mongols from the top of the local political hierarchy and positioned Buddhist trülkus as local leaders.[53] Magistrate Zhuang was right that the Qing military campaign dispossessed the Mongols and Tibetans and stripped them of their social, political, and economic resources; but at the same time, the campaign and Qinghai's relatively marginal position within the Qing administrative framework (Qinghai was under the jurisdiction of Gansu) created a political vacuum that Tibetan Buddhist trülkus readily moved to occupy. By the late Qianlong reign in the second half of the eighteenth century, these highly placed Buddhist trülkus, including the emperor's Buddhist teacher, capitalized on the Qing's imperial ambitions and regained their prestige, to which the Qing imperial patronage of Tibetan Buddhist trülkus contributed greatly in much of the eighteenth century, under the Qianlong emperor's rule.

It was one thing to conquer a region and turn it into an imperial frontier but quite another to sustain imperial governance. The Qing imperial endeavors exhibited a range of governing practices. These included the more strong-arm policy of replacing local chieftains with state-appointed civilian officials in southwestern areas under the Qing's rule, known as *gaitu guiliu* (transforming chieftainships into district administrators), as well as the more favorable alliances formed with the southern and eastern Mongols.[54] The Qing emperors found Buddhist trülkus most suitable for Amdo. Zhuang Junyuan's tenure in Xining came roughly a century after the Qianlong emperor had completed territorial expansion.[55] The subprefect magistrate's acute observation reflects reverberations of Qing imperial management long in the making. In their lengthy negotiation for power and authority, the Qing state and Tibetan Buddhists found common ground that sustained their presence in this crucial region.

For the Qing imperial rulers, courting elites helped them proclaim their universal sovereignty, and the emperors conferred titles and showered the Tibetan Buddhist trülkus with gifts publicly and elaborately. Field officials like Nayancheng had made feasible recommendations to continue governing the region without vastly increasing the state's administrative presence, whether civilian or military. It aligned with the Qing's imperial governing practice elsewhere, not just on the fringes. At the core of the Qing's bureaucratic configuration was an effort to match a deployed official's pragmatic expertise with the specific sociocultural situations in the administrative unit to which he was assigned.[56] The Qing state heavily invested in understanding spatial governance based on the unique challenges and opportunities that each of the "blocs" presented to the administrative layout.[57] Statecraft was geared toward pragmatic governance that relied upon individual governors. Yet, these governing personnels found themselves relying upon local elites in their day-to-day practices.

To both the Yongzheng and the Qianlong emperors, these Buddhists were transformed as part of the imperial elites, a crucial asset whose interests needed to be keenly preserved as the Qing broadcast its "imperial imaginaries."[58] To emphasize the exercise of a publicly orchestrated show of favor or grace to a certain subset of imperial subjects, the imperial rulers drew on more encompassing strategies that included religious and performative aspects of the imperial encounter with borderland peoples. This gave them more space to explore flexible imperial practices as opposed to a narrowly (and overly) defined ideology that exclusively served the needs of imperial rulers in the metropole.

MONASTIC DISPOSSESSION AND REPOSSESSION OF RESOURCES

Undoubtedly, the Qing troops severely damaged the monastic institutions in terms of both their physical capacity and their social influence. In response, Buddhists' accounts gravitated toward measures to resist their destruction: "Then [when the Nian troops arrived] the two monasteries of Gönlung Jampa Ling and Serkhok monastery were destroyed."[59] Amdo monasteries downsized both in scale and in number shortly after the suppression. For instance, Kumbum Jampa Ling (est. 1583), the largest Tibetan Buddhist monastery in Amdo at the time, was staffed with only three hundred "weak and well-behaved" monks after the revolt. The astonishing contrast between the monastery before and after the Qing campaign indicates that "Qing forces razed entire Tibetan Buddhist monastic villages, decimated their temples and residential quarters, and slaughtered their resident monks virtually wholesale."[60] Indeed, the Qing army's damage to the Buddhist communities was traumatizing. "Who doesn't cherish life?" the young third Changkya, Rolpai Dorje, of Gunlong monastery told General Yue Zhongqi (1686–1754) when the general asked the eight-year-old why he hid away. Rolpai Dorje continued, "When we heard a killing army was coming, we were frightened and fled."[61]

FIGURE 1.2. The residence of the Changkya trülku line, Gönlun Jampa Ling, Amdo. Photo by Lan Wu, July 2011.

The situation was in fact far more complicated than has been traditionally understood. In the 1903 *Monastic Chronicle of Kumbum Monastery*, the thirty-third abbot of Kumbum Jampa Ling, Lobzang Tsultrim Gyatso (1845–1915), offered a curious account of what happened to Kumbum Jampa Ling during the Labsang Danjin Uprising. At the time of the Qing attack in 1723–1724, Kumbum Jampa Ling was headed by Lobzang Dondrub (d. 1724), its twentieth abbot.[62] Lobzang Dondrub was said to have been very involved in the uprising, and he himself was also a close kinsman to Lobzang Danjin.[63] Although he met his end as the Qing court razed the monastery to the ground, most of the monks were spared. When the Qing troops arrived at Kumbum Jampa Ling on January 20, 1724, many of the monks ran for their lives, with the exception of three hundred elderly monks.[64] A new abbot was selected, and the three hundred elderly monks received official licenses that certified their monastic affiliations. Shortly after the 1724 campaign, a certain respected lama named Lobzang returned from China and regathered the former young monks, after which the monastery once again prospered.[65] The number of monks residing in Kumbum Jampa Ling in 1741 grew to at least nine hundred. On July 17 that year, several dozen Oirat Zunghars made their offerings at Kumbum Jampa Ling on their way to Central Tibet to pay respect to the deceased fifth Panchen Lama. The pilgrims were said to have offered one tael of silver to each of the monks performing rituals, which totaled 814 taels, and they offered 92 taels for each of the monks assisting the abbot and general business in the monastery.⁶⁶ By the time Wenfu came to Amdo in 1810, the monastery had housed approximately two thousand monks. This account was further confirmed in the writings of the third Tukwan, Lobzang Chokyi Nyima: "[The] monastery was taken over [by the Qing troops] a while ago, but except for the major criminal [the abbot] and thirty-some old monks whose homes were not in the vicinity, the whole monastery was not damaged."⁶⁷

These two accounts detailed in the Tibetan language underscored the very conditions based on which the Buddhists in Qinghai rewrote the collective memory of the Qing's imperial undertakings. The destruction was real, but not irreversible. The real rescue was said to lie in the imperial ruler's hands. The third Changkya, Rolpai Dorje, returned to his home region of Amdo for the first time in 1749, twenty-five years after he was captured and taken to Beijing at the tender age of eight. Before he left Beijing for Amdo, the highly venerated Buddhist dignitary approached the Qianlong emperor regarding conferring imperial tablets on Kumbum Jampa Ling, Gönlung Jampa Ling, and Serkhok Monastery, lest they be ruined by corrupt officials—a view that the emperor happened to hold, or so it was said.⁶⁸ To a certain extent, the political void filled by the Qing's administrative mechanism offered monasteries a valuable opportunity to secure the protection of their own assets. There is no better example than the monastic repossession of resources, especially land, to showcase the Qing's imperial management, which enabled the Buddhist institution to grow; let us now turn to it.

In his palace memorial, General Nian Gengyao was truly bewildered by the power that these large Tibetan Buddhist monasteries wielded; he loudly complained about the economic resources that these monasteries had amassed. How could they collect taxes and yet be exempt from paying some form of tax to the state? Again, Nian Gengyao's frustration stemmed from his ignorance of the very threads of the social fabric in this socially composite region with deeply seated, centuries-long Buddhist influence. He saw the monasteries as a competing force for economic resources that

FIGURE 1.3. Lhamo Dechen Monastery, Amdo. Photo by Lan Wu, June 2010.

ought to be controlled solely by the imperial state. He agonized over the wealth that these monasteries had accumulated, among other privileges. Quite simply, in the general's mind, the monasteries thwarted the state and needed to be curtailed and regulated in order to reduce their political and economic power. His fear was real, and his worries validated, but his bold measures reflected the way the imperial state miscalculated the enormous power that trülkus and monasteries wielded in the Buddhist world. Much of the grim struggle faced by appointed officials concerned rectifying the situation. Sorting out the economic relationship between Buddhist institutions and the laity was one of the most pressing issues for Qing field officials. This section therefore discusses how the monasteries availed themselves of the state's governing practices to support their monastic community, reclaim land, and acquire more land, which buoyed up the monasteries after the Qing state annexed the region.

After imperial operations disbanded the monastic communities in the campaign of 1723, the Qing state developed a range of practices to bring the monks into its administrative orbit. One of the two pillars of the new financing mechanism was to require monks to register with the state, which gave the recognized monks an ordination permit (Ch.: *dudie*). The origin and changes of the permit practice have drawn ongoing scholarly interest.[69] For the specific region under discussion, it seemed that a sort of permit system was established shortly after the campaign.[70] Those with a permit were on an official roster and received a stipend either in kind—"clothing grain" (Ch.: *yidanliang*)—or in silver—"clothing silver" (Ch.: *yidanyin*).[71] The creation and systematization of monk rosters and stipends were intended to dispossess the monasteries of wealth and realign the power hierarchy in the critical region. The Qing's inclination was to redefine the regional political hierarchy, not to upend it. To carry that out, the state rebuilt the monasteries, renamed them, and repopulated them, albeit with restrictions. The rebuilt monasteries were often those that had been large and influential in the pre-Qing years. They were forced to adopt a financing system that at least nominally bound them closely to the Qing imperial state. The true value of the state's patronage of the monasteries lay in the symbolic positioning of the Qing state at the pinnacle of the transformed political structure of the region. To the imperial state, its administrative investment remained minimal; meanwhile, it broadcast imperial benevolence through redefining once-powerful social institutions.

As for the monasteries, how did they respond to the new overlord that had taken hold of the lifeblood of the monastic economy? Monks in two monasteries in the Datong and Guide counties, adjacent to the prefecture seat of Xining, were not bothered when their stipends went missing or miscalculated, whether due to corruption or simply to ineptitude. On one occasion, more than half of the state-allocated stipend to Datong County's Tongkhor Ganden Chokhor Ling went missing.[72] The monasteries had their own sources of income that mitigated the meager financial support from the imperial state.[73] Ultimately, the monasteries did not lose ties with the local communities, and the state's governing practices did not deprive them of the resources needed for their survival and growth.

The Qing imperial state did not do away with these established monasteries; instead, the state found it beneficial to support them, albeit with restrictions in place. It was a question of how big and influential a monastery could be, as well as how much power it could potentially mobilize. In its policies, the Qing state inadvertently facilitated the process of the monasteries reclaiming and expanding their landholding as it navigated this uncharted territory. The Qing's struggle to grant authority while curbing the influence of regional powers was not unique to the Qing; other early modern empires negotiated with their respective regional leaders as well. The Kurdish leaders accepted Ottoman imperial rule so as to drive out the Ottoman-dispatched census takers or tax collectors.[74] Other migrant or nomadic groups likewise received more power or autonomy because the Ottoman bureaucracy was small in number, and it was more economical to handle the matter in this way than to focus on collecting taxes.[75] To maintain social order in a volatile region was pivotal for vast empires such as the Ottoman and the Qing. For Qing imperial governance, oscillating between circumventing and supporting influential Buddhist monasteries gave the institutions leverage to reclaim their dispensation and grow, a perennial issue faced by a string of Qing field officials.

In comparison to the monks' living costs, monastic wealth accumulation was a greater concern for the Qing state, as land was crucial to the survival and flourishing of the Buddhist monasteries. It generated rental income and crops, both of which were major resources for monks and their monasteries. The Qing state was fully aware of the economic potential of land and thus confiscated land from Amdo's monasteries in 1724. Did the state approach render the monastic economy hors de combat? It is undeniable that many monasteries experienced a downturn because of imperial injunctions, but their economic connections with local communities did not cease, as stipulated by the official statutes. Shortly after the devastating attack in 1724, Kumbum Jamyang Ling reclaimed all its land through unspecified clever tactics; it even retained official licenses to certify its ownership of the land.[76] State backing of the monastic landholding rights would only be possible when a strong state presence was established. Before the military campaign in 1724, the political structure in Amdo was highly fluid and influenced by a much larger geopolitical current. For more than two centuries, first during the Qing imperial administration and then during the Nationalist regime after the downfall of the Qing, Kumbum Jampa Ling made full use of the political framework to its own advantage.

If anything, government protection did not limit monastic power, but rather reinforced its influence. In 1922, perhaps for the first time, Kumbum Jampa Ling was concerned about its landholding rights. At that time, the monastery was brought under the control of the Republic of China. A number of steles were erected that year that documented all exchanges with the official confirmations of farmland, pastureland, real estate, and monastic buildings in Kumbum Jampa Ling between the monastery's establishment in 1583 and 1920.[77] Kumbum Jampa Ling's then-abbot, Akyā trülku, and other prominent trülkus, including a Serkhi trülku, appealed to Ma Qi (1869–1931), the executive officer and a local Muslim warlord, and Li Zhou, the local administrative official, to certify Kumbum Jampa Ling's property.[78] The state-warranted steles validated Kumbum Jampa Ling's ownership of all the property, publicly and legally. Through this validation, the monastery obtained state recognition and thus protection of its privilege to receive offerings in the form of land, goods, or silver. The Qing imperial—and later Nationalist—political context did not dispossess the monasteries of their wealth; instead, they enabled these monasteries to retain and acquire more economic resources.

Other than protecting their landholding rights, the monasteries were also a site for collecting resources in the form of donations or offerings. A stele in the left corner of an assembly hall known as the "Nine-Room Hall" (Ch,: *jiujian tang*) documented Zeku District's Hor kyi shédru wanggyel's pledge to donate five hundred liters of grain—half of his annual harvest—to the Kumbum Jampa Ling for the religious events hosted there.[79] Donations continued to be part of the inward economic flow into the monastery. A stele erected circa 1905 shows that Mongols from afar offered land and tenants associated with the lands to Kumbum Jampa Ling.[80] How then should the diverse types of economic flows into the monasteries, especially donations or offerings, be considered? The main concern was how to reconcile the supposedly complex handling of wealth within Buddhist monasticism. Instead, religious figures engaged in socioeconomic practices because of their soteriological or devotional dispositions, and monastery livelihood was reliant on managing wealth and their unique position in the religious economy.[81] For Tibetan Buddhists, entry to monasticism did not sever one's ties with their family, nor did it preclude their acceptance of economic aid from patrons.[82] More specifically, for Amdo monasteries under Qing rule, their capacity of wealth accumulation was further enhanced by the proliferation of Buddhist trülku lines. All Geluk trülkus were monastic in nature, with their residence (Tib.: *nang chen*) or estate (Tib.: *labrang*) in one or more monasteries. In turn, they brought wealth to the monasteries. Many of the trülku lines themselves, like that of the fifth Tongkhor, Sonam Gyatso, could decisively change a line of trülku and its associated estates for one of the most influential monasteries in eastern Tibet up to the modern era. The two institutions intersected and were potent social forces commanding land and other forms of wealth, but it would be erroneous to assume that monasteries and the trülku practices viewed wealth as solely transactional. Wealth also entered a new realm of the religious economy, moving in and out of the monastic context.[83]

Buddhism provided a pragmatic mechanism to assign value to land through rituals, which had real economic leverage in the circulation of land. Through rituals, a patch of land had the potential to be redefined in the market. Take land acquisition, for example. First, stolen land was disqualified from donations or offerings; this factor depreciated its monetary potential from a purely economic standpoint. Even when a patch of land was donated or offered to a monastery, the monastery still needed to perform rituals to "acquire" the land properly; otherwise, it could lead to inauspicious consequences for the monastery.[84] Likewise, rituals could enhance value or totally change the nature of a land patch. When the first Jamyang Zhepa, Jamyang Zhepai Dorje (1648–1721/2), returned to Amdo to establish the Labrang Tashikhyil in 1709, he painstakingly performed extensive rituals because the location was believed to be contaminated by poisonous snakes and other beasts. Moreover, several creeks were said to originate from the location designated for building the main assembly hall. To ensure the prosperity of the monastery-to-be, he spent at least one week purifying the land and reorganizing the spirits associated with the location.[85] The ritually transformed site then in no way hindered the Labrang Tashikhyil's growth. These scenarios demonstrated how Buddhist institutions did not confront the imperial Qing state as economic resources became a contested site for power and legitimacy; instead, they shored up their wealth with an established Buddhist vocabulary.

Other tools to allow the monasteries to seize upon a new imperial structure included land purchases through middlemen. In the summer of 1739, a man named Daerji sold a piece of arable family land to Chuzang Gön Ganden Mingyur Ling (est. 1649) because he felt it was "inconvenient to cultivate the piece of land."[86] In addition to selling the land, he transferred all corvée associated with the land to the monastery. As the seller declared in the written contract, "all transactions are final and no further negotiation is needed."[87] In 1742, Chuzang Gön Ganden Mingyur Ling purchased another piece of land from a Yang household for exactly the same reason.[88] Except for a few descriptions of the land in the two contracts, the contracts exhibited identical formats and styles of language, even with the same middleman: He Jincai. This alludes to the possibility that land transactions between local people and Chuzang Gön Ganden Mingyur Ling were not uncommon. Even though the monastery was only a small one, it continued to purchase lands from the local people more or less routinely, shortly after the Qing annexed Amdo. Like the abovementioned Kumbum Jampa Ling, Chuzang Gön Ganden Mingyur Ling appealed to the Nationalist government in 1927 for protection of its landholding rights. The two deeds cited here formed the basis for its argument—that is, the monastery had lawfully purchased the land in 1739–1742 under Qing imperial rule. The Nationalist government readily certified the monastery's ownership of the two patches of land.

Through the acquisition of land and its associated labor service, monasteries became a legitimate social force commanding economic resources.[89] If anything, the Qing imperial intervention and later the Nationalist state recognition allowed Tibetan Buddhist monasteries in this volatile region to retain their resources within a political and legal framework. Monasteries became a central actor acquiring land in Qinghai. This contrasts sharply with pre-Qing and early Qing rule. Land deeds preserved from the Kangxi and Yongzheng reigns suggest that land transactions took place

TABLE 1.1
Land Transfer Documents, Amdo

Seller	Buyer	Middleman	Date*	Cat. no.	Stated reason for property sale
Liu, Yuning	Liu, Mengqi	Dong, Xingzhao	01/27/1672	463001-5-6-4	cash shortage
Xu, Loulong	Fan, Maolong	Xu Guolin and Xu??	12/03/1697	463001-5-6-2	abandoned
Luo, Junxi	Luo, Yuxiu	Li, Yang Qiao; Luo??	08/12/1703	463001-5-6-3	abandoned
?	Luo Yuxiu	Fan, Maolong	04/04/1727	463001-5-6-3	abandoned
Xu, Aibang	Luo, Kefa	Xu Wang	10/11/1727	463001-5-7-2	abandoned
Ma Pin's family	Liu, Chaobin	Zheng Quanyou; Ma Jinchang	05/10/1730	463001-5-7-1	cash shortage

Note: Dates are given in the Chinese lunar calendar in the format mm/dd/yyyy.

between two households. The Qing imperial campaign undoubtedly changed the social and political hierarchy in the region, but these changes were complicated and sometimes worked to the advantage of those already in power in pre-Qing times.

The year 1723 was indeed a watershed moment in the modern history of Qinghai, bringing an imperial framework that fundamentally changed its geopolitical position in Inner Asia. The imperial campaign rendered the region hierarchical and subordinated Qinghai local elites to the metropole to perpetuate an inequitable relationship, but this course of action did not go uncontested.[90] The strength of Qing imperial governance lay in its incredible flexibility and its adaptation to spatially specific circumstances. The evolving power dynamics between the Qing imperial apparatus and Qinghai elites demonstrated the very process through which the Qing rulers crafted their vision of empire. It was not a singular creation of state-engineered hegemony; rather, it grew out of ongoing negotiations with heterogeneous social groups. For the borderland peoples, each of them carried significant clout in their own way. Unlike Taiwan, Xinjiang, or the Qing's southwestern frontiers, Amdo did not experience an influx of Han Chinese migrants under Qing rule to transform its ethnographic profile and economic patterns.[91] Hereditary leaders in Amdo did not receive official recognition as their counterparts had and did not become Qing imperial representatives at the local level. Even though these Buddhist trülkus received titles and other imperial favors, as well as financial support from the imperial state, they remained independent from official administrative operations. I demonstrate that it was precisely because of their distance from the official apparatus that Amdo's local agents of management achieved more autonomy than ruling elites in other regions.

What enabled them to claim their agency and independence was the religious backing derived from Tibetan Buddhism. Buddhist institutions and the region's historical linkages to the Buddhist world provided local elites with pragmatic and institutional mechanisms to transform their liability into an asset as two campaigns unfolded in the border region. The Qing imperial expedition brought about destruction, disruption of social life, and monastic dispossession of economic resources—in short, a new political reality. But the story of Qing imperial governance is incomplete without recognition of its struggle to rule and its reliance upon the Buddhist institutions—monasteries and Buddhist trülku practices—that the imperial state patronized. The state's need to produce knowledge about the region gave rise to Qinghai's hereditary leaders, who then consciously redefined their identity through imperially sanctioned Buddhist institutions. However, their sources of authority did not derive from Qing imperial recognition; rather, it was rooted in a sprawling Geluk knowledge network established even before the founding of the Geluk mandalic Ganden Podrang government in 1642. The prolonged campaign to seek more patrons outside Central Tibet and form alliances with military strongmen allowed the Geluk School to convert or build monasteries to the east, including in Amdo and Mongolia. The Geluk Buddhists plowed on, trying to recruit more support to outperform more established schools in Central Tibet.

This Buddhist missionary campaign had two broad impacts on the geopolitical history of Inner Asia. Locally, Buddhist monasteries and trülku lines recreated their collective memories and articulated their regional identities. The emergence of Amdo as a distinct cultural and linguistic bloc took place in the middle of the seventeenth century and crystallized in historical narratives in the eighteenth and nineteenth centuries. This coincided with the power consolidation of Lhasa's Ganden Podrang government and the monastic expansion of the Geluk School. Even though Amdo in the eighteenth and nineteenth centuries was dominated by Geluk monasteries, the distance and difference from Lhasa made Amdo Buddhists ideal candidates to help Qing rulers bridge the gap between Beijing and Lhasa. Beyond Amdo, earlier Geluk Buddhists who engaged with Mongols were initially sent to the Manchu court in Mukden. Later, they were sent to the Qing court in Beijing, which I will address in the next chapter, on manufacturing Buddhist knowledge in the Qing imperial capital.

Chapter Two

MANUFACTURING

The third Changkya, Rolpai Dorje, was a man who needs no introduction among scholars of Qing-Tibet relationships.[1] He was captured in Amdo in 1724, when the Qing troops defeated Lobzang Danjin, the leader of the Qoshot Mongol in Kokonuur. After the third Changkya Rolpai Dorje was brought to Beijing, he was raised alongside the reigning Yongzheng emperor's fourteenth son, Hongli, who in due course would ascend to the throne and adopt the temple name of Qianlong (r. 1735–1796). Approaching the end of his first decade of rule in 1744, the Qianlong emperor asked his childhood schoolmate and then-religious teacher, "How did the precious Buddhist teachings spread in Tibet? What kinds of Buddhists have appeared? And how did schools where [people] can practice Buddhist teachings appear?"[2] Upon hearing the third Changkya Rolpai Dorje's detailed responses, the emperor concluded that

> it relied upon schools [Tib.: *lopdra*], where Buddhist teachings can be studied, to spread [Buddhism] far and for a long time. Previously, Sakya Pandita and Phagspa built monastic learning colleges this way, but they remain only in name now. During my ancestors' reigns, [they] promoted Buddhism. My father and the second Changkya established such a monastery in tsodün [Dolonnuur], but there has not been a monastic learning college

in the capital city [Tib.: *gyelkhap chenpo*]. If we two, *yönchö*, build a monastery within the palace (Tib.: *podrang chenpo*), [where] sutra and tantra [Tib.: *do ngak*] can be studied thoroughly, Buddhism will be spread and sustained.³

The following year, Yonghegong, the "palace of harmony and peace," was to become a Tibetan Buddhist monastery within the palace where sutra and tantra were the subjects of teaching. This was also where the infamous *Proclamation on Lamas* was issued in 1792. This chapter explains the efforts the Qianlong emperor undertook to build a monastic learning college in the capital city in the 1740s, a decade marked by massive investment in Buddhist knowledge production. It thus situates the institutional history of Yonghegong within the Qing imperial enterprise of manufacturing Buddhist knowledge, which brought together Buddhists and the Qing imperial rulers as they developed strategies to grow side by side. By using the term "manufacturing," I underscore the scale of knowledge production as well as the process of systematizing and institutionalizing Buddhist knowledge that enabled it. The sheer quantity of imperially sponsored Buddhist material production is simply awe-inspiring: more than two dozen new Tibetan Buddhist monasteries dotted Beijing's urban landscape, Buddhist images were mass-produced, and Buddhist canons were translated, printed, worshipped, and gifted. This fulfilled the Qing's imperial universalist promises and broadcast imperial imagery to its audience, but the epistemological foundation lay in the hands of Buddhists, who found a niche as the Qing rulers continued to raise the Buddhist stakes in their imperial governing practice. Yonghegong, like many other built environments, "long served empire as a means of broadcasting power."⁴ Its institutional history offers a window into the Qianlong emperor's efforts to solidify his vision of the Qing empire widely and publicly. His dependence on Buddhist prelates, most of whom had close ties with Qinghai and Mongolia, enabled them to chart an alternative Buddhist sphere overlapping and crisscrossing the Qing's administrative divides. In light of these dynamic geopolitical circumstances, Yonghegong must be seen as more than a cloistered imperial Tibetan Buddhist monastery; it was also an outpost in a sprawling Buddhist knowledge network in the Qing empire's Inner Asia. The abovementioned conversation between the Qianlong

MANUFACTURING

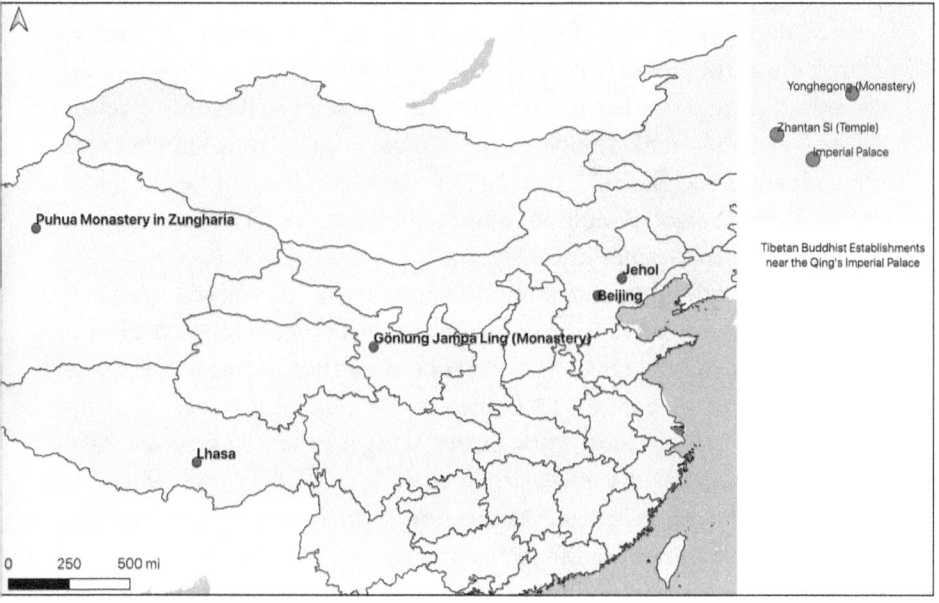

MAP 2. Sites discussed in chapter 2. Created by Lan Wu, adopting the shapefile of CHGIS, 2016, "1820 Layers GBK Encoding," https://doi.org/10.7910/DVN/2K4FHX, Harvard Dataverse, V1.

emperor and the third Changkya, Rolpai Dorje, delineated a historical connection to preceding regimes and spatial breadth into Mongolia.

"LAMA TEMPLE": A HISTORY

Yonghegong is located in the northeastern corner of Beijing's inner city, a short walk from the Imperial Palace at its center. Yonghegong has meant different things to different peoples throughout its history. It was an urban spectacle before the founding of the People's Republic of China in 1949, and it drew Beijing's dwellers and visitors to its fantastic Cham dance (Tib.: *cham*), vernacularly known to Beijing residents as the "ghost dance" for its costumes and masks worn by monks. Going further back in time, it was a cloistered monastery that was reserved for the Qing ruling family and visiting Tibetan Buddhists. Its peculiarity earned it the name of Lama Temple in the vernacular. "Lama" became the synonym for Tibetan

Buddhism in Qing documents, and Yonghegong's name rose in prominence among Tibetan Buddhist monasteries in the Qing capital. True to form, it was the largest Tibetan Buddhist monastery in Beijing, where the sangha lived and studied. It was principally restricted to Buddhist teachers from Tibet and monk disciples from Mongolia, collectively known in the Qing literature as "lama."[5] Although the term itself was only applicable to a small number of Buddhists, often trülkus, it bespoke the enigmatic nature of the space since its early years.

Before Yonghegong rose to prominence, it was the princely residence the Kangxi emperor had bestowed upon his fourth son, Yinzhen, the future Yongzheng emperor. During his reign of more than a decade, the Yongzheng emperor gradually transformed it into a Buddhist space. Near the end of his rule in the early 1730s, eighty Mongolian monks received state-allocated pensions.[6] Its quieter time came to an end in 1746, when the Qianlong emperor celebrated its opening in an elaborate ceremony as a base to teach hundreds of Mongolian monks.

Yonghegong was not always the gathering site for Mongolians in the capital. The Zhantan Temple was especially favored by and had continued to attract Mongolian pilgrims to Beijing in the eighteenth and nineteenth centuries.[7] The Zhantan Temple was tied closely to the Kangxi emperor, who commemorated its founding with an inscription.[8] By the 1740s, Yonghegong overtook other Tibetan Buddhist monasteries and became the central focus of Buddhist activities in the city. The changes came after the Qianlong emperor incorporated Yonghegong under his governing arm and streamlined its management. In 1744, the Department of the Imperial Household created an office supervising affairs concerning Yonghegong.[9] For the entire Qianlong reign, all appointed officials overseeing Yonghegong's business had been imperial princes, who were the bedrock for effectual rule.[10] Prior to this institutionalized management, Imperial Prince Guo, Yunli (1797–1738), had masterminded its transformation in the transitional years of the 1730s, between the Yongzheng emperor and the Qianlong emperor. It was not until 1812 that someone outside the inner circle of rule began to manage Yonghegong. Sungyūn (1752–1835) began to direct the institution while serving as minister of the Department of Personnel (1811–1813), and afterward the minister of the Department of Rites (1813–1819). This may reflect both Yonghegong's decline in Qing imperial strategy and the weakened position of imperial relatives in state business in the nineteenth century. The long Qianlong reign witnessed a marked shift in the Qing's imperial governance of its Inner Asian communities and the impact on how Buddhists articulated their notions of belonging to the transformed Buddhist Inner Asia facilitated by Qing practices. No place was more fitting than Yonghegong to represent that contested process.

This chapter aims to bring together two sides of a story. On the one hand, Yonghegong was a part of the Qing's imperial landscape. I borrow the term "imperial landscape" from Stephen Whiteman's article on the Qing's imperial summer resort in Jehol, wherein Whiteman uses this term to refer to all sorts of designed landscapes sharing certain characteristics. They include gardens, temples, park-palaces, and traveling palaces, which formed a "stage for performances of rulership."[11] These imperial built environments were pivotal for the imperial rulers to communicate their vision of empire. Yonghegong's transformation into a Tibetan Buddhist monastery in the 1740s was part of a much grander enterprise to assert the Qianlong emperor's authority widely among Buddhists, but the process leading to that vision remains relatively underexplored. On the other hand, architectural undertakings were a process, or, as Whiteman puts it, "events" that took time to reach their final physical forms. Rather than seeing Yonghegong as a complete, definite, and static space in the 1790s, this chapter examines the reciprocal relationship between two forces as they came into close contact. Yonghegong did not evolve into a site with these connotations until the final decade of the eighteenth century, nor was its transformation a result of the Qing imperial court's efforts alone. It was where Mongolian monks lived alongside visually articulated Tibetan Buddhist iconography and Chinese architecture.[12] These convergent modes of expression and representation were the hallmarks of Tibetan Buddhist practice in the Qing empire and evolved over a long period of time.

The discussion that follows explores Yonghegong's physical, financial, and institutional changes between the cited conversation of the Qianlong emperor with his Buddhist teacher in 1744 and the rhetorical criticism of the Buddhist trülku practice in 1792. All these aspects of Yonghegong's history will reveal that it was a discursive space created through negotiation between powers and the flow of Buddhist materials and ideas. Beijing, with its burgeoning Buddhist monasteries, was reimagined as an outpost in expanding the Buddhist knowledge network with Buddhist teachers travelling in Inner Asia.[13]

SPATIAL PRACTICE: THE MAKING OF AN IMPERIAL BUDDHIST MONASTERY

From the outside, with its layout and yellow roofs, Yonghegong resembled many Qing imperial estates. The transformation started under the rule of the Yongzheng emperor, who spent his years as an imperial prince there. This was also where his coffin was housed before he was officially interred in his mausoleum.[14] In the final year of his life, the Yongzheng emperor still aimed to renovate his erstwhile princely residence into a Buddhist temple (Ch.: *fo tang*). In the late spring of 1735, Haiwang, the director of the Department of the Imperial Household, submitted a budget of 26,381 taels of silver for new additions to meet the emperor's needs: "I (Haiwang) have ascertained that, in order to make the space look like a temple-hall, it will

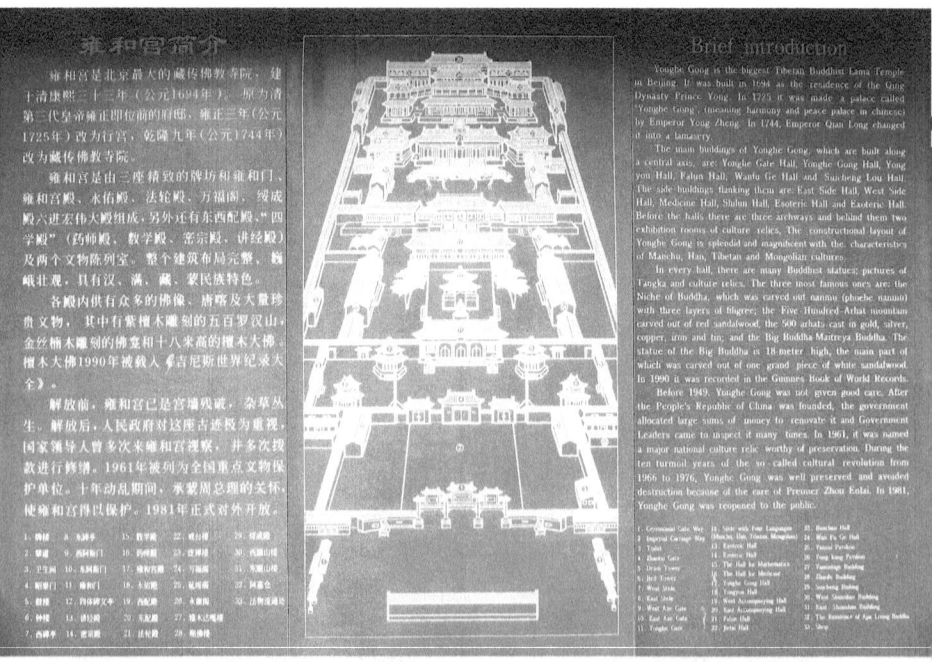

FIGURE 2.1. Yonghegong layout. Photo by Gray Tuttle.

need to have one arch added; five screen walls; two bell/drum towers; two flagpoles; two pavilions housing steles; five chanting rooms; two rear buildings; eighty relocating rooms; one hundred and six small rooms." Apart from these additions, Haiwang also reported that some of the railings needed repainting, and new statue niches (Ch.: *fo kan*) and other ceremonial implements were to be added, which were budgeted at 6,712 taels of silver. This was part of a seemingly larger project to transform Yonghegong into a Buddhist palace. He commissioned 49 new Buddhist images to be made, at an estimated cost of 3,381 taels.[15] This sizeable investment in Yonghegong reflected the emperor's interest in Buddhism.[16] Throughout his reign, he strengthened his ties to Buddhists and Buddhist practices. His connection with the second Changkya, Ngawang Lobzang Choden (1642–1714), during the dignitary's stay in Beijing was decisive for him in elevating the third Changkya, Rolpai Dorje, within the imperial household.[17] Buddhism permeated the emperor's everyday life as well. In November 1730, a Buddhist statue (Ch.: *fo*) was placed in his bedroom ("Xinuange") in the imperial palace for two hours and then moved to Yonghegong, accompanied by four ushers and commandants in official attire.

> To Yonghegong (1730.11.24): A Buddhist statue [*fo*] was invited to the Xinuange of the Yangxindian between 11 a.m. and 1 p.m., and was (respectfully) presented there between 1 p.m. and 3 p.m. . . . between 7 a.m. and 9 a.m. on November 23, [the Buddhist statue] was then relocated to Yonghegong, received by four ushers [Ch.: *yin dao yuan*] and imperially . . . drummer commandants [Ch.: *yuzhang gushou jiaowei*] dressed in official attire.[18]

How do we understand the protocol of welcoming and hosting Buddhist statues in this manner? Two issues are at stake. First of all, these Buddhist materials in Yonghegong were more than tangible objects; Buddhist images were embodiments of the Buddha, as Janet Gyatso insightfully points out: "In the Tibetan religious context, a work of art that is a Buddhist image (kudra) is not merely a symbolic representation of an ultimate Buddhist truth. Nor is it simply an icon, a rendering of the ideal form of a member of the Buddhist pantheon. It is both of those things but, to the extent that it embodies the form of the Buddha or deity, the image also conveys the presence of that Buddha in its own right."[19] Moving these Buddhist objects around within the imperial estates created a discursive

Buddhist space that was mobile and fluid, like all practiced places.[20] The time when the *fo* stayed in the emperor's private room assigned the place a time variable and turned it into a momentary Buddhist space. The movement of many Buddhist materials within the imperial estates, including parks, gardens, and palaces, added a nuanced layer to the everyday life of the imperial household. The ruling family's very identity was saturated with Buddhist practices, to which I will return in my discussion of imperial governance in chapter 4. For now, it should be noted that other mobile Buddhist elements similarly changed Qing imperial spatial practices centering on Buddhism. Secondly, these portable Buddhist objects changed the spatial practice of imperial Buddhism, defining a Buddhist space and transcending monastic physical confines. When Yonghegong was reinvented as a Buddhist monastery, in 1744 the seventh Dalai Lama, Kelzang Gyatso, sent five hundred yellow hats from Lhasa, one for each of the young monks enrolled in Yonghegong's four monastic colleges.[21] Yellow hats were often synonymous with the Geluk School in the Qing imperial vocabulary since the eighteenth century. The Geluk School was commonly called the Yellow Hat School, as seen in the *Proclamation on Lamas*. Ornament and clothing are vital to articulating the social aspects of a body.[22] Through dressing the young monks with highly emblematic yellow hats, the seventh Dalai Lama intervened in making an imperial Buddhist space. The young monks' headdress was inevitably a site in which their religious association with the Yellow Hat School of Tibetan Buddhism came to be defined, articulated, and circulated. Unlike the physical site of Yonghegong, the monks wearing the yellow hats were mobile and thus moved Geluk power in and out of the cloistered monastery. By performing elaborate rituals for the imperial court, the yellow hats also entered the everyday life of the imperial family. The imperial household almost always highly demanded various sumptuous rituals throughout the year. The monks' bodies in saffron garments and yellow hats travelled through space to make Tibetan Buddhism a visible presence in the Qing imperial court.

The five hundred yellow hats were a small portion of the lavish gifts that the seventh Dalai Lama, Kelzang Gyatso, sent in 1745. He also sent a series of forty-one tapestries (Tib.: *thangka*) to commemorate Yonghegong's transformation. He composed congratulatory verses on several tapestries.

One of them is an illustrated life story of Shakyamuni, the historical Buddha. In this painting, an image of the seventh Dalai Lama was positioned above the Shakyamuni to give a strong sense of the Geluk presence in articulating its power in an imperial space. The tapestries filled the monks with awe when they were displayed at the Pavilion of Infinite Happiness (Ch.: *wanfu ge*).[23] This particular building has also been housing a colossal Maitreya Bodhisattva, the Buddha of the future, which is fifty-nine feet tall and made from a single piece of sandalwood—another gift from the seventh Dalai Lama, Kelzang Gyatso, to celebrate the opening of Yonghegong.[24] The Maitreya statue was five feet taller than a Maitreya statue made in Dolonnuur (to be discussed in chapter 3) that was assembled in Ikh Khüree, the largest camp monastery in Khalkha. In her exploration of Ikh Khüree and Mongolian Buddhist art, Uranchimeg Tsultemin discusses the special connection between Maitreya and Geluk power. In their installation of a Maitreya statue, both the Qianlong emperor and the Khalkha Mongols articulated a convergent vision of Buddhist and secular power.[25]

These Buddhist images and statues were intended to represent the enlightened body, speech, and mind (Tib.: *sku gsung thugs rten*).[26] Buddhist images and tapestries are receptacles of the Buddha's body; stupas and stamped-clay (Tib.: *tsa-tsa*) objects are those of the Buddha's mind; and books and *dhāranis* are where the Buddha's speech resides.[27] The celebratory gifts and compositions of the seventh Dalai Lama, Kelzang Gyatso, rendered the imperial space a Buddhist place. The interior of the built environment was a site for negotiation and constitution of its architectural identity. The multistage transformation of Yonghegong's physicality—a princely mansion, an imperial Buddhist space, and finally a Geluk Buddhist monastery—reflected the very process through which new meanings were inscribed, and how the built environment was subject to pluralistic interpretations as Qing rulers and Buddhists found common ground.

The spatial practice was in many ways theatrical, in that Yonghegong's interior space provided both Buddhists and Qing rulers a stage on which to construct a unique Buddhist identity under the Qing.[28] It communicated the emperor's universalist vision of the Qing empire, while simultaneously incorporating Yonghegong into the growing Tibetan Buddhist world.

In the Qing's Inner Asia, shared architectural designs established a mutually intelligible visual language that defined the Buddhist space. Yonghegong, whether by design or circumstance, served as a prototype for many Qianlong-period temples built between 1759 and 1780 that appeared in Beijing's suburbs and at the imperial summer resort in Jehol to the north. Many of these Qing Tibetan Buddhist spaces shared a common architectural attribute: Tibetan architectural motifs and ornamentations with Chinese layouts and buildings.[29] There was an imperial Buddhist temple inspired by Yonghegong, including the landscape called "Ritian linyu" in the now-defunct garden: Yuanming Yuan (the Garden of the Perfect Brightness) in Beijing's northwestern suburbs.[30] There was also the Shuxiang Temple (the Manjushri Image Temple) in Jehol, which was said to draw its architectural inspiration from Yonghegong as well.[31] Both temples were intended to serve only the imperial household members: the former was an imperial garden that the Qing ruling family frequented, and the latter was possibly one of the very few Tibetan Buddhist monasteries staffed exclusively by Manchu bannermen. Yonghegong and the monasteries it inspired provided the Qing ruling family with accessible and holistic experiences across space.

MONASTIC WEALTH AND RELIGIOUS VALUE IN YONGHEGONG

The tension between monastic wealth and religious renunciation of materialism was not easily reconciled, and the reasons are manifold. First, monastic land acquisition was not unfamiliar to China; in fact, land transactions in medieval China defined the relationship between the laity and large monasteries through land, securing economic stability that provided and validated its social role.[32] Access to imperial power was crucial to Chinese Buddhist communities.[33] By the Qing period, imperial patronage continued to play a central role in monastic growth. Yonghegong was likely one of the biggest beneficiaries among more than forty Tibetan Buddhist establishments in Beijing in the Qianlong reign in much of the eighteenth century, and given that Tibetan Buddhism at the time enjoyed more imperial patronage than Chinese Buddhism, Yonghegong might have had more resources than any other Buddhist institutions in Beijing. Large land endowments granted to Yonghegong were thus in many ways understood in research in light of Chinese Buddhist monastic practices. However,

Yonghegong was different, and dissecting its monastic wealth is one way to correct this misapprehension.

Second, the misconception of monastic wealth outlived the imperial history of China. In the Republican decade of 1927–1937, Yonghegong's monks were said to go out of their way to solicit bribes from visitors, for which they were despised. In Juliet Bredon's account, a Russian bought his way in with a box of biscuits, which only invited more monks to request a toll at each of the many gates on his way out.[34] This anecdote reveals the seemingly inconceivable connection between monastic wealth and religious renunciation in modern times. Religious institutions of all kinds experienced increasing marginalization in social and political contexts across the world, of which modernization and secularization were the hallmarks in the first half of the twentieth century. The monks' quest for wealth was depicted as moral and ethical decay and fueled the rejection of religious forces in light of the new political realities of modernization and secularization. But as a matter of fact, Buddhist doctrine does not prohibit monks from involving themselves in property matters and so forth, even in early India.[35] Wealth was fundamental for monasteries to function. For an imperially sponsored monastery, Yonghegong's manifold financial disposition revealed the contested process through which the Qing empire and Geluk Buddhist Inner Asia intersected and grew symbiotically.

Yonghegong was the largest Tibetan Buddhist monastery in Beijing during the Qing. Over time it decreased in size, and the number of monks eventually shrank to 315 in 1941. The number was 550 in 1908, in the final years of the Qing, preceded by a much bigger community numbering between 1,000 and 2,000 from 1860 to 1900. Going further back to 1766, a Korean visitor to Beijing estimated the number of monks was "at least several thousands."[36] This number seems even more remarkable given that Yonghegong was converted into a Tibetan Buddhist learning center specifically for banner-designated monk disciples, and the number seemed stable and hovered around five hundred for the first two decades after the conversion in 1744. It remains unclear how the Korean observer came up with the number or if the official roster was not fully enforced. Either way, the monk population in Yonghegong was higher in the eighteenth century and then decreased gradually over time. The faltering monk population could suggest changing rhetoric from the imperial ruler toward Tibetan Buddhism. The Qianlong emperor's agenda markedly changed after he finalized expansions started by his grandfather and consolidated power toward the end of his reign, in the final years of the eighteenth century.

What enabled Yonghegong to accumulate wealth was its affiliation with imperial rulers at a time when they had expanded the empire and inevitably became more diverse. To be sure, the Department of the Imperial Household endowed the monastery with several land purchases from twenty-seven counties near Beijing since 1745, in addition to financing regular upkeep.[37] These patches of land were instituted as Yonghegong's "incense-lamp land," which were designed to support the monastery's routine religious functions.[38] The patches of land measured approximately 400 qing (about 100 acres), and were collectively expected to generate more than 8,570 taels of silver. The amount was very generous, considering the price of rice in Beijing in 1745 was around 1.5 taels of silver per kilogram. The first recorded land purchase was conducted by Ayuxi, a vice director of Lifanyuan.[39] In this document dated 1745, Lifanyuan reported a purchase of property measuring seven qing ninety-two mu with 18 rooms in Sanhe County, from Tongning, a junior imperial guard (Ch.: *lanling* [blue-plumes] *shiwei*) of the White Banner. The real estate cost was 533 taels of silver (70 taels of silver with an annual interest rate of 0.013 taels of silver), among other expenses reported in the same document.[40] This was the first of two land purchases in which Ayuxi bought land from Tongning for Yonghegong. The next purchase came five years later, again in the Sanhe District, for eighty mu. In the same document, Ayuxi also reported a property purchase from Liu Yongzhou, an imperial college student (Ch.: *jiansheng*) in the service of a Han Chinese military officer in the Embroidered White Banner. Altogether, Ayuxi tallied 540 taels of silver for the lands.[41] Ayuxi was one of two known Qing officials purchasing land for Yonghegong. Additional documents may yield a more definitive conclusion as to the exact amount of land owned by Yonghegong during the Qianlong reign, but the extant texts show useful patterns of land transaction for religious institutions. Almost all the land sold to Yonghegong belonged to banner households whose allocated property was near the capital and whose financial situation had become dire. This conformed to the pattern by which land in the early and mid-eighteenth century cycled through banner households and back to the imperial household, albeit with value reassigned and meanings changed.[42] Yonghegong's land acquisition practice within this established pattern was a useful reminder that Tibetan Buddhist monasteries were integral to Qing imperial governance.

Yonghegong would have enjoyed much greater prosperity had the revenue from the endowed land been delivered to Yonghegong as expected. This was, unfortunately, not the case. The land revenues were consistently in arrears for decades, and all the rulers tried to recover these revenues to no avail. The Qing imperial household struggled to collect land-generated revenue from more than two dozen counties, which resulted in roughly two-thirds of the promised endowments remaining unpaid.[43] The supposed sharecropping revenue from the twenty-seven counties near Beijing was reckoned ten thousand taels of silver, had it been collected.[44] Lai and Chang meticulously collected materials to show that over twenty thousand taels of silver supposedly generated from endowed land remained uncollected between 1750 and 1767, and the overdue revenue only grew greater over the next century.[45] It remains unknown what caused these problems. Fang Guancheng, viceroy of Zhili, which surrounded the capital, reported in 1767 that he was simply too busy to collect the rent. He then suggested that the Qianlong emperor assign this duty to the Department of the Imperial Household.[46] The overdue revenue remained an unsolved problem for the succeeding Jiaqing and Daoguang emperors. The Jiaqing emperor urged officials to collect the revenues for thirty-eight years, starting from the late Qianlong reign in the 1790s. The Jiaqing emperor's endeavors did not yield the expected results, and the unpaid land revenue for Yonghegong persisted throughout his rather short reign.[47] The Daoguang emperor fought to collect thirteen years of overdue revenue between 1821 and 1834. Unfortunately, neither effort bore any fruit, as the accumulated debt for this century was enormous.[48]

But did the uncollected revenues cause financial stress to Yonghegong's operation? To answer that question, one must delve into the actual management of the monastery and understand how imperial patronage functioned. One oft-overlooked source of income was rentals on Yonghegong's premises, and this was a continuation from an earlier time rather than an invention of its more prosperous phase after its conversion in 1746. Between 1740 and 1743, a quarter of the 563 vacant rooms to the east of the Yonghegong complex had generated a total annual revenue of more than two hundred taels.⁴⁹ The rental income consistently covered routine maintenance in these years. A report dated to 1740 goes as follows: "Total income was 324 liang 8 qian, within which 33 liang 5 qian 2 fen was withdrawn to repair all wooden 'screen walls' [*yingbi*] and 5 damaged windows/doors of a guard room [*kangshoufang*] in the 11th month of this year . . . the actual remaining rent of 291 liang 7 qian 4 fen 8 li is kept in the 'office,' to be withdrawn for maintenance if needed."⁵⁰ The multiple economic sources seemed to be part of the attempt of the Qing rulers to establish Yonghegong to be as financially independent and sustainable as possible. Yonghegong's greatest asset was not monetary input from the imperial household, but rather recognition of the monastery as an imperial monastery. The imperial family's sponsorship put it on a par with major patrons of large Buddhist monasteries. In Tibet, affluent aristocrats or kings offered financial support to monasteries before they had amassed enough to develop their own real estate.⁵¹ Precisely because of this generous imperial patronage, it is easy to forget that Yonghegong was a complex institution that best reflected the negotiated nature of Buddhist praxis under Qing imperial undertakings.

At its core, Yonghegong resembled the Geluk monasteries that one can find in many locales in the Himalayas and Mongolia since at least the seventeenth century, when Tibetan Buddhist monasteries prevailed in many areas. Its imperial affiliation did not distinguish it from major monastic organizations. Two underexplored issues have contributed to this distorted understanding of Yonghegong and how Buddhists resisted being fully transformed as the Qing made inroads into Inner Asia. First, monastic wealth did not translate into individual monks' financial wellbeing. Dreyfus, in his detailed account of Geluk monasticism, notes that the monks "were often supported by their families (the large monasteries provided food for their members only within the context of a ritual in the assembly hall) and supplemented this stipend by doing rituals for the laity."⁵² For the five hundred or more monk disciples, their home banners were responsible for clothing and feeding them. Lai Hui-min estimates that six thousand taels of silver were expected to meet the needs of the five hundred monks in 1744.⁵³ By the Jiaqing reign (1796–1799), the Mongolian banners delivered 5,600 taels of silver to Yonghegong each year to support eighty young monk disciples.⁵⁴ These numbers explain how Yonghegong's monastic practices upheld prevailing organizational and operational schemes among Tibetan Buddhist monasteries in Inner Asia. Each Mongolian banner contributed able monks to its four monastic colleges and was responsible for replacing inept monks with more adept ones.[55] Yonghegong thus became a space where Mongolians exhibited their new identities: young Mongolian monks represented their home banners as defined by the Qing imperial organization. Meanwhile, they strengthened their Buddhist connections through a monastic space defined by Buddhist elements, teachers, materials, and highly systematic monastic curricula, which were beyond the purview of the Qing administration. This ostensibly paradoxical relationship of the Qing, Tibetan Buddhists, and Mongolians was materialized in imperial Buddhist spaces such as Yonghegong.

The hundreds and sometimes thousands of Mongolian monk disciples made their ends meet in more than one way as well. While studying in Yonghegong, the monks also received payments from the imperial household for the ritual services they routinely provided. At services, sponsoring patrons customarily provided tea and other perishable foodstuffs for the participating monks.[56] The laity presented food at a ritual service, which helped translate their material wealth into social capital via Buddhist rituals. In that process, the monastery also maintained connections

FIGURE 2.2. The main assembly hall, Yonghegong, Beijing. Photo by Gray Tuttle.

with its patrons outside the monastery. In other words, rituals became a mechanism that transformed material worth into religious merit that brought social value to both the monasteries and their supporting patrons. The perishable foods offered to the monks at ritual services therefore ought to be considered part of the monastic wealth that helped sustain the monastic body.

What further complicated monastic life was that the teachers and the monk disciples in the four colleges did not share sources of support. The invited head monks and teachers from Lhasa were on the official payroll and received stipends from the Department of the Imperial Household.[57] For instance, records from the 1810s showed that 4 custodians received 2 taels of silver, 246 monks (unspecified ranking) received 2 taels, and 254 monks received 1 tael per month. The sum was minimal and insufficient for these Buddhist teachers to get by in Beijing at the time, but the official stipend was only one of several sources of income for them; some were richer than Manchu imperial princes on account of the offerings they regularly received from Mongolian princes and the Qing imperial family.[58]

As Yonghegong's main patron, the ruling family also dictated its monastic makeup. This tripartite coalition set Yonghegong apart from other Tibetan Buddhist monasteries of the time. It simultaneously served the three parties within a single space in which each of them found common ground. However, Yonghegong's multifaceted organization and financial situation were not immediately obvious, an oversight resulting from our lack of access to archives and a general misconception of monastic operations within the context of Tibetan Buddhism. Its obscurity has partly contributed to a distorted understanding of the multilateral relationship. Instead, the commonly accepted understanding was that the imperial family financed Yonghegong monks.[59]

Breaking down the financial compound of Yonghegong is crucial to demystifying this cloistered space and clarifying its position within the Qing imperial governing practice, otherwise Yonghegong is often misunderstood. From a princely mansion to a large Tibetan Buddhist monastery, the fundamental difference in space in the Yongzheng reign and the Qianlong reign was not its scale, but rather its transformation into a Tibetan Buddhist monastery conforming to monastic traditions established in Tibet. It indeed received considerable imperial patronage, but its uncollected revenues and the separation between teachers and the enrolled monk disciples were rarely addressed. What caused the greatest confusion was taking it out of the Tibetan Buddhist monastic context, which strictly and clearly divides the individual from the sangha. Monastic collective wealth ensured the functional operation of the monastery, which the Qing emperors supported. The Qing rulers did not invent the practice, but rather continued it. Monastic dependency on a state or strong political party was one of the earliest modes of monastic wealth accumulation.[60] To Inner Asian Buddhists, Yonghegong was an institutional outpost that connected the dots of this transregional Buddhist world.

MONASTIC OUTPOST OF BUDDHIST INNER ASIA

The year 1746 saw a grand opening ceremony that marked Yonghegong's new era as the largest Tibetan Buddhist monastery in the capital city of Beijing. Such a grand opening was important to both the Qing imperial rulers and the Geluk Ganden Podrang Buddhist government. The spectacle was constitutive of their respective rules and their continuous determination to expand and exercise their influence. To the Qing, the new emperor had yet to complete the expansion and power consolidation that had kept his grandfather and father busy. To the Geluk power in Lhasa, the seventh Dalai Lama was very much in the throes of political struggle, a hallmark of the eighteenth-century political history of Tibet.[61] Yonghegong's opening ceremony betokened its position in the entangled history of Qing and Tibet.

Their relationship was neither a confrontation nor a collaboration, but rather a historically grounded encounter with subsequent negotiations to find a delicate balance that met their respective needs. Along with the ever-shifting geopolitical matrix, they each sought to find the common ground that sometimes brought them together more harmoniously, and at other times less so. In that process, Buddhist practice and monastic institutions kept the negotiations going and smoothed out wrinkles. Monastic institutions like Beijing's Yonghegong and Amdo's large Geluk monasteries functioned to train young monks and sustain a dynamic Buddhist intellectual network. Yonghegong was mostly restricted to its main patron: the Qing imperial household and the Mongolian banners, of which the latter were more articulated after 1746, when the site began to house Mongolian monk disciples. This section focuses on representational attributes of the institution, especially within the context of a cross-cultural Buddhist knowledge network in the Qing's Inner Asia.

This Buddhist knowledge network intrinsically hinged upon the growing Geluk School. Yonghegong adopted the Tibetan name of Ganden Jinchak Ling upon conversion in 1744, which echoed that of Ganden Namgyel Ling, also simply known as the Ganden Monastery, one of the "three great seats." This monastery stood outside Lhasa and was founded by Tsongkhapa's disciples in 1409. Lhasa's Ganden Monastery was the first of the three main great Geluk monasteries in Central Tibet. Ishihama Yumiko argues that the intimate link between Beijing's Ganden Jinchak Ling (Yonghegong) and Lhasa's Ganden Monastery indicated Yonghegong's strong connection to the Lhasa-based Geluk School. Ishihama compares three monastic establishments: Beijing's Yonhegong, Amdo's Labrang Tashikhyil, and the Ganden Monastery in Khalkha Mongolia, all of which contain "Ganden" in their names. Ishihama makes a convincing case that they collectively marked missionary success in the east and the strength of the Geluk School's mass monasticism.[62] This model of Geluk monasticism, with a reliance upon diverse and strong local patrons and an emphasis on systematic monastic curricula, mitigated the financial stress of maintaining its growing monastic constituencies, and in the meantime created a Buddhist intellectual community with a shared schooling experience and collective memory. More importantly, each of the major monasteries at a key nodal point in Buddhist Inner Asia helped created consistency in curricula and teaching staff. The mandalic knowledge system proved especially valuable for the nascent Geluk power. The Geluk School lacked historical ties to the affluent aristocrats in Central Tibet, like other more established schools; what contributed instead to the success of the Geluk School was its infrastructural innovations: monasteries and Buddhist trülkus, who combined the flexibility of mobile Buddhist teachers and the stability of immobile Tibetan Buddhist monasteries.

Erudite Buddhist scholars proved essential to expanding the Geluk School's monastic curricula and kept the mandalic Buddhist monastic infrastructure functional. The seventh Dalai Lama, Kelzang Gyatso, recognized that and justified his decision based upon historical precedent: "Previously, when Buddhist teachings had not yet been disseminated in Tibet, learned Buddhist scholars were invited from places like India, and

[Tibet] has been enjoying continuous success [in] disseminating Buddhist teachings. If [the emperor] intended to increase the learning of Buddhist knowledge, it would certainly meet with success through the unique minds of the learned Buddhist masters."[63] Who were the first crop of Buddhists on this mission to spread Buddhist teachings in Yonghegong? Among the initial twenty-two teachers invited to Yonghegong in 1744 were some of the highly accomplished teachers from one of the three Geluk seats in Lhasa: Drepung Monastery. Many of them came from its oldest philosophical monastic college—Gomang College, which produced many celebrated Geluk Buddhist scholars, especially from Amdo in eastern Tibet.[64] As I discussed in the preceding chapter, the cluster of Buddhist prelates helped shape the Qing's Inner Asian cultural landscape, which the Qing imperial rulers had negotiated since the late seventeenth century. In addition to the learned Buddhist teachers, monastic disciplinarians (Tib.: *grwa tshan gi dge bskos*) came from Lhasa.[65] The mutual interdependence between the Geluk Buddhists and the Qing emperors set the tone for geopolitical realignment in early modern China. Institutions like Yonghegong facilitated an active and continuous flow of Buddhists and Buddhist materials within this dynastic space.[66] These famed Buddhists and symbolic gifts redefined an imperial Buddhist place as a node of convergence within a Buddhist world that crisscrossed the Qing empire's Inner Asia.

Yonghegong's dual function as an imperial Buddhist institution determined that each of its appointments must be deliberate. Its first abbot (Tib.: *khen po*) was the seventh Tatsak Jedrung, Lobzang Pelden Gyeltsen (1708–1758). He was a confidant to the reigning seventh Dalai Lama, a good friend of the third Changkya, Rolpai Dorje, and spent the last years of his life teaching in Yonghegong, dying at his post in 1758.[67] In his final years, the seventh Tatsak Jedrung, Lobzang Pelden Gyeltsen, and the Geluk power by extension, continued to play a crucial role in shaping the Qing's imperial enterprise, especially in reviving Tibetan Buddhism in Zungharia after the downfall of the Zunghar state. The Qianlong emperor continued to fight with the Zunghar state in Central Asia, which had threatened the Qing in three successive reigns for over half a century, starting in 1687. The Zunghar state's highly contested succession issue after the death of Galdan Tseren in 1745 offered the Qianlong emperor a unique opportunity to attack the Zunghars in the bitter winter of 1754–1755. The Qing mobilized massive troops to push into Ili, a critical site that the

Zunghars had dominated and used as a political center, and removed Dawachi (d. 1759), the last leader (khan) of the Zunghar state. The Ili campaign decisively changed the geopolitical structure in the region and ushered in a new era of a more assertive Qing imperial presence.

The Qing takeover of Ili delivered the coup de grâce to the Zunghar state. In that swift military advancement, the troops also destroyed the two major Tibetan Buddhist monasteries in the Zunghar stronghold.[68] Monasteries continued to feature prominently in the Qing's massive efforts to develop its own governing infrastructure. In this process, Tibetan Buddhism seemed to play a salient role in Qing reconstruction projects. The Zunghars had repeatedly requested to have Tibetan Buddhist teachers sent to Zungharia, and the Qing court did not refuse such a demand, but insisted on sending someone from Beijing. Several months after taking the city of Ili in February 1755, Fuheng (1722–1770), a confidant of the Qianlong emperor, asked the Lhasa Amban to recommend a replacement for the seventh Tatsak Jedrung, Lobzang Pelden Gyeltsen (1708–1758), the then-abbot of Yonghegong.[69] By October of that year, the Qianlong emperor summoned the seventh Tatsak Jedrung, Lobzang Pelden Gyeltsen, to Jehol to meet with him before imminently heading to Ili. A month later, the Lhasa Amban reported with a recommendation ready, but the seventh Tatsak Jedrung had halted his trip to Ili in December, and he died in Beijing three years later without going to Ili after all.[70] It remains unclear what caused him to abort his mission. Nonetheless, the Qing imperial state intended to assert its power through the two crucial Tibetan Buddhist institutions, and Yonghegong's abbot seemed to be an ideal candidate for reestablishing monastic centers in Zungharia. The conclusion of the Qing-Zunghar war and the destruction of the two monasteries in Zungharia left the Qing emperor with little choice but to rebuild the area.

The Zunghar state had developed close ties with the Geluk School in Tibet since at least the mid-seventeenth century. One of the crucial early leaders of the Zunghar, Galdan (1644–1697), spent years studying in Central Tibet and only gave up his Buddhist studies in 1671, when his brother was assassinated by a rival. Before 1671, there were approximately eighteen Tibetan Buddhist institutions, half of which were mobile monasteries, and others were stupas or temples of varied sizes.[71] The next two Zunghar leaders had continued to invest in religious infrastructures, building new or reconstructing damaged monasteries, inviting Buddhist teachers from Central

Tibet, and offering land or households to develop sustainable financial support, and the number of monks likely reached several thousand by the mid-eighteenth century.[72] Tibetan Buddhism once again proved critical in the Qing's Buddhist sphere in Inner Asia. This curious scenario reminds us how Tibetan Buddhism and the Qing's imperial enterprise found each other mutually beneficial. In 1767, the Qing relocated the Lama Si in Suiding City to the north bank of the Ili River, east of Huiyuan City, and renamed it Puhua Temple; it housed more than one thousand monks at the time.[73]

The seventh Tatsak Jedrung, Lobzang Pelden Gyeltsen, had significant influence among Geluk Buddhists. He accompanied the seventh Dalai Lama to Kham's Gartar Monastery when the minor head of the Ganden Podrang government was driven out of Lhasa and stayed there for a few years, starting in 1728. His post as the Yonghegong abbot positioned him well to take on the complex situation in the newly annexed city of Ili. His dual identity as a respected Buddhist associated with the Ganden Podrang and an esteemed Buddhist in the Qing imperial court secured a delicate balance as the Qing attempted to remap its Inner Asian landscape. His successor, the eighth Tatsak Jedrung, Yeshe Lobzang Tenpai Gongpo (1760–1810), was much more involved in the Qing's negotiations with Tibet and other Buddhists.[74] Despite the Qianlong emperor decrying the overwhelming Buddhist trülku practice in the final decade of his rule, the practice was crucial to his success in imperial formation and continued to influence Qing governance, even after he publicly disassociated himself from this Buddhist institution in his *Proclamation on Lamas*.

Even though the Qianlong emperor did impose limits on the trülku practice, he still found it indispensable as imperial governance became more sophisticated. Yonghegong operated as an institutional base for Buddhist dignitaries to continue influencing the Qing-Tibet relationship. In 1777, Ngawang Tsultrim (1721–1791) of Amdo's Chone region departed his abbacy in Yonghegong for Lhasa to fill the political vacuum left by the death of the seventh Demo, Ngawang Jampel Delek Gyatso (d. 1777), the first regent (Tib.: *rgyal tshab*), which was compounded by the reluctance of the young eighth Dalai Lama, Jampel Gyatso (1758–1804), to take control of the Ganden Podrang government.[75] In many ways, Ngawang Tsultrim was an ideal candidate for this delicate act. He spent almost all his twenties and thirties in Lhasa, studying and connecting with some of the most learned Buddhists of the time. By the time he came to Beijing in 1762, he was already highly regarded among the circle of Geluk Buddhists. His return to Lhasa in a changed political landscape further attested to the power of Buddhist practice and Qing reliance on it. Ngawang Tsultrim's political career ran to the very end of his life, when he was on his second mission to Lhasa in 1790, in the aftermath of the Gurkha War. He was posthumously recognized as first in the line of Tsemonling and established a new trülku lineage, which continued the influence in the Qing handling of Tibet, especially through serving as regents in Central Tibet.[76]

These two Buddhists were part of a circle of prominent Geluk Buddhists instrumental in shaping the Qing's imperial undertaking, and whose credentials were deeply rooted in their connection with the Lhasa-based Geluk Ganden Podrang Buddhist government and their own scholarly achievements. Their unique assets made them especially influential and allowed them to gain a stake in the Qing's imperial governing practices, but they were not in Beijing just for the sake of Qing imperial expansion and power consolidation. In 1744, the third Changkya, Rolpai Dorje, wrote to Ngawang Chokden (1677–1751), whom he encountered on his mission to meet the seventh Dalai Lama in Kham, and who later went on to become the fifty-fourth Ganden Tripa, the leader of the Geluk School.[77] In this exchange, the third Changkya, Rolpai Dorje, described his stay in Beijing this way: "I am presently in the capital city of the [Qing] empire [Tib. *rgyal khab chen po*], because of the benevolence of the [Qianlong] emperor. Owing to his many decrees, I have had abundant things in this lifetime; but bearing the teacher's [your] teachings and advice, and the Geluk teachings, for the sake of Buddhism, [I] work and pray night and day."[78] Here, the third Changkya, Rolpai Dorje, registered the Qing's imperial patronage as advantageous to Geluk teachings, and by extension to Tibetan Buddhism. His assertion helps to understand why Geluk Buddhist dignitaries partook in the Qing's growing imperial ambitions. It was the continuation of a prolonged effort on the part of Buddhists to strengthen the patron base for the young Geluk School. This did not start with the Qianlong emperor's patronage, and it was not to end with him. This historical precedent and inspiration are subjects I will further explore in the next two chapters.

Yonghegong's close connection with the imperial household also provided a platform for establishing other Buddhist practices within Qing imperial governance. Nothing attracted urban dwellers more than the fantastic Cham dance, a costumed Tibetan Buddhist ritual dance performed by monks wearing richly decorated masks. The dance is a form of meditation and religious offering. Only monks experienced in tantric rites would participate in a full-fledged Cham dance and recite tantric hymns, and the dance was often orchestrated by fifty to sixty musicians. The Cham dance became institutionalized as part of the Geluk knowledge repository since the late seventeenth century under the fifth Dalai Lama.[79] It soon became a powerful means by which religious rites and rituals became central to Buddhist practices. As a highly institutionalized bodily Buddhist practice, the Cham dance became a site in which the Qianlong emperor directed his religious energy.

In 1755, the Qianlong emperor decreed that a Cham dance team was to form in the imperial inner quarters, and he went so far as to order the dancers' costumes to be made in his imperial workshop, with assistance from his religious teacher, the third Changkya, Rolpai Dorje.[80] Like Yonghegong and his other Buddhist endeavors, the Cham dance practice was part of his manufacture of Buddhist knowledge. He sponsored an annual Cham dance as a form of religious practice. The ritual was likely part of long-standing Buddhist practices in Jehol until the twentieth century.[81] This performative and public Buddhist ritual also functioned to recreate collective historical memory and to reinforce a shared communal identity. Many of the dances had their roots in Buddhist history. In 1903, Berthold Laufer obtained a black hat from Beijing, which was likely made for a Cham dance performed at Yonghegong. The "Black Hat" (Tib.: *zhva nag*) Cham dance revolves around the assassination of the Buddhism-hating King Lang Darma, a ninth-century Tibetan imperial ruler who was killed by a monk disguised as a "Black Hat" magician. The twenty-one "Black Hat" dancers appeared in the second-to-last part of the dance and performed wearing ceremonial black hats to commemorate this Buddhist victory. The historical connection with Tibet's imperial past and Buddhist escape from the purge was relived through the Buddhist ritual in this far outpost of Tibetan Buddhist institutions under imperial patronage.

The grandeur of the dance gathered urban residents, foreign visitors, and petty vendors; it created a cultural focus in a cosmopolitan city with plenty of attractions each day. In the 1930s, onlookers would climb onto the lion statues, trees, and flagpoles. On one occasion, a courtyard was so packed that the flagpoles collapsed after too many spectators attempted to climb up them to see the dance.[82] The popularity of these rituals underscores the sustained interest that a cloistered imperial Buddhist space generated after restricting access for more than a century.

Rituals meant different things to laity and the monastic community separated by walls. Religious ritual events define a collective identity and "serve to organize time much as the pilgrimage routes organize space."[83] For the sanghas, Lhasa's Great Prayer Festival, known as Monlam Chenmo, was one of the most important festivals in Tibetan Buddhism since the fifteenth century, along with Buddhist scholars' public debates and novice monks' ordination ceremonies.[84] Shortly after Yonghegong was converted into a Tibetan Buddhist monastery, the Qianlong emperor had monks conduct this festival in his presence in 1746. Through a series of characteristic Buddhist rituals, Yonghegong was transformed into a practiced Buddhist space in which the Qianlong emperor assertively established himself and the Qing empire as part of the cross-cultural Buddhist knowledge network.

Even though Yonghegong was immobile, what it represented traveled far. The *Proclamation on Lamas* was carved on a stone stele that still stands in Yonghegong. On three separate occasions after the stele was erected in Beijing, rubbings of the text were sent to various frontier locales.[85] The circulations of the text, albeit in a different medium, helped communicate the Qing vision of a universal empire, in which Yonghegong and its connection with Tibetan Buddhism played a key role. To define Yonghegong as an imperial Buddhist institution also inadvertently advanced Buddhist interests, as the Geluk mandalic Buddhist government relied heavily upon monasteries to exert its influence and recruit patrons.

The flow of people was diverse, including Mongolian monk disciples, teachers from Tibet, visiting Buddhists of all kinds, and patrons from near and far. Yonghegong was reimagined as a key site of convergence that connected parts of Buddhist inner Asia under the Qianlong emperor's rule. Precisely because of the movement of Buddhist elements, the Qing capital was provincialized as a part of the Buddhist world. The circuit of a Buddhist institutional blueprint further stresses how the Tibetan Buddhist world and the expanding Qing empire grew symbiotically.

Learned Buddhists from Tibet shaped intellectual parameters for Mongolian monks and extended Buddhist influence in the capital city. The second Akyā, Lobzang Tenpai Gyeltsen (1708–1768), exemplified this slate of Amdo-associated Buddhists.[86] He was the twentieth throne holder of Amdo's Kumbum Jampa Ling's Tantric College (Tib.: *rgyud pa grwa tshang*) before 1748.[87] The years of the second Akyā, Lobzang Tenpai Gyeltsen, in Yonghegong established him as a respected master among Mongolian monks. His instructions on ritual, *lamrim* practices, and other writings shaped the intellectual parameters for aspiring Mongolian monks such as Lobzang Tsultrim (1740–1810).[88]

Lobzang Tsultrim enrolled in one of the Yonghegong's monastic colleges in 1763, when he was twenty-three, after having studied for years in Dolonnuur (more on this in chapter 3) and traveled to Amdo with his uncle to further his Buddhist studies. He spent seven years in Yonghegong, an experience that not only equipped him with Buddhist knowledge but also introduced him to some of the most influential Buddhist teachers in the Qing court, including the third Changkya, Rolpai Dorje.[89] Back home, he earned the respect of his countrymen for his commitment to Buddhist dissemination through translations and compositions and through printing Buddhist texts in his more advanced age. He was venerated as a prolific Buddhist scholar, fondly remembered by Chahar Mongolians as the "geshe from Chahar." The title of "geshe" is technically reserved for monks who have received a high academic degree in Buddhist philosophy, but it is unclear when and where Lobzang Tsultrim could have received such a degree. The "geshe" designation indicates that Tibetan Buddhist knowledge in and after the Qianlong reign gained social recognition in Mongolia. Lobzang Tsultrim tirelessly worked to compile texts in Mongolian, translate Tibetan texts, and, upon returning home, print Buddhist texts in his newly expanded monastery. His voluminous writings covered almost all aspects of the Buddhist knowledge system, including language, dialectics, arts and crafts, Buddhist philosophy, and the science of medicine.[90] His devotion to spreading Buddhism among his countrymen was lifelong, and his quest for Buddhist knowledge started in Dolonnuur, 224 miles north to Beijing, on the southern edge of the Mongol steppe.

He was typical of many young Mongolian monks. For them, Yonghegong was a desirable institution within which they could pursue their Buddhist studies. While studying in Beijing's Yonghegong, they cemented their ties with the imperial center that also functioned as a Tibetan Buddhist monastic outpost. Tibetan Buddhists were not only taught through texts, but also by some of the most remarkable Tibetan Buddhist scholars in a Geluk monastic college. These Mongol monk disciples experienced Tibetan Buddhism in a provincialized Beijing in Buddhist Inner Asia.

In 1792, a stele bearing the *Proclamation on Lamas* was installed in a courtyard in Yonghegong, wherein the emperor expressed his concerns about a Buddhist practice that he had explicitly championed for most of his regime and offered his solution to sever the tie between influential families and Buddhist trülku lines. It is an oversight to erase the process of making a space and consider the final phase of a built environment as the only form of it that matters, since space has a history too. Yonghegong's institutional history reveals the dynamic process through which the Qianlong emperor crafted and then publicized his vision of a universalist empire. Theatrical acts of governance were key to understanding the mass production of Buddhist materials in the early Qianlong reign, including the conversion of Yonghegong into a mass monastery to teach Buddhist subjects to hundreds or thousands of Mongolian monks, as well as some Han Chinese.

Manufacturing a dynamic Buddhist Inner Asia under Qing rule demanded commitment and investment from more than one party. The Qing imperial rulers undeniably took the lead in supporting the unique Buddhist culture with their public and zealous patronage of Buddhist art and literature, but the Mongolians and Buddhists from Tibet were constitutive of the Buddhist world as well. Their presence and their influence on the establishment of Yonghegong made this monastery simultaneously a Buddhist space for practice and a node of convergence within the expansive Buddhist knowledge network. To serve the mutual interest of the imperial rulers, Mongolian monks, and Buddhist teachers from Tibet, the construction of Yonghegong as an imperial Buddhist monastery was a delicate act of seeking common ground between the Qing empire and the sprawling Geluk monastic presence in Inner Asia. For the Qing rulers, Yonghegong provided a platform on which to construct a symbolic center that acted out the imperial imaginary and projected their vision of an all-encompassing empire. It served as a means of establishing imperial legitimacy when the emperor routinely received Inner Asian Buddhists on their rotational visits to Beijing. For the Geluk Buddhist prelates, Yonghegong was a home away from home where they augmented their ties with patrons who were by then the ruling elites of the Qing, including Mongolian princes and the imperial household. During their extended stays in Yonghegong, they trained a large number of young Mongolian monks, who advanced in their Buddhist studies and returned to their banners to propagate Buddhist teachings, found monasteries, or treat patients.

The tripartite relationship had developed in many ways to respond to internal fractures in Tibet. The outcast young seventh Dalai Lama, Kelzang Gyatso, grew under the influence and protection of many Buddhists outside of Lhasa, relying heavily upon these regional powers to drive out other contestants for ultimate power in Tibet. The Geluk Ganden Podrang Buddhist government continued to rule Tibet, with occasional challenges. The real strength of the Geluk School lay in its monastic constituencies and the growing number of the trülku lines, which both the Qing rulers and Mongolian princes keenly supported. The Buddhists traveled to or resided in many Geluk monasteries across many regions, which allowed a loosely defined but closely tied Buddhist community to take shape in Inner Asia. Yonghegong manifested the interdependence of all the involved parties as a node connecting a series of nested monasteries that functioned as monk-disciple pipelines for more advanced Buddhist studies. The monastic network became more and more robust in eastern Tibet, where monasteries turned east for more patrons and greater influence. The next chapter will discuss what led to these eastward activities and how they influenced Qing imperial governance and the geopolitical history of Inner Asia in the eighteenth century.

Chapter Three

ASSEMBLIES

Before "Chahar Geshe" Lobzang Tsultrim (1740–1810) holed up in Beijing's Yonghegong to gain more advanced Buddhist knowledge, he was one of several hundred Mongolian monks studying in Dolonnuur in the eighteenth century. Dolonnuur was a small town in the Shiliin Gol League of the southern Mongolian region of Chahar. It came to be known as the site where the Qing Kangxi emperor convened an assembly of Khalkha Mongols on June 3, 1691.[1] At this convocation, the Kangxi emperor conferred titles on and granted material goods to these leaders in exchange for their submission to the Qing; subsequently, the Khalkha Mongols were regrouped administratively into thirty-two banners.[2] The Qing's reorganized Mongolian administrative structure—i.e., the banner and league system—was intended to nurture a sense of imperial belonging under the Qing through replicating the Manchu social organization. Beyond this single event, the town has remained largely underexplored by scholars—aside from art historians, who recognize its importance in Buddhist art production in the second half of the nineteenth century. However, it was a town of many functions in the Qing empire's Buddhist Inner Asia.

One of the direct outcomes of the Kangxi emperor's assembly in 1691 was the construction of the Blue Temple (Mon.: Köke süme; Ch.: Huizong si).[3] When it was completed in 1711, young Mongolian monk disciples like Lobzang Tsultrim enrolled there to start their Buddhist studies. Two

ASSEMBLIES

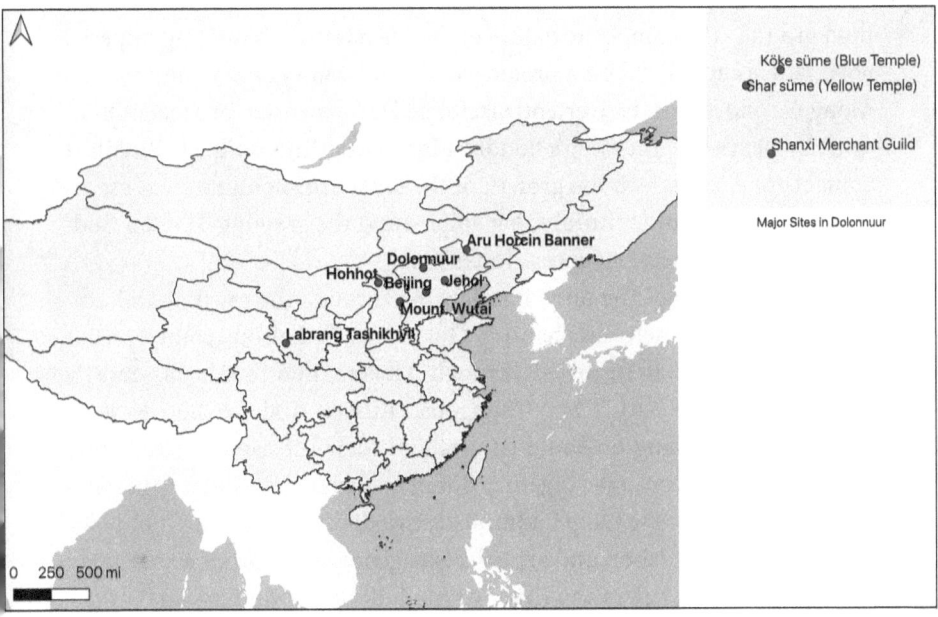

MAP 3. Sites discussed in chapter 3. Created by Lan Wu, adopting the shapefile of CHGIS, 2016, "1820 Layers GBK Encoding," https://doi.org/10.7910/DVN/2K4FHX, Harvard Dataverse, V1.

decades later, the succeeding Yongzheng emperor decreed that another monastery would be built nearby. The new Yellow Temple (Mon.: Shar süme; Ch.: Shanyi Si) was the emperor's offering to the third Changkya, Rolpai Dorje, who was captured six years prior, in the Yongzheng emperor's campaign against the Oirat Qoshot Mongols in Amdo. Together, the two monasteries made Dolonnuur a vibrant Buddhist hub that attracted Buddhists, artisans, and merchants across Inner Asia year-round since the early decades of the eighteenth century. This chapter examines what drew these diverse mobile groups to this town. The chapter title, "Assemblies," calls attention to how Dolonnuur's Yellow Temple and Blue Temple—the two Tibetan Buddhist monasteries—established a nodal point in Buddhist Inner Asia to which diverse groups gravitated. Groups consisted of Buddhist teachers from Tibet, Mongolian pilgrims, monk disciples, and merchants, as well as impoverished Chinese migrant laborers. They brought knowledge, market demands, labor, and capital and formed a new type of social place in Dolonnuur that captured the negotiated process through which the Qing imperial rulers and Inner Asian Buddhists found common ground. The composite nature of the town reflects how Qing imperial governance capitalized on a prolonged Buddhist missionary enterprise in Mongolia and how it inadvertently facilitated the expansion of Tibetan Buddhist influence into the Qing's Buddhist Inner Asia. This uniquely Buddhist contact zone, as seen in the growth of the town of Dolonnuur, was essential to both the multicultural Qing empire and the growing Tibetan Buddhist knowledge network across Inner Asia.

Humans were not the only ones flowing through the town of Dolonnuur. By the mid-nineteenth century, Dolonnuur had also become a major production site that funneled through Tibetan Buddhist arts—mostly bronze sculptures—to Tibet, Mongolia, Russia, and farther west to Europe.[4] The making of Buddhist arts and their subsequent circulation beyond Mongolia brought together different social circles that otherwise were kept apart by the Qing's administrative divisions. The flows of texts, Buddhist teachers, labor, and art objects engendered a porous social space that both the Qing rulers and Inner Asian Buddhists found useful for their respective agendas.

Located roughly 224 miles north to Beijing, Dolonnuur shares many environmental attributes with other places straddling the pastoral and agricultural zones along the Great Wall. It is dry and windy, though its name—which means "seven lakes"—suggests the existence of water sources nearby, at least once upon a time. Thanks to its historical importance, Dolonnuur's rough terrain did not preclude monks, pilgrims, artisans, merchants, or improvised farmers from coming here. Located in the vicinity of the Upper Camp (Ch.: *shangdu*), it was one of three Mongol Yuan capitals where the Yuan emperors spent their summers.[5] Since the turn of the eighteenth century, it had evolved and exuded greater appeal not only for Mongols but also for the Manchus.

Before examining Dolonnuur's rapid growth since then, a concise historical overview of all the major actors in the preceding seventeenth century is in order. I begin this chapter by sketching out how the various Mongol groups solved their conflicts in the sixteenth and seventeenth centuries, before many of them were subjugated and redefined within the Qing's banner system. I then consider the impact of the Dolonnuur assembly in 1691 on changing the dynamics in resolving disputes. Finally, I will focus on the emergence of Dolonnuur as a manifold space for a range of social actors in the eighteenth century and describe its ultimate dominance in Buddhist art production in Mongolia by the mid-nineteenth century. By tracing these evolutions, this chapter shows how Buddhist Inner Asia and the Qing empire's Inner Asia overlapped and were mutually productive as the Qing set out to redefine political hierarchy in Inner Asia.

CONFLICTS AND ASSEMBLIES IN THE SIXTEENTH AND SEVENTEENTH CENTURIES

After the Yuan Mongol forces were defeated by Ming troops in 1368, the Mongols retreated north and were plagued by internal struggles that spanned the second half of the fourteenth century to the middle of the seventeenth century. The Yuan remnants self-styled its rump state as Yuan, which clearly emphasized its continuity from the more powerful Great Yuan state established by Kublai Khan in 1271. In actuality, Mongol identity in the ensuing centuries was not at all static. The rise of Manchu power to the east and increasingly complex politics within Tibet to the southwest further complicated the geopolitical dynamics.

The Manchu's relentless expansions might have forced the Mongols and the Oirats to reevaluate their tenuous relationship; indeed, their respective leaders convened an assembly and pledged alliance on September 20, 1640.[6] The Great Code (Mon.: Yeke Cayaja) of 1640 not only created a sense of a collective defense coalition between the Khalkha Mongols and the Oirats. It was also vital for the post-Yuan Mongols in their creation of a shared communal identity.[7] Even though the alliance did not really halt the rise of the Manchus, the assembly should be considered within the long process of geopolitical construction in this volatile century. In Inner Asia, assemblies and the associated formation of confederations were a tried-and-true political mechanism to mediate conflicts or redefine relationship among stakeholders.[8] There had been several assemblies between the consequential 1640 assembly and the Dolonnuur assembly in 1691. But the assemblies and confederations formed on these occasions were rarely seen on this scale.

In the study of Mongolian history, the Great Code of 1640 has been the primary topic of interest, and the Dolonnuur assembly in 1691 has been viewed as part of the Mongols' submission to the Kangxi emperor. But they were not the only assemblies that bore historical weights, others were lesser-known and only concerned scholars of Mongolian history. For instance, three arbiters called upon the Khalkha Mongols to meet at Khüree (modern-day Ulaanbaatar) in late summer 1686. Agreements were made, violated, then remediated.[9] The three arbiters were the first Jebstundamba Hutuktu (1635–1723), representing the Khalkha left wing; the Lifanyuan minister, Alani, representing the Qing state; and the forty-fourth Ganden Tripa, Ngawang Lodrö Gyatso (1635–1688), representing the fifth Dalai Lama, the founder of the Geluk's mandalic Ganden Podrang Buddhist government.[10] In fact, this assembly in 1686 was intended to resolve conflicts between different leaders within the Khalkha Mongols over refugees and scarce resources. What triggered the refugee crisis and the ensuing social economic challenges went back decades. The last ruler of the Chahar Mongols, Ligdan Khan (1588–1634), attempted to reunite the Mongols in the early decades of the seventeenth century. The chaos caused by his failed attempts outlived him and spilled over to other Mongol communities. People fled to the Khalkha Mongol territory further north—predominantly its right wing—which was led by a succession of the Jasagtu Khans. Fights to contain the refugees and overconsumed economic resources eventually dragged the Khalkha's left-wing Tüshiyetü Khan into a series of exhausting negotiations, most of which proved fruitless.[11]

The presence of Tibetan Buddhists also reflects the geopolitical complexity of the area. Tibetan Buddhist participation suggests that another variable was part of the already intricate relationship between the Mongols, the Oirats, and the rising Manchu power. Tibetan Buddhist intermediaries were to assume an indispensable role in many of the regional parlays. The Qing Kangxi emperor clearly saw them as effective in mediations. Right after the 1686 Khüree meeting, the emperor requested that the fifth Dalai Lama, Ngawang Lobsang Gyatso, send a learned Buddhist to teach Buddhism in Beijing; thus, the forty-fourth Ganden Tripa, Ngawang Lodrö Gyatso (in office 1682–1685), set out with a disciple, the second Changkya, Ngawang Lobzang Chöden (1642–1714), to Beijing in 1687.[12] Ngawang Lodrö Gyatso was an ideal candidate for this mission. A year prior to his trip to Beijing, he represented the fifth Dalai Lama at the Khüree meeting. His trips to Mongolia and Beijing established a distinct channel of interaction between the Qing imperial court and the Buddhist Ganden Podrang government. After Ngawang Lodrö Gyatso died on his way back to Lhasa after this mission, Ngawang Lobzang Chöden, who was traveling with him, wielded substantial influence in Kangxi's court. For example, he received the title "anointed universally compassionate great state preceptor" (Ch.: *guanding pushan guangji da guoshi*) in 1706, and he was tasked with managing the Blue Temple in Dolonnuur until he retired to Amdo.[13] Ngawang Lobzang Chöden's successor in the line of Changkya trülkus was Rolpai Dorje, and the Yongzheng emperor offered this trülku Dolonnuur's Yellow Temple. These Buddhist mediators, mostly from Amdo, continued to influence geopolitical shake-ups in Qing Inner Asia. Dolonnuur monasteries helped perpetuate the legacy of these Amdo Buddhist trülkus in Mongolia. The two religious infrastructures intertwined and facilitated the outreach of the Geluk's mandalic Buddhist government.

Earlier Tibetan Buddhist missionary efforts in Mongolia that predated the rise of the Manchus and the founding of the Qing were indispensable factors that made all of this possible. Buddhists like Ngawang Lodrö Gyatso and Ngawang Lobzang Chöden traveled between Beijing and Lhasa, a practice to be systematized in the eighteenth century by the Yongzheng and Qianlong emperors. The long-lasting Geluk preaching among the Mongols led to the establishment of a number of Tibetan Buddhist monasteries in various locales. These monastic establishments helped Tibetan Buddhists—especially Geluk Buddhists—to bolster their influence in Mongolia, where many patrons made offerings and donations critical to the rise of the Geluk School. For the Qing emperors, these monasteries provided a platform from which they could broadcast a vision of Buddhist Inner Asia under the Qing.[14] Two decades after the Kangxi emperor constructed the Blue Temple, the succeeding Yongzheng emperor clearly understood the importance of these Buddhist institutions and invested heavily in building more monasteries in Urga and Dolonnuur that were said to cost two hundred thousand taels of silver.[15] These individuals' engagements—first in the assemblies and later on in Beijing—underscore the groundwork laid by earlier Buddhist missionaries who traveled to Mongolia before the rise of the Manchu in the early seventeenth century.[16]

All the while, Ming-dynasty China took over many regions that were once under the control of the Yuan Mongol state in China proper. Even after the Ming's troops sacked the Mongol's new capital city of Karakorum (near the Erdene Zuu in Mongolia) in 1380, the Mongols continued to threaten the Ming's border regions. In 1421, the third Ming emperor, Yongle (r. 1403–1424), relocated the Ming's capital city up north to modern-day Beijing, which had also served as the principal capital for the Mongol Yuan state. Emperor Yongle also personally led campaigns to push the Mongols farther north. The first eight decades of the Ming's rule were defined by the Ming's forceful military operations as a way to keep the Mongols at bay until 1449.[17] The Ming's persistent offenses did not eliminate the Mongols; indeed, their weakened and fragmented forces continued to pose challenges to the Ming.

The continuous military confrontations between the Ming and the Mongols had allowed the Oirat to grow even stronger. They had already established themselves as a fixture farther north, even before the demise of the Yuan Mongol state in 1368, which left little room for the Mongols to regain their strength. The Mongols and the Oirat came into direct conflict when the Ming's trading partner changed from the Mongols to the Oirat at the turn of the fifteenth century. The change in trade further fueled conflicts among the Ming, the Mongols, and the Oirat. Because both the Mongols and the Oirats desired to dominate border trade with the Ming, their competition for trading privileges often led them to raid the Ming's border towns when their demands were not met.[18] Early in the fall of 1449, the Oirat ruler Esen Khan captured the reigning Ming emperor, Zhengtong, in a major military victory at Tumu, some fifty miles northwest of Beijing, the Ming's capital at the time. The Ming's campaign was "unnecessary, ill-conceived, and ill-prepared."[19] It was a military disaster that caused Ming society to redefine its priorities. Inland territorial expansions and seaborne voyages were halted; instead, the state turned inward, and Ming society had to deal with the trauma long after the incident.[20] After the Manchu relocated its capital to Beijing, the Qing emperors had yet to consolidate their power. In 1661, the eight-year-old Aisin Gioro Hiowan yei ascended to the throne as the Kangxi emperor. At the start of his reign, four designated regents held power. It would be two decades before the Kangxi emperor removed the regents and purged the Ming loyalists. In the 1680s, the Kangxi emperor was engrossed in fighting with Galden, the leader of the Zunghar state who drove the Khalkha Mongols southward. The Khalkha Mongols and the Manchu troops severely debilitated the Zunghar Mongols in Ulan Butung in 1690, but they failed to put an end to the Zunghar threat. Thus, the Dolonnuur assembly can be understood as the Kangxi emperor's continuous effort to assert Manchu power in this contest for ultimate control of the region.

The interlocked history of all these stakeholders was a defining feature of the era after the Mongol Yuan collapsed. Indeed, no single power could decisively claim supremacy until the Khalkha Mongols' meeting with the Kangxi emperor at Dolonnuur in 1691. Dolonnuur's transformation into a key Buddhist center was an important episode in the prolonged struggle by several successive Manchu emperors to eradicate the threatening Zunghar state of the Oirat throughout many of their reigns. Indeed, the Dolonnuur assembly redefined the power hierarchy in Inner Asia.

A NODE OF BUDDHIST TEACHINGS IN MONGOLIA IN THE EIGHTEENTH CENTURY

The town of Dolonnuur was first associated with the Qing's assembly. As described above, it was then associated with two major Tibetan Buddhist monasteries. Around the 1840s, it emerged as a promising production site for Buddhist arts—especially bronze sculptures—which circulated as far as Europe. Over the course of one and a half centuries in the Qing, the town itself had grown to attract sizable numbers of visitors as well as many who settled down to call this place home. When Évariste Régis Huc (1813–1860), a French Catholic priest, made his way to Dolonnuur in 1844, he met increasing numbers of Chinese and Mongolian travelers. Indeed, this made him realize that they were approaching "the great town of Tolon-Noor [Dolonnuur]."[21] The well-traveled route leading up to the town of Dolonnuur was marked by a succession of cemeteries that defined the town proper. Lacing one large cemetery that encircled the town were vegetable gardens that grew a few necessary esculents like leeks, spinach, hard bitter lettuces, and cabbages—all of which appeared miserable to Huc's eyes.[22] The scale and diversity of visitors in Dolonnuur at this time was the upshot of negotiations. Its continuous evolution captured the changing and overlapping nature of Inner Asia under the Qing with the influence of Tibetan Buddhism.

The Dolonnuur monasteries represented the imperially sponsored Tibetan Buddhist monasteries found in and near the Qing's political centers. Administratively, an office was created in Dolonnuur in 1701 to oversee Tibetan Buddhist affairs before the construction of the Yellow Temple was complete. The Office of Lama Seals and Affairs (Ch.: Lama yinwu chu) was an administrative body that the Qing state created to meet the growing demands of handling the monastic population when large monasteries began to house monk disciples. In 1745, a year after Beijing's Yonghegong was converted into a Tibetan Buddhist monastic college, a similar office was established in Beijing.[23] The office was also installed at important Tibetan Buddhist sites under the Qing's rule, such as Mukden, Jehol, Hohhot, Beijing, and Mount Wutai, the last of which was headed by Geluk monks trained in Central Tibet.[24] Isabelle Charleux has assessed that this office existed in monasteries with an official title, thereby recognized by the Qing's Lifanyuan.[25] If Charleux's assertion is correct, then this specific administrative organ could exist in many imperially sanctioned monasteries regardless of their size or monastic population, not just in core cities like Beijing and Dolonnuur. This would mean that monasteries that had received the seal from Lifanyuan and an official title would have a "place to keep the seal," the origin of this office's name. Further research on this office's evolvement and responsibilities may shed new light on how involved the Qing imperial state was in the day-to-day management of institutional affairs in approximately 1,340 monasteries in southern Mongolia at the turn of the twentieth century.[26] In the case of Dolonnuur's two monasteries, it was clear that a fully staffed office was set up with one chief governing Lama (Man.: *Jasak i da lama*), two chief Lamas (Man.: *da lama*), and two vice chief Lamas by the early Qianlong reign in the mid-eighteenth century.[27] The day-to-day administrative tasks seem to have been handled by one managing monk (Man.: *damci*), and then by two after 1878.[28] This office's continual presence in Dolonnuur not only attests to an increasingly systematic approach to Tibetan Buddhist affairs under the Qing but also reveals that the Qing imperial support was not the only reason why Tibetan Buddhism flourished in Mongolia. The earlier missionary undertakings sowed seeds among the Mongols, and the Qing's investment further facilitated broadening the impact of Tibetan Buddhism in Mongolia with key institutions. Even though the Qing's patronage ebbed after the Qianlong reign, Buddhists continued to play a key role among the Mongols.

The Dolonnuur monasteries served multiple functions at once. For example, they were a resting spot for many Buddhist pilgrims en route to

Beijing, Mount Wutai, or the Qing's imperial summer resort in Jehol nearby, and farther west to Amdo and Central Tibet. The most famous visitor may have been the sixth Panchen Lama, Lobzang Palden Yeshe, in 1780.[29] The monasteries also provided shelter for the Buddhists residing in Beijing who could not tolerate its summer heat. In addition, the town of Dolonnuur was a site for commerce and a flourishing center for Buddhist art production. Above all, it was where many young Mongolian monks, like Lobzang Tsultrim from Chahar, began their monastic lives. Dolonnuur was a platform from which the Qing state capitalized on the longstanding interest of Mongolians in Buddhism, and where the Geluk Buddhists labored to disseminate Buddhism by exploiting a key infrastructural mechanism.

At the age of seven, Lobzang Tsultrim took novice vows with his uncle, with whom he began to study the Mongolian and Tibetan languages. A decade later, he went to one of the two Dolonnuur monasteries to hone his linguistic skills, which proved crucial for his voluminous literary production in the two languages. When he turned twenty, he visited the monastery again, this time to be ordained by one of the most revered Geluk scholars at the time. This scholar was the second Sertri, Lobzang Tenpai Nyima. This Buddhist dignitary routinely spent his summers in Dolonnuur during his prolonged stay in Beijing, where he was tasked with overseeing many projects, including converting Yonghegong. Lobzang Tsultrim spent most of his twenties studying in Yonghegong, where he was so diligent that he only went to the market twice in his seven-year stay. Among his teachers, Lobzang Tsultrim seemed to be close to the second Akyā, Lobzang Tenpai Gyeltsen, and to Chone Ngawang Tsultrim (1721–1791).[30] The two Buddhists were both prolific writers and influential in the circle of Buddhists privileged in the Qing court. Chone Ngawang Tsultrim was later appointed as a regent in Tibet and exercised considerable power in politics. He was likely the most high-profile Buddhist trülku in the Qianlong court after the death of the emperor's Buddhist teacher, the third Changkya, Rolpai Dorje. This was especially the case between 1777 and 1786, when he was appointed as the regent of Tibet, while the eighth Dalai Lama focused on his studies.[31] He was entrusted with mediating between Qing officials and the Tibetan administration when disagreement arose between them in the aftermath of the Gurkha war between Tibet and Nepal in 1791.[32] He was posthumously recognized as the first Tsemönling, which started a new trülku line.

By the late Qianlong reign in the 1780s and 1790s, a cluster of Buddhist trülkus moved between Lhasa and Beijing and established themselves as key mediators in Buddhist Inner Asia. Their political undertakings were certainly helpful in reconsidering how the Qing politics had evolved in its dealing with Tibet in this crucial century, but their roles went beyond the political realm. As one of the two pillars in providing infrastructural framework, these Buddhist trülkus trained many monk disciples, like Chahar's Lobzang Tsultrim, who went on to compose, translate, and print texts in the Mongolian language. These trülkus also conducted rituals and built or renovated monasteries in their home regions. If large Tibetan Buddhist monasteries shaped the contours of Buddhist Inner Asia by mapping Tibetan Buddhism on Inner Asian landscape, then knowledge transmitted through teachings, texts, and interpersonal relationships gave Buddhist Inner Asia much-needed energy and set it in motion. The two religious infrastructural elements collectively and ingeniously contributed to the creation and growth of Buddhist space that not only directly challenged the Qing empire's Inner Asia, but also relied upon a reconfigured Inner Asia under the Qing. The space was conductive for young monks like Chahar Lobzang Tsultrim to thrive and access knowledge and authority in places closer to home. Elements that contributed to his social development include his writings, his monastic training, and the intellectual orbit into which his years in these large Geluk monasteries brought him. This last element revealed the profound impact that Tibetan Buddhism had on Mongolian Buddhist practice since the eighteenth century. In the meantime, young Mongolian monks were being passed through the Dolonnuur monasteries. This not only facilitated their establishing connections with the Qing state but also fostered their gravitation towards Buddhist hubs farther to the west in the Himalayas. For the many young monk disciples, their Buddhist identity was defined by representing their home banner, enrolling in an imperially sanctioned Tibetan Buddhist monastery, studying under erudite Geluk trülkus, and immersing themselves in a knowledge network closer to home. Institutionally, the two monasteries helped sustain a vast Buddhist knowledge network by providing an anchor for Buddhists all across Inner Asia.

After he returned to his home in southern Mongolia, Lobzang Tsultrim traveled to Dolonnuur monasteries to receive more teachings. He also met with the sixth Panchen Lama, Pelden Yeshe (1738–1780), when the latter passed through Dolonnuur en route to Beijing in 1780.[33] Lobzang Tsultrim was among the many Buddhists who came to attend teachings and make offerings to the famed sixth Panchen Lama.[34] Dolonnuur was the last stop before the sixth Panchen Lama reached Beijing, where an audience with the famed Buddhist was most likely reserved for the privileged few. Buddhist monasteries like those in Dolonnuur allowed lesser-known Buddhists and many young Buddhists to forge a relationship with Buddhist authorities like the sixth Panchen Lama. Indeed, in 1782, Lobzang Tsultrim translated the collected works (Tib.: *gsung 'bum*) of the sixth Panchen Lama, Pelden Yeshe, into the Mongolian language, after the sixth Panchen Lama died of smallpox in Beijing. Monastic training and the intellectual network formed and extended through texts, visits, and teachings created a community that transcended physical and temporal restrictions. Lobzang Tsultrim set out to translate texts from Tibetan into Mongolian and to compile texts in the Mongolian and Tibetan languages. As part of his Buddhist engagement, he also gave lectures, performed rituals, and founded the Čagan Agulan Monastery, wherein he managed to print many Buddhist texts.[35] As recently as 2000, the local government reported that this monastery was known as one of the three major Mongolian-language printing centers in Mongolia.

Without Buddhists' persistent missionary efforts from the sixteenth to eighteenth centuries and without the Qing's heavy investment in nurturing Buddhist culture among Mongolians, young Mongolian monks like Lobzang Tsultrim would have needed to go to Amdo or more likely even to Lhasa to obtain more advanced Buddhist knowledge. The interconnected formation of Buddhist Inner Asia under these specific historical circumstances provided Lobzang Tsultrim with resources, inspiration, and connections to claim his Buddhist identity and grant him agency. The multilayered Buddhist network went beyond the rulers in both the Qing and the Geluk's Ganden Podrang government. Indeed, their negotiation helped create a Buddhist community that was found within a network of Tibetan Buddhist monasteries in Mongolia. The Qing rulers sponsored the constructions of the two monasteries and assigned quotas for each banner to send young Buddhist monks. However, Buddhist trülkus and teachers helped shape the town of Dolonnuur into a place for many: monk disciples, teachers, the laity, and merchants. Trülkus attracted pilgrims, patrons, and monk disciples from near and far.

Lobzang Tsultrim was a sterling student and achieved laudable goals that were unmatched among his peers. However, concerns scattered in letters exchanged between the monasteries and the banners show that not every monk sent there was content with his fate. For example, a monk by the name of Tsewang fell behind in the Tibetan-language curriculum. His struggle ultimately led the monastery to request his home banner to send a more competent monk in his place.[36] Illness resulted from many conditions such as stress. In 1789, Yeshe, a young monk from the Khalkha Secen Khan's Jasak Banner was reported as falling ill because he struggled to adapt to monastic life. Yeshe was promptly replaced by Sherab, who was also from his banner.[37] The expectations of monk disciples could cause unbearable stress for some and prompted them to flee. A certain Lobzang of the Khalkha Mongol Banner reported to the monasteries about his difficulties in acclimating to Dolonnuur and stated his desire to withdraw. After his request was denied, Lobzang left without permission. The monasteries deemed his request ungenuine, because he had failed the language curriculum. Regardless of the explanation, Lobzang's home banner in Khalka was responsible for replacing him with someone more suitable for Buddhist studies in Dolonnuur. Until then, the Dolonnuur monasteries reallocated Lobzang's duties, including sutra recitations on his behalf, to another monk.[38] To the Dolonnuur monasteries, merit-generating Buddhist practices were of ultimate importance.

The monasteries insisted that they did not accept "ill" or "lazy" monk disciples.[39] In 1789, a monk by the name of Baidai, who came from the Sain Noyan Banner of the Khalkha Mongol, fell ill and died. Tosalaci, the head of his banner, was asked to send an "intelligent" young monk to replace him and twenty-one taels of silver to cover the replacement's living expenses in Dolonnuur.[40] On another occasion in 1789, the monasteries felt the need to request the Jarud Banner of the Juu Uda League in eastern Mongolia to send a monk to replace Tashi, who was similarly challenged in reciting sutras in the Tibetan language.[41] Sutra recitations were so important that the monasteries loaned money to their monks when several banners could not send money for two consecutive years, in 1787–1788. At that time, many Mongolians could not make ends meet, because of hazardous weather from the start of the decade.[42] With the decline of the Qing's financial support, and perhaps due to the equally struggling Mongol banners, in the second half of the nineteenth century, many impoverished monks were drafted into the labor force for transportation projects out of necessity.⁴³ It reminds us not to assume the monastic community was a monolithic whole where every member had the same access to or inspiration for Buddhist knowledge. In that sense, Dolonnuur's monasteries epitomized the complexity of Tibetan Buddhist monasteries in Tibet.⁴⁴

The monasteries were not the only party concerned with religious affairs in Dolonnuur; so were the Mongolian banners. Each Mongolian banner sent a designated number of young monks for study and to represent their respective banners. During the eighteenth century, approximately 400 monks from 106 Mongolian banners called Dolonnuur monasteries home. The monks' banners covered their living costs, whereas their teachers were on the official payroll, like their counterparts in Yonghegong. A Khalkha Mongol banner explicitly wrote that the money from this banner was intended for Buddhist sutra recitations.⁴⁵ The banner also wrote to follow up on a previous communication wherein the monasteries attempted to raise funds to build a new hall and received five hundred taels of silver from this banner. In this letter, the Khalkha banner requested that the monasteries inform them whether the money was used for supporting the recitation of sutras in this newly constructed hall.⁴⁶ The exchanges shed light on the unique political economy of merit that existed in the Qing's Buddhist Inner Asia. With imperially sanctioned Tibetan Buddhist monasteries, these young monk disciples helped funnel through Mongol patrons' material wealth and translated it into Buddhist merits. The Qing's support of Tibetan Buddhist monasteries legitimatized and normalized Mongols' deep historical connection with Tibetan Buddhism. Through the Geluk Buddhists and these monasteries, the banner-representing monk disciples helped further dissimilate its teachings among the Mongols.

The Geluk School's rise to dominance was intimately connected with the Mongols. It was not until the enthronement of the fourth Dalai Lama—who was a Mongol—as the abbot of the Drepung monastery in 1603, along with the military support that such an enthronement entailed, that the Geluk School began to have any forceful political presence in Central Tibet.⁴⁷ The institution of Tibetan Buddhist trülku also provided Mongols with a means to exercise a certain power over monastic and political contestations in Tibet; ultimately, they used it to sever deep-seated familial ties between the Tibetan aristocracy and Tibetan Buddhist monastic estates.[48] For the Buddhists, their connections with the line of the Dalai Lama became a valuable asset, and many of them grew more powerful over time. In 1578, Altan Khan met with Sönam Gyatso, the third Dalai Lama avant la lettre. At their meeting in Amdo, Altan Khan requested that Sönam Gyatso send a representative to return with him to Köke Khota (modern-day Hohhot in China's Inner Mongolia Autonomous Region). In response, Tongkhor Yonten Gyatso (1557–1587) spent four years in the Altan Khan's territory, until 1582. During his stay, Yonten Gyatso was regarded as "the highest of the spiritual leaders there."[49] He was probably the first recorded Buddhist to represent Geluk power in Mongolia.[50] Yonten Gyatso was recognized as the second trülku of the Tongkhor line of reincarnation, which continued to grow in influence. A century and a half later, the fifth Tongkhor trülku, Sönam Gyatso, successfully installed his own nephew as the second Jamyang Zhepa, an architect of Amdo's Labrang Tashilkhyil, as documented in the first chapter of this book.

This historical context was overtaken by the more visible systematic Qing imperial engagements launched in the Qianlong reign. Nevertheless, the Mongolian banners' commitment to optimal Buddhist practice bespoke a Buddhist culture apart from the court, whose perspectives have dominated historical analysis on this issue. The shift from more sporadic and individually driven missionary efforts to this institutional practice was a long process. Without the Qing imperial promotion of Tibetan Buddhist monasteries and the historical ties cultivated by earlier Buddhists, this new Buddhist culture would not have developed.

Dolonnuur joined Buddhist monastic clusters in Mount Wutai, Beijing, and the imperial summer resort of Jehol to meet the institutional needs of Buddhist eastward expansion into the Qing's Inner Asia. Monasteries like those in Dolonnuur functioned as nodal points linking the cross-cultural knowledge network. For decades, Mongols had enrolled in major Geluk monasteries to advance their intellectual capacity. With the establishment of Dolonnuur monasteries and Beijing's Lama Temple, Mongols could obtain systematic Geluk monastic education on the Mongol steppe or at places closer to it. The two monasteries rendered Dolonnuur a new institutional center of Tibetan Buddhist gathering. The highly systematized Geluk monastic curriculum and its stress on Tibetan-language skills made

Geluk mass monasticism key for sustaining the knowledge network beyond Tibet.

MOBILE BUDDHISTS AND IMMOBILE MONASTERIES

Forging connections with Mongolian communities went further back, before the series of assemblies outlined in the beginning of the chapter, even before Sönam Gyatso—the future third Dalai Lama—met with the Altan Khan in 1578.[51] More than a handful of Tibetan Buddhists of diverse sectarian, regional, and ethno-cultural backgrounds set out to meet several Mongolian headmen.[52] These earlier missionary peregrinations were spatially expansive and less holistic than the cluster of Buddhists discussed in the book so far. Yet, they were no less impactful than the trips of those who set foot in Mongolia in the eighteenth century. Indeed, the sporadic journeys of these early Buddhist vanguards created a historical precedent that helped the Qing emperors develop their universalist governing philosophy and drove home their vision of a pluralist empire. The creation of a Buddhist Inner Asia was the end result of century-long interactions among the Mongols, Tibetan Buddhists, and, later on, the Qing imperial state.

Undoubtedly, the Qing's imperial expansions inadvertently boosted these Geluk Buddhist missionary endeavors—perhaps more so in the eighteenth century, when the numbers of Tibetan Buddhist trülkus and monasteries increased drastically both in Tibet and Mongolia. The Qing's imperial patronage intensified in the second half of the Qianlong reign. At the turn of the nineteenth century, patronage ebbed when the town established itself as a major production site for Tibetan Buddhist art—principally bronze sculptures—which continued to attract Tibetan Buddhists. The Mongolians had held these Buddhist teachers from Tibet in high regard since the sixteenth century. By 1844, when the Catholic priest Évariste Régis Huc made his way to Dolonnuur, he was told that "the nearer you approach the West... the purer and more luminous will the doctrine manifest itself."[53] Indeed, Tibet and Buddhists from Tibet continued to be held as the ultimate source of authority in Buddhist Mongolia. It is worth reiterating that the Qing imperial enterprise—including territorial expansion and Buddhist patronage—was crucial in making sites like Dolonnuur nodes of convergence.[54]

ASSEMBLIES

To many Inner Asian Buddhists, the Qing's engagement with Tibet provided major and minor Buddhists alike with greater space and more opportunities to meet their goals. The Qing state reconfigured various Mongolian groups, which in many ways changed the missionary trajectory for many Tibetan Buddhists. Unlike earlier vanguards in the sixteenth and seventeenth centuries, Geluk trülkus in the late eighteenth century traveled in a different political and religious landscape. At this time, large monasteries received the Qing's imperial patronage. To be sure, Inner Asia was not an open land without any restrictions. The Qing state put in place restrictions and regulations to discourage travels by Tibetan Buddhists in Mongolia.

The Qing's imperial patronage could only extend to so many established Buddhist trülkus, but it did not stop many others from availing themselves of state initiatives to fund monasteries and produce Buddhist knowledge. Such efforts helped move these trülkus in the newly defined Inner Asia in the Qing empire. The sites marked by these peripatetic Buddhists were not just points on a map, such as Beijing or Lhasa; they were nodes of connections with an expansive Buddhist network. These imperially sponsored monasteries provided institutional common ground for Buddhists across regional and linguistic divides to develop their Buddhist community and shared Buddhist knowledge. These peripatetic Buddhists brought with them embodied Buddhist knowledge as they traveled within Buddhist Inner Asia, connected by monastic establishments. Their travels helped transcend linguistic and geographical divides and made a sense of communal belonging tangible. Two important factors facilitated their transregional travels: the Geluk School's long-standing missionary efforts to the east since the late sixteenth century and the Qing empire's growing territorial claims. By the eighteenth century, most of the post-Yuan Mongolian groups to the north, south, and east were brought into the Qing imperial orbit in some fashion. This geopolitical realignment redrew the cultural landscape in Inner Asia. Within this setting, Buddhists from Tibet had cultivated patrons since the sixteenth century, but during this time things were different. Unlike early Tibetan Buddhist vanguards, most Buddhists in Mongolia in the eighteenth century were Geluk trülkus with significant resources to mobilize. Their resources included the imperially sponsored Tibetan Buddhist monasteries, which served as institutional outposts allowing these Buddhists to reach farther north and east.

Dolonnuur became a meeting point for Buddhists of various resources. Some rested their tired bodies on their multistop trips, like the second Jamyang Zhepa, Konchok Jigme Wangpo, or the more famed sixth Panchen Lama, Lobzang Palden Yeshe; others established residence there. At one point the number of trülku estates reached thirteen. Many of them would move between Beijing and Dolonnuur, the latter sheltering them from the miserable summer heat of Beijing. This tradition went back to the first decade of the 1700s, when the Blue Temple was hardly ready to receive young monks. The second Changkya, Ngawang Lobzang Chöden, spent his summers in Dolonnuur compiling ritual texts, giving teachings, and meeting with Buddhists, as did Ngawang Lodrö Gyatso.[55] In 1734, the second Serkhi, Lobzang Tenpai Nyima, reportedly ordained more than two hundred people and gave numerous Buddhist teachings in one summer.[56] As more trülkus were bureaucratized and spent considerable time in Beijing, they followed suit and routinely came to Dolonnuur to give teachings and meet with the laity.[57] In 1762, for instance, the third Changkya, Rolpai Dorje, found it taxing to give lectures every day for fifteen consecutive days in Dolonnuur.[58] For these prominent Buddhist scholars, teachings and writings were essential to their Buddhist identity. The Geluk School accentuated total dedication to Buddhist learning, and its rigorous monastic curricula helped produced a slate of Buddhist men of letters. It was crucial for the Geluk School to reach farther across Mongolia. The Qing's imperial patronage and territorial expansion facilitated the Geluk's eastward ventures across administrative and linguistic boundaries.

Many Buddhists traveled beyond the major monasteries founded by the Qing imperial household. Between 1769 and 1772, the second Jamyang Zhepa, Konchok Jigme Wangpo, the then-abbot of Amdo's Labrang Tashikhyil, traveled tirelessly in Mongolia.[59] He made multiple stops to dine with Mongolian princes, to give Buddhist teachings to large crowds, and to collect offerings throughout southern and eastern Mongolia.[60] In this three-year journey, he also stopped in Beijing—even though it was not his final destination. During his stay in Beijing, the second Jamyang Zhepa, Konchok Jigme Wangpo, had some truly curious experiences that are recounted in his spiritual biography. His point of contact was the Qianlong emperor's Buddhist teacher and imperial preceptor, the third

Changkya, Rolpai Dorje. Rolpai Dorje had proposed to introduce the second Jamyang Zhepa to the emperor. He declined, apparently, although his reasons are not explained in his spiritual biography. Instead, he stood with the Rolpai Dorje's retinue when the emperor came to visit him at his residence in the now-defunct Songzhu Temple.[61] He took a tour of the imperial gardens on the outskirts of Beijing and other Buddhist sites in the capital.[62] The second Jamyang Zhepa, Konchok Jigme Wangpo, was looking for more patrons in these crucial early years of his monastery. Reaching further east made sense. His trips set the course for several eminent Amdo Buddhists later on and proved his strategies successful in retaining patrons among the Mongols. The trülku lineage of Detri made substantial efforts over time to cultivate its tie to the eastern Mongolian region. I will turn to this development now.

CRAFTING BUDDHIST ART IN BUDDHIST INNER ASIA

In 1808, the third Detri, Jamyang Tubten Nyima (1779–1862), of Amdo's Labrang Tashikhyil, commissioned two foundries in Dolonnuur to produce a brass statue of Mañjuśrī (Tib.: Jamyang künzik) and numerous other Buddhist figures. In 1822, these objects made their way to the Labrang Tashikhyil and found a home at Kelzang Lhakhang, a new temple that Jamyang Tubten Nyima had built next to his residence on the southeastern edge of the Labrang Monastery complex. These two buildings were the first real estate owned by this trülku, whose line of succession had remained in the residence of the Jamyang Zhepa reincarnation line, the founding lineage of the Labrang Tashikhyil. In the same year, Jamyang Tubten Nyima was named abbot of the Labrang Tashikhyil. In an 1823 essay commemorating the opening of this temple, Jamyang Tubten Nyima acknowledged his patron's generous support and rejoiced in the building's exquisite statues. He had gone a long way—both figuratively and literally—to find a patron.

The Mongolian leader of the Aru Horchin Banner in the eastern Mongolian league of Juu Uda provided indispensable funds for the large construction project.[63] The connection between this Mongolian patron and the Detri trülku line continued until the end of Qing rule.[64] Labrang Tashikhyil had long cultivated patrons in eastern Mongolia. Around 1770, the second Jamyang Zhepa founded a monastery in Baarin Left banner (modern-day Chifeng in the Inner Mongolia Autonomous Region). This monastery—Gilubar zuu (Ch.: Houzhao miao, Shanfu si; Mon.: Sain buyantu süme)—was known as the Little Wutai Shan. This appellation associated it with one of the most important Tibetan Buddhist sites in north China among Buddhists of Inner Asia.[65] Eventually, Labrang Tashikhyil strove to maintain a strong patron base in the Juu Uda League.[66] Labrang Tashikhyil was not alone in cultivating ties with faraway Mongolian patrons. Gönlung Monastery, another influential Amdo monastery, also registered efforts made since the second half of the eighteenth century by one of its minor trülku lines to work with patrons from Inner Mongolia.[67]

The reasons behind the apparent surge in interest since the mid-Qianlong reign are manifold. Sullivan has suggested that Amdo monasteries lost local patrons after the Lobzang Danjin Uprising and the withdrawal of the Oirat rulers in this region in 1723–1724, which renewed Amdo trülkus' efforts to find patrons in Inner Mongolia.[68] If we look at these individuals' travels since the turn of the nineteenth century, it is possible that the shifting patron base was a primary driving force that spurred their eastward journeys. But Amdo's connections with Mongolia to the east had long been in the making. Tibetan Buddhists had cultivated local ties before the Manchu rose to dominance; moreover, the Manchu Qing's imperial patronage helped create Buddhist Inner Asia through sponsorships of monasteries like the two in Dolonnuur. The lateral interactions away from the Qing imperial enterprise and the political center were the cornerstone of the resurgence of Geluk trülkus' actions in Inner Mongolia between the mid-Qianlong reign to the end of the Qing empire in 1911.

In addition to these journeys, many of these Buddhists were prolific writers who left behind voluminous records on their trips. In their literary renderings, Buddhist trülkus extended their socioeconomic influence far and beyond their monastic bases. In his discussion of Labrang Monastery's growth and development, Nietupski notes that Amdo trülkus' travels were awe-inspiring, which left a vivid impression on the communities they and their large entourages visited. The embellished processions certainly helped maintain a powerful image of Tibetan Buddhism in the areas they traveled in, and they might have increased the size of their patron pools as people witnessed the grandeur. But more importantly, the literary narratives recounting these events defined such endeavors as "corvée responsibility."[69] Here, we must bear in mind that the contractual nature of corvée allowed the Buddhist trülkus to invent a new mechanism in order not only to expand their socioeconomic power in their own lifetimes but also to allow later generations of the trülku line to exert influence over the communities. Needless to say, the corvée responsibility might not have been conceived in the same way by the communities. But the language used in the literature helped shape the relationship between a monastery and its far-flung patron communities.

This curious case reveals two intriguing issues regarding Buddhist art production in the Qing. Earlier Buddhist missionary undertakings and more concerted efforts from the Qing rulers helped cement the authority of Buddhists in Inner Asia. Buddhist trülku lines and Tibetan Buddhist monasteries grew rapidly. Peter Schwieger has tallied the registered trülku lines under the Dalai Lama jurisdiction in Central Tibet, western Tibet, and the western part of eastern Tibet. According to Schwieger, these rose by 40 percent in the eighteenth century, and he records thirty trülkus in the Mongolian and Chinese areas in the same document.[70] The drastically increased number of Tibetan Buddhists with a nest of Buddhist monasteries drove demand for texts and artworks to articulate Buddhism's connection with both the religious centers in Tibet and the political center in Beijing. For many Buddhists like Jamyang Tubten Nyima, Dolonnuur's composite art production site offered a way to bridge the gap between supply and demand for Buddhist statues.

Admittedly, Dolonnuur was not the only site where Tibetan Buddhist arts were produced in the Qing. In Beijing, the Qing's imperial studio was responsible for cataloguing and producing many Tibetan Buddhist art objects. Patricia Berger's seminal research has revealed the complexities of a process through which art production was part of the negotiations in the Qing's imperial enterprise.[71] Even though the imperial studio enjoyed incomparable resources and access to artists and artisans, it was not the only place where Tibetan Buddhist arts were made in the Qing. In fact, Bogdo Gegen Zanabazar (1635–1723), the first Jebtsundamba Khutuktu of Khalkha, developed such a distinct style that his gilt bronze sculptures defined an entirely new school of artistic expression.[72] In either case, Tibetan Buddhist arts were produced for specific recipients. In Beijing's imperial studio, most of the arts produced were intended for the imperial household or as gifts to Tibetan Buddhist dignitaries. Those made under the tutelage of Zanabazar were certainly not meant for the growing market with a higher demand for Buddhist arts. This, I believe, sets Dolonnuur apart from these better-studied sites in the Qing.

So, what made Dolonnuur unique? For the time being, without massive investment from the Qing imperial household in these costly projects, the drastically increased number of Buddhist trülkus—and of Buddhists in general—in the Qianlong reign still looked to establish connections with patrons. To that end, a reference to the Qing's imperial recognition was important for them in order to draw the laity and expand their patron pool. Foundries in Dolonnuur evolved with the increasing demand from this specific market: Inner Asian Buddhists' commissions for Buddhist arts to bring home. By the mid-nineteenth century, Dolonnuur overtook Hohhot and became a vital metalworking production site for many Buddhists in Inner Asia, north China, eastern Tibet, Russia, and a few places in Europe.[73] Yulia Elikhina and Victoria Demenova examine fifty-three sculptures identified as the "Dolonnuur school." The fact that a distinct artistic school was named after the town of Dolonnuur indicates the far reach of Dolonnuur's sculpture production.[74] Not all the fifty-three objects were made in Dolonnuur workshops. Some of them were produced in workshops in Urga (modern-day Ulaanbaatar), Buddhist regions of Russia, or parts of Europe. Their shared attributes include the mixed technique: hammered metal for the body and the base, cast metal mostly for limbs and occasionally for the head, thin-sheet hammered decorations attached to the sculpture. In addition, most of the sculptures that fell within the Dolonnuur school were gilded. Compared with Buddhist sculptures made in Mongolia and Beijing, Dolonnuur's products were cheaper, principally because the repoussé technique was more cost-effective: this hammering technique required less energy (fuel) and material (metal) than the lost-wax casting technique, which was popular in northern China.[75] Bartholomew further reveals that the region of Chahar was rich in iron. This fact might help explain why the repoussé technique dominated bronze production in Dolonnuur, but additional research would be needed for a conclusive assessment of technological preferences.[76]

By the time the third Detri, Jamyang Tubten Nyima, visited Dolonnuur, its artists had assiduously developed strategies for courting potential customers. There were approximately ten blacksmith shops, many of which were run by the Chinese who had migrated there in the eighteenth century. The Chinese craftsmen were quite refined, as related in Huc's travelogues.[77] Among them, a shop by the name of Yuheyong was often credited with making large Tibetan Buddhist statues; some of the commissioned works were so big that they could easily take up to three years to complete.[78] The third Detri, Jamyang Tubten Nyima, noted in a description of his journey that the owner of the Ayushi Foundry had thrown an elaborate banquet in his honor during an earlier visit, when he came to secure his order.[79] His massive order, including one Mañjuśrī statue and one thousand Buddhist deities, were too great for the Ayushi Foundry to complete in a timely manner. As a result, the production of the Mañjuśrī statue was postponed. Additionally, Jamyang Tubten Nyima dispatched two monks to help prepare production of the statues of the thousand Buddhist deities.[80] This practice of collaboration between multiple shops offered the Dolonnuur foundries flexibility and minimal expenses on regular staffing, which reflected a market experiencing high demand for Buddhist artifacts. All in all, this art-production process embodied the nature of the Dolonnuur's commerce at a contact zone. It drastically differed from Beijing's imperial studios in terms of its lack of resources, but it made up for this with its influx of people, techniques, and styles.

Arts produced in Beijing and Dolonnuur certainly shared some attributes; in fact, they both found their inspiration in an earlier artistic tradition. Patricia Berger's study of Tibetan Buddhist art made in eighteenth-century Beijing suggests that the Qing rulers encouraged a combination of Tibetan, Nepalese, and Chinese styles when making Tibetan Buddhist art. The combination made literal visual connections with the Mongol Yuan dynasty (1271–1368). In Kublai Khan's court (r. 1260–1294), Nepalese-style Tibetan Buddhist art was associated with Mongol imperial authority.[81] The Qing emperors' pursuit of political power through religious art began in 1697, when the Zhongzheng Hall Scripture Recitation Office (Ch.: Zhongzhengdian hanjing chu) was designated as the imperial workshop for Tibetan Buddhist art.[82] The Kangxi emperor seemed particularly captivated by this heterogeneous Tibetan Buddhist style. He shared Kublai Khan's concerns regarding the need to stabilize a nascent empire; both leaders were conquest rulers whose attention necessarily focused on territorial expansion and administrative integration. Like Kublai Khan, the Kangxi emperor capitalized on the power of Tibetan Buddhist art and communicated his understanding of Buddhist cosmology to his Inner

Asian subjects through art. The Kangxi emperor was not alone in his invocation of the Mongol Yuan state. Uranchimeg Tsultemin has demonstrated that the famed Zanabazar of Mongolia likewise made the Nepali Newari style central to his artistic creation.[83] These references to the specific art forms attested to the salient role played by art and artisanal knowledge in making Inner Asia simultaneously a Buddhist space and an imperial unit within the Qing empire.

The overlapped and contested space in Inner Asia also compelled craftsmen and Buddhist monks alike to move across regions. These traveling bodies brought the Qing court a host of ideas and techniques, which in turn supported the increasing need and desire to craft a universalist imperial agenda to accommodate its diverse subjects. While facial finishes and gestures of artworks were visibly in the Nepalese style, the craftsmanship was nevertheless Chinese, identified with "the heavy precise casting, deep gold gilding, and the attention to the intricacies of looped and swirled drapery."[84] Valrae Reynolds also suggests that the Kangxi emperor made a conscious effort to emulate the Sino-Tibetan art tradition popular in the fifteenth century, during Ming Yongle emperor's reign.[85] The Kangxi emperor inserted his authoritative voice into the knowledge network that centered on Tibetan Buddhist knowledge. The following sculpture was made in the eighteenth century at Dolonnuur. It attested to this particular style. Featuring "large and flat lotus petals, the large jewel inlays, the flame shape of the hair, and a smooth roundness in the body contours of this statue all indicate an eighteenth-century origin from Dolonnuur."[86] This newly articulated artistic tradition showcased a mutually defined Tibetan Buddhist knowledge network wherein the Qing imperial court and Tibetan Buddhists came together to form a Qing Buddhist culture. As seen in this sculpture and many other in this style, Nepalese influence, especially the smooth facial structure and bodily gestures, was noticeable. However, the peculiar design of the lotus base departed from earlier Kangxi-era statues. What contributed to the difference could be Buddhist artists in the Khalkha Mongolian community.[87] The evolving Tibetan Buddhist artistic style was reflective of the interdependent nature of the Tibetan Buddhist network and the Qing culture, which embraced multiple sources of inspiration.

Circulation of these Dolonnuur Tibetan Buddhist artworks highlighted the parameters of the Tibetan Buddhist knowledge network. They reached far beyond the Mongol steppe or the Qing's imperial capital city, where Tibetan Buddhist monasteries appeared in the eighteenth century.[88] In the nineteenth century, a local Mongol leader from the Üjümücin banner prepared a large Tibetan Buddhist statue for his trip to Lhasa for an audience with the Dalai Lama. The statue was so big that it took a team of eighty-eight camels to transport its components before they were assembled in Lhasa.[89] Tsultemin notes that a similar project was carried out in the same manner, this time up north in Ikh Khüree, the largest camp monastery in Khalkha, outside modern-day Ulaanbaatar. In 1833, a fifty-four-foot Maitreya statue was installed by Agwaan Khaidav in a new monastery built specifically to house the statue, which was assembled there but made in Dolonnuur by twelve Chinese artists. Indeed, the chief artist could very likely have been a bronze artisan from the aforementioned Ayushi Foundry.[90] Like these two colossal statues, most Buddhist art objects were made to order, produced in a modular fashion for easier transportation, and then finally assembled on the site of installation and worship. The great demands in the eighteenth and nineteenth centuries gave rise to a market-driven Buddhist art production site in Dolonnuur. It became a key node attracting people, capital, and labor, which in turn defined a distinct Buddhist art market that met the needs of Buddhists from Mongolia as well as Tibet. These Buddhist artworks, large or small, connected Buddhists in Inner Asia as they traveled across domains in different cultural or linguistic settings. The multidirectional movement of Buddhists and the knowledge they possessed, produced, reproduced, and circulated wove together and formed the institutional and intellectual common ground for Buddhist followers to articulate a shared Buddhist identity.[91]

This section on Buddhist art production complements more invested studies of the "Khalkha style," especially the perhaps most celebrated Mongolian Buddhist artist, Zanabazar, and the distinct artistic style that he propelled.[92] As an accomplished artist with significant religious backing, Zanabazar transformed the Mongolian Buddhist art landscape in his lifetime. His contributions, influences, and accomplishments cannot be overstated in our understanding of Buddhist art in recent centuries of Mongolian history. But arts produced elsewhere in Mongolia have yet to receive due attention. Unlike an individual-driven high art form, as I have shown in this section, Tibetan Buddhist bronze arts produced in Dolonnuur was market driven. The foundries there employed cheap labor and collaborated with other foundries to meet the market demand. Making bronze Buddhist sculptures was not the only activity they engaged in at Dolonnuur. This bustling town was full of business opportunities.

AN INLAND ENTREPÔT

In 1740, when Huc approached Dolonnuur on his journey through Inner Asia, he saw in the distance "glittering under the sun's rays, the gilt roofs of two magnificent Lamaseries."[93] South of this was the less glamorous part of the town: a marketplace. Huc was genuinely lost upon entering the town of Dolonnuur, an experience that he called "fatiguing and full of perplexity." He described the town critically:

> [It] is not a walled city, but a vast agglomeration of hideous houses, which seem to have been thrown together with a pitchfork. The carriage portion of the streets is a marsh of mud and putrid filth, deep enough to stifle and bury the smaller beasts of burden that not unfrequently fall within it, and whose carcasses remain to aggravate the general stench; while their loads become the pretty of the innumerable thieves who are ever on the alert. The foot-path is a narrow, rugged, slippery line on either side, just wide enough to admit the passage of one person.[94]

Such disorganization contrasted sharply with the "magnificent" monasteries that were just across the river and slightly shy of two miles away. Commonly referred as a "trading town" (Ch.: *maimai cheng*), this area welcomed diverse crowds, including travelers like Huc.[95] He clearly had a low opinion of this jumbled town that tired him out with its "tortuous streets," as he put it.[96] At the same time, he also knew that he had come to the right place. For itinerant merchants, laborers, monks, and missionaries, Dolonnuur was a key resting place for restocking their supplies and gathering information about what lay ahead of them. This was exactly why Huc was there. Despite Dolonnuur's harsh environment, he observed that "its population [was] immense, and its commerce enormous."[97] By the mid-nineteenth century, the town of Dolonnuur had grown to be somewhat global. Russian merchandise poured into the place; nomads sold livestock such as camels, oxen, and horses; in turn, they brought home tobacco, linen, and tea.[98] Peddlers and storeowners each found their callings in the market. Later on, when Japan looked to southern Mongolia to advance its interests, one Japanese observer lamented that Japan had missed out on this market.[99] By the late nineteenth century, animal hides shipped from Dolonnuur reached roughly 27.5 tons (50,000 *jin*) and fed a constant demand that existed even beyond the Qing's territory.[100]

What Huc witnessed in Dolonnuur seems to clearly contradict Joseph Fletcher's seminal characterization of Mongolia in the nineteenth century. The dire situation described in Fletcher's general historical narrative includes mention of a "thoroughly decayed nomadism" and Geluk monasteries that increasingly drew manpower away from production and turned them into bondmen—donations made by Mongol leaders ("the jasaks" in Fletcher's account) to monasteries. Monastic institutions and Buddhist trülkus, the two religious infrastructural mechanisms under discussion here, further compounded their damage to Mongolian society by operating as moneylenders.[101] Both meticulous studies that Tsai and Dear have put forward attest to and add nuances to Fletcher's general historical observation.[102] From an exclusive economic standpoint, both of the religious institutions absorbed resources and contributed to the decline of nomadic pastoralism, but the economic activities in the area did not collapse. The very fact that Dolonnuur rose to become a major production site of Buddhist sculpture in the second half of the century indicates that a different type of commodity continued to sustain the economy. An important difference was who benefited from the changes. Clearly, in this case, the nomadic Mongols were not the benefactory.

This inland entrepôt shared many traits with trading ports across regions in early modern times.[103] It was porous, heterogenous, and subject to changing geopolitical circumstances. Dolonnuur was emblematic of this type of place. The assemblage of merchants, monks, and other social groups filled the space with vitality and appeal. What differentiated Dolonnuur from other nodal trading ports was its heavy reliance on monastery-centered networks of commerce and religious activities that brought together a slate of social agents from different regions across cultural domains.

The two monasteries there provided people from all walks of life in Inner Asia with a space to access the multifaceted network. The monasteries were part of a regional religious nexus including Mount Wutai, Beijing, and Tibet.[104] Monks studied here, rested on their trips to other monasteries, met with patrons and erudite Buddhist teachers, and purchased Buddhist art. The great demand drew labor and capital from other regions. Migrant farmers rented plots from landowning Mongolians to avoid heavier taxes in their home regions south of the Great Wall, including the Shanxi and Zhili regions. In the seventeenth century, the Qing rulers tried to discourage farmers from settling in southern Mongolia, including in Dolonnuur. In 1655, the Shunzhi emperor proclaimed a ban on Han Chinese settlement in Mongolia.[105] But population growth drove struggling farmers north, so that by the 1720s—before the Blue Temple was constructed—an increasing number of migrant farmers had begun to form settled communities in these places. They brought a labor force, capital, and kinship networks, embodying knowledge that contributed to a prosperous economy at the crossroads.[106] By 1749, places like Dolonnuur or Guihua (modern-day Hohhot) saw the presence of several hundred thousand Han Chinese, some of whom engaged in commercial trading or provided affordable labor to all kinds of businesses in the regional trading network.[107] Farther north, in Khalkha, resettled Han Chinese were part of the local economy, providing their labor input and trade engagements.[108] By the early Qianlong reign in the 1750s, the Qing imperial policy regarding Han Chinese migration into Mongolia had changed from hesitance to acceptance, which set in motion a greater volume of people relocating to Mongolia.[109]

Migrant farmers were not the only ones who called Dolonnuur home. Along with the financially struggling farmers, merchants also traveled north to establish their businesses in Mongolia. Some of them found sites for their business farther north in Khalkha, not surprisingly near large monasteries and in other congregate areas like military bases.[110] But there was also a group of merchants who commanded privilege and resources. Much of the commerce in southern Mongolia was under the control of powerful merchants and their firms, known as the "dragon-permit merchants" (Ch.: *longpiao shangren*). The "dragon" connoted these merchants' connection to imperial power. They provided the key logistical infrastructure for Qing troops as they pushed aggressively into challenging terrain early in the Qing; in turn, they received special trading privileges to support lucrative business, especially in the Qing's northern territory.[111] A fortunate few were among the merchant community that invested heavily in Mongolia. Known as "sojourning merchants in Mongolia" (Ch.: *lümeng shang*)—a term that reflected their seasonable trading patterns—these merchants rarely maintained a permanent residence on the steppe. Instead, they and their firms traded in places like Dolonnuur in the summer and retreated south when their business was done. Many of them came from the neighboring Shanxi, Shandong, and Henan provinces and established a transregional trading network spanning northern parts of Qing China. Southern Mongolia became a key node within the sprawling trading network that they established. Among these Chinese merchants, the Shanxi merchants and their guild house (Ch: *huiguan*) were the most influential, with their corporate system known as the Eight Grand Shops. This imperially sanctioned merchant network brought capital and business opportunities not only to nomads from the steppe, monks, and pilgrims across Inner Asia, but also to impoverished farmers fleeing difficult circumstances by migrating south to Mongolia, as well as to poor monks who struggled to get by, as mentioned above.

Ordinary people made their ends meet by bartering along the way. The wealthy ones, like many Mongolian princes, made the best use of their required rotation to visit the imperial capital. The Mongol leaders' rotational visit to Beijing was one of the principal systems through which the Qing rulers defined their relationship with Mongols in Mongolia.[112] Buddhist and secular leaders in Mongolia were divided into two systems, each of which designated one subset of leaders who came to Beijing in rotation. As the Qing imperial expansion grew, the practice replicated into other areas—first Inner Mongolia in 1648, then the Khalkha Mongols in 1691, Mongols in Amdo in 1725, after Lobzang Danjin and his supporters were defeated, and finally the Oirat Zunghars, when the Zunghar state vanished.[113] Once they arrived in Beijing, they were directed to a place commonly known as Tartar Hall (Ch.: *dada guan*), which was near the Hanlin Academy and the Imperial Carriage Park. British travelers in the early twentieth century observed a "Mongolian Market, where the Children of the Steppes [Mongols] came to barter their turquoises and [animal] skins for the luxuries of civilization."[114] En route to Beijing, these Mongolian princes also helped Chinese merchants circumvent tax collection at the border checkpoints. One case enraged the Qianlong emperor and resulted in confiscation of that Mongol prince's property.[115] Southern Mongolia was deeply integrated into multiple networks of commerce in a process involving diverse parties. Southern Mongolian ties to the region were historically specific. They were contingent upon interactions between the Qing imperial state and prolonged Buddhist dissemination in Mongolia but the pressure of food shortages in the north China plain in difficult times also had an impact.

The economic system on the ground in Dolonnuur was more spontaneous than state dictated, but it was bustling nonetheless. As described above, the two monasteries built and sponsored by the Kangxi and Yongzheng emperors provided a key driving force for the rise of Dolonnuur. They paved the way for the bourgeoning commerce that defined this space, and the sprawling business networks in turn helped broker trade. These networks built on established kinship business practices and brought capital and logistic measures that enabled transregional trade. This set Dolonnuur apart from other monastery-centered commercial hubs in Inner Asia, where monasteries had drawn flows of people and goods around religious gatherings. Some of the large monasteries engaged in trade with their own operational arms or had amassed enough resources to be part of the economic life of their localities. But in Dolonnuur, the economic activities were less organic than they were in other Inner Asian hubs, like the eastern Tibetan region of Amdo discussed in chapter 1. The imperially regulated and highly monopolized trading network measured the gap between what Qing imperial governance intended to do with its distinct Buddhist Inner Asian communities and what it was actually able to accomplish.

Again, the friction in Dolonnuur did not invalidate the Qing's effectual rule or, for that matter, Inner Asian Buddhists' lack of power in their negotiations. The combination of religious, social, and commercial networks in Dolonnuur illustrated the very process of push and pull as Qing rulers developed flexible governing practices, and their need for flexibility was compounded by the relentless eastward expansion of Buddhist power. The two powers' encounter and search for common ground brought about a new type of relationship that connected multiple networks.

In the context of the interpenetration of Buddhist Inner Asia and the Qing empire's Inner Asia, this chapter focused on the tripartite relations between the Mongols, Qing imperial rulers, and Buddhists from Tibet. In these interactions, Buddhist objects traveled across immobile monastic institutions and played a defining role in shaping the encounter. Monasteries provided venues in which the Qing and the Inner Asian Buddhists could find common ground. However, the creation and development of Dolonnuur differed from the border region of Amdo and from Beijing's Yonghegong. In many ways, Dolonnuur further attested to the Qing's flexible imperial governance. Instead of adopting new coercive measures to assimilate the Mongols, the Qing capitalized on existing social practices already at work. Tibetan Buddhist missionary undertakings, gradually dominated by the rising Geluk School, shaped social life in Mongolia on many levels. Pilgrims, merchants, monks, and people of all sorts of means converged in places like Dolonnuur, where they traded as well as practiced Buddhism. The Qing rulers' investment in Buddhist monasteries bespeaks the deep-seated Buddhist influence in Mongolia. The Qing's policies of reinstalling Amdo's monastic order reflected the plasticity of imperial rules; Beijing's reinvented Buddhist imperial space in Yonghegong established a channel to maintain smooth negotiations and communications between Beijing and Lhasa. These spatial governing practices reflect the processes through which the Qing and the Geluk Ganden Podrang power grew symbiotically and became mutually dependent. Monasteries large and small emerged as nodes of various capacity where these Buddhists developed their knowledge network, which crisscrossed the Qing's administrative divides. Similarly, Dolonnuur provided an institutional mechanism for Inner Asian Buddhists to position themselves within both Buddhist and imperial frameworks.

But Dolonnuur was different. It was an assemblage of many features, a site of multiple and overlapping networks of merchants, monks, the laity, and migrant farmers. Flows of merchandise and knowledge and the profits from them made the town of Dolonnuur at once hard to define and full of vitality. Even though its emergence was indeed marked by Qing imperial ambitions and struggles to achieve its goals, the actual social practices in Dolonnuur were not determined by imperial rules. The binary perspective that has often locked the metropole and frontier into a rigid power hierarchy can only go so far. Here, lateral connections among various Mongolian banners in this nodal site as well as those of Buddhists from Tibet and the laity in Mongolia were ever present. Young Mongolian monks established themselves as Buddhists in the Qing through their connections with these monasteries. This connection was equally important to the mandalic expansion of the Geluk Ganden Podrang and to Qing imperial governance. It was precisely because of this mutual interest that sites like Dolonnuur flourished.

This prosperity drew multiple social actors and resources to the site. For Buddhists from Tibet, Dolonnuur not only articulated their connection with Qing imperial narratives but also materialized that connection in tangible ways. The lateral connection between Tibet and Mongolia was not always from Tibet to the east, nor was it from Beijing to Mongolia or Tibet. Buddhists from Tibet brought Buddhist objects back west. These multidirectional flows of Buddhist elements suggest that a much more holistic Buddhist space defined the Qing's Buddhist Inner Asia, where a shared communal identity was created and sustained through mutually intelligible Buddhist languages, visual or textual. This knowledge network stemmed from long-standing Buddhist missionary endeavors; indeed, historical memory weighed heavily on the Mongolians, even predating the Manchu rulers relocating their capital to Beijing.

Erudite Buddhists embodied and transmitted this knowledge. Some of them were monastic figures. By exploiting the Geluk School's nested monastic sites, they were able to extend their influence to many areas within Buddhist communities in Inner Asia. While those who ventured into the Buddhist knowledge world were not necessarily monastic figures, monasteries and the institution of Buddhist trülkus were key religious infrastructures facilitating the dissemination of Buddhism and they impacted important aspects of the way the Qing developed its imperial rule. What enabled erudite Buddhists to be so effective and why it is important to know what they did will be discussed in the next chapter.

Chapter Four

GOVERNANCE

The preceding three chapters have each addressed a specific place within the Qing empire where Tibetan Buddhists exercised their influence and complicated spatial narratives. The present chapter closes the circuit by exploring Tibetan Buddhist influence inside the imperial core. Central to the religious impact on the Qing's governing practices in the first half of the eighteenth century were several imperial clansmen. While all of them served in some capacity within the Qing's bureaucratic apparatus, they were deeply engaged in Tibetan Buddhist social-textual communities that were defined by the act of writing. By focusing on their experiences, I aim to address two interconnected issues. First, this chapter asks how the Tibetan Buddhist knowledge regime defined one's cultural belonging. Second, these Buddhist statesmen partook of the Qing's intensified quest to know its shifting territory, producing as well as displaying that knowledge.[1] The Qing's imperial expansions required the state to produce knowledge; at the same time, the statesmen deep in the enterprise appropriated the state's quest for that knowledge and created a Buddhist intellectual outpost moored to the Buddhist epicenter in Tibet through writing. Their literary production firmly grounded them within Buddhist Inner Asia, and the act of writing offered them a path to the Buddhist world.

Two imperial officials, Gombjab (Tib.: mGon po skyabs, 1690?–1750) and Prince Guo (Yunli, 1697–1738), participated in producing and circulating

GOVERNANCE

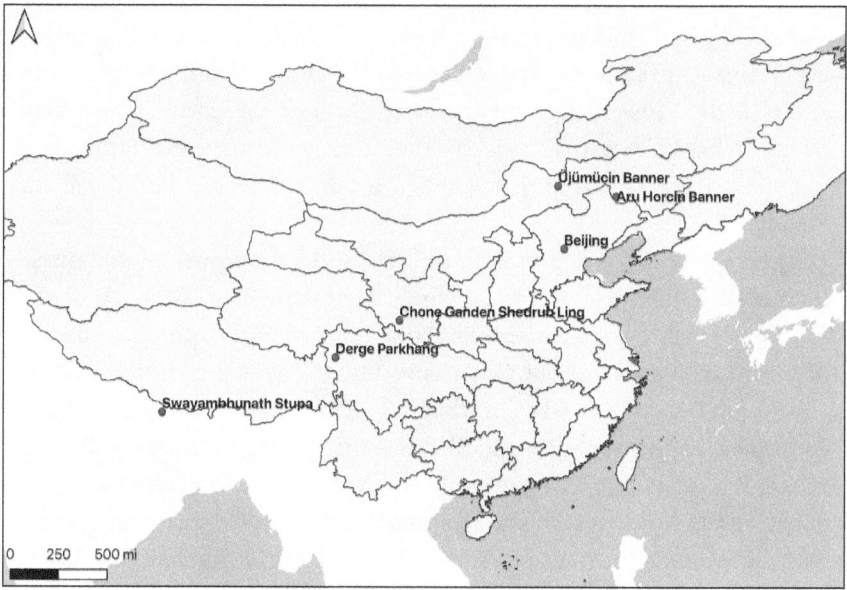

MAP 4. Sites discussed in chapter 4. Created by Lan Wu, adopting the shapefile of CHGIS, 2016, "1820 Layers GBK Encoding," https://doi.org/10.7910/DVN/2K4FHX, Harvard Dataverse, V1.

Tibetan Buddhist knowledge while holding key state appointments in the first half of the eighteenth century. They both were part of the ruling Aisin Gioro clansmen, Gombjab through marriage, and Prince Guo through birth. Unlike the monastic figures discussed in preceding chapters, they were Tibetan Buddhist laity employed in the Qing's complex administrative apparatus. Gombjab was a Qing imperial court appointee and a lay Tibetan Buddhist from Mongolia.[2] He was born to a Mongolian noble family in the Üjümücin Banner of the Xilin Gol League in southern Mongolia sometime in the latter half of the seventeenth century. After 1709, when he married a princess of seventh rank within the imperial clan and thereby received the title of "ceremonial companion" (Ch.: *yibin*), Gombjab spent most of his adult life in the capital city.[3] A polyglot career man, Gombjab put his linguistic skills to good use as head of the Lifanyuan's Tibetan Language School (Ch.: Xifan xue), a bureaucratic pipeline for prospective scriveners. The second figure, Prince Guo, was active at the crucial moment when the Yongzheng emperor recalibrated his close kin's access to ultimate power and "transformed them into pillars of the imperium."[4] The first-rank imperial prince was a younger brother of the reigning Yongzheng emperor and a capable statesman handling many key affairs in the Yongzheng and the early years of the ensuing Qianlong reigns. What follows will show how their stories illustrate the multivalent socio-textual communities revolving around Tibetan Buddhism in Beijing.

Their political and personal endeavors in the imperial enterprise marked the start of a period of "high territoriality," a hallmark of the Qianlong reign. I borrow the term "high territoriality" from a discussion of a shift of Russian territorial science under the rule of Catherine the Great (1762–1796).[5] The ways in which Russian ruling elites produced and consumed territorial knowledge left a mark on their understanding of tsarist Russia. It also ultimately affected the imperial statecraft and the public's growing interest in knowing about the expanded Russian territory. Textual accounts introduced a wide array of topics on Russian territories, including geographical, historical, and cultural information; handbooks on how to consume territorial knowledge nurtured a strong sense of belonging among the literate Russian public. In the case of the Qing, the turn of the nineteenth century saw growing concerns among statesmen—many were Han Chinese—who developed an interest in geography and the people living on the imperial fringes.[6] The two figures under study in this chapter predated those concerned about the shifting geopolitical realities in the nineteenth century; they were motivated not by political considerations but cultural ones. Their interests in Tibetan Buddhism nonetheless contributed to an increasingly cosmopolitan intellectual currents within the capital in the eighteenth century.

Here, we must expand our analytical scope to include different types of knowledge production and consumption. If Beijing was not the only variable lens—and it ought not to be—through which to understand how knowledge and power intertwined deeply, then why and what these Buddhist statemen wrote would shed light on how Tibetan Buddhist knowledge was a source for them to create themselves as authorities in Buddhist Inner Asia. These Buddhist laymen's writings offer us an opportunity to see Tibetan Buddhism as more than a political tool that helped the Qing imperial rulers develop state policies in their newly annexed territories. Instead, Tibetan Buddhism was a knowledge system that bore significant cultural weight and gained them access to an intellectual network revolving around the act of writing.

As the three preceding chapters have shown, the Qing's contested and prolonged expansion processes forced the Qing ruling elites to adopt new ways of understanding and claiming sovereignty over the imperial territory. The territorial expansions were as much about the annexed territories as about the metropolis, since new frontiers brought about changing territoriality in terms of sophisticated practice and knowledge about the places and their relations to the imperial core. This chapter investigates how the Qing imperial governance adapted to evolving geopolitics as a result of territorial expansions. It also looks at how the Buddhist-knowledge regime helped shape the ruling elites' experience through their interactions with Buddhists who spent considerable time in the Qing's political hubs.

Returning to the Qing's imperial capital facilitates my efforts to include a range of governing practices and experiences within the analytical parameters. I deliberately use "governance" rather than more conventional terms such as "state" or "administration." This choice allows me to raise questions about who and what constituted the imperial state in Qing empire—a critical issue that research on other early modern empires has likewise addressed. For example, Christine Philliou examines the life of Stephanos Vogorides, who was an Orthodox Christian living in the Phanar quarter of Istanbul and became an influential mediator between the Porte and foreign diplomats. Vogorides's familial connections and patronage network crossed formal administrative and confessional boundaries. Vogorides's life highlighted how informal modes of governance proved equally important to and mutually dependent upon a formal governing structure.[7]

However, until very recently, it has been commonplace to begin the conversation about the Qing's imperial governance with its drive to expand as a conquest regime or its military prowess. Some research focuses on the "militarization of culture" by the Qianlong emperor and argues that the Qing's conquest did not take place just on the battleground but also in many steles, banquets, rituals, and multimedia art production, all of which were strategies for the conqueror to legitimate his right to rule even after his military campaigns ended.[8] Others have explained how wars were planned on the battleground and later fought, provisioned, and commemorated back in the imperial court.⁹ Still others explore the nature of Qing imperial rule through close examinations of the imperial ideology and the imperial household.¹⁰ Tibetan Buddhism has featured more or less prominently in some of the existing studies, but often only to the extent that it supported how emperors exercised their power in conciliating the Mongols, thus reducing religion to a mere political tool. Recent research on specific regions along the Qing borderlands has consistently challenged these existing narratives and showed that the Qing's rule relied upon local ruling elites, but the emergent studies often focus on the locales, and, in doing so, squarely place the frontier regions at the imperial margins and within the political realms. In this chapter, I hope to show how the Qing's imperial core was influenced by Qing expansion as much as those living on the fringes. Tibetan Buddhism was one such social force that shaped the everyday lives of those within the imperial household and, by extension, their role in the empire through their bureaucratic assignments.

Another productive line of inquiry has followed the Qing's institutional innovations. In these discussions, the Lifanyuan has received scholars' sustained attention.¹¹ Collectively and separately, the Department of the Imperial Household (Ch.: Neiwu fu) and the Lifanyuan were set apart from other constituent administrative arms of the state. This is because the primary focus of the Department of the Imperial Household concerned the affairs of the Qing ruling family, while the Lifanyuan dealt with frontier communities—especially the Mongols and Tibetans. While it is useful to understand the inner working mechanisms of these two distinct governing bodies, their singularity reinforces the historiographical division of inner and outer court. The fact that Buddhist imperial clansmen straddled multiple government organs within the imperial administration reflects its internally heterogeneous character. The multiplicity of the state made the Qing resilient to shifting geopolitics. Bartlett makes a strong case that the inner court "ministers" often held bureaucratic posts in the outer court in her seminal study of the Grand Council (Ch.: Junji chu; Man.: Coohai nashūn i ba).¹² These ministers were the imperial ruler's confidants, who enjoyed what Bartlett called an "extralegal dynamic" with the ruler. While I agree with Bartlett's description of the concurrent appointments of able imperial kinsmen, I see them as constituting part of the state with their own agency, rather than solely as the ruler's right-hand men in governance. During the Qianlong reign, high territoriality entailed the production of legible knowledge about the empire and its diverse geographical expanse. For the specific case of Qing Buddhist Inner Asia, the present chapter continues to question the faulty assumption that the Qianlong emperor and his religious teacher were responsible for creating a court-driven Tibetan Buddhist knowledge network after the 1740s. Instead, what follows will show that the heightened sense of territoriality and the Qing's imperial governance were built upon earlier erratic and unofficial interactions initiated outside of administrative considerations. Ultimately, this chapter aims to locate the influence of Tibetan Buddhism beyond the Qing ruler's personal covert religious realm, which has received due attention from scholars. Instead, it demonstrates how the very staffing practices of the mid-Qing led to a greater impact of Buddhism on Qing imperial governance.

GOMBJAB'S TEXTS AND PARATEXTUAL BUDDHIST COMMUNITIES

While heading the Tibetan Language School, an administrative arm within Lifanyuan, Gombjab oversaw several translation projects. He was uniquely positioned to acquaint himself with some of the most influential Buddhist scholars residing in Beijing. Gombjab put his linguistic aptitude to good use: a prolific writer himself, Gombjab is remembered for his literary legacy in multiple languages. Of his oeuvre, two texts are particularly helpful in thinking about how Buddhist social-textual communities transcended linguistic and geographical barriers. One text is a historical account of Buddhist dissemination in the Tibetan language, and the other is a Chinese how-to manual for making Buddhist statues. Each of the texts reveals a Buddhist community reliant upon the production and circulation of textual knowledge; together, they show how the Buddhist knowledge network in Qing Buddhist Inner Asia was full of vitality. The network was facilitated by the Qing's territorial expansion to the west and by the Geluk School's infrastructural reach to the east.

In the mid-1740s, while managing the Tibetan Language School, Gombjab compiled an account of the history of Buddhism in China in his spare time. The text, *Enchanting Earring of the Omniscient Minds: An Explanation for the Spread of the Dharma in the Land of China* (hereafter, *History of Buddhism in China*), delineated how Buddhism diffused in the place known today as China.¹³ Gombjab was puzzled by the Tibetan rendering of "rgya nag" in its reference to "China."¹⁴ Even though the term "rgya nag" refers to China in modern Tibetan, in the eighteenth century it did not correspond to the contemporary Chinese state's territorial confines or to its cultural sphere. Gombjab instead positioned the land of rgya nag within Buddhist cosmology and literary sources.¹⁵ The text begins with a topographic description of China. It then unfolds into a historical narrative that has adopted the Chinese dynastic chronicle as its temporal framework. Gombjab's literary reconstruction of the land of China captures the very process through which Buddhist elites appropriated the Qing imperial undertakings. Take his description of Mount Wutai, for example, which had begun to establish a more sustainable and visible connection to the Qing imperial household by the mid-eighteenth century, when Gombjab penned this historical narrative.¹⁶ The Qianlong emperor made multiple trips to this mountain range, built new temples, and cemented his image as Manjushri, the Buddha of Wisdom there. Gombjab repeatedly refers to Mount Wutai in his description of Chinese political geography, a testimony to Mount Wutai's prominence among Inner Asian Buddhists. The site has only grown in importance since Gombjab's time. Multilingual guidebooks about the sacred site circulated widely among Inner Asian Buddhists, especially in the nineteenth century, when the Qing's imperial patronage waned.¹⁷ Gombjab's allusion to this imperial site reveals how Buddhists under the Qing internalized Qing imperial practices: first in the literary realm, as in Gombjab's *History of Buddhism in China*, and then in everyday practice, such as in pilgrimages undertaken by Mongols in the late eighteenth and nineteenth centuries.¹⁸ Gombjab's text was written in the early days of a wave of knowledge production by many Geluk scholars since the mid-eighteenth century. Unlike many literary giants contemporary to him, Gombjab was not a monastic figure. This very fact reminds us that the act of writing helped many like Gombjab define their sense of religious belonging. The historical backdrop against which Gombjab and other imperial clansmen operated was the more prevalent Tibetan Buddhist knowledge network that went beyond the political negotiations of the Qing empire and the Dalai Lama's Buddhist government.

The text was written in a highly formulaic Tibetan Buddhist literary genre known as the "origin of Buddhism" (Tib.: *chos 'byung*). This discursive literary form emerged in the eleventh century and gained popularity among Buddhists in the ensuing centuries. History writing in the Tibetan cultural sphere was deeply ingrained in religious literature, partially because men of letters were often Buddhists who were trained in Buddhist literature.[19] Also, the form is generally specific to a particular region and religious traditions.[20] Gombjab's text is one of the first Tibetophone accounts in the genre of origin of Buddhism written by a Mongolian.[21] Mongolian Buddhists adopted this particular genre from the Tibetan Buddhist literary tradition as early as the seventeenth century.[22] Its adoption ushered in a new era for Mongolian Buddhists by reconceptualizing both their history and the centrality of Buddhism within the Mongolian historical narrative. Johan Elverskog has made the following insightful observation regarding this literature in the late eighteenth century:

> These works shifted away from the predominantly historical-genealogical narratives of the Mongol *ulus* (Mongols' communal identity) found in earlier histories and in their place offered stories resolving around the transmission of Dharma, and the Buddhist works contributed to the idea of the Qing as a transethnic Buddhist community, and the earlier histories that focused on specific genealogies and localized groups helped foster the localization of Mongol identity.[23]

This transethnic Buddhist community was largely sustained by the practice of writing. The imagined Buddhist Inner Asia centered on Tibetan-language Buddhist writings and was facilitated by a thriving print culture in an expanding Qing empire. The culture of the book in Tibetan Buddhism and the Qing's imperial territorial expansion was at the nexus of knowledge production. Buddhists of diverse linguistic and cultural backgrounds seized upon the discourse of writing, and their textual production cultivated a distinctive Buddhist community.[24] Gombjab's mastery of Tibetan Buddhist literature and history made his text more accessible to Buddhists, who similarly drew from shared literary and historical sources to produce their work. At that time, the Buddhist knowledge regime forged under the Qing with Buddhists' eastward movement provided a communication bridge between Buddhist laity and monastic figures.

Gombjab then proceeded to explain Buddhist dissemination in China. He posited that the Buddha was born during the reign of the Emperor Zhao of the Western Zhou (r. 1027–977 BC)—a point that drew a Buddhist scholar's attention and to which I will return later in the chapter. Buddhism was introduced to China during the reign of the Ming Emperor of Eastern Han (r. AD 28–75), according to Gombjab.[25] His concise account of the political development in imperial China ends with a discussion of when the Manchu-Mongolian marriage alliance originated. He writes that two consorts of Ligdan Khan (1588–1634) of the Chahar Mongols married into the Manchu imperial family upon the death of their husband in 1734. The death of this last Mongolian strongman concluded the fragmentary politics that plagued the Mongolian confederates since the mid-fourteenth century. Gombjab adeptly recasts Mongol submission to the Manchu rulers as ordained by a sacred Buddhist statue, which the two consorts found and handed over to the Manchu ruler Hong Taiji (1582–1643). For what it's worth, Ligdan Khan's consorts became prominent members of the imperial household, secondary only to Hong Taiji's empress in 1736, on the eve of Manchurian entry into China proper. Their submission at this watershed moment fortified the Manchu ruler, who rightly placed Ligdan Khan's widows in the inner court of the Mukden Place. Over the course of a century, the Mongolian-Manchu marriage alliance had become institutionalized and expanded the pool of ruling elites beyond ethnolinguistic limits.[26] Mongolian aristocrats were often entrusted with important state managerial tasks, especially in the newly annexed regions in Qing Inner Asia. Gombjab's Mongolian aristocratic upbringing and his career in the Qing imperial administration epitomized the practice that he believed accounted for Mongolian incorporation into the Qing empire, a process in which Tibetan Buddhism played a pivotal role. However, the other side of the same coin is equally important but has been underexplored. Gombjab's text and his reference to Buddhism in shaping the Mongolian-Manchu connection bespeak more wide-ranging and longer interactions among Tibetan Buddhists, Mongolians, and Manchus. The dissemination of Tibetan Buddhist literature was neither a goal nor a consequence of Qing state patronage; instead, it was part of the very historical context in which the Qing invested in Buddhist enterprises. By the mid-eighteenth century, Mongolian elites within the Qing administrative apparatus had gained unprecedented access to the Tibetan Buddhist knowledge regime. The brief opening section of *History of Buddhism in China* demonstrates Gombjab's mastery of Tibetan Buddhist literature. In this text, he devises a genealogical structure to outline the spread of Buddhism, which was a hallmark of history writing in Tibetan Buddhist literature.[27]

This strategy enabled Gombjab to establish an intellectual genealogy and define his religious belonging. To Gombjab, it was crucial to Buddhist dissemination that many Buddhists labored to produce and circulate Buddhist texts. Gombjab held these Buddhist intellectuals in high regard, perhaps partially because he himself saw such engagements as integral to his Buddhist identity. Gombjab's unique lay Buddhist background did not hold him back from pursuing Buddhist knowledge. His resourceful interpretation of Buddhist dissemination in China was how he cemented his position within a Tibetan Buddhist intellectual circle outside Central Tibet, where Geluk monstic trainings gravitated toward debate and memorizations, and writing came to be cherished among Tibetan Buddhists to the east.[28]

Gombjab was a sedentary statesman whose official duties pinned him to Beijing, yet his text (or copies of it) traveled to the eastern Tibetan region of Kham and even farther away, to the Kathmandu valley in modern Nepal. The text's fascinating journey showcases the contours of a cross-cultural Buddhist knowledge network forged across Qing Buddhist Inner Asia. In 1747, Katok Ridzin Tsewang Norbu (1698–1755) of the Karma Kagyü School wrote a letter to Gombjab. Katok Ridzin Tsewang Norbu was a trusted confidant of the seventh Dalai Lama, Kalzang Gyatso, as well as an erudite Buddhist scholar and an observant political commentator. He wrote to Gombjab during his second stay in Nepal, in 1748. He also made two more trips to Nepal, first in 1728 and a final trip between 1751 and 1755. This particular trip in 1748 was to restore the famed Swayambhūnāth Stūpa. While commending Gombjab for his contribution to the "history of Dharma," he took Gombjab to task for several issues discussed in his account.[29] Among his thirteen questions, Tsewang Norbu was chiefly concerned about the source materials that Gombjab used for his discussion of the historical Buddha's birth year. Katok Tsewang Norbu believed that reliable Indian Buddhist texts approached the sites quite differently.[30] The discrepancies among their opinions could perhaps be attributed to the sources that Gombjab drew upon in writing this manuscript. In the colophon, he listed three books as his sources. However, Bira believes that Gombjab consulted Chinese-language books in preparing this manuscript.[31] With the given textual sources, it is hard to conclude decisively what sources Gombjab actually drew on, and if so, how he selected them. Tsewang Norbu listed his sources of information in the letter and urged Gombjab to do so as well. There is no confirmation as to whether Tsewang Norbu's letter ever reached Gombjab's hands, but the letter attested to a diverse Buddhist intellectual network that was not always defined by sectarian differences. The knowledge network was oriented toward intellectual curiosity independent from the exceedingly political agenda of the Qing state. Rather, Qing imperial governance—both territorial expansion and administrative flexibility—facilitated the long-standing Buddhist literary traditions in Inner Asia.

How did Gombjab's text reach Tswang Norbu in Nepal? Its curious journey to Nepal via Dergé from Beijing attests to the cultural and political dynamics of the communicative space across regions and cultures as the Qing empire expanded and Buddhists realigned their power in the Himalayas, especially with the nascent Geluk's Ganden Podrang government in Central Tibet. Its emergence and growth forced many to withdraw, including influential Geluk figures such as Jamyang Zhepai Dorje, who found the Labrang Tashikhyil in Amdo; many who retreated to their places of origin were Buddhists of other sectarian affiliations. The power shift gave rise to new cultural centers such as Dergé.[32] Gombjab's text indicates that the manuscript made its way to Dergé; in the colophon, the author states that "to get the authoritative opinions on it, I [Gombjab] sent this manuscript along several other works to Situ Panchen in Dergé by the postal relay stations ... the manuscript was printed at the Dergé Printing House [Tib.: Derge Parkhang]."[33] Situ Panchen Chökyi Jungné visited the Kathmandu Valley in 1748, when Tsewang Norbu resided there. It is unknown whether Situ Panchen Chökyi Jungné brought a copy to Katok Tsewang Norbu on this trip, but their mutual connection to Dergé suggests that connections between Dergé and Kathmandu were not infrequent. The Dergé Parkhang was an institutional and physical component of the Gönchen Monastery in Dergé.[34] As one of the five major monasteries of the Dergé king, it had a long history of shifting religious identities since its inception in 1448.[35] In 1729, Situ Panchen Chökyi Jungné (1700–1774) established a printing house with support from the royal house of Dergé and focused on printing the Tibetan Buddhist Canon (Kangyur and Tengyur), as well as texts about Tibetan medicine and collected works of eminent monks.³⁶ Productions of the Buddhist canon—including editing, translating, and printing—also bore weight beyond the political realm; they provided Buddhists a source of merit.³⁷ The Dergé king's sponsorship of production of woodblock Buddhist canons reflected the centrality of Buddhist knowledge production in an expansive Buddhist space in the Himalayas. Several cultural hubs emerged and cemented their political capital through sponsoring Buddhist canon productions. In eastern Tibetan regions—both Kham and Amdo—new regional principalities such as Dergé and Chone defined their cultural centrality through financing these expensive undertakings.³⁸ Similar to the Dergé king, rulers of the Chone principality also sponsored the production of the woodblocks for the Kangyur (works thought to be traceable to the word "ka" spoken by the Buddha) in 1731, for which the eleventh ruler of Chone has been remembered ever since. In the seventeenth and eighteenth centuries, both Ligdan Khan of Chahar Mongols and the Qing rulers ventured to produce Buddhist canons. The Qing's imperial Buddhist canon-production project included editing, translating, printing, offering, or gifting Buddhist canons. The centrality of Buddhist canonical texts established the Qing capital as an important Buddhist center, an image that the Qing rulers were eager to nurture.³⁹

How did Gombjab describe his motivation for writing this historical account of Buddhist dissemination in China? In the colophon to his *History of Buddhism in China*, Gombjab credits Sertri Lobzang Tenpai Nyima (1689–1762) for encouraging him to write the chronicle:

> The Sertri imperial preceptor gave me a bronze statue and a nice horse. He instructed me to write a book of this kind; I could do nothing but take up the task. I excerpted from manuscripts such as *ma ha tsi na'i rgya rabs kyi yig tshang gzhung chen mo* [The extensive official records of Chinese dynastic history], *bla chen rnam thar* [Biograpies of Buddhist masters], and *sde snod gsum gyi dkar chag* [Early and later catalogues of the Buddhist Tripitaka] to draft this book, titled *History of Buddhism in China* [Tib.: *rgya nag chos 'byung*] ... he had given me his blessing by presenting me with gifts, including a bronze statue.⁴⁰

The second Sertri, Lobzang Tenpai Nyima, has received increasing attention in recent scholarship.⁴¹ Hailing from a Mongolian family in Amdo, he was invited to serve as the principal teacher to Changkya Rolpai Dorje (1717–1786).[42] Like his disciple, Lobzang Tenpai Nyima also received the title of imperial preceptor. His trülku line had played a vital role in the Kangxi reign and wielded power in the ongoing negotiations between Beijing and Lhasa. Together with Changkya Rolpai Dorje, he was instrumental in translating Tibetan Buddhist canonical texts. He also helped convert Yonghegong into a Buddhist learning center in the capital city and worked on cataloging Buddhist art collections in the Qing imperial palaces. Gombjab's linguistic expertise and administrative assignments on Buddhist canon production made him no stranger to the many Buddhist trülkus living in Beijing. The inclusion of Lobzang Tenpai Nyima's name in the colophon to his *History of Buddhism in China* gained Gombjab a foothold in the coterie of diverse erudite Buddhists with political influence. Gombjab's *History of Buddhism in China* redrew a Buddhist space that overlapped with Qing imperial governance. The social-textual Buddhist community sustained Buddhists across Qing Inner Asia and brought them closer to the cultural and political centers in the Himalayas. The transcultural movements of people, institutions, ideas, and texts would not have been possible without the Geluk's religious infrastructure, the stabilizing Buddhist monasteries, and the mobile Buddhist trülkus, especially those who were bureaucratized as the Qing's demand for Buddhist knowledge production grew in the 1740s. The paratextual community that revolved around Gombjab's *History of Buddhism in China* involved mostly highly placed Buddhists within a confined circle of Buddhist trülkus. The other text compiled by him is evidence not only of how porous the network was but also of how the movement of Buddhist texts and ideas was multidirectional.

The second text authored by Gombjab was a how-to manual of Buddhist art production. The *Canon of Buddhist Iconometry* (Ch.: *Foshuo zangxiang liangdujin jie*) was completed in 1741. It was one of the first Chinese-language manuals for making Tibetan Buddhist statuary. To him as well as to many of his contemporaries, crafting Tibetan Buddhist statues correctly was more than an aesthetic concern; it was a matter of practicing Tibetan Buddhism correctly. Buddhist artworks correspond to the very material existence of the Buddhahood: "enlightened body, speech, and mind."[43] Gombjab cautioned that craftsmen could not easily make a statue without the correct measurements. His frustration grew when he noticed that "[existing] manuals of making Buddhist statuary do not derive from Buddhist canons."[44] To him, the appropriate measurements of a Buddhist statue were of utmost importance, but this was due to philosophical rather than aesthetic reasons. He notes that a statue with incorrect measurements was an essentially inhospitable site for a Tibetan Buddhist deity to manifest. Unfortunately, extant manuals did not conform to Tibetan Buddhist canonical texts, as Gombjab claimed, so they were not helpful with respect to the crafting Tibetan Buddhist statues. His objection to the ostensibly erroneous manuals reflected a well-circulated sophisticated understanding of Buddhist knowledge authority and production across regions. Gombjab was certainly not the only one who asserted the centrality of Buddhist canonical texts in making Buddhist art. The third Changkya, Rolpai Dorje, produced a widely popular text used primarily in Mongolia, titled "Three Hundred Icons." These were two of a handful of manuals in circulation in the eighteenth century.[45]

Beijing was not the only site where the Buddhist knowledge regime was crucial to political realignment processes. In Central Tibet, Buddhist knowledge codification was brought into play in the state-building process that kept the fifth Dalai Lama and his regent Sangye Gyatso busy for decades. It created new institutions, treatises, and practices in Tibet.[46] There, knowledge making was intensely political. Janet Gyatso has discussed a fascinating case in which empiricism directly challenged textual knowledge and became a new source of legitimacy as power struggles intensified in Tibet. At the heart of this debate lay this question: how many bones are there in the human body? Buddhist canons stated 360 as the number of bones. However, a physician close to the fifth Dalai Lama had a different opinion and figured the best way to settle the discrepancy would be to actually count them. Around 1670, Darmo Menrampa and his students publicly dissected human corpses in a park in Lhasa. They concluded that there are 365 bones because there are nine sections of the skull, not four.[47] This remarkable episode bespoke perhaps a pan-Tibetophone Buddhist knowledge regime: Buddhists embraced pluralistic sources of authenticity and authority and explored a wide range of subjects. The multitude might explain the elasticity of the Buddhist knowledge network and what enabled it to grow.

Let's return to the text itself. One question is, is it possible for craftsmen to make use of a manual that was rooted in the authoritative textual tradition, as Gombjab asserted? Although his text might not have served its purpose well, his intention was to rectify erroneous manuals and recalibrate the production process of statuary. The most substantial section of all the manuals is not the instructions that supposedly gave how-to information; rather, it is the five prefaces that take up much of the space in *Canon of Buddhist Iconometry*. All the blurbs sang Gombjab's praises and helped the text gain currency in Beijing's Buddhist circles. Endorsements came from prominent figures, including one official, one imperial prince, two monks, and the most well-known Buddhist figure of the Qing empire.

The set of prefaces merits further consideration; unfortunately, much of what can be said now remains speculative until more sources come to light. The second through the last prefaces were composed within a short span of seven months in a single year. The manuscript changed hands about every two months between two monks, one official, and the Qianlong emperor's Buddhist teacher. Its trajectory suggests a vibrant intellectual network that frequently brought together people who did not run in the same circles. The first two prefaces were written by powerful figures in the 1740s, the early years of the Qianlong reign. In recent decades, discussion of the third Changkya, Rolpai Dorje, has been prominent in research on Tibet in the Qing empire. The first preface, although written last chronologically, was penned by none other than Prince Zhuang, the first-rank imperial prince who was instrumental in converting Yonghegong and who developed a keen interest in Buddhist knowledge. Gombjab's claims in his preface raise several questions. What constituted authentic Tibetan Buddhist epistemology in eighteenth-century Buddhist Inner Asia? What motivated Buddhists to write, share, and comment on Buddhist knowledge production? He disapproved of these manuals because they were not rooted in the authoritative texts of the Buddhist canon.

TABLE 4.1
Prefaces to the *Canon of Buddhist Iconometry*

Preface order	Author	Date
1	Prince Zhuang	The eighth day of the eighth month, 1748
2	The third Changkya, Rolpai Dorje	The fifth day of the seventh month, 1742
3	Monk Ding Guang	The fourteenth day of the first month, 1742
4	Official Ming Ding	The twelfth day of the fifth month, 1742
5	Monk Ben Cheng	The fourteenth day of the third month, 1742

The prefaces thus illustrated a socio-textual community that was much more diverse and multidirectional. The commissioner of this text was a case in point. Gombjab credited a monk by the name of Jingjue visiting from Taozhou (Tib.: watsé) in southern Gansu for encouraging him and allegedly providing the "earliest and most precise" Tibetan-language manual. My search for Monk Jingjue was perhaps more serendipitous than anything else. While doing archival research on the changing power dynamics in Amdo, I stumbled upon the name of Ngawang Trinlé Gyatso (1688–1738/1739), the abbot of Chone Gönchen (Ganden Shedrub Ling) in modern-day southern Gansu Province in the early decades of the eighteenth century. His older brother Makzor Gonpo (Chinese surname: Yang) was crowned as the head of Chone, a semi-independent principality that grew to be a cultural center for Buddhists in Qing Inner Asia.[48] By custom, the Yang family's eldest son inherited the title of chieftain, while one of the younger sons occupied the monastic abbacy. Together with his elder brother, Ngawang Trinlé Gyatso visited the Kangxi emperor's court in Beijing in 1716; he received the title of "imperial preceptor" and a tablet inscribed "Chanding Si" for his monastery. Ngawang Trinlé Gyatso then returned to Amdo and devoted his time to the monastic affairs in this Chandi Si, known to the locals as Chone Ganden Shedrub Ling.[49] The title and the tablet embodies Qing imperial endorsement, and thus enabled the abbot and his monastery to define their relationship with a new patron. As for many Buddhist trülkus and monasteries in Inner Asia, Ngawang Trinlé's visit and subsequent recognition from the Qing court was part of the mutual effort from both Buddhists and Qing imperial rulers to find common ground as their spheres overlapped and their powers grew. But the process was long and contested; it predated the proliferation of Tibetan Buddhist trülkus in the Qianlong reign.

Title conferral was a tactic that the Kangxi emperor deployed, like the Mongol Yuan and Ming China. Early Qing emperors granted titles to Buddhists like Ngawang Trinlé Gyatso, but the imperial guesture did not establish him as a fixture in the Qing Inner Asian political agenda, as the Kangxi emperor still labored to consolidate his power in Inner Asia and was deeply invetseted in the war against the Zunghar state. His name—Chi Lian—was most likely a partial phonetic transcription of his Tibetan name, Trinlé.[50] The only possible meeting between him and Gombjab had to have taken place in 1716, during his trip to Beijing, but it is also possible that this trip marked the start of their epistolary relationship. Ngawang Trinlé Gyatso's most commemorated accomplishment was overseeing the production in the 1720s–1730s of the Tibetan Buddhist canonical texts of the Kagyur in Chone from engraving to final printing.[51] Around the same time, Gombjab was involved in translation projects of the Chinese canon and, later on, of their Mongolian versions.[52] Even though he was preoccupied by these official and commanding projects, he was excited by the rare chance of having an authoritative text to work with, so much so that Gombjab claimed that he translated the manual in a mere month.

Ngawang Trinlé capitalized on the larger sociopolitical changes at the time to turn his technical literacy into cultural literacy, and to use his case to remind the reader of the importance of seeing Tibetan Buddhism beyond the Qing's political intervention in its Inner Asian Buddhist world. Ngawang Trinlé Gyatso appears to have been well versed in the Chinese language; indeed, he may perhaps have been more comfortable with it than he was with the Tibetan language.[53] His linguistic detour through the Chinese language to textual authority in the Tibetan language suggests several new analytical trends in Qing Buddhist Inner Asia: knowledge transmission occurred in a multidirectional fashion, linguistic and ethnic boundaries were less meaningful in the eighteenth century, and finally, the heavily routinized and monitored movements of Buddhists were compromised by approved travel and letter exchanges. In the process, the Geluk School's insistent emphasis on writing and literary production shaped the socio-textual community centered on the Buddhist knowledge regime. The act of writing helped make the cross-cultural Buddhist network porous and accessible.

A BUDDHIST STATESMAN: IMPERIAL PRINCE GUO (1697-1738)

Gombjab was not the only one who vowed to make Buddhist knowledge more accessible to the laity. The seventeenth son of the Kangxi emperor, Prince Guo (Yunli), held several key administrative posts in the Yongzheng reign. In 1723, soon after the Yongzheng emperor had ascended the throne, he headed the Lifanyuan. After leading the Ministry of Works (Ch.: Gongbu), he was appointed as the minister overseeing the Ministry of Revenue (Ch.: Hubu) in 1733.[54] In his second year in this post, Prince

Guo led an unusual mission to prepare the displaced seventh Dalai Lama, Kelzang Gyatso, for his return to Lhasa. The seventh Dalai Lama had been living in exile in Kham since 1727. The Qing imperial government had removed him from Lhasa in response to the political turmoil in Tibet.[55] Twelve years old at the time, the newly recognized Dalai Lama did not have the political capital to rule Tibet. His young age and support from the Qing government only intensified the struggle for authority.[56] Polhané Sönam Topgyé (1689–1747), an astute political figure, became the "king" of Tibet and provided Tibetan politics with relative stability. The seventh Dalai Lama struggled to find his authority among various powerful contestants for ultimate control; instead, he was ensconced in Kham until 1733. Aiming to restore the power of the seventh Dalai Lama—and by extension that of the Qing imperial state in Central Tibet—Prince Guo's trip was of no small significance, but such a mission certainly fell outside the purview of the Ministry of Revenue, the post that Prince Guo held at the time. It might have fallen within the purview of the Lifanyuan, but he had left his post there five years prior. What motivated his becoming a proxy representing the imperial interest at this politically complicated time?

The prince was more than a veteran statesman and a trustworthy kinsman to the emperors. Prince Guo's erudition in Buddhist literary knowledge made him a safe choice to handle the subtle religio-political situations in Tibet. Prince Guo was no stranger to the circle of Beijing's Tibetan Buddhist dignitaries who moved in the space between Lhasa and Beijing during the eighteenth century, most of whom were Geluk trülkus by then. The growing number of Geluk trülkus in Beijing signaled an interdependency that ensured a Qing imperial grip on politics in Lhasa as well as a stronger Ganden Podrang government. Establishing this interdependency was a long process embroiled in conflict that at times could go in any direction. Prince Guo's interactions with these Geluk prelates in Beijing offer a fascinating dimension to the political maneuvers on both sides. He caused some unease among the Geluk lamas, whose trülku lines had been deeply involved in Inner Asian politics for more than a half a century. The preceding three chapters have demonstrated how Qing territorial expansion created a space for these Geluk trülkus to assert their agency in Qing Buddhist Inner Asia. By the eighteenth century, some of these lines spent substantial time each year in Beijing and at other important Buddhist sites in the regions bordering China proper and Mongolia, including Mount Wutai and Dolonnuur. Their growing influence and long stays created a space for members of the ruling elites to participate in the evolving social-textual Buddhist intellectual network.

Even though this network consisted mostly of Geluk trülkus, it was neither static nor exclusively dominated by the Geluk School, at least not before the Qianlong emperor's more systematic investment in Buddhist knowledge production in the 1740s. The spiritual biography of the third Changkya, Rolpai Dorje, recounted the process through which the Geluk School gradually dominated the network—or, at least, dominated the narratives of the network. The prince was said to have attempted to influence the third Changkya's education by inviting two Kagyü trülkus to Beijing in 1732 to serve as his principal teachers. Unfortunately, both passed away en route to Beijing, their deaths most likely caused by smallpox, which posed a fatal threat to Inner Asians not acclimated to local conditions. However, the spiritual biography claims the second Tukwan, Ngawang Chökyi Gyatso (1680–1736), was responsible for their deaths by casting spells on the two trülkus out of fear of their influence over the young Rolpai Dorje's learning.[57] The account then claims an ultimate win by the Geluk School when the role of principal teacher went to the second Sertri, Lobzang Tenpai Nyima, whose previous reincarnation was pivotal in brokering peace among the Mongols, as shown in chapter 3. The second Sertri, Lobzang Tenpai Nyima, also commissioned Gombjab to compile the *History of Buddhism in China*, discussed above. When the famed Geluk teacher arrived at the capital city, he received a welcome from Prince Guo, whose wife arranged the bestowal of appropriate titles and gifts on the learned Buddhist scholar.[58] The biography was written in 1792–1794, when these Amdo trülkus had established a stronger presence in the Qing imperial court. In this biography, the prince's ostensibly sectarian adherence and his changed attitude toward the teacher later on could be due to reconstruction created in hindsight in the biography, which was written many decades later, in a changed political landscape. Regardless, this eventful scenario suggests that the Geluk School had yet to solicit unwavering support within the imperial core in the transitional years of the Yongzheng and Qianlong reigns.

It was not just that the Geluk School had yet to establish its dominance in the Qing's negotiations with Tibetan Buddhists. For Buddhist laity like

Prince Guo and Gombjab, their interest in Buddhist knowledge did not seem to be much affected by sectarian differences in Tibetan Buddhism. One-third of the extant 958 titles in Prince Guo's private collection were Tibetan manuscripts or Mongolian translations of Tibetan "treasures" (Tib.: *gter ma*).[59] Even though they vary in their themes, the "treasures" are all texts or material objects that "treasure discoverers" (Tib.: *gter ston*) have unearthed from a place or from their own minds. Main treasure subjects consist of recounting history, spiritual biographies, or teachings and practices.[60] Treasure texts provided a means of authentication and asserted authority in a Buddhist culture centered on literacy. Treasure texts were most prominent in the Nyingma School of Tibetan Buddhism, which endured attacks from Geluk writers since the time of the fifth Dalai Lama, Sonam Gyatso, in the middle of the seventeenth century. Even though the Nyingma School experienced a resurgence among Tibetan Buddhists in the Himalayan regions in the eighteenth century, it drew criticism from the increasingly powerful Geluk scholars at the time. Prince Guo's keen interest in practices and writings beyond the Geluk School caused distress among Geluk trülkus, as attested in the writings of Sumpa Khenpo Yeshe Peljor (1704–1788).[61] However, Prince Guo did not seem overburdened by sectarian tensions. In 1736, he welcomed the second Sertri, Lobzang Tenpai Nyima, and the third Changkya, Rolpai Dorje, the top two Geluk dignitaries in Beijing. Prince Guo's embrace of multiple Buddhist traditions in the Yongzheng-Qianlong transitional years reflected the fact that the Geluk's firm dominance over Qing's interaction with Buddhists came in tandem with the Geluk's growing religious infrastructural presence in Qing Inner Asia. The mass production of Tibetan Buddhist knowledge in the Qianlong reign allowed Geluk trülkus to define the Buddhist Inner Asia of the Qing as a Geluk space within its network of monasteries; both institutions were the cornerstones of Geluk expansion into Inner Asia, whose formation was facilitated by Qing imperial expansion. On another occasion, seeing a rainbow above his residence after meeting with a Buddhist monk prompted Prince Guo to make a generous donation to the monk's monastery. Prince Guo's oeuvre belies the faulty assumption that the Geluk School was an ahistorical force that had established itself firmly in the Qing court.

Prince Guo's voluminous Buddhist writings indicate that Tibetan Buddhism was more than just a tactical instrument that Qing emperors found useful in their negotiations with local elites. Instead, the gradual process of incorporating Tibetan Buddhism into the everyday lives of the Manchu ruling elites provided an important context for their visions of how to manage the frontier. During the transitional years between the Yongzheng and Qianlong emperors in the 1730s, trustworthy kinsmen like Prince Guo played a pivotal role in shaping the Qing imperial agenda.[62] His other pursuits suggested that his interest in Buddhist knowledge was more philosophically oriented, an aspect that has yet to receive due attention in studies of Qing-Geluk interactions in the Qing era. For instance, Prince Guo was so immersed in Tibetan Buddhist knowledge that he composed consecration ritual manuals (Tib.: *rab gnas*). As Yael Bentor has argued, ritual can be understood "as a process of the localization of the omnipresent 'divine power' for the sake of those who do not realize its true nature."[63] Bearing this in mind helps to understand what Prince Guo aimed to accomplish. He was trying to simplify knowledge to make it comprehensible, to the extent that even a little child would be capable of grasping it without much difficulty.[64] His affinity for a more accessible ritual was perhaps part of an emergence of explanatory consecration ritual manuals, which differed from previous, more prescriptive ones. This is evident when his work is compared with earlier manuals written since the twelfth century. The shift toward explanatory styles, as Bentor argues, targeted both lay and monastic audiences of consecration rituals.[65] Both Prince Guo and Gombjab seem to have been concerned with the issue of accessibility; their concern is indicative of the porosity of the Buddhist knowledge regime as it spread east.

That century also witnessed a heightened sense of frontiers, as the Qing empire grew bigger territorially and more comprehensive administratively. Making sense of the sprawling empire requires understanding its growth as a long and deliberate process. The center's perceptions of and perspectives on the margins developed over time. A travelogue penned by Prince Guo on his mission to prepare the seventh Dalai Lama for his return to Lhasa reflects aspects of this evolving process of understanding. *Diary to Tibet* (Ch.: *Xizang riji*) documented the places through which Prince Guo made his way to Litang in western Sichuan in 1735. His travelogue consistently refers to the earliest extant geographical text in imperial China, *A Treatise on All Districts from the Yuanhe Reign* (Ch.: *Yuanhe junxian zhi*) that the official Li Fifu (758–814) wrote during the Tang dynasty. Another source text was *Commentary on the Waterways Classics* (Ch.: *Shuijing zhu*), which was composed in the Tuoba Northern Wei dynasty (386–534/535). After crossing a river in what is a Beijing suburb today, Prince Guo commented that "the Liuli river... was called 'Sacred water/river' [Ch.: Sheng shui] according to the *Commentary on the Waterways Classics*, or 'Encircling-City water/river' [Ch.: Huicheng shui] if the *Yuanhe Treatise* was consulted."[66] He was particularly keen to understand the rivers he crossed and continued to consult the two texts regarding their changing names. For more recent changes, his account bore political weight. Toward the end of his trip, on the sixteenth day of the twelfth month in 1734, he arrived at Hualinping (located in modern-day Kardzé in the Tibetan Autonomous Prefecture in Sichuan Province) and noted the following:

> A flat base of the valley is surrounded by high and precipitous mountains. If guarded well, it would be hard to transgress the area. It has been the boundary between the Han-Chinese and Qiang people since the Tang and Song periods (618–1279), and now Chinese and Tibetans ["fan" in the text] cohabit here. The vice-commander's office was relocated to Taining, and a post of brigade vice vommander [Ch.: *dusi*] was established here.[67]

Prince Guo's geohistorical account deviated from state-sponsored conventional gazetteers. In his writing, he wove together Chinese dynastic geographical texts along with his daily observations of the new border regions. As he approached Dartsedo shortly after, he explained that the place's Chinese name of Dajianlu was acquired in the early Kangxi reign; he also noted that Qing troops had been stationed there to guard the newly annexed area ever since. The place had grown in significance; since 1730, it had served as the new seat of Yazhou Prefecture.[68] His experience as reflected in his account provided an incentive for the Qianlong emperor to produce more legible knowledge about its territories, a sense of "high territoriality." It was reflective of a long historical process through which systematic knowledge about the Qing's imperial fringes was acquired in expeditions and subsequent negotiations with frontier elites, including Buddhists in Inner Asia.[69] This more nuanced territorial thinking had to be considered in light of the changing political perspectives of the world and the position of the Qing in that world. Territorial parameters and knowledge of the people, social practices, and mundane life in these new imperial spaces needed to be displayed and made available. Precisely because statecraft in the late Qianlong reign was so sophisticated, it is easy to assume that high territoriality was conceptualized at the top and carried out on the ground, but Prince Guo's unusual interest and deep knowledge in Tibetan Buddhism complicate such an assumption.

Another imperial prince similarly partook of the production and circulation of Buddhist knowledge in the crucial Yongzheng-Qianlong transitional year in 1735–1736. Prince Zhuang (Yunlu, 1695–1767) was two years senior to Prince Guo; both were confidants to the deceased Yongzheng emperor and were appointed to the transitional interim council when the Yongzheng emperor died. Prince Zhuang led a four-person transitional interim council and was later appointed to the Grand Council, along with his brother.[70] While in charge of the Department of the Imperial Household in the final years of the Yongzheng emperor's rule, he oversaw the renovation of Yonghegong prior to its conversion into a large Tibetan Buddhist monastery.[71] His other appointments also included heading the Ministry of Construction in 1736 and Lifanyuan in 1739, even though his tenure in Lifanyuan only lasted for a year before he was stripped of the title.[72] Besides his high-profile political posts, the prince was mostly known for his leading role in the codification and institutionalization of mathematical, musical, and astronomic knowledge in the Qing court.[73] Unlike his earlier writings on mathematics and music in the 1710s, however, Prince Zhuang spent much of his post-bureaucracy years after the 1740s focused on a wide range of Buddhist topics. He sponsored and compiled multilingual texts on Buddhist art production and ritual performance, and he wrote a quadrilingual compendium of orthoepy of *dhāraṇī* and mantras in Manchu, Chinese, Mongolian, and Tibetan.[74] In 1756, the Qianlong emperor appointed him to manage the production of 360 Tibetan Buddhist statues for the imperial palace.[75] For his contribution, the emperor rewarded Prince Zhuang with the entire set of 360 statues. The prince seemingly valued the set; he placed them in his private shrine room and commissioned artists to draw paper illustrations of the entire collection for preservation.[76] Beatrice Bartlett argues that imperial clansmen had gradually lost power and key posts over the course of the Qianlong rule.[77] It seems that both of the imperial princes devoted significant amounts of time to Tibetan Buddhism as their influence in court politics decreased. Their familiarity with the Tibetan Buddhist intellectual circle in Beijing and their knowledge of Buddhist art and literature offered them a favorable opportunity to keep up with court life in the changed political climate in the eighteenth century. The deep engagements of these two first-rank imperial princes in multiple sites of knowledge are suggestive of the cosmopolitan nature of Qing rule.[78]

One may question what the princes' private intellectual pastimes—even the Qianlong emperor's, for that matter—had to do with Qing imperial governance. After all, by the mid-eighteenth century, imperial kinsmen were transformed into civil servants of the state and had no military power to threaten the throne.[79] Indeed, neither Prince Guo nor Prince Zhuang was any more equipped to overthrow their brother than their nephew was. Nevertheless, the long process of transforming imperial clansmen into bureaucrats opened other doors to them; with the transformation, they also earned credentials in governing practices as the empire grew more diverse and needed more tools to rule. Precisely because of their pluralistic intellectual appetites, they remained at the very center of the Qing rule and were able to establish an unofficial platform for negotiating with multiple interest groups at the behest of the rulers before the state crafted feasible governing strategies.

Qing imperial governance has been a fruitful field of study in recent decades. One of the major historiographical approaches is a deep-seated belief that the Qing state operated in two halves. The imperial household and its Inner Asian alliances were the focus of the "inner court" arm, including the Department of the Imperial Household and the Lifanyuan, in which Tibetan Buddhists were a key target of administrative undertakings. In contrast, the regions of China proper that had long been governed by imperial dynasties fell within the state apparatus, or the "outer court." But how much did this division ring true in the Qing? The roles of each of the two princes in imperial management were informed by their personal interests and clearly straddled these supposed boundaries. This calls into question the assumed artificiality of the division when thinking about Qing imperial governance.

Another long-running assumption, which similarly suffers from a teleological perspective, has also prejudiced our thinking about Tibetan Buddhism. Tibetan Buddhism was and still is a religion, and I do not dispute that categorization. Rather, I want to call attention to the limitation this categorization has in terms of historical inquiry. We are largely informed by the proposition that political power should be separated from the numinous. More commonly known as separation of church and state, this notion is applied erroneously to modern polities in general.[80] As I have discussed earlier in this book, such a categorization lodged Tibetan Buddhism in a skewed power hierarchy. Exacerbating the problem, Tibet's Ganden Podrang government never intended to steer clear of religion. The adamant assertion of this division nonetheless has also undercut Tibetan Buddhism as a knowledge system. Some have identified the impact of Western science in China; others have focused on agents from within;[81] but Tibetan Buddhism has rarely been considered a body of systematic knowledge in the studies of Qing-Tibet relations.[82] Instead, in research on the Qing, subject matter related to Tibetan Buddhism is more likely to be found in sections on religion, along with Daoism, Shamanism, or (Chinese) Buddhism. When the Qianlong emperor tasked Tibetan Buddhist trülkus with classifying, organizing, and making Tibetan Buddhist images, we understand this as more of a political move than a process of knowledge production.[83] The assumption is that the emperor's "private" and "religious" undertakings had to be politically saturated. At the time, the cosmopolitan Qing empire was governed by men of letters who were versed in many realms of knowledge. For at least some of these learned men, Tibetan Buddhism was not an exceptional body of knowledge divorced from the rest of their lives or the governance of the empire.

CROSS-CULTURAL BUDDHIST KNOWLEDGE NETWORK IN QING BUDDHIST INNER ASIA

Qing imperial rule also impacted the ways in which Tibetan Buddhists understood the world and their outlook on geography. Since the mid-sixteenth century, Tibetan Buddhist vanguards had long been enlisted to solve political conflicts, especially among the Mongol strongmen.[84] The Qianlong emperors took their involvement to a new level: bureaucratization.[85] A cluster of Geluk trülkus, mostly from Amdo, became a fixture in Qing Inner Asian politics through expansive engagements. By the end of the Qianlong reign in the 1790s, a number of these Geluk hierarchs acquainted themselves with intellectual circles in Beijing that included officials and the imperial family as well as foreign missionaries. In 1830, the fourth Tsenpo Mindrol Nominhan, Jampel Chokyi Tendzin Trinle (1789–1838), wrote a 410-folio manuscript entitled *The Detailed Description of the World* (Tib.: *Dzam ling chen pö gyé shé nö chü kün sel mé long zhé jap zhuk so*).[86] Jampel Chokyi Tendzin Trinle, the abbot of an influential Amdo Geluk monastery—Serkhok Monastery (Ch.: Guanghui si)—spent more than two decades in Beijing and frequently stayed in Dolonnuur's monasteries. He wrote this manuscript in the final decade of his life; in it, he introduced a quasi-anthropogeography of the world, with uneven attention to different parts of the world. He was more meticulous in his description of European countries and provocatively located Shambhala— the Buddhist Pure Land—in Spain. This identification earned him criticism from other contemporary Buddhist scholars.[87] His writing process itself is perhaps more instructive than the actual manuscript. His writing exhibits the realization of a vibrant intellectual network that had been long in the making among Buddhists in the Qing empire.

Jampel Chokyi Tendzin Trinle did not travel globally; rather, he learned about the world through conversation. He identified a certain "Alexander" in Beijing as a key informant. When certain topics seemed beyond his reach, he wrote to other scholars. When the seventh Panchen Lama, Palden Tenpai Nyima (1782–1853), received a letter from the curious Jampel Chokyi Tendzin Trinle about the Arctic Circle, he referred him to European sources.[88] Jampel Chokyi Tendzin Trinle's geographical account of the world was not a simple quest for knowledge. Rather, it reflects a dynamic system of knowledge making that was deeply grounded in Buddhist philosophy. Jampel Chokyi Tendzin Trinle joined a long tradition in reimagining India as the holy land of Buddhism, even though India at the time was dominated by Hinduism and Islam.[89] Physical distance did not undercut this intellectual network. Rather, texts and letters created a socio-textual community that sustained a Buddhist space transcending geographical limits. What facilitated the literary space was also Qing imperial expansion and political realignment. One of the two Buddhists credited with comissioning Jampel Chokyi Tendzin Trinle to write his geographical text was Kagyurwa Mergen Nomönhen. While further research may definitively confirm his identity, this particular Kagyurwa Mergen Nomönhen may have belonged to a prominent line of reincarnation active in Beijing's imperial court and Mongolia.[90] The title "Kagyurwa" refers to Buddhists who have deep knowledge of the word of the

Buddha (Tib.: *bka'*), and several Buddhists earned this title in the eighteenth century. Such knowledge was facilitated by the imperially supported Buddhist canon printing projects. A certain Kagyurwa was closely associated with Prince Guo in his Buddhist writing and translation projects,[91] but "Mergen" in his title was unmistakably a Mongolian name, which suggests his connection to the Mongols. Finally, in writing this world geography text, Jampel Chokyi Tendzin Trinle made an effort to make his text more accessible, just as Prince Guo and Gombjab had done in their works; clearly, he did this in hopes that one day informed young people could travel around easily. He opted for a straightforward free-verse style.[92] All of these Buddhist men of letters seemed concerned about accessibility because it was imperative for facilitating Buddhist knowledge production and transmission.[93] Why did writing become a vital attribute of the notion of belonging for Buddhists in this particular time and place? Writing-facilitated Buddhist authenticity was intricately connected to the politics of the Buddhist knowledge network fostered in the first half of the Qing empire.

Neither writing nor printing was a static process isolated or independent from socio-historical development in Tibet or, later on, in Qing Buddhist Inner Asia. For Buddhists in Tibet, the dynamic editorial choices of canonical tantras reflected the rise to power of the new schools (Tib.: Sarmapa) that had a great impact on the Geluk School later on.[94] For these later lineages, textual authenticity and thus inclusion in the canon were determined by their proven Indian origins. Some of the tantric texts produced by the new schools and excluded from the canons were considered treasures by the Nyingma School.[95] The Geluk School's efforts to codify a range of Buddhist knowledge subjects such as ritual traditions, medicine, and philosophy started in the seventeenth century, and the more costly canon productions were done through the generous sponsorship of its Mongolian and Manchu patrons.[96] In other words, the Geluk's Buddhist knowledge regime was closely tied to its expansion into Inner Asia, first among the Mongolians, then among the Mongolians under the Qing, and among the Qing imperial rulers; all of these leaders resided outside of Central Tibet, and all were looking for support for their political legitimacy.

Recent studies have shown that the Qing empire's encounter with Tibetan Buddhists was beyond the singular Qianlong emperor and his religious teacher, and was about more than political legitimacy.[97] I hope this chapter adds another dimension to the ongoing explorations of their interactions. Tibetan Buddhism was also a knowledge system that could expand how we think about epistemology in late imperial China. Considerable scholarly attention has been placed on the Jesuits' activities when it comes to knowledge production in the Qing; however, more recent reappraisals consider local agency among literati in China to be an important factor.[98] However, it is clear that non-Han Chinese officials have been afforded little significance in the social history of knowledge making in the Qing. Even though the city of Beijing was spatially segregated, ideas traveled and people moved. Gombjab was not the only multilingual Mongolian statesman, and Buddhism was not the sole focus of intellectual inquiry. The Mongolian bannerman Faššan (Fashishan, 1753–1813) brought together painters, calligraphers, and court artists to produce paintings to commemorate his grand residence in Beijing.[99] A Hanlin Academy scholar himself, Faššan wrote over three thousand poems in Chinese; other multilingual ruling elites of ethnically Mongolian and Manchu heritage were also prolific in literary traditions prevalent among Han Chinese scholars.[100] Toward the end of the Qianlong reign and for much of the nineteenth century, Han Chinese scholars became increasingly aware of the Qing's territorial reach and the diverse subjects brought under Qing rule. They were concerned over how the Qing state produced knowledge of Inner Asia in shifting geopolitical realities around the world in the nineteenth century. As maritime empires—the British in particular—moved to colonize the Indian subcontinent, many Han Chinese scholars felt an urgent need to shift a localized approach to managing Inner Asian frontiers to a more holistic understanding of world geography and foreign policies in this critical region.[101] Not all Han Chinese scholars studied Inner Asians or Tibetan Buddhism out of political need; Gong Zizhen (1792–1841), for example, embraced Buddhism and studied Inner Asian communities in the belief that cultural exchange would enrich and supplement native (that is, Chinese) intellectual currents.[102] A more inclusive consideration will change not only how we think about the cultural history of knowledge making and circulation, but also how we understand the cosmopolitan Qing empire as it was experienced by its diverse scholars.

So far, my discussion has been mostly focused on Buddhist textual knowledge, but texts have their own limits in transmitting knowledge, even how-to manuals. It is questionable whether Gombjab's translation of

146

GOVERNANCE

the *Canon of Buddhist Iconometry* could serve its purpose to produce aesthetically pleasing statues that could host Buddhist deities. If so, what about visual forms of Buddhist knowledge? A picture is worth a thousand words. In an image from a collection of fifty-eight paintings, the deity on the top left and the mountain on the top right, both surrounded by clouds, demonstrate what the visualization is supposed to generate in the associated meditation. The series was commissioned by a Mongolian banner leader in eastern Mongolia in the eighteenth century to facilitate visualization in Buddhist practice, as Karl Debreczeny insightfully points out.[103] Cartographical references were similarly essential in reinforcing site-specific historical memory among Buddhist pilgrims, such as at Mount Wutai.[104] Long-standing literary practices motivated these Buddhists to produce or circulate knowledge about Buddhist sites and practices in a more transmittable and flexible manner.

Writing was central among Buddhists, especially among those Geluk trülkus who traveled more frequently within Qing Inner Asia. Additionally, the Qing imperial expansion created an alternative landscape that Buddhists saw as even more connected spatially. Qing imperial governance also had an impact on Buddhist knowledge making on many fronts. Beijing became a hub attracting Buddhist trülkus; in turn, cosmopolitan living changed their worldview. Their travels and writings recalibrated Buddhist literary practices and created new sites of Buddhist imagination.[105] With the shifting Buddhist landscape in Qing Inner Asia, Chinese-speaking Tibetan Buddhists and Mongolian Buddhists could also negotiate their identities and partake in making a unique Buddhist culture that transcended linguistic boundaries.[106] To arrive at this point, we must not only recognize the central place that writing held in Buddhist practices but also acknowledge that, since the rise of the Geluk School's power in Tibet in the fifteenth century, the centrality of textuality had become a Buddhist hallmark.

The final chapter brings closure to a circulatory Buddhist-knowledge regime propelled by the Geluk School as it expanded its patron pool outside Tibet. This growth was facilitated by the Qing's imperial expansion into Inner Asia. Even though the present chapter continues to address the overlap of the two powers as they both sought sources of support and

GOVERNANCE

expansion of their respective spheres of influence, it focuses more on the years that predated the formation of the Qing's imperial governance practice and the inner workings of the court. In so doing, it shows how the Qing's imperial enterprise not only facilitated Buddhist expansion, but also was shaped in that process. The preceding three chapters have examined the religious infrastructures that enabled Buddhist knowledge to travel far and perpetuate itself. Stationary monasteries connected mobile Buddhists; these gave the network both stability and fluidity. Within the dynamic Buddhist space of Qing Inner Asia, the act of writing made the network more porous; writing was instrumental in developing a paratextual community centered on producing and circulating Buddhist knowledge. It allowed individuals, especially Buddhist laity, to partake in a Buddhist world and create a notion of Buddhist belonging. The socio-textual community constructed a fluid religious space that overlapped with the Qing's administrative divisions and transcended linguistic barriers. Qing Inner Asia was thus transmuted into a Buddhist space within the empire.

The imperial expansion and governing practices that the Qing rulers had invested in for approximately a century inadvertently facilitated the circulation of Buddhist knowledge. Tibetan Buddhism provided the institutional and intellectual common ground on which the Qing rulers negotiated the terms on two fronts. First of all, the Qianlong emperor has long been seen as a sophisticated political figure who employed Tibetan Buddhist art to meet his political and spiritual needs. Indeed, there was a mass production of Buddhist images of varied forms, expensive projects to translate and print Buddhist canons, and numerous Tibetan Buddhist monasteries appearing in Beijing and Inner Asia during the emperor's six-decade rule. These dominant, imperially sanctioned endeavors certainly overshadowed other regional hubs like Dergé and Chone. The emergence and eventual prominence of these regional cultural kernels located on the fringes of the Himalayan Buddhist space depended in part on the rising power of the Geluk's Ganden Podrang government, as well as on the Qing's enthusiastic support of the Geluk Buddhists' undertakings to the east. These multiple sites launched their own Buddhist knowledge-making enterprises: monasteries in Amdo and Kham printed texts, while studios in Dolonnuur found their niche in the market for Buddhist art. The Qing's Buddhist Inner Asia consisted of multiple centers, each of which functioned as a node of convergence. In other words, the Qing court strove to define itself as a Buddhist hub in this newly redefined space in Inner Asia. Its support of Buddhist infrastructures afforded Buddhists more venues to articulate their Buddhist belonging; it also made Buddhist knowledge more mobile, and finally, the Qing imperial rulers allowed regional powers to claim their cultural authority with the new platform based on Buddhist knowledge making.

Buddhist knowledge production also offered Buddhist men of letters a way to assert their agency in the Qing's imperial enterprise. Their embodied knowledge defined the collaborative process through which texts, statues, and architecture were produced massively in and around the Qing imperial space. The act of writing itself perhaps was more crucial to these Buddhists than the particular subject matters of their writing. This was especially so in the case of Gombjab's iconometric manual. Although it might be challenging to use this manual as a technical reference, in the way that how-to texts are often intended, the text nonetheless created a socio-textual community based on Buddhist knowledge and helped this community articulate their notion of Buddhist identity in this dynamic knowledge regime. The mutual interest of both powers propelled a distinctly Qing Buddhist culture that was heavily invested in writing. Tibet's Ganden Podrang government built its strength on mass monasticism and the tradition of literary production. The seventeenth and eighteenth centuries witnessed a growing desire for the young Geluk School to expand its patron base, particularly outside Tibet, where the more-established schools had parceled out aristocratic support. For Mongolian leaders and then for the Manchu rulers, Tibetan Buddhism provided a unique asset for their political ambitions: Tibetan Buddhism upheld a historical memory that was indispensable to their legitimacy claims. All of these developments had emerged before the mid-eighteenth century, when the Qianlong emperor made inroads in places his predecessors had long fought to include in the Qing imperial territory.

Looking closely at Tibet, internal competition for financial support came in tandem with growing Mongolian interest in Tibet, as well as its Buddhist legacy from the Mongol Empire centuries earlier. The Mongols' northward retreat after the demise of the Mongol Empire led to a series of alliances and conflicts within its constituents. The rise of the Manchu Jin polity further complicated the geopolitical history of Inner Asia. However, by the mid-eighteenth century, these power struggles diminished, because the Zunghar state as a polity vanished, and Tibet's political landscape shifted significantly. The Qing empire became well positioned to decide the regional order and the future direction of political development, but this hegemony arose at the very end of a long series of historical developments that we have just begun to understand. In the process, Tibetan Buddhist knowledge provided the institutional and philosophical common ground that allowed the Qing to craft a unique Buddhist space in Inner Asia.

EPILOGUE

A Balancing Act

On my visit to Dolonnuur in summer 2010, the newly painted walls of the Yellow Temple were glaring, and gigantic marble pillars stood outside the temple in an empty plaza. The temple's grandeur suggests a return of Tibetan Buddhism to a town that has lost its relevance in the modern era; a short walk of five minutes to the west, however, the dilapidated Blue Temple was nearly unrecognizable. I stood on tiptoes attempting to see what was behind the short and shabby walls, but the silence inside spoke loudly: it was deserted, and nothing was left for tourists to see. The two monasteries represent the two ends of the spectrum of Tibetan Buddhist monastic institutions, and examples of both are numerous in contemporary China, a state that has left little to no space for religious institutions to claim a voice in national politics. The Chinese Communist Party's approach to many religious institutions, including Tibetan Buddhist monasteries, has tended to paralyze religious infrastructures. The sangha has been dispossessed of its institutional base, and the built environment repurposed as tourist attractions to generate revenue for the local government. Tourism gives the physical facility of a monastery a fresh start, but redefines its nature in that process.

The damage caused by state policy was indeed irreversible. However, the noticeable absence of religion in national politics has not rendered

EPILOGUE: A BALANCING ACT

Tibetan Buddhists entirely powerless. In fact, the Tibetan Buddhist trülkus have continued to play an indispensable role in local communities, albeit with more restrictions and fewer resources. This depletion of resources reveals both the strength and vulnerability these Buddhists embody in modern times: they are forced to retreat to the religious realm and severely marginalized in politics, their involvement in which is heavily scrutinized. Even so, the model of resistance and domination does not capture the full range of interactions of the Chinese Communist Party and the religious communities. Fernanda Pirie's extensive fieldwork in nomadic communities in eastern Tibet between 2003 and 2007 revealed that local officials could not maintain social order without negotiating with tradition and without relying upon religious and communal leaders to resolve conflicts. The Chinese state's governing mechanisms, such as law enforcement and the criminal justice system, did not reduce violence or restore social order. From resolving pasture disputes to de-escalating intra-ethnic conflicts, venerated Tibetan Buddhist trülkus and communal leaders were called upon to mediate, and the resolution was acknowledged in socially accepted ceremonies.[1]

Like these Tibetan Buddhist trülkus, some Tibetan Buddhist monasteries have similarly shown their vitality in contemporary China. To be sure, political campaigns and outright coercive state policies irrevocably damaged numerous monasteries in the high socialist era in the 1960s and 1970s, like the Blue Temple in Dolonnuur. But some monasteries, like the Yellow Temple, availed themselves of state initiatives and found a way to revive and somewhat regain local religious authority. The paths to revival varied for many religious communities and were definitely difficult, but many areas in Buddhist Inner Asia saw some level of Buddhist institutional revitalization. Ben Hillman shows the complex power relationship between leaders of a Tibetan Buddhist monastery in western China and local government officials since the 1990s. In this remarkable confrontation, some monks from this anonymous monastery attacked officials from the county bureau of ethnic and religious affairs, and the tension spilled out into the local community, but the skirmish did not result in violence or juridical interventions.[2] On other occasions, local government officials actively sought help from prominent Buddhist figures to defuse tensions between communities lest armed conflicts ensue.[3] These episodes show the resilience of religious infrastructural mechanisms, even as the state's governing apparatus has continued to coerce them in recent decades.

Tibetan Buddhists were not the only religious group that worked with the state beyond the resistance and hegemony model. There is no question that the Chinese state has depleted religious institutions of resources, but it does not completely deprive these religious actors of agency. Thomas Borchert details how the Buddhist community of the Dai People's Autonomous Prefecture of Sipsongpanna (Ch.: Xishuangbanna Daizu zizhi Zhou) work within the state's regulatory frameworks, but do not share the state's agenda in carrying out their religious practices.[4] Needless to say, the adversity they face is unnecessarily grim, but the resistance model does not reflect the full extent of religious activities and vitality in contemporary China. Instead of creating the binary paradigm of "minority religious figures" versus the state, it would be equally helpful to think that the state-sanctioned religious realms did not remove agency from these religious figures. Some Tibetan Buddhist men of letters in the socialist state asserted their "moral agency" under political restraints. Buddhist intellectuals expressed their ethnical values, upheld religious practices, and continued to promote Buddhist studies even when they had to navigate a perilous political environment.[5] Of course, the cases recounted here are not meant to paint a rosy picture as if religious communities—Tibetan Buddhists or others—have been enjoying due freedom and autonomy in the recent history of China. It is profoundly disheartening to see how Buddhist institutions have been disfranchised right in front of our eyes.

The modern promise of separation between state and religion is only partly responsible for the depreciation of religion. Tibetan Buddhism in modern Chinese politics has occupied a more sensitive position, not only because of its far-reaching transcultural sphere of influence, but also because of ethnicity (Ch.: *minzu*). When the nation-state held sway in global history at the beginning of the twentieth century, China was struggling. In the face of adversity, Chinese intellectuals were dismayed by the Manchu Qing's inability to respond to the threats to China's sovereignty. To many, a modern China was envisioned as a free and independent nation. China needed to be a nation that "enjoys equal rights with other great nations in international affairs."[6] To the many Chinese men of letters, the Manchu rulers of Qing China were simply not up to the task. Instead, they were destructive and obstructive of China's modernization, and ethnicity was highly politicized in the context of nationalism in fin de siècle China. Social Darwinism provided these revolutionary-minded intellectuals with a trope to generate social debates about China's recent humiliating past. In this context, ethnicity and/or nationality had to be addressed to achieve national sovereignty in the new world order. As Benno Weiner puts it, "nation-states, even those with pluralistic aspirations, are prone to homogenize as they demand new types of expressions of loyalty and identity from their citizens."[7]

Nationalist revolutionaries such as Sun Yat-sen (1866–1925) and Chen Tianhua (1875–1905) also deployed the concept of ethnicity to mobilize support for their anti-Qing and anti-Manchu movements. To them, to establish a modern China, "all responsibility to obey the Manchus is abolished" because "China belongs to the Chinese. Our countrymen should all recognize that this is the China of the Han race." How best to achieve this goal? Zou Rong (1885–1905) wrote: "Let us overthrow the barbaric government established by the Manchu people in Beijing."[8] His articulation of a China comprising an exclusive Han race would amount to disaggregating close to half of the Qing imperial territory, a fact that he and his contemporaries had to address. The discourse of ethnicity might have helped propel nationalist sentiment in the early revolutionary years, but Tibetan Buddhist practices and teachers continued to influence national politics in the 1930s and 1940s. Shared religious identity and the influence wielded by these Buddhists helped unify the people to form a modern China, however politically fractured it may have been.[9] Finding a balance between these two pressing challenges proved difficult for modern Chinese regimes.

At the turn of the twentieth century, Han Chinese literati developed mounting concerns over territorial reaches and the people living on these imperial fringes, which were two separated but interconnected issues. To many of them, it was deeply worrying that the Qing state relied heavily upon local ruling elites, doing little to protect those territories as the "great game" between the British Empire and tsarist Russia advanced through Central Eurasia, including Tibet, Mongolia, and Xinjiang. In many cases, local elites were excluded or alienated from the modern state-building process. The issue might have more to do with Han scholars' anti-Qing rhetoric suggesting an overhaul of the entire political system than with historical developments on the ground in Tibet. Exterior pressure made them acutely dissatisfied with how the Qing imperial court had governed these critical border regions. Since the 1880s, there were greater efforts to generate public support to replace imperial institutions at work in the borderlands with administrative apparatus in China proper; the outcomes, however, were unpredictable and uneven.[10] Of course, territory was not the only pressing issue for these Chinese scholars with respect to Qing governing practices. The modern Chinese state as they envisaged it must also separate religion from politics, and ethnicity became more and more pronounced in defining nationhood. If anything, the changed tone toward both the borderlands and the people living there was reflective of the modern state-making process in China that collapsed historical processes into a roadblock that needed to be cleared as China moved along with the rest of the world into the modern era.

Dominance of nationalist historical reconstruction and the statemaking process also present a unique challenge when appraising the Qing's imperial governance in Inner Asia. Going further back in history, Qing imperial rulers saw Tibetan Buddhism in a different light. To understand the complexity and subtlety of the role of Buddhist forces in holding together Qing imperial territory, we must eschew the established norms of national history or divided ethnic studies before either concept gained traction in the twentieth century, or we start from the wrong place with the modern nationalist framework in mind. Many of the places and figures discussed in this book have yet to receive due attention in the study of Qing imperial governance, but they were important in their own right. The sites and figures that wove together the Buddhist knowledge network often slipped under the radar in a political historical narrative focused only on the metropoles—in this case, either Beijing or Lhasa. To explain how the two powers grew symbiotically, a different kind of narrative has given Inner Asia both tension and vitality. This fluid network responded to changing geopolitical realities at the eastern terminus of the Eurasian continent. It was resistant to political push and pull and in many ways shaped the power negotiation between the two metropoles.

The *Proclamation on Lamas*, with which this book began, marked a notable shift in the Qing imperial imagination. Here, the Qianlong emperor faced a different empire than he had inherited from his father almost six decades previously: the Zunghars were finally reined in after nearly a century of taxing warfare; the Qing's territories doubled, its imperial subjects diversified, and its population tripled. The Qianlong emperor

EPILOGUE: A BALANCING ACT

crafted, articulated, and displayed a new vision of the Qing empire and adopted new strategies to realize that vision. The apex of Qing growth and prosperity overshadowed the decades of contested processes through which the emperor had envisaged an all-encompassing empire.

The Qing imperial perspectives offer one side of the story, but it was not the only side that mattered. The Geluk's Ganden Podrang Buddhist government had likewise striven to expand its sphere of influence and to command more economic and social resources to fuel its growth and expansion. Its strength lay in its flexible infrastructural mechanisms: mobile Buddhist trülkus were moored to immobile Buddhist monasteries. These two pillars rendered the mandalic Ganden Podrang polity more resilient. Back in the days when General Nian Gengyao led the expedition to Amdo, he was puzzled by the power wielded by these two types of Buddhist institution. The general's court memorial provided a pretext for imposing restrictions on Buddhist institutions when the Qing first came into close contact with the vast Buddhist network on the eastern fringe of the Himalayan Buddhist world. Much of what I have discussed in the preceeding chapters addresses the tensions in their initial encounter as well as the subsequent negotiations to survive the changing geopolitical terrain, which was a process of finding common ground between them. It was a delicate balancing act that sometimes worked, and at other times did not.

Many factors contributed to this vacillation. During the eighteenth century, the Kangxi, Yongzheng, and Qianlong emperors each faced different but equally daunting tasks in consolidating power, expanding Qing territory, and crafting a plausible imperial vision for all subjects. But it misses the mark to see the Qing imperial enterprise as a series of state-engineered projects to claim space far afield. In the Himalayas, the rising Geluk School of Tibetan Buddhism was striving to recruit more patrons and looked to the east. It had long cultivated ties with a slate of Mongol strongmen, who had tried in vain to revive the Mongol empire after Ming China drove them back north. These historical ties underlay the Qing's imperial policies toward its Inner Asian Buddhist subjects. The Qing's territorial consolidation created space for these Buddhists to travel, expand their patron pools, and exert Buddhist influence. In that process, the distinctive Geluk monasticism played a pivotal role in sustaining the fluid religious network. Its flexibility was compounded with the Tibetan Buddhist trülku practice, another resourceful Buddhist institution upon which Qing rulers relied. The mobile Buddhists and immobile monasteries offered the religious network both the crucial stability and elasticity that the Geluk's mandalic Buddhist government needed to negotiate with the growing Qing empire.

The year after the Qianlong emperor's proclamation was made public, the golden-urn practice was institutionalized in his more comprehensive policy framework in governing Tibet, *The Twenty-Nine-Article Statute on the Restoration of Tibet*. The politically tinged rhetoric and the more forceful administrative intervention had broad ramifications for the geopolitical history of Tibet and the Qing in the nineteenth century. Their search for common ground created a Buddhist Inner Asia that had an enduring influence on the geopolitical history of the peoples now living in Tibet, Mongolia, and China.

NOTES

INTRODUCTION

1. Pekka Hämäläinen, *Lakota America: A New History of Indigenous Power* (New Haven, CT: Yale University Press, 2019), 204.
2. Tak-Sing Kam, "The DGe-Lugs-Pa Breakthrough: The Uluk Darxan Nangsu Lama's Mission to the Manchus," *Central Asiatic Journal* 44, no. 2 (2000): 161–76. Kim Sung Soo [Jin Chengxiu], *Ming Qing zhiji Zangchuan Fojiao zai Menggu diqu de chuanbo* [Tibetan Buddhism in Mongolia during the Ming and Qing] (Beijing: Shehui kexue wenxian chubanshe, 2006); Matthew Kapstein, ed., *Buddhism Between Tibet and China* (Boston: Wisdom Publications, 2009).
3. On the agency of Mongols and Tibetan Buddhism in Mongolia, see Vesna Wallace, ed., *Buddhism in Mongolian History, Culture, and Society* (Oxford: Oxford University Press, 2015), xv; Uranchimeg Tsultemin, *A Monastery on the Move: Art and Politics in Later Buddhist Mongolia* (Honolulu: University of Hawai'i Press, 2021), 8.
4. Kim S. S., *Ming Qing zhiji Zangchuan Fojiao zai Menggu*.
5. C. A. Bayly et al., "AHR Conversation: On Transnational History," *American Historical Review* 111, no. 5 (December 2006): 1441–64; James C. Scott, *The Art of Not Being Governed: An Anarchist History of Upland Southeast Asia*, Yale Agrarian Studies Series (New Haven, CT: Yale University Press, 2010); Sebouh David Aslanian, *From the Indian Ocean to the Mediterranean: The Global Trade Networks of Armenian Merchants from New Julfa* (Berkeley: University of California Press, 2011); Engseng Ho, *The Graves of Tarim: Genealogy and Mobility Across the Indian Ocean* (Berkeley: University of California Press, 2006); Arash Khazeni, *Sky Blue Stone: The Turquoise Trade in World History* (Berkeley: University of California Press, 2014); Julia A. Clancy-Smith, *Mediterraneans: North Africa and Europe in*

INTRODUCTION

an Age of Migration, c. 1800–1900 (Berkeley: University of California Press, 2012); Alison Games, "Atlantic History: Definitions, Challenges, and Opportunities," *American Historical Review* 111, no. 3 (2006): 741–57.

6. Peregrine Horden and Nicholas Purcell, "The Mediterranean and 'the New Thalassology,'" *American Historical Review* 111, no. 3 (2006): 722–40; Markus P. M. Vink, "Indian Ocean Studies and the 'New Thalassology,'" *Journal of Global History* 2, no. 1 (May 2007): 41–62.
7. Engseng Ho, "Inter-Asian Concepts for Mobile Societies," *Journal of Asian Studies* 76, no. 4 (November 2017): 907–28.
8. Thomas J. Barfield, *The Perilous Frontier: Nomadic Empires and China*, Studies in Social Discontinuity (Cambridge, MA: Basil Blackwell, 1989), 12.
9. Evelyn Rawski, *Early Modern China and Northeast Asia: Cross-Border Perspectives*, Asian Connections (Cambridge: Cambridge University Press, 2015); Evelyn Rawski, "The Qing in Historiographical Dialogue," *Late Imperial China* 37, no. 1 (2016): 1–4; Nianshen Song, *Making Borders in Modern East Asia: The Tumen River Demarcation, 1881–1919* (Cambridge: Cambridge University Press, 2019).
10. Gray Tuttle and Johan Elverskog, eds., "Wutaishan and Qing Culture," special issue, *Journal of the International Association of Tibetan Studies* 6 (December 2011); Stacey van Vleet, "Medicine, Monasteries and Empire: Tibetan Buddhism and the Politics of Learning in Qing China" (PhD diss., Columbia University, 2015). For other transregional studies within the Qing, see Luman Wang, "Money and Trade, Hinterland and Coast, Empire and Nation-State: An Unusual History of Shanxi Piaohao, 1820–1930" (PhD diss., University of Southern California, 2014); Richard Belsky, *Localities at the Center: Native Place, Space, and Power in Late Imperial Beijing* (Cambridge, MA: Harvard University Asia Center, 2006); Amy Gordanier, "The (Male) Divas of Beijing: Trade Networks, Professional Ties, and the Road to Stardom in Eighteenth-Century China" (paper abstract, American Historical Association Annual Meeting 2016), https://aha.confex.com/aha/2016/webprogram/Paper19382.html.
11. David Bello, *Across Forest, Steppe and Mountain: Environment, Identity and Empire in Qing China's Borderlands* (New York: Cambridge University Press, 2015); Jonathan Schlesinger, *A World Trimmed with Fur: Wild Things, Pristine Places, and the Natural Fringes of Qing* (Stanford, CA: Stanford University Press, 2017).
12. Karen Barkey, *Bandits and Bureaucrats: The Ottoman Route to State Centralization* (Ithaca, NY: Cornell University Press, 1996); Karen Barkey, *Empire of Difference: The Ottomans in Comparative Perspective* (Cambridge: Cambridge University Press, 2008).
13. Bayly et al., "AHR Conversation," 1442; see also Sven Beckert's contribution in this forum at 1459.
14. Wen-Shing Chou, *Mount Wutai: Visions of a Sacred Buddhist Mountain* (Princeton, NJ: Princeton University Press, 2018), 12.
15. Matthew W. King, *Ocean of Milk, Ocean of Blood: A Mongolian Monk in the Ruins of the Qing Empire* (New York: Columbia University Press, 2019), 14.
16. King, *Ocean of Milk*, 7.
17. Jodi L. Weinstein, *Empire and Identity in Guizhou: Local Resistance to Qing Expansion* (Seattle: University of Washington Press, 2013); C. Patterson Giersch, *Asian Borderlands: The Transformation of Qing China's Yunnan Frontier* (Cambridge, MA: Harvard University Press, 2006).

INTRODUCTION

18. Rian Thum, *The Sacred Routes of Uyghur History* (Cambridge, MA: Harvard University Press, 2014); James Millward, *Beyond the Pass: Economy, Ethnicity, and Empire in Qing Central Asia, 1759–1864* (Stanford, CA: Stanford University Press, 1998); Justin Jacobs, *Xinjiang and the Modern Chinese State* (Seattle: University of Washington Press, 2016); Kwangmin Kim, *Borderland Capitalism: Turkestan Produce, Qing Silver, and the Birth of an Eastern Market* (Stanford, CA: Stanford University Press, 2016).
19. Opinions on when the Qing imperial expansion concluded varied. See Perdue, *China Marches West*, xiv. I choose the 1760s as the concluding event, when the Qianlong emperor defeated the Zunghar state in the Ili campaign in 1765, which I will discuss more extensively in chapter 3.
20. Michiel Baud and Willem Van Schendel, "Toward a Comparative History of Borderlands," *Journal of World History* 8, no. 2 (October 1997): 211–42.
21. For competing powers in Eurasian Asia, see Peter Perdue, *China Marches West: The Qing Conquest of Central Eurasia* (Cambridge, MA: Belknap Press of Harvard University Press, 2005).
22. For the inscription in Chinese and Tibetan, see Zhou Runnian, "Beijing Yonghegong yuzhi 'Lama shuo' beiwen jiaolu kaquan" [Studies of the *Proclamation on Lamas* at Beijing's Yonghegong], *Xizang yanjiu* 3 (1991): 87–98.
23. See Zhou, "Beijing Yonghegong yuzhi 'Lama shuo,'" 90–91 for the Tibetan text and 93–94 for the Chinese text.
24. Peter Schwieger, *The Dalai Lama and the Emperor of China: A Political History of the Tibetan Institution of Reincarnation* (New York: Columbia University Press, 2015), 193.
25. Schwieger, *The Dalai Lama and the Emperor of China*, 1–49.
26. Schwieger, *The Dalai Lama and the Emperor of China*, esp. 185–208.
27. Max Oidtmann, *Forging the Golden Urn: The Qing Empire and the Politics of Reincarnation in Tibet* (New York: Columbia University Press, 2018).
28. The characterization of the Qianlong emperor as a universalist emperor started with David Farquhar, "Emperor as Bodhisattva in the Governance of the Ch'ing Empire," *Harvard Journal of Asiatic Studies* 38, no. 1 (1978): 5–34. A more recent exemplary work on the Qianlong emperor's Buddhist engagement is Patricia Berger, *Empire of Emptiness: Buddhist Art and Political Authority in Qing China* (Honolulu: University of Hawai'i Press, 2003).
29. Major works include Evelyn Rawski, *The Last Emperors: A Social History of Qing Imperial Institutions* (Berkeley: University of California Press, 1998); Zhang Yuxin, *Qing zhengfu yu Lama jiao* [Qing government and Tibetan Buddhism] (Lhasa: Xizang renmin chubanshe, 1988).
30. "Inner Asia" has been a contested term in historical research. This geographical area fell largely within the orbit of the Qing empire in the seventeenth and eighteenth centuries, during its territorial expansion. It stretched east to Manchuria, north to Mongolia, and west to the eastern edge of the Tibetan plateau. Nicola Di Cosmo proposed "Inner Asia" as an analytical parameter in his "State Formation and Periodization in Inner Asian History," *Journal of World History* 10, no. 1 (1999): 3n8.
31. The third Changkya Rolpai Dorje remains the most thoroughly researched Tibetan Buddhist in the Qing historiography. See Xiangyun Wang, "Tibetan Buddhism at

the Court of Qing: The Life and Work of lCang-Skya Rol-Pa'i-Rdo-Rje (1717–1786)" (PhD diss., Harvard University, 1995); Xiangyun Wang, "The Qing Court's Tibet Connection: Lcang Skya Rol Pa'i Rdo Rje and the Qianlong Emperor," *Harvard Journal of Asiatic Studies* 60, no. 1 (2000): 125–63; Marina Illich, "Selections from the Life of a Tibetan Buddhist Polymath: Changkya Rolpai Dorje (Lcang Skya Rol Pa'i Rdo Rje), 1717–1786" (PhD diss., Columbia University, 2006); the third Tukwan, Lobzang Chokyi Nyima, *Zhangjia Guoshi Ruobiduojie zhuan* [Biography of the imperial preceptor Changkya Rolpai Dorje], trans. Lianlong Ma and Qingying Chen (Beijing: Zhongguo Zangxue yanjiu zhongxin, 2007). For a concise biography, see https://treasuryoflives.org/biographies/view/Chankya-Rolpai-Dorje/3141.

32. The High Qing often focuses on the rise of the Qing between the pacification of the Revolt of the Three Feudatories in the 1680s and the Opium Wars in the 1830s.

33. For the Qoshot Mongols' rule in eastern Tibet, see Uyunbilig Borjigidai, "The Hoshuud Polity in Khökhnuur (Kokonor)," *Inner Asia* 4 (2002): 181–96.

34. The tenth Zhamarpa, Chodrub Gyatso: Buddhist Digital Resource Center (hereafter BDRC) P831; the sixth Panchen Lama, Lobzang Pelden Yeshe: BDRC P168.

35. Pamela Crossley, *A Translucent Mirror: History and Identity in Qing Imperial Ideology* (Berkeley: University of California Press, 2002); Mark C. Elliott, *The Manchu Way: The Eight Banners and Ethnic Identity in Late Imperial China* (Stanford, CA: Stanford University Press, 2001); Rawski, *The Last Emperors*; Joanna Waley-Cohen, *The Culture of War in China* (London: I. B. Tauris, 2006); Perdue, *China Marches West*. The cluster of publications around the new millennium offered a refreshing perspective on the nature of the Qing's governance. For its receptions in the Chinese scholarly community, see Liu Fengyun and Liu Wenpeng, eds., *Qingchao de guojia rentong: Xin Qingshi yanjiu yu zhengming* [The identity of the Qing state: Research and debates on the new Qing history] (Beijing: Zhongguo renmin daxue chubanshe, 2010); Di Cosmo, "State Formation and Periodization"; William T. Rowe, *Saving the World: Chen Hongmou and Elite Consciousness in Eighteenth-Century China* (Stanford, CA: Stanford University Press, 2002); R. Kent Guy, *Qing Governors and Their Provinces: The Evolution of Territorial Administration in China, 1644–1796* (Seattle: University of Washington Press, 2013).

36. Giersch, *Asian Borderlands*; Johan Elverskog, *Our Great Qing: The Mongols, Buddhism and the State in Late Imperial China* (Honolulu: University of Hawai'i Press, 2006); Thum, *The Sacred Routes of Uyghur History*; Weinstein, *Empire and Identity in Guizhou*; Emma Jinhua Teng, *Taiwan's Imagined Geography: Chinese Colonial Travel Writing and Pictures, 1683–1895* (Cambridge, MA: Harvard University Asia Center, 2006); John Robert Shepherd, *Statecraft and Political Economy on the Taiwan Frontier, 1600–1800* (Stanford, CA: Stanford University Press, 1993).

37. Yingcong Dai, *The Sichuan Frontier and Tibet: Imperial Strategy in the Early Qing* (Seattle: University of Washington Press, 2009); Xiuyu Wang, *China's Last Imperial Frontier: Late Qing Expansion in Sichuan's Tibetan Borderlands* (Lanham, MD: Lexington Books, 2011); William M. Coleman, "Making the State on the Sino-Tibetan Frontier: Chinese Expansion and Local Power in Batang, 1842–1939" (PhD diss., Columbia University, 2014); Jann Michael Ronis, "Celibacy, Revelations, and Reincarnated Lamas: Contestation and Synthesis in the Growth of Monasticism at Katok Monastery from the 17th Through 19th Centuries" (PhD diss., University of Virginia, 2009); Yudru Tsomu, "Local Aspirations and National

INTRODUCTION

Constraints: A Case Study of Nyarong Gonpo Namgyel and His Rise to Power in Kham (1836–1865)" (PhD diss., Harvard University, 2006); Karl Debreczeny, "Ethnicity and Esoteric Power: Negotiating the Sino-Tibetan Synthesis in Ming Buddhist Painting" (PhD diss., University of Chicago, 2007); Paul Nietupski, *Labrang Monastery: A Tibetan Buddhist Community on the Inner Asian Borderlands, 1709–1958* (Lanham, MD: Lexington Books, 2010); Paul Nietupski, *Labrang: A Tibetan Buddhist Monastery at the Crossroads of Four Civilizations* (Ithaca, NY: Snow Lion Publications, 1999); Max Oidtmann, "Between Patron and Priest: Amdo Tibet Under Qing Rule, 1792–1911" (PhD diss., Harvard University, 2014); Brenton Sullivan, "The Mother of All Monasteries: Gönlung Jampa Ling and the Rise of Mega Monasteries in Northeastern Tibet" (PhD diss., University of Virginia, 2013).

38. David Ruegg, "Mchod yon, yon mchod and mchod gnas/yon gnas: On the Historiography and Semantics of a Tibetan Religio-social and Religio-political Concept," in *Tibetan History and Language: Studies Dedicated to Uray Géza on His Seventieth Birthday*, ed. Ernst Steinkeller (Vienna: Arbeitskreis für Tibetische und Buddhistische Studien Universität Wien, 1991), 441–53; David Ruegg, "The Preceptor-Donor (yon mchod) Relation in Thirteenth-Century Tibetan Society and Polity, Its Inner Asian Precursors and Indian Models," in *Tibetan Studies: Proceedings of the 7th Seminar of the International Association of Tibetan Studies, Graz 1995*, ed. H. Krasser et al. (Vienna: Österreichische Akademie der Wissenschaft, 1997), 857–72. For Chinese dynastic influence on the Qing's creation of universalist empire, see Natalie Köhle, "Why Did the Kangxi Emperor Go to Wutai Shan? Patronage, Pilgrimage and the Place of Tibetan Buddhism at the Early Qing Court," *Late Imperial China* 29, no. 1 (2008): 73–119.

39. Schwieger, *The Dalai Lama and the Emperor of China*, 27.

40. David Snellgrove and Hugh Richardson, *A Cultural History of Tibet* (Boston: Shambala, 1995), 178–79.

41. Alexander Gardner, "The Twenty-Five Great Sites of Kham: Religious Geography, Revelation, and Non-sectarianism in Nineteenth-Century Eastern Tibet" (PhD diss., University of Michigan, 2006); Dominique Townsend, *A Buddhist Sensibility: Aesthetic Education at Tibet's Mindröling Monastery*, Studies of the Weatherhead East Asian Institute, Columbia University (New York: Columbia University Press, 2021).

42. Derek Maher, "The Lives and Time of 'Jam Dbyangs Bzhad Pa," in *Proceedings of the Tenth Seminar of the IATS, 2003*, vol. 3, *Power, Politics, and the Reinvention of Tradition: Tibet in the Seventeenth and Eighteenth Centuries*, ed. Bryan J. Cuevas and Kurtis R. Schaeffer (Leiden: Brill, 2006), 129–44.

43. Georges B. J. Dreyfus, "The Shuk-Den Affair: History and Nature of a Quarrel," *Journal of the International Association of Buddhist Studies* 21, no. 2 (1998): 232–33.

44. For changing Tibetan sectarian conflict, see Carl S. Yamamoto, *Vision and Violence: Lama Zhang and the Politics of Charisma in Twelfth-Century Tibet*, Brill's Tibetan Studies Library 29 (Leiden: Brill, 2012); Schwieger, *The Dalai Lama and the Emperor of China*, 50–70.

45. Federica Venturi, "To Protect and to Serve: The Military in Tibet as Described by the Fifth Dalai Lama," *Cahiers d'Extrême-Asie* 27, no. 1 (2018): 28.

46. Gray Tuttle, ed., *Mapping the Modern in Tibet* (Andiast: International Institute for Tibetan and Buddhist Studies, 2011); see especially Janet Gyatso, "Moments of

INTRODUCTION

Tibetan Modernity: Methods and Assumptions," in Tuttle, *Mapping the Modern in Tibet*, 2–3.
47. Gyatso, "Moments of Tibetan Modernity," 5–6.
48. Pekka Hämäläinen, *The Comanche Empire* (New Haven, CT: Yale University Press, 2009), 182.
49. Hämäläinen, *The Comanche Empire*, 2–3.
50. Stanley Tambiah, "The Galactic Polity in Southeast Asia," *HAU: Journal of Ethnographic Theory* 3 (2013): 508.
51. Tambiah, "The Galactic Polity," 509.
52. Tambiah, "The Galactic Polity," 514.
53. Rebecca French, "The Cosmology of Law in Buddhist Tibet," *Journal of the International Association of Buddhist Studies* 18, no. 1 (July 1995): 114.
54. Georges B. J. Dreyfus, "Law, State, and Political Ideology in Tibet," *Journal of the International Association of Buddhist Studies* 18, no. 1 (July 1995): 137.
55. Venturi, "To Protect and to Serve," 28.
56. Perdue, *China Marches West*, esp. 133–302.
57. Perdue's *China Marches West* includes extensive historiography on the Zunghars, mostly in the Japanese and Russian languages. The following publications are largely new research, after Perdue's monumental study. On their military operations, see Hosung Shim, "The Zunghar Conquest of Central Tibet and Its Influence on Tibetan Military Institutions in the 18th Century," *Revue d'Etudes Tibétaines* 53 (March 2020): 56–113. On the political formation of the Zunghar Khanate, see Richard Taupier, "The Rise of the Jöüngars Based on Primary Oyirod Sources," *Inner Asia* 21, no. 2 (October 2019): 140–61. On the four Oirat confederation, see Lhamsuren Munkh-Erdene, "The 1640 Great Code: An Inner Asian Parallel to the Treaty of Westphalia," *Central Asian Survey* 29, no. 3 (September 2010): 269–88. On the legacy of the Zunghar's rule in Qing Xinjiang, see David Brophy, "The Junghar Mongol Legacy and the Language of Loyalty in Qing Xinjiang," *Harvard Journal of Asiatic Studies* 73, no. 2 (2013): 231–58.
58. Okada Hidehiro, *Kōkitei no tegami* [Emperor Kangxi's letters] (Tokyo: Fujiwarashoten, 2013).
59. Oidtmann, *Forging the Golden Urn*, 14–15, 37–39.
60. Leonard W. J. van der Kuijp, "The Dalai Lamas and the Origins of Reincarnate Lamas," in *The Tibetan History Reader*, ed. Gray Tuttle and Kurtis R. Schaeffer (New York: Columbia University Press, 2013): 335–47.
61. Schwieger, *The Dalai Lama and the Emperor of China*, 71–145.
62. Oidtmann, *Forging the Golden Urn*.
63. Isabella Charleux, *Nomads on Pilgrimage: Mongols on Wutaishan (China), 1800–1940*, Brill's Inner Asian Library 33 (Leiden: Brill, 2015).
64. Chou, *Mount Wutai*, esp. 51–78.
65. Brenton Sullivan, *Building a Religious Empire: Tibetan Buddhism, Bureaucracy, and the Rise of the Gelukpa*, Encounters with Asia (Philadelphia: University of Pennsylvania Press, 2021), 13.
66. Berthe Jansen, *The Monastery Rules: Buddhist Monastic Organization in Pre-Modern Tibet* (Berkeley: University of California Press, 2018), 106, 112.
67. José Cabezón and Dorjee Penpa, *Sera Monastery* (Somerville, MA: Wisdom Publications, 2019).

INTRODUCTION

68. For a detailed institutional history of Labrang Monastery, see Nietupski, *Labrang Monastery*.
69. Ishihama Yumiko, *Shincho to Chibetto Bukkyo: Bosatsuo to Natta Kenryutei* [Qing China and the Tibetan Buddhist world: The Qianlong emperor who had become a Buddhist king], Waseda Daigaku Gakujutsu Sosho 20 (Tokyo: Wasedadaigakushuppanbu, 2011), 105–27.
70. For Jehol [Rehe], see Stephen H. Whiteman, "From Upper Camp to Mountain Estate: Recovering Historical Narratives in Qing Imperial Landscapes," *Studies in the History of Gardens and Designed Landscapes* 33, no. 4 (October 2013): 249–79; Stephen H. Whiteman, *Where Dragon Veins Meet: The Kangxi Emperor and His Estate at Rehe* (Seattle: University of Washington Press, 2020); Ruth W. Dunnell et al., eds., *New Qing Imperial History: The Making of Inner Asian Empire at Qing Chengde* (London: Routledge, 2004).
71. Vesna Wallace has persistently warned against such an interpretation of Buddhism. See Wallace, *Buddhism in Mongolian History, Culture, and Society*.
72. Elverskog, *Our Great Qing*.
73. Melvyn Goldstein, "Tibetan Buddhism and Mass Monasticism," in *Des moines et des moniales dans le monde: La vie monastique dans le miroir de la parenté*, ed. Adeline Herrou and Gisele Krauskopff (Press Universitaires de Toulouse le Mirail, 2010), https://case.edu/affil/tibet/tibetanMonks/documents/Tibetan_Buddhism_and_Mass_Monasticism.pdf, 1. Page reference is to the online edition.
74. Goldstein, "Tibetan Buddhism and Mass Monasticism," 2.
75. Sullivan, *The Mother of All Monasteries*, esp. 113–32; Gray Tuttle, "A Tibetan Buddhist Mission to the East: The Fifth Dalai Lama's Journey to Beijing, 1652–1653," in *Tibetan Society and Religion: The Seventeenth and Eighteenth Centuries*, ed. Bryan Cuevas and Kurtis Schaeffer (Leiden: Brill, 2006), 65–87.
76. For case studies of mass monasticism and its varied forms, see Nicolas Sihlé, "Quasi-generalized, Mostly Temporary, Monasticism Among Boys: An Uncommon Form of Tibetan 'Mass Monasticism,'" *The Himalayas and Beyond: The Center for Himalayan Studies Blog*, July 10, 2011, https://himalayas.hypotheses.org/85#footnote_1_85; Sullivan, *The Mother of All Monasteries*; Jansen, *The Monastery Rules*; Elizabeth Reynolds, "Tibet Incorporated: Institutional Power and Economic Practice on the Sino-Tibetan Borderland, 1930–1950" (PhD diss., Columbia University, 2020).
77. For a thorough study of Tsongkhapa's writings and their role in Geluk's rise to dominance, see Sonam Tsering, "The Role of Texts in the Formation of the Geluk School in Tibet During the Mid-fourteenth and Fifteenth Centuries" (PhD diss., Columbia University, 2020).
78. For more, see Georges B. J. Dreyfus, "An Introduction to Drepung's Colleges," The Tibetan and Himalayan Library, http://www.thlib.org/places/monasteries/drepung/essays/#essay=/dreyfus/drepung/colleges/s/b1.
79. Townsend, *A Buddhist Sensibility*, 79–81.
80. Indrani Chatterjee, *Forgotten Friends: Monks, Marriages, and Memories of Northeast India* (Oxford: Oxford University Press, 2013).
81. Aslanian, *From the Indian Ocean to the Mediterranean*, 181–82.
82. Barkey, *Bandits and Bureaucrats*. Christine M. Philliou, *Biography of an Empire: Governing Ottomans in an Age of Revolution* (Berkeley: University of California

Press, 2010); E. Natalie Rothman, *Brokering Empire: Trans-Imperial Subjects between Venice and Istanbul* (Ithaca, NY: Cornell University Press, 2011); Resat Kasaba, *A Moveable Empire: Ottoman Nomads, Migrants, and Refugees* (Seattle: University of Washington Press, 2009).

83. In addition to the scholarship on the Ottoman Empire cited above, there is other literature on intermediaries in other imperial polities, such as Alida C. Metcalf, *Go-Betweens and the Colonization of Brazil, 1500–1600* (Austin: University of Texas Press, 2005); Maya Jasanoff, *Edge of Empire: Lives, Culture, and Conquest in the East, 1750–1850* (New York: Vintage Books, 2006); Ian W. Campbell, *Knowledge and the Ends of Empire: Kazak Intermediaries and Russian Rule on the Steppe, 1731–1917* (Ithaca, NY: Cornell University Press, 2017); Thomas R. Metcalf, *Imperial Connections: India in the Indian Ocean Arena, 1860–1920* (Berkeley: University of California Press, 2007).

84. An inspiring study of the local administrator-entrepreneurs on the Muslim oases of the Tarim Basin is K. Kim, *Borderland Capitalism*. For the Buddhist role in state formation in the Republic China, see Gray Tuttle, *Tibetan Buddhists in the Making of Modern China* (New York: Columbia University Press, 2005).

85. For upholding this point of view, see Sarah H. Jacoby, *Love and Liberation: Autobiographical Writings of the Tibetan Buddhist Visionary Sera Khandro* (New York: Columbia University Press, 2014).

86. Kurtis R. Schaeffer, *The Culture of the Book in Tibet* (New York: Columbia University Press, 2009).

87. Berger, *Empire of Emptiness*.

88. Alfred Gell, *Art and Agency: An Anthropological Theory* (Oxford: Clarendon Press, 1998); Finbarr B. Flood, *Objects of Translation: Material Culture and Medieval "Hindu-Muslim" Encounter* (Princeton, NJ: Princeton University Press, 2009).

89. David Armitage, "Three Concepts of Atlantic History," in *The British Atlantic World, 1500–1800*, ed. David Armitage and Michael J. Braddick (Basingstoke: Palgrave Macmillan, 2002), 23.

1. CAMPAIGNS

1. Michiel Baud and Willem Van Schendel, "Toward a Comparative History of Borderlands," *Journal of World History* 8 2 (October 1997): 211–42.

2. Amdo is more of a cultural and linguistic space that consists of most of modern Qinghai Province, with the exception of Golok, southern Tibetan-speaking areas of Gansu Province, and Northern Sichuan Province. Gray Tuttle, "An Overview of Amdo (Northeastern Tibet) Historical Polities," The Tibetan and Himalayan Library, http://www.thlib.org/tools/about/wiki/An%20Overview%20of%20AMDO%20%28Northeastern%20Tibet%29%20Historical%20Polities.html.

3. Sam Van Schaik, *Tibet: A History* (New Haven, CT: Yale University Press, 2011), 50–52.

4. David Farquhar, "Emperor as Bodhisattva in the Governance of the Ch'ing Empire," *Harvard Journal of Asiatic Studies* 38 1 (1978): 5–34; Zahiruddin Ahmad, *Sino-Tibetan Relations in the Seventeenth Century*, Serie Orientale Roma (Rome: Istituto italiano per il Medio ed Estremo Oriente, 1970).

1. CAMPAIGNS

5. The region was later renamed to Shaan-Gan region in 1731.
6. Amdo has become a productive research theme in recent years. See the Amdo-related publication https://www.iaaw.hu-berlin.de/en/region/centralasia/research/projects/current/amdo-research-network/pictures/arn-literaturliste-12_2018.pdf.
7. Gray Tuttle, "Challenging Central Tibet's Dominance of History: The Oceanic Book, a 19th-Century Politico-Religious Geographic History," in *Mapping the Modern in Tibet*, ed. Gray Tuttle (Andiast: International Institute for Tibetan and Buddhist Studies, 2011), 135–72.
8. Kurtis R. Schaeffer, Matthew Kapstein, and Gray Tuttle, *Sources of Tibetan Tradition* (New York: Columbia University Press, 2013), 588; Sumpa Khenpo Yeshe Panjor's *The Annals of Kokonor* is often cited as a major historical account of Buddhist dissemination in Amdo. The text was part of Sumpa Khenpo Yeshe Panjor's collected works, and later edited as a stand-alone text. For the author's biography, see Samten Chhosphel, "Sumpa Khenpo Yeshe Peljor," The Treasury of Lives, https://treasuryoflives.org/biographies/view/Sumpa-Khenpo-Yeshe-Peljor/5729. For more on this work, see Hanung Kim, "Renaissance Man from Amdo: The Life and Scholarship of the Eighteenth-Century Amdo Scholar Sum Pa Mkhan Po Ye Shes Dpal 'Byor (1704–1788)" (PhD diss., Harvard University, 2018), 9n16.
9. Monastic power consolidations were one aspect of the complex social practices here in these centuries. See Ling-Wei Kung, "The Transformation of the Qing's Geopolitics: Power Transitions Between Tibetan Buddhist Monasteries in Amdo, 1644–1795," *Revue d'Etudes Tibétaines* 45 (April 2018): 110–44.
10. Zhuang Junyuan, "Hungzhong gongyu ji" [Pastime journals in Huangzhong], in *Lidai Riji Congchao* [Anthology of diaries in Chinese history], ed. Li Delong and Yu Bing (Beijing: Xueyuan chubanshe, 2006), 99–101.
11. Naoto Katō, "Lobjang Danjin's Rebellion of 1723: With a Focus on the Eve of the Rebellion," in *The Tibetan History Reader*, ed. Gray Tuttle and Kurtis Schaefer (New York: Columbia University Press, 2013), 411–36; Luciano Petech, "Notes on Tibetan History of the 18th Century," *T'oung Pao* 52 4-5 (1966): 276–92.
12. Katō, "Lobjang Danjin's Rebellion of 1723," 418.
13. Nian Gengyao, *Nian Gengyao Man Han zouzhe yibian* [The annotated palace memorials of Nian Gengyao in Manchu and Chinese], ed. Ji Yonghai et al. (Tianjin: Tianjin guji chubanshe, 1995), 286–87.
14. For a concise description of Governor-General Nian Gengyao's attempt to chart an imperial vision in Qinghai, see "Nian Gengyao and the Incorporation of Qinghai" in Peter C. Perdue, *China Marches West: The Qing Conquest of Central Eurasia* (Cambridge, MA: Belknap Press of Harvard University Press, 2005), 310–14.
15. *Qinghai shanhou shiyi shisantiao* was also known as *Tiaochen Xihai shanhou shiyi*. Jinyue Qinghai Menggu shi'er shi was also known as *Gongcheng Qinghai jinyue shi'er shi*. See Narachaogetu, "Shi shu Qingchao dui Qinghai Mengzang minzu defang de lifan" [A preliminary discussion of Qing China's legislation in the Mongolian and Tibetan areas of Qinghai], *Neimenggu shehui kexue: Hanwenban* [Social science of Inner Mongolia (Chinese edition)] 1 (2008): 67–71; He Feng, "Cong 'Fan Li' kan Qing wangchao dui Qinghai zangqu de guanli cuoshi" [The Qing's management of Qinghai Tibetan region: A study of the Tibetan injunctions], *Qinghai Shehui kexue* [Qinghai social science bulletin] 6 (1996): 72–76.

1. CAMPAIGNS

16. Requests regarding applying the Qing legal codes to Amdo were rejected in 1736, 1740, 1743, and finally 1748, when the Qianlong emperor decided not to introduce Qing legal codes to Amdo, given that they would not be well understood in the distant region. For more, see Liu Hainian and Yang Y., eds., "Regulations of Qinghai Tibetans, Xining," in *Collections of Rare Chinese Legal Codes* (Beijing: Kexue chubanshe, 1994), 2:376–404, esp. 2:379–80.
17. Some have interpreted the Qing as a colonial power in Amdo; see Max Oidtmann, "Between Patron and Priest: Amdo Tibet Under Qing Rule, 1792–1911" (PhD diss., Harvard University, 2014).
18. *Neige daku dang'an* [Archives of the grand secretariat of the Qing dynasty], Institute of History and Philosophy, Academia Sinica, Taipei, cat. no. 116320-001, dated May 7, 1808 (converted to the Gregorian calendar).
19. The official title of the post is *Qinchai banli Qinghai Menggu fanzi shiwu dachen* (imperial commissioner administering affairs of Mongols and Tibetans in Qinghai) (1724–1911), but the position was bureaucratized in 1736, the first year of the Qianlong reign, with *banshi dachen* officially designated to the official holding the post. See Cai Jiayi and Zhu Guangmei, "Xining banshi dachen de shezhi jiqi dui Qinghai diqu de guanzhi" [Establishment of the *Xining banshi dachen* and its management of Qinghai], *Qinghai minzu yanjiu, shehui kexue ban* [Qinghai nationality research: Social science edition] 1 (1990): 30–35. In his manuscript, Qiguang made a similar claim that by 1736 the post was likely changed to *Xining banshi dachen*, or *Xining Amban* in Qing histography. See Qiguang, *Daqing diguo shiqi Menggu de zhengzhi yu shehui: Yi Alashan Qoshot bu wei yanjiu Zhongxin* [Politics and society of the Mongols in the Qing empire: Research centered on the Alashan Qoshot Mongols] (Shanghai: Fudan daxue chubanshe, 2013), 202.
20. R. Kent Guy, *Qing Governors and Their Provinces: The Evolution of Territorial Administration in China, 1644–1796* (Seattle: University of Washington Press, 2013); Daniel Koss, "Political Geography of Empire: Chinese Varieties of Local Government," *Journal of Asian Studies* 76 1 (February 2017): 159–84.
21. Three officials were appointed to this post during Yongzheng reign and twenty-five during Qianlong reign. Official rotations were on a three-year schedule, though few of them stayed for three years, and many held the post more than once.
22. Wenfu, *Qinghai shiyi jielue* [Concise reports on Qinghai affairs] (Xining: Qinghai Renmin Chubanshe, 1993), 1. He was holding the *Xining banshi dachen* post between 1808 and 1811.
23. Gábor Ágoston, "A Flexible Empire: Authority and Its Limits on the Ottoman Frontiers," *International Journal of Turkish Studies* 9 (2003): 19.
24. C. A. Bayly, *Empire and Information: Intelligence Gathering and Social Communication in India, 1780–1870* (Cambridge: Cambridge University Press, 1999), 56–57.
25. Bayly, *Empire and Information*, 58.
26. Ian Campbell, *Knowledge and the Ends of Empire: Kazak Intermediaries and Russian Rule on the Steppe, 1731–1917* (Ithaca, NY: Cornell University Press, 2017).
27. Guy, *Qing Governors and Their Provinces*, 203–4.
28. Michael Szonyi, *Practicing Kinship: Lineage and Descent in Late Imperial China* (Stanford, CA: Stanford University Press, 2002); David Faure, *Emperor and Ancestor: State and Lineage in South China* (Stanford, CA: Stanford University Press, 2007).

1. CAMPAIGNS

29. Peter Schwieger, *The Dalai Lama and the Emperor of China: A Political History of the Tibetan Institution of Reincarnation* (New York: Columbia University Press, 2015), 17–49.
30. Rachel M. McCleary and Leonard W. J. van der Kuijp, "The Market Approach to the Rise of the Geluk School, 1419–1642," *Journal of Asian Studies* 69 1 (2010): 149–80.
31. C. Patterson Giersch, *Asian Borderlands: The Transformation of Qing China's Yunnan Frontier* (Cambridge, MA: Harvard University Press, 2006); John E. Herman, "From Land Reclamation to Land Grab: Settler Colonialism in Southwest China, 1680–1735," *Harvard Journal of Asiatic Studies* 78 1 (2018): 91–123; Xiuyu Wang, *China's Last Imperial Frontier: Late Qing Expansion in Sichuan's Tibetan Borderlands* (Lanham, MD: Lexington Books, 2011).
32. The fifth generation of the Tongkhor incarnation's dates were given as 1686–1754. See brag dgon dkon mchog bstan pa rab rgyas (1800/1–1866), *Yul mdo smad kyi ljongs su thub bstan rin po che ji ltar dar ba'i tshul gsal bar brjod pa Deb ther rgya mtsho* [The ocean annals of Amdo] (Lanzhou: Kan su'u mi rigs dpe skrun khang, 1982); Sonam Dorje, "The Fifth Tongkhor, Ngawang Sonam Gyatso," The Treasury of Lives, https://treasuryoflives.org/biographies/view/Fifth-Tongkhor-Sonam-Gyatso/2755.
33. Zha Zha, "Lidai Jiamuyang hutukutu de jiating Beijing yanjiu" [A primary research on the family backgrounds of each Jamyang Zhepa], *Zangxue yanjiu zhongxin qikan: zhexue yu shehui kexu ban* [Journal of Tibet Nationalities Institute: Philosophy and social sciences] 27 5. (September 2006): 19–25. The Xining Amban could be either Kuishu (in office 1788–1792) or Tekeshen.
34. Tsering Namgyal, "The Third Rongpo Drubchen, Gendun Trinle Rabgye," The Treasury of Lives, http://treasuryoflives.org/biographies/view/Rongwo-Drubchen-03-Gendun-Trinle-Rabgye/5436.
35. Zha Zha, "Lidai Jiamuyang hutukutu de jiating Beijing yanjiu." For the active role played by the nephew of the second Jamyang Zhepa in Labrang Monastery, see Max Oidtmann, *Forging the Golden Urn: The Qing Empire and the Politics of Reincarnation in Tibet* (New York: Columbia University Press, 2018), 155–56.
36. Dorje, "The Fifth Tongkhor, Ngawang Sonam Gyatso."
37. Elliot Sperling, "Tibetan Buddhism, Perceived and Imagined, Along the Ming-Era Sino-Tibetan Frontier," in *Buddhism Between Tibet and China*, ed. Matthew Kapstein (Somerville, MA: Wisdom Publications, 2009), 173.
38. Tongkhor Gonpa, BDRC G 239.
39. The precise location of the dka 'bzhi tribe remains unknow so far. It is not found elsewhere in the text.
40. *Zhabs drung 'jam pa'i dbyangs rim byon gyi 'khrungs rabs rnam par thar pa gsal bar byed pa'i rin po che baidurya'i me long* [Biographies of the successive Stong 'khor reincarnates] (Beijing: Krung go'i Bod rig pa dpe skrun khang, 2005), 237–39.
41. See chapter 2 for more on this topic.
42. Wenfu, *Qinghai shiyi jielue*, 14.
43. Oidtmann, *Forging the Golden Urn*.
44. Thebo-Trinlé Ozer (Chenlie Aosai), "Introduction to the Zhabdrung Karpo Lineages," unpublished manuscript, 258–59.

1. CAMPAIGNS

45. Thebo-Trinlé Ozer, "Introduction to the Zhabdrung Karpo Lineages," 19. For the fifth Zhabdrung Karpo, Khetsun Gyatso, see Tsehua, "The Fifth Zhabdrung Karpo, Khetsun Gyatso," The Treasury of Lives, http://treasuryoflives.org/biographies/view/Fifth-Zhabdrung-Karpo-Khetsun-Gyatso/8860.
46. Nayancheng, *Nayancheng Qinghai Zouyi* [Nayancheng's memoirs on Qinghai affairs] (Xining: Qinghai renmin chubanshe, 1997), 49.
47. Van Schaik, *Tibet*, 50–52.
48. Nayancheng, *Nayancheng Qinghai Zouyi*, 49.
49. Nayancheng, *Nayancheng Qinghai Zouyi*, 49.
50. Max Oidtmann discusses *Nayancheng Qinghai Zouyi* in "A 'Dog-Eat-Dog' World: Qing Jurispractices and the Legal Inscription of Piety in Amdo," *Extrême-Orient Extrême-Occident* 40 (2016): 151–82. And for the lineage's role in Mongolia since the mid-seventeenth century, see Uranchimeg Tsultemin, *A Monastery on the Move: Art and Politics in Later Buddhist Mongolia* (Honolulu: University of Hawai'i Press, 2021), 201.
51. Paul Nietupski, *Labrang Monastery: A Tibetan Buddhist Community on the Inner Asian Borderlands, 1709–1958* (Lanham, MD: Lexington Books, 2010), 141–45. The sixth Gungtang, Jigme Tenpai Wangchuk (1926–2000, BDRC P5591) has settled a number of disputes in southern Gansu Province over the course of the twentieth century, most recently in 1995; occasionally he was even asked by local communities to settle pasture disputes in the adjacent Sichuan Province, where he was born. Xiaoying Meng and Xiaoyan Meng, "Jiexi dangdai Gannan muqu minjian jiufen tiaojie zhongde Zangzu buluo xiguanfa" [A study of the customary laws in civil conflicts in nomadic Tibetan communities in southern Gansu region], *Zhongguo Zangxue* [China's Tibetan studies] 1 (2010): 90.
52. Relevant works include Alida C. Metcalf, *Go-Betweens and the Colonization of Brazil, 1500–1600* (Austin: University of Texas Press, 2005); Maya Jasanoff, *Edge of Empire: Lives, Culture, and Conquest in the East, 1750–1850* (New York: Vintage Books, 2006); Bayly, *Empire and Information*; Campbell, *Knowledge and the Ends of Empire*.
53. Zhuang, "Huangzhong gongyu ji," 76, 100–101.
54. John E. Herman, "The Cant of Conquest: Tusi Offices and China's Political Incorporation of the Southwest Frontier," in *Empire at the Margins: Culture, Ethnicity, and Frontier in Early Modern China*, ed. Pamela Crossley, Helen Siu, and Donald Sutton (Berkeley: University of California Press, 2006), 135–70.
55. Peter C. Perdue, "Nature and Nurture on Imperial China's Frontiers," *Modern Asian Studies* 43 1 (2009): 248.
56. Guy, *Qing Governors and Their Provinces*, 17; Koss, "Political Geography of Empire."
57. William T. Rowe, *Saving the World: Chen Hongmou and Elite Consciousness in Eighteenth-Century China* (Stanford, CA: Stanford University Press, 2002).
58. Nancy Kollmann, *The Russian Empire 1450–1801* (Oxford: Oxford University Press, 2017), 129.
59. The third Tukwan, Lobzang Chokyi Nyima, *khyab bdag rdo rje sems dpa'i ngo bo dpal ldan bla ma dam pa ye shes bstan pa'i sgron me dpal bzang po'i rnam par thar pa mdo tsam brjod pa dge ldan bstan pa'i mdzes rgyan* [The major biography of the

1. CAMPAIGNS

third Changkya, Rolpai Dorje] (Lanzhou: Kan su'u mi rigs dpe skrun khang, 1989), 93. Hereafter this text is referred to as *Major Biography*.
60. Marina Illich, "Selections from the Life of a Tibetan Buddhist Polymath: Chankya Rolpai Dorje (Lcang Skya Rol Pa'i Rdo Rje), 1717–1786" (PhD diss., Columbia University, 2006), 3.
61. Yue Zhongqi was a general who launched the pacification campaign with General Nian Gengyao. The third Tukwan, Lobzang Chokyi Nyima, *Major Biography*.
62. BDRC P4480. His title is also listed as "Achithu nomonhan," though no further information is available to establish how this title came to him.
63. Sertok Lobzang Tsültrim Gyatso (1845–1915, BDRC P251), *sku 'bum byams pa gling gig dan rabs don ldan tshangs pa'i dbyangs snyan* [Monastic chronicle of Kumbum Monastery] (Xining: mtsho sngon mi rigs dpe skrun khang, 1982), 59 (BDRC W 19838). Hereafter this text is referred to as *Monastic Chronicle of Kumbum Monastery*.
64. Sertok Lobzang Tsültrim Gyatso, *Monastic Chronicle of Kumbum Monastery*, 61.
65. Sertok Lobzang Tsültrim Gyatso, *Monastic Chronicle of Kumbum Monastery*, 61.
66. Zhongguo diyi lishi dang'an guan annotated, *Qingdai Junjichu Manwen aocha dang* [Tea offering archives in the Manchu language of the grand council during the Qing] (Shanghai: Shanghai guji chubanshe, 2010), cat. no. 03-1741-1-15, 125–30.
67. The third Tukwan, Lobzang Chokyi Nyima, *gling bsad sgrub bstan pa'i 'byung gnas chos sde chen po dgon-lung-byams-pa-gling gi dkar chag dpyod ldan yid dbang 'gugs pa'i pho nya* [The monastic chronicle of Gönlung Jampa Ling] (Xining: mtsho sngon mi rigs dpe skrun khang, 1988), 65.
68. The third Tukwan, Lobzang Chokyi Nyima, *Major Biography*, 139.
69. State-controlled Buddhist registers had appeared earlier in Chinese dynastic history. See Michael J. Walsh, *Sacred Economics: Buddhist Monasticism and Territoriality in Medieval China*, Sheng Yen Series in Chinese Buddhist Studies (New York: Columbia University Press, 2010), 78–82; Timothy Brook, "At the Margin of Public Authority: The Ming State and Buddhism," in *Culture and State in Chinese Society: Conventions, Accommodations, and Critiques*, ed. Theodore Huters, R. Bin Wong, and Pauline Yu (Stanford, CA: Stanford University Press, 1997), 164–65.
70. It remains unclear when and how the *dudie* practice was implemented in Qinghai. Research on this specific region includes Brenton Sullivan, "The Mother of All Monasteries: Gönlung Jampa Ling and the Rise of Mega Monasteries in Northeastern Tibet" (PhD diss., University of Virginia, 2013), 351.
71. Yang Ying, *Xining fu xin zhi* [New chronicle of Xining], vol. 15 (Xining: Qinghai renmin chubanshe, 1988), 51.
72. Bai Wengu and Xie Zhanlu, "Qingdai Lama yidanliang zhidu tantao" [A survey on the lama's stipend practice of the Qing], *Zhongguo zangxue* [China Tibetology] 3 (2006): 7.
73. Bai and Xie "Qingdai Lama yidanliang zhidu tantao," 7. See also Xu Ke, *Qingbi leichao* [Qing petty matters anthology] (1916; repr., Beijing: Zhonghua shu ju, 1984), 1:224–25.
74. Ágoston, "A Flexible Empire," 21.
75. Resat Kasaba, *A Moveable Empire: Ottoman Nomads, Migrants, and Refugees* (Seattle: University of Washington Press, 2009), 105.

1. CAMPAIGNS

76. The succeeding abbot was a lama of a minor incarnate lineage of Kumbum Jampa Ling. His tenure as the monastery's abbot ran between 1724 and 1728. Other information pertaining to this figure remains unavailable.
77. Chen Qingying, *Zhongguo xibei wenxian congshu, Xibei shaoshu minzu yuyan wenxian* [Collections of bibliographical materials in minority languages in northwestern China] (Lanzhou: Lanzhou guji chubanshe, 1990), 154:457. For more, see Sertok Lobzang Tsültrim Gyatso, *Monastic Chronicle of Kumbum Monastery*, 1986.
78. Chen, *Zhongguo xibei wenxian congshu*, 472.
79. Sertok Lobzang Tsültrim Gyatso, *Monastic Chronicle of Kumbum Monastery*, 222.
80. Sertok Lobzang Tsültrim Gyatso, *Monastic Chronicle of Kumbum Monastery*, 251–52.
81. Walsh, *Sacred Economics*, 5–6.
82. For more, see Martin Mills, *Identity, Ritual and State in Tibetan Buddhism: The Foundations of Authority in Gelukpa Monasticism* (London: Routledge Curzon, 2003).
83. Sample data on livestock management in Amdo can be found at http://www.tibetanculture.weai.columbia.edu/livestock-of-monasteries-in-amdo/. Thanks to Qichen Qian for pointing me to this source.
84. For instance, see rituals related to land examination in 'jam dbyangs bzhad pa'i rdo rje, "sa chog," in *gsung 'bum/_'jam dbyangs bzhad pa'i rdo rje* [Collected works of bgangwang tsondru] (South India: Gomang College, 1997), 1:511–36 (BDRC W21503). For procedures regarding taming the lands for monastery building, see, for example, Thub bstan legs bśad rgya mtsho, *Gateway to the Temple: Manual of Tibetan Monastic Customs, Art, Building, and Celebrations: Originally Entitled A Requisite Manual for Faith and Adherence to the Buddhist Teaching, Including the Way of Entering the Door of Religion, the Root of the Teaching, the Method for Erecting Temples, the Resting Place of the Teaching, and Cycle of Religious Duties, the Performance of the Teaching*, Bibliotheca Himalayica, series 3, vol. 1 (Kathmandu: Ratna Pustak Bhandar, 1979), 29–34.
85. dkon mchog rgyal mtshan, *gyibla brang bkra shis 'khyil gyi gdan rabs lha'i rnga chen* [History of Bla brang Bkra shis 'khyil] (lan kru'u: Kan su'u mi rigs dpe skrun khang, 1987), vol. 1 (BDRC W00KG09686). The main ritual related to the land discrimination is "sa chog" or "sa dpyad." See entry on "sa dpyad," in Dung dkar blo bzang 'phrin las, *Dung Dkar Tshig Mdzod Chen Mo* [Dungkar Tibetological great dictionary] (Beijing: Zhongguo zangxue yanjiu chubanshe, 2002), entry 2051. For more on the ritual "sa chog," see Yael Bentor, "Literature on Consecration (Rab Gnas)," in *Tibetan Literature: Studies in Genre*, ed. Jose Ignocio Cabezon and Roger Jackson (Ithaca, NY: Snow Lion Publications, 1996), 290–311; Mkhas grub dpal bzang po, *Rgyud Sde Spyiḥi Rnam Par Gźag Pa Rgyas Par Brjod* [Mkhas Grub Rje's fundamentals of the Buddhist tantras], Indo-Iranian Monographs (The Hague: Mouton, n.d.), 1; Thub bstan legs bśad rgya mtsho, *Gateway to the Temple*.
86. The exact date of the land-transferring contract is the twelfth day of the sixth month of the fourth Qianlong reign, which is July 17, 1739, in the Gregorian calendar.
87. Qinghai Archive, cat. no. 463001-05-89-3-4, *Qingshi gongcheng* [Qing history project], Renmin University of China, Beijing.
88. Qinghai Archive, cat. no. 463001-05-89-5-6.

89. For Chinese Buddhist institutional financial management, see Timothy Brook, *Praying for Power: Buddhism and the Formation of Gentry Society in Late-Ming China* (Cambridge, MA: Harvard University Press, 1994); Weiwei Luo, "Land, Lineage and the Laity: Transactions of a Qing Monastery," *Late Imperial China* 36 1 (2015): 88–123; Walsh, *Sacred Economies*. For Tibetan monasteries, see Berthe Jansen, *The Monastery Rules: Buddhist Monastic Organization in Pre-Modern Tibet* (Berkeley: University of California Press, 2018), especially chapters 5 and 6.
90. The definition of "empire" as an organizational framework to define relationship between two powers is seen Ronald Grigor Suny and Terry Martin, eds., *A State of Nations: Empire and Nation-Making in the Age of Lenin and Stalin* (Oxford: Oxford University Press, 2001), 25.
91. For Yunnan, see Giersch, *Asian Borderlands*. For Guizhou, see Jodi L. Weinstein, *Empire and Identity in Guizhou: Local Resistance to Qing Expansion* (Seattle: University of Washington Press, 2013). For Xinjiang, see James Millward, *Beyond the Pass: Economy, Ethnicity, and Empire in Qing Central Asia, 1759–1864* (Stanford, CA: Stanford University Press, 1998). For Taiwan, see John Robert Shepherd, *Statecraft and Political Economy on the Taiwan Frontier, 1600–1800* (Stanford, CA: Stanford University Press, 1993).

2. MANUFACTURING

1. A selected list of publication in the English language on the third Changkya, Rolpai Dorje, includes Xiangyun Wang, "Tibetan Buddhism at the Court of Qing: The Life and Work of LCang SKya Rol-Pa'i-Rdo-Rje (1717–1786)" (PhD diss., Harvard University, 1995); Marina Illich, "Selections from the Life of a Tibetan Buddhist Polymath: Chankya Rolpai Dorje (Lcang Skya Rol Pa'i Rdo Rje), 1717–1786" (PhD diss., Columbia University, 2006); Patricia Ann Berger, *Empire of Emptiness: Buddhist Art and Political Authority in Qing China* (Honolulu: University of Hawai'i Press, 2003). Translations of his spiritual biography include the third Tukwan, Lobzang Chokyi Nyima, *Zhangjia Guoshi Ruobiduojie zhuan* [Biography of the imperial preceptor Changkya Rolpai Dorje], trans. Lianlong Ma and Qingying Chen (Beijing: Zhongguo Zangxue yanjiu zhongxin, 2007). Hereafter this text is referred to as *Major Biography*. Please note that his name is transliterated differently in these publications.
2. The third Tukwan, Lobzang Chokyi Nyima, *Major Biography*, 218.
3. The third Tukwan Lobzang Chokyi Nyima, *Major Biography*, 218–89, emphasis added. Note that mtsho bdun is the Tibetan rendering of Dolonnuur, a place that features centrally in the next chapter.
4. Nancy Kollmann, *The Russian Empire, 1450–1801* (Oxford: Oxford University Press, 2017), 141.
5. Susan Naquin, *Peking: Temples and City Life, 1400–1900* (Berkeley: University of California Press, 2000), 49; Evelyn Rawski, *The Last Emperors: A Social History of Qing Imperial Institutions* (Berkeley: University of California Press, 1998), 231–63.
6. Wang, "Tibetan Buddhism at the Court of Qing," 94.
7. Isabelle Charleux, "From North India to Buryatia: The Sandalwood Buddha from the Mongols' Perspective," *Palace Museum Journal* 154, no. 2 (2011): 81–100.

2. MANUFACTURING

8. Zhang Yuxin, *Qingdai Lamajiao beiwen* [Tibetan Buddhist stelae of the Qing dynasty] (Tianjin: Tianjin guji chubanshe, 1987), 19.
9. Qi Meiqin, *Qingdai Neiwufu* [Department of the Imperial Household in the Qing dynasty] (Shenyang: Liaoning minzu chubanshe, 2009), 83.
10. Rawski, *The Last Emperors*, 96–126.
11. See Stephen H. Whiteman, "From Upper Camp to Mountain Estate: Recovering Historical Narratives in Qing Imperial Landscapes," *Studies in the History of Gardens and Designed Landscapes: An International Quarterly* 33, no. 4 (2013): 272.
12. Kevin R. E. Greenwood, "Yonghegong: Imperial Universalism and the Art and Architecture of Beijing's 'Lama Temple'" (PhD diss., University of Kansas, 2013), 2.
13. Vladimir L. Uspensky, *Prince Yunli (1697–1738): Manchu Statesman and Tibetan Buddhist* (Tokyo: Institute for the Study of Languages and Cultures of Asia and Africa, 1997), 111.
14. Frist Historical Archives of China and Yonghegong Administration Office, *Qingdai Yonghegong Dang'an shiliao* [Yonghegong archival documents in the Qing dynasty] (Beijing: Zhongguo minzu sheying yishu chubanshe, 2004), vol. 1. Hereafter this source is referred to as *Yonghegong Archives*.
15. *Yonghegong Archives*, vol. 1, cat. no. 35, 73.1735.5.8.
16. One exemplary work on the Yongzheng emperor's Buddhist connection is Jiang Wu, *Enlightenment in Dispute: The Reinvention of Chan Buddhism in Seventeenth-Century China* (Oxford: Oxford University Press, 2008), 163–85.
17. For the second Changkya, Ngawang Lobzang Choden, see Tsering Namgyal, "The Second Changkya Ngawang Lobzang Choden," The Treasury of Lives, https://treasuryoflives.org/biographies/view/Second-Changkya-Ngawang-Lobzang-Choden/3758 (BDRC P209).
18. *Yonghegong Archives*, vol. 1, 1–2. The Yangxindian (hall of cultivating mind), was the emperor's private room and the core of the ruling power during the Yongzheng reign; see Wu Hung, "Emperor's Masquerade: 'Costume Portraits' of Yongzheng and Qianlong," *Orientations* 6, no. 7 (July/August 1995), 25; for *jiaowei*, see entry 2486, Charles O. Hucker, *A Dictionary of Official Titles in Imperial China* (Stanford, CA: Stanford University Press, 1985), 238.
19. Janet Gyatso, "Image as Presence: The Place of the Work of Art in Tibetan Religious Thinking," in *The Newark Museum Tibetan Collection*, vol. 3, *Sculpture and Painting*, ed. Valrae Reynolds, Amy Heller, and Janet Gyatso (Newark, NJ: Newark Museum, 1986), 171.
20. Denise Baxter, "Introduction: Constructing Space and Identity in the Eighteenth-Century Interior," in *Architectural Space in Eighteenth-Century Europe: Constructing Identities and Interiors*, ed. Denise Baxter and Meredith Martin (London: Routledge, 2016), 1–12.
21. The third Changkya, Rolpai Dorje, *skal bzang rgya mtsho'i rnam thar* [The biography of the seventh Dalai Lama, Kelzang Gyatso], 2 vols. (Lhasa: bod ljongs mi dmangs dpe skrun khang, 1990) (BDRC W2625).
22. John Hay, "The Body Invisible in Chinese Art?," in *Body, Subject, and Power in China*, ed. Angela Zito and Tani E. Barlow (Chicago: University of Chicago Press, 1994), 44; Martin A. Mills, *Identity, Ritual and State in Tibetan Buddhism: The Foundations of Authority in Gelukpa Monasticism* (London: Routledge Curzon,

2. MANUFACTURING

2003); Benjamin Bogin, *The Illuminated Life of the Great Yolmowa* (Chicago: Serindia Publications, 2013).
23. The same account also appeared in the seventh Dalai Lama's biography, written by none other than the third Changkya, Rolpai Dorje. In the biography, the tapestries were again considered as present to celebrate the establishment of Yonghegong as a Buddhist learning center. For more, see the third Changkya, Rolpai Dorje, *skal bzang rgya mtsho'i rnam thar*, 241.
24. Greenwood, *Yonghegong*, 16, 209.
25. Uranchimeg Tsultemin, *A Monastery on the Move: Art and Politics in Later Buddhist Mongolia* (Honolulu: University of Hawai'i Press, 2021), 181.
26. The third Tukwan, Lobzang Chokyi Nyima, *Major Biography*, 221. For the descriptions of the tapestry series, the original Tibetan text reads as follows: "Sangs rgyas kyi rnam thar dpag bsam 'khri shing gi bris thang grang."
27. Yael Bentor, "Literature on Consecration (Rab Gnas)," in *Tibetan Literature: Studies in Genre*, ed. José Cabezón and Roger Jackson (Ithaca, NY: Snow Lion Publications, 1996), 291; Giuseppe Tucci, *mc'od rten ets'a ts'a nel Tibet Indiano ed Occidentale: Contributo allo studio dell'arte religiosa tibetana e del suo sigificato* [Stupas and tsa-tsa in Indian and Western Tibet: Contributions to the study of Tibetan religious art and its significance], Indo-Tibetica 1 (Roma: Reale Accademia d'Italia, 1932).
28. Berger, *Empire of Emptiness*, 116. Here Berger argues that Yonghegong from the beginning was a project of multiple redefinitions, its identity changed according to its content. For "universalism," see Greenwood, "Yonghegong."
29. Gary Liu, "Archive of Power: The Qing Dynasty Imperial Garden-Palace in Rehe," *Meishu shi yanjiu jikan* [Journal of art history] 28 (2010): 48.
30. Naquin, *Peking*, 316n50.
31. Forêt Philippe, *Mapping Chengde: The Qing Landscape Enterprise* (Honolulu: University of Hawai'i Press, 2000), 50–53.
32. Michael J. Walsh, *Sacred Economies Buddhist Monasticism and Territoriality in Medieval China*, Sheng Yen Series in Chinese Buddhist Studies (New York: Columbia University Press, 2010), 3.
33. Michael J. Walsh, "The Economics of Salvation: Toward a Theory of Exchange in Chinese Buddhism," *Journal of the American Academy of Religion* 75, no. 2 (2007): 357.
34. Juliet Bredon, *Peking: A Historical and Intimate Description of Its Chief Places of Interest* (Shanghai: Kelly and Walsh, 1922), 156.
35. Berthe Jansen, *The Monastery Rules: Buddhist Monastic Organization in Pre-Modern Tibet* (Berkeley: University of California Press, 2018), 88.
36. Naquin, *Peking*, 344. Chen Qingying, *Zhongguo xibei wenxian congshu, xibei shaoshuminzu yuyan wenxia* [Collections of bibliographical materials in minority languages in northwestern China] (Lanzhou: Lanzhou guji shudian, 1990), 154:585.
37. Hsiang-Ling Ho, "Qianlong huangdi dui Beijing simiao zhi zanzhu" [The Qianlong emperor's patronage of religious establishments in Beijing] (master's thesis, Soochow University, 2005), 84.
38. Lai Hui-min and Chang Su-ya, "Qing Qianlong shidai de Yonghegong—yige jingji wenhua cengmian de kaocha" [Yonghegong under the Qing Qianlong reign: A culture and economic perspective], *National Palace Museum Research Quarterly* 23,

2. MANUFACTURING

no. 4 (June 2006): 144. The "incense-lamp land" is a variation of "incense-fire land." Possibly, this is because Tibetans lit lamps filled with butter as offering to the Buddhas, while Chinese Buddhists focused on lighting incense as an offering to the Buddhas. Most of the Qing court documents used the former term. Lai and Chang, "Qing Qianlong shidai de Yonghegong," 133. Some of the documents designated the revenue as *Yonghegong yongyuan xianggong zhi fei* (Yonghegong infinite incense [supply costs]). Some of the documents simply refer to finances to Yonghegong as the Yonghegong *bushi yinliang* (donation taels), which is confusing, as it's not clear how much of it went to land purchase. Within the context of Tibetan Buddhism, this type of land is also referred to as "monk fields," which provided a form of support for monks. See Jansen, *The Monastery Rules*, 94.

39. Ayuxi's official title was *yuanwai lang*. Hucker's entry 8251 translates it as "vice director of a government agency." Hucker, *A Dictionary of Official Titles*, 597.
40. *Yonghegong Archives*, vol. 4, cat. no. 76, 240. Several points remain unclear: The "Sanhe County" is in the Zhili province, and it was one of the major endowed lands of the Yonghegong. Only further research can determine whether the lands were administered by local government or by the Mongol banner. Ning Chia, in her study of the Lifanyuan, discusses the management of the Yonghegong (or Yung-ho-kung in her transliteration) in relation to the Lifanyuan. For more, see Ning Chia, "The Li-Fan Yuan in the Early Ch'ing Dynasty" (PhD diss., Johns Hopkins University, 1992), 211.
41. *Yonghegong Archives*, vol. 5, cat. no. 93, 271–72.
42. Xiaomeng Liu, *Qingdai Beijing qiren shehui* [Social life of Qing bannermen in Beijing] (Beijing: Zhongguo shehui kexue chubanshe, 2016).
43. Naquin, *Peking*, 75, 66, 335.
44. Ho, "Qianlong huangdi," 2.
45. Lai and Chang, "Qing Qianlong shidai de Yonghegong," 144–45.
46. For Fang Guancheng's report, see *Gongzheng dang Qialong chao zouzhe* [Memorials from the Qianlong reign], vol. 28, *Memorials by Fang Guancheng* (December 1767 to January 1768), 512–53 (Taipei: Guoli Gugong bowuyuan, 1982).
47. In February–March 1811, the Ministry of Revenue communicated with the Department of the Imperial Household concerning the due endowment income for 1770–1808. See *Neige daku dang'an* [Archives of the grand secretariat of the Qing dynasty], Institute of History and Philosophy, Academia Sinica, Taipei, cat. no. 142669-001. See also *Yonghegong Archives*, vol. 17, cat. nos. 9, 10, 15, 19, 20, 27, 28, 36, 37, 38, 59, 60, 103, 104, 105, 108, 112, 142 (1822), 152 (1825), 153 (1825).
48. Ishihama Yumiko, *Shincho to chibetto bukkyō: bosatsuō to natta kenryūtei* [Qing China and the Tibetan Buddhist world: The Qianlong emperor who had become a Buddhist king], Waseda Daigaku Gakujutsu Sosho 20 (Tokyo: Wasedadaigakushuppanbu, 2011), 130–47. In 1834 (DG 14th year, 4th month, 27th day), the Department of Personnel (Ch.: Li Bu) again communicated with the Department of the Imperial Household concerning the due income from the endowments between 1821 and 1834. See *Neige daku dang'an*, cat. no. 185258-001. Evelyn Rawski, "The Imperial Way of Death: Ming and Ch'ing Emperors and Death Ritual," in *Death Ritual in Late Imperial and Modern China*, ed. James Watson and Evelyn Rawski (Berkeley: University California Press, 1990), 228–53. For the Daoguang reign, see

2. MANUFACTURING

Yonghegong Archives, vol. 17, cat. no. 160 (1826 with lists); vol. 18, cat. nos. 1, 4, 6, 12, 15, 17, 18, 21, 23, 24, 27, 32, 33, 36, 41, 45, 47, 51, 55, 58, 63, 68, 73, 76, 77. For later reigns, see *Yonghegong Archives*, vol. 17.
49. *Yonghegong Archives*, vol. 3, 50–51 (1740); 84–85 (1741); 97 (1742); 205 (1743).
50. *Yonghegong Archives*, vol. 3, 50–51.
51. Jansen, *The Monastery Rules*, 86.
52. Georges B. J. Dreyfus, *The Sound of Two Hands Clapping: The Education of a Tibetan Buddhist Monk* (Berkeley: University of California Press, 2003), 41. For ritual services provided by monks, see especially Jansen, *The Monastery Rules*, 86.
53. Lai Hui-min, *Tian huang gui zhou: Qing huangzu de jieceng jiegou yu jingji shenghuo* [Qing imperial lineage: Its hierarchical structure and economic life] (Taipei: Zhongyang yanjiuyuan jindaishi yanjiusuo, 1997), 85n27.
54. Lai, *Tian huang gui zhou*, 16. Naquin also talks about the actual number of residing monks in Yonghegong throughout its history; see Naquin, *Peking*, 585.
55. *Yonghegong Archives*, vol. 16; see Mongolian letters regarding funds for monks. Different accounts do not always agree with the names of the four colleges. However, detailed information confirms that the configuration was modeled after Geluk's great monasteries in Lhasa. See Chen, *Zhongguo xibei wenxian congshu*, 154:920–29; Wei Kaizhao, *Yonghegong manlu* [Leisurely collections of Yonghegong] (Zhengzhou: Henan Renmin chubanshe, 1985), 141–43; Miaozhou, *Meng Zang Fojiao shi* [History of Buddhism in Mongolia and Tibet], vol. 7, section 2. The third Tukwan, Lobzang Chokyi Nyima, *Major Biography*, fl. 49–50. Another place mentioning the makeup of the four monastic colleges of the Yonghegong is tshe 'phel, "lcang skya ngag dbang blo bzang chos ldan," in *chen po hor gyi yul du dam pa'i chos ji ltar byung ba'i bshad pa rgyal ba'i bstan pa rin po che gsal bar byed pa'i sgron me* [History of Buddhism in Mongolia] (Xining: mtsho sngon mi rigs dpe skrun khang, 1993), 1:235–36 (BDRC W21994).
56. Dreyfus, *The Sound of Two Hands Clapping*, 65. Jansen, *The Monastery Rules*, chap. 5.
57. Hui-Min Lai, "The Yung-ho Temple in the Ch'ien-lun Era: A Culture and Economic Perspective," *National Palace Museum Research Quarterly* 23, no. 4 (2006): 144.
58. Lai, *Tian huang gui zhou*, 16. Jin Liang, *Yonghegong zhilue* [A concise history of Yonghegong] (Beijing: Zhongguo Zangxue yanjiu zhongxin chubanshe, 1994), 114.
59. Naquin, *Peking*, 584–85.
60. Jansen, *The Monastery Rules*, 91–92.
61. The most complete history of Qing Tibet in the eighteenth century is Luciano Petech, *China and Tibet in the Early 18th Century* (Leiden: Brill Archive, 1950).
62. Ishihama Yumiko, *Shinchō to chibetto bukkyō: Bosatsuō to natta kenryūtei* [Qing China and the Tibetan Buddhist world: The Qianlong emperor who had become a Buddhist king], Waseda Daigaku Gakujutsu Sosho 20 (Tokyo: Wasedadaigakushuppanbu, 2011). For more on Tibetan Buddhist mass monasticism, see Brenton Sullivan, *Building a Religious Empire: Tibetan Buddhism, Bureaucracy, and the Rise of the Gelukpa*, Encounters with Asia (Philadelphia: University of Pennsylvania Press, 2021).

2. MANUFACTURING

63. The seventh Dalai Lama, Kelzang Gyatso, *gsung 'bum/_bskal bzang rgya mtsho* [Collected works of skal bzang rgya mtsho] (gangtok: dodrup sangye, 1975); the third Changkya, Rolpai Dorje, *skal bzang rgya mtsho'i rnam thar*, 311.
64. Dreyfus, *The Sound of Two Hands Clapping*. The third Tukwan, Lobzang Choyi Nyima, *Major Biography*. For the Geluk School's monasticism, especially its development in the eighteenth century, see Sangye Gyatso Desi, *dga'-ldan chos 'byuṅ Baiḍūrya ser po* [Yellow Beryl: The history of Dge-lugs-pa sect and its monasteries in Tibet] (Beijing: Kruṅ-go Bod kyi śes rig dpe skrun khang, 1991). In addition to the monastic establishments of the Gelukpa School, it is noteworthy that the academic degrees in the Geluk School also took shape in the initial years of the eighteenth century. See, for instance, Tarab Trülku, *A Brief History of Tibetan Academic Degrees in Buddhist Philosophy*, NIAS Report Series, no. 43 (Copenhagen: NIAS, in association with the Royal Library, 2000), 18, 20. I thank Gray Tuttle for sharing this source with me.
65. The seventh Dalai Lama, Kelzang Gyatso, *khri chen sprul sku blo bzang bstan pa'i nyi ma dpal bzang po'i rnam thar pa dpyod ldan yid dbang 'gugs pa'i pho nya* [The biography of the second Serkhi Lobzang Tenpai Nyima], in *gsung 'bum/_bskal bzang rgya mtsho*, f. 420.
66. Uspensky, *Prince Yunli*, 111.
67. Sonam Dorje, "The Seventh Tatsak Jedrung, Lobzang Pelden Gyeltsen," The Treasury of Lives, http://www.treasuryoflives.org/biographies/view/Seventh-Tatsak-Jedrung-Lobzang-Pelden-Gyeltsen/9693 (BDRC P 7054). For blo bzang dpal rgyan's biographical information, see mi 'gyur rdo rje ed, *Bod Kyi Gal Che'i Lo Rgyus Yig Cha Bdams Bsgrigs* [Selections of historical documents on Tibetan Buddhism of Tibet], Par theṅs 1. Gaṅs Can Rig Mdzod 16 (Lhasa: Bod-ljoṅs Bod yig dpe rñiṅ dpe skrun khang, 1991), 285–86. When he died in 1758, he was succeeded by the second Gungtang, another important Buddhist, but the second Gungtang held the position for less than a year, until 1760. Information on his time in Yonghegong has yet to come to light.
68. For more on the two monasteries, see Caiwujiapu, "Qingchao shiqi de Xinjiang Zhunga'er hanguo zangchuan Fojiao" [Tibetan Buddhism in Zungharia in Xinjiang under the Qing], *Xinjiang shifan daxue xuebao: Zhexue shehui kexue ban* [Bulletin of Xinjiang Normal University: Social science edition] 3 (2005): 66–73.
69. Dorje, "The Seventh Tatsak Jedrung, Lobzang Pelden Gyeltsen." For the related requests, see *Yonghegong Archives*, vol. 6, cat. nos. 75 and 76, 238–42. Fuheng's appointments at the time were grand secretary and grand minister of the Department of the Imperial Household concurrently controlling the Imperial Guardsmen (*Daxueshi ling shiwei neidachen*); see Hucker, entry 3771, *A Dictionary of Official Titles*, 315.
70. *Yonghegong Archives*, vol. 6, cat. nos. 81 and 82, 251–55.
71. Wang Li, *Mingmo Qingchu Dalai Lama xitong yu Menggu zhubu hudong guanxi yanjiu* [Interactions between the Dalai Lama line and Mongol communities in the Ming-Qing transitional period] (Beijing: Minzu chubanshe, 2011), 80–81.
72. Wang, *Mingmo Qingchu Dalai Lama xitong*, 105–14.
73. He Bin, Yanghui Xie, and Huocheng xianzhi bianzuan weiyuanhui, eds., *Huocheng Xianzhi* [Huocheng county gazetteer] (Ulumuqi: Xinjiang renmin chubanshe, 1998), 11.

2. MANUFACTURING

74. Liz Flora, "The Eighth Tatsak Jedrung, Yeshe Lobzang Tenpai Gongpo," The Treasury of Lives, https://treasuryoflives.org/biographies/view/Eighth-Tatsak-Yeshe-Lobzang-Tenpai-Gonpo/5328 (BDRC P302).
75. BDRC P1788.
76. Samten Chhosphel, "The Sixty-First Ganden Tripa, Ngawang Tsultrim," The Treasury of Lives, http://www.treasuryoflives.org/biographies/view/Trichen-61-Ngawang-Tsultrim/5652.
77. Xiangyun Wang, "The Qing Court's Tibet Connection: Lcang Skya Rol Pa'i Rdo Rje and the Qianlong Emperor," *Harvard Journal of Asiatic Studies* 60, no. 1 (2000): 131; Samten Chhosphel, "The Fifty-Fourth Ganden Tripa, Ngawang Chokden," The Treasury of Lives, https://treasuryoflives.org/biographies/view/Trichen-54-Ngawang-Chokden/6526 (BDRC P412).
78. The third Tukwan, Lobzang Chokyi Nyima, *Major Biography*, 208.
79. René de Nebesky-Wojkowitz, *Tibetan Religious Dances: Tibetan Text and Annotated Translation of the 'Chams Yig* (The Hague: Mouton, 1976), 43–47.
80. The third Tukwan, Lobzang Choyi Nyima, *Major Biography*.
81. Nebesky-Wojkowitz, *Tibetean Religious Dances*, 64.
82. "yi guan Yonghegong dagui" [Memory of watching the Ghost Festival at Yonghegong], *Liyuan huakan* [Li Yan pictorial journal] 282 (1944): 15.
83. Matthew Kapstein, *The Tibetans* (Malden, MA: Wiley-Blackwell, 2006), 239.
84. Vladimir L. Uspensky, "The 'Beijing Lamaist Centre' and Tibet in the 17th to early 20th Centuries," in *Tibet and Her Neighbors: A History*, ed. Alex McKay (London: Thames and Hudson, 2004), 110–11.
85. *Yonghegong Archives*, vol. 3.
86. Helmut Eimer, "Preliminary Remarks on the Second A-Kya," in *Tibetan Studies in Honor of Hugh Richardson: Proceedings of the International Seminar on Tibetan Studies, Oxford, 1979*, ed. Michael Aris and Aung San Suu Kyi (Warminster: Aris and Phillips, 1979), 97–103. Even though Eimer identified Lobzang Tenpai Gyeltsen as the first one in this line of reincarnation, he was in fact the second in line (1708–1768, BDRC P3912). For his biographical account, see Mi-nyag Mgon-po, *Gangs-Can Mkhas Dbang Rim Byon Gyi Rnam Thar Mdor Bsdus Bdud Rtsi'i Thigs Phreng* [Concise biographies of historical Tibetan scholars] (Beijing: Mtsho-sngon Zhin-chen Zhin-hwa dpe tshong khang gis bkram, 1996). The "second A-Kya" in his analysis is the third in line (Lobzang Jamyang Gyatso, 1768–1816, BDRC P322). The first one recognized in this line of reincarnation was Sherab Zangpo (1633–1707, BDRC P3825).
87. This date was inferred from his successor, Yeshe Kelzang, who was enthroned in 1748 as the head of the Tantric College.
88. Exemplary works drawn from his writings and inspired by him are included in Chahar Geshe Lobzang Tshutrim's *gsum 'bum* [Collected works], BDRC W23726, vols. ka, ga, nga, ca, ja, and ta.
89. Matthew W. King, "'Miscellaneous Writings' of Čaqar Gebši Luvsančültem," in *Sources of Mongolian Buddhism*, ed. Vesna Wallace (Oxford: Oxford University Press, 2020), 153–56.
90. BDRC P4797. For his biographical information in Tibetan, see ko źul grags pa 'byung gnas, *Gangs Can Mkhas Grub Rim Byon Miṅ Mdzod* [Biographical dictionary of prominent Tibetans in Tibet] (Lan chou: Mtsho sgnon Žing chen Žin hwa dpe khang gis bkrams, 1992), 539–41 (BDRC W19801). For a Mongolian account of

2. MANUFACTURING

his life, see Oyuncimeg, *Monggol sudulul-un nebterkei toli: Sasin surtaqun* [Encyclopedia of Mongolian studies: Volume on religion] (Hohhot: Ölbör Monggol-un-Arad-un Keblel-un Qoriy-a, 2007), 465–66.

3. ASSEMBLIES

1. For more information on Dolonnuur (Dolonnor), see Isabelle Charleux, *Catalogue of the Main Monasteries of Inner Mongolia*, 2006, https://halshs.archives-ouvertes.fr/halshs-01788006/document, 221–34.
2. Johan Elverskog, *Our Great Qing: The Mongols, Buddhism and the State in Late Imperial China* (Honolulu: University of Hawai'i Press, 2006), 24; Shigeru Tayama, *shindai ni okeru Mōko no shakai seido* [The Mongolian social system in Qing dynasty] (Tokyo: Tōkyō Bunkyō Shoin, 1954).
3. There have been debates on the meaning of the temple's Chinese name, Huizong si, particular the meaning of "zong." Henry Serruys, "A Study of Chinese Penetration Into Chahar Territory in the Eighteenth Century," *Monumenta Serica* 35 (1981–1983): 539–40.
4. Isabelle Charleux, "The Making of Mongol Buddhist Art and Architecture: Artisans in Mongolia from the Sixteenth to Twentieth Centuries," in *Meditation: The Art of Zaabazar and His School, catalogue trilingue (polonaise, anglaise, mongol) de exposition éponyme organisée au Asia and Pacific Museum*, ed. Elvira Eevr Djaltchinova-Malets (Warsow: Państwowe Muzeum Etnograficzne w Warszawie, 2010), 59–105, https://halshs.archives-ouvertes.fr/halshs-00702140/document.
5. Ishihama Yumiko, *Shincho to Chibetto Bukkyo: Bosatsuo to Natta Kenryutei* [Qing China and the Tibetan Buddhist world: The Qianlong emperor who had become a Buddhist king], Waseda Daigaku Gakujutsu Sosho 20 (Tokyo: Wasedadaigakushuppanbu, 2011), 228; Xiangyun Wang, "Tibetan Buddhism at the Court of Qing: The Life and Work of LCang SKya Rol-Pa'i-Rdo-Rje (1717–1786)" (PhD diss., Harvard University, 1995), 85.
6. This argument is put forth in both Sh. Natasgdorj, *Khalkhyn tüükh* [History of Khalkha] (Ulaanbaatar: Ulsyn khebleiin khereg erkhlekh khoroo, 1963), 34; Junko Miyawaki, "Qalqa Mongols and the Oyirad in the Seventeenth Century," *Journal of Asian History* 18, no. 2 (1984): 152. Both sources are cited in Lhamsuren Munkh-Erdene, "The 1640 Great Code: An Inner Asian Parallel to the Treaty of Westphalia," *Central Asian Survey* 29, no. 3 (September 2010): 269n2, 285.
7. David Sneath, *The Headless State: Aristocratic Orders, Kinship Society, and Misrepresentations of Nomadic Inner Asia* (New York: Columbia University Press, 2007); Munkh-Erdene, "The 1640 Great Code"; Elverskog, *Our Great Qing*.
8. Thomas J. Barfield, *The Perilous Frontier: Nomadic Empires and China*, Studies in Social Discontinuity (Cambridge, MA: Basil Blackwell, 1989), 27. For the role of the confederation in state formation of the Xiongnu empire, see Nicola Di Cosmo, *Ancient China and Its Enemies: The Rise of Nomadic Power in East Asian History* (Cambridge: Cambridge University Press, 2004), 165–66.
9. Heilong, "Kulunboleqi's huimeng Mengguwen dang'an yijie" [Annotation and translation of Mongolian archives on the Khüree assembly], *Manzu yanjiu* [Manchu minority research] 1 (2017): 43–52; Wuritu, "A Research Study on the Political

3. ASSEMBLIES

Activities of the First Jebtsundamba Khutuktu" (PhD diss., University of Inner Mongolia, 2010); Miyawaki, "The Qalqa Mongols and the Oyirad in the Seventeenth Century," 140n9. Miyawaki suggests that the assembly did not take place because the Zunghar troops made rapid advancements into Khalkha areas, and there was little time for a large assembly to be organized.

10. The third figure under discussion is inferred from Tibetan sources. See Samten Chhosphel, "The Forty-Fourth Ganden Tripa, Lodro Gyatso," The Treasury of Lives, http://treasuryoflives.org/biographies/view/Trichen-44-Lodro-Gyatso/2872. Wuritu identifies him as a different figure whose title in the eighteenth century was Galden Sirutu and who was active in Mongolia. Wuritu, "A Research Study."
11. Kim Sung Soo [Jin Chengxiu], *Ming Qing zhiji Zangchuan Fojiao zai Menggu diqu de chuanbo* [Tibetan Buddhism in Mongolia during the Ming and Qing] (Beijing: Shehui kexue wenxian chubanshe, 2006).
12. Samten Chhosphel, "The Forty-Fourth Ganden Tripa, Lodro Gyatso"; Tsering Namgyal, "The Second Changkya, Ngawang Lobzang Choden," The Treasury of Lives, http://treasuryoflives.org/biographies/view/Second-Changkya-Ngawang-Lobzang-Choden/3758.
13. The third Changkya, Rolpai Dorje, *skal bzang rgya mtsho'I rnam thar* [The biography of the seventh Dalai Lama, Kelzang Gyatso], 2 vols (Lhasa: bod ljongs mi dmangs dpe skrun khang, 1990), 271 (BDRC W2625); Blo bzang tshe 'phel, *chen po hor gyi yul du dam pa'i chos ji ltar byung ba'i bshad pa rgyal ba'i bstan pa rin po che gsal bar byed pa'i sgron me* [History of Buddhism in Mongolia] (Xining: mtsho sgnon mi rigs dpe skrun khang, 1993).
14. Elverskog, *Our Great Qing*, 15n35.
15. Wang, "Tibetan Buddhism at the Court of Qing," 82.
16. Kim, *Ming Qing zhiji Zangchuan Fojiao zai Menggu*; Gray Tuttle and Lan Wu, "Tibetan Buddhist Vanguards in Mongolia, 1576–1644" (forthcoming).
17. Peter C. Perdue, *China Marches West: The Qing Conquest of Central Eurasia* (Cambridge, MA: Belknap Press of Harvard University Press, 2005), 61; Arthur Waldron, *The Great Wall of China: From History to Myth*, Cambridge Paperbacks: Oriental Studies, History (Cambridge: Cambridge University Press, 1998), 72–164.
18. Perdue, *China Marches West*, 144–45.
19. Johan Elverskog, "The Tumu Incident and the Chinggisid Legacy in Inner Asia," *Silk Road* 15 (2017): 142.
20. Elverskog, "The Tumu Incident."
21. Évariste Régis Huc, *Travels in Tartary, Thibet, and China During the Years 1844–5–6*, trans. W. Hazlitt (London: Vizetelly, 1857; Project Gutenberg, 2010), 31, 32. Page references are to the Project Gutenberg edition.
22. Huc, *Travels in Tartary*, 32.
23. The term Lama yinwu chu is translated variously as the Department of Lama Correspondence, e.g., in Kevin R. E. Greenwood, "Yonghegong: Imperial Universalism and the Art and Architecture of Beijing's 'Lama Temple'" (PhD diss., University of Kansas, 2013), 230; and as the Office of Lama Seals and Service, e.g., in Max Oidtmann, *Forging the Golden Urn: The Qing Empire and the Politics of Reincarnation in Tibet* (New York: Columbia University Press, 2018), 161. Both sources use the term to describe an office known as the Jingcheng Lama yinwuchu. Oidtmann

asserts the office was established in 1745, right after Yonghegong was converted to a Tibetan Buddhist monastery.

24. Wen-Shing Chou, *Mount Wutai: Visions of a Sacred Buddhist Mountain* (Princeton, NJ: Princeton University Press, 2018), 6n26, 181.
25. Isabelle Charleux, "Buddhist Monasteries in Southern Mongolia," in *The Buddhist Monastery: A Cross-Cultural Survey*, ed. Pierre Pichard and François Lagirarde (Paris: École Française d'Extrême-Orient, 2003), https://halshs.archives-ouvertes.fr/halshs-00409747/document, 15.
26. Charleux, "Buddhist Monasteries in Southern Mongolia," 15.
27. Zhao Yuntian, ed., *Qianlongchao neifu chaoben "Lifanyuan zeli"* [Lifanyuan regulations in the Qing's Qianlong reign] (Beijing: Zhongguo Zangxue yanjiu zhongxin chubanshe, 2006), 127.
28. Coyiji, *Neimenggu Zangchuan fojiao siyuan* [Tibetan Buddhist monasteries in Inner Mongolia] (Lanzhou Shi: Gansu minzu chubanshe, 2014), 116. Zhao, *Qianlongchao neifu chaoben "Lifanyuan zeli,"* 154.
29. For more, see Gray Tuttle, "A Tibetan Buddhist Mission to the East: The Fifth Dalai Lama's Journey to Beijing, 1652–1653," in *Tibetan Society and Religion: The Seventeenth and Eighteenth Centuries*, ed. Bryan Cuevas and Kurtis Schaeffer (Leiden: Brill, 2006), 65–87.
30. Lobsang Tsultrim refers to both as his teachers.
31. Samten Chhosphel, "The Sixty-First Ganden Tripa, Ngawang Tsultrim," The Treasury of Lives, http://treasuryoflives.org/biographies/view/Trichen-61-Ngawang-Tsultrim/5652.
32. Samten Chhosphel, "The Sixty-First Ganden Tripa Ngawang Tsultrim"; for Qing officials' assessment of his position in the Gurkha war, see Oidtmann, *Forging the Golden Urn*, 59.
33. For information regarding the sixth Panchen Lama (Blo bzang dpal ldan ye shes), see BDRC P168. See also Elverskog, *Our Great Qing*, 2.
34. The third Tukwan, Lobzang Chokyi Nyima, *khyab bdag rdo rje sems dpa'i ngo bo dpal ldan bla ma dam pa ye shes bstan pa'i sgron me dpal bzang po'i rnam par thar pa mdo tsam brjod pa dge ldan bstan pa'i mdzes rgyan* [The major biography of the third Changkya, Rolpai Dorje] (Lanzhou: Kan-suu mi rigs dpe skrun khang, 1989), 275–76. Hereafter this text is referred to as *Major Biography*.
35. Mi nyag mgon po, ye shes rdo rje, thub bstan nyi ma, dpal rdor, lha mo skyabs, *gangs can mkhas dbang rim byon gyi rnam thar mdor bsdus* [Biographical dictionary of eminent Tibetans in Tibet], 2 vols (Beijing: krung go'i bod kyi shes rig dpe skrun khang, 1996–2000) (BDRC W25268); Alexander Fedotov, "Some Aspects of the Influence of Tibetan Literature Over Mongolian Literary Tradition," in *Tibetan Studies: Proceedings of the 4th Seminar of the International Association for Tibetan Studies, Schloss Hohenkammer, Munich, 1985*, ed. Helga Uebach and Jampa L. Panglung (Munich: Kommission für Zentralasiatische Studien, Bayerische Akademie der Wissenschaften, 1988), 159. For Lobsang Tsultrim's literary productions extending back to Chahar, see Ü (Ünenci-yin) Tuyaġ-a, *Monggol Keblel-Ün Teüke* [History of Mongolian-language printing] (Hohhot: Öbör Monggol-un Surġan Kümüjil-ün Keblel-ün Qoriy-a, 2010), 248–54. Matthew King identifies this monastery in the Tibetan-source as Dga' ldan chos 'dzin gling. See Matthew W. King, *Ocean of Milk, Ocean of Blood: A*

3. ASSEMBLIES

Mongolian Monk in the Ruins of the Qing Empire (New York: Columbia University Press, 2019), 154.
36. National Archives of Mongolia, Ulaanbaatar, cat. no. M-166-1, item 1.
37. National Archives of Mongolia, cat. no. M-166-1-2, item 45.
38. National Archives of Mongolia, cat. no. M-166-2, item 81.
39. National Archives of Mongolia, cat. no. M-166-1-2, item 81.
40. National Archives of Mongolia, cat. no. M-166-1-2, item 7.
41. National Archives of Mongolia, cat. no. M-166-1-2, item, 35.
42. National Archives of Mongolia, cat. nos. M-166-2-21, M-166-2-22. For an ecological history in the eighteenth-century Mongol steppe, see David A. Bello, "Relieving Mongols of Their Pastoral Identity: Disaster Management on the Eighteenth-Century Qing China Steppe," *Environmental History* 19, no. 3 (July 2014): 480–504.
43. Devon Dear, "Holy Rollers: Monasteries, Lamas, and the Unseen Transport of Chinese–Russian Trade, 1850–1911," *International Review of Social History* 59, no. S22 (December 2014): 84.
44. José Cabezón and Penpa Dorjee, *Sera Monastery* (Somerville, MA: Wisdom Publications, 2019); Paul Nietupski, *Labrang Monastery: A Tibetan Buddhist Community on the Inner Asian Borderlands, 1709–1958* (Lanham, MD: Lexington Books, 2010).
45. National Archives of Mongolia, cat. no. M-166-2, item 78.
46. National Archives of Mongolia, cat. no. M-166-2-78.
47. Gray Tuttle, "Tibetan Buddhism Among the Mongol and Manchu Noble Families Before the Rise of Dge-Lugs Hegemony (1576–1651)" (master's thesis., Harvard University, 1996).
48. Peter Schwieger, *The Dalai Lama and the Emperor of China: A Political History of the Tibetan Institution of Reincarnation* (New York: Columbia University Press, 2015), chap. 2; Gray Tuttle, "The Role of Mongol Elite and Educational Degrees in the Advent of Reincarnation Lineages in Seventeenth Century Amdo," in *Tibet's Turbulent Seventeenth Century and the Tenth Karmapa*, ed. Karl Debreczeny and Gray Tuttle (Chicago: Serindia Publications, 2016), 235–62.
49. Walther Heissig, *A Lost Civilization: The Mongols Rediscovered* (New York: Basic Books, 1966), 29. For a more detailed biographical account, see Sonam Dorje, "The Second Tongkhor, Yonten Gyatso," The Treasury of Lives, https://treasuryoflives.org/biographies/view/Second-Tongkhor-Yonten-Gyatso/3708; Hurcha, Coyiji, and Wuyun, *Zangchuan Fojiao zai Menggu diqu de chuanbo yanjiu* [Research on the dissemination of Tibetan Buddhism in Mongolia] (Beijing: Minzu chubanshe, 2012), 66–69.
50. Tongkhor is located in an eastern suburb of Xining city, Qinghai Province. Zahiruddin Ahmad, *Sino-Tibetan Relations in the Seventeenth Century*, Serie Orientale Roma (Rome: Istituto italiano per il Medio ed Estremo Oriente, 1970), 90. Here Ahmad states that a diplomatic office was set up at Tongkhor to maintain the relationship between the Geluk School and the Mongols.
51. Tuttle, "Tibetan Buddhism Among the Mongol and Manchu Noble Families."
52. Tuttle, "Tibetan Buddhism Among the Mongol and Manchu Noble Families."
53. Huc, *Travels in Tartary*, 37.
54. Other sites include Mount Wutai and the Qing imperial summer resort in Jehol. For Mount Wutai in the Qing, see Chou, *Mount Wutai*; Gray Tuttle and Johan

Elverskog, eds., "Wutaishan and Qing Culture," special issue, *Journal of the International Association of Tibetan Studies* 63 (December 2011). For Jehol, see Stephen H. Whiteman, *Where Dragon Veins Meet: The Kangxi Emperor and His Estate at Rehe* (Seattle: University of Washington Press, 2020); Philippe Forêt, *Mapping Chengde: The Qing Landscape Enterprise* (Honolulu: University of Hawai'i Press, 2000); Ruth W. Dunnell et al., eds., *New Qing Imperial History: The Making of Inner Asian Empire at Qing Chengde* (London: Routledge, 2004); Anne Chayet, *Les Temples de Jehol et leurs modèles tibétains* [The Jehol temples and their Tibetan models] (Paris: Editions Recherche sur les civilisations, 1985).

55. Brenton Sullivan, "Monastic Customaries and the Promotion of Dge lugs Scholasticism in Amdo and Beyond," *Asian Highlands Perspectives* 36 (2014).
56. The seventh Dalai Lama, Kelzang Gyatso, *khri chen sprul sku blo bzang bstan pa'i nyi ma dpal bzang po'i rnam par thar pa dpyod ldan yid dbang 'gugs pa'i pho nya* [The biography of the second Serkhi Lobzang Tenpai Nyima], in *gsung 'bum/_bskal bzang rgya mtsho* [Collected works of skal bzang rgya mtsho] (gangtok: dodrup sangye, 1975–1983), vol. 10, ff. 345–448 (BDRC W2623).
57. The third Gungtang, Konchok Tenpai Drome, *Kun mkhyen 'jam dbyangs bzhad pa sku 'phreng gnyis pa rje 'jigs med dbang po'i rnam thar* [The biography of the second Jamyang Zhepa, Konchok Jigme Wangpo] (Lanzhou: kan su'u mi rigs dpe skrun khang, 1990).
58. The third Tukwan, Lobzang Chokyi Nyima, *Major Biography*, 214.
59. For more on the second Jamyang Zhepa, see Samten Chhosphel, "The Second Jamyang Zhepa, Konchok Jigme Wangpo," The Treasury of Lives, http://www.treasuryoflives.org/biographies/view/Jamyang-Zhepa-02-Konchok-Jigme-Wangpo/2996; Nietupski, *Labrang Monastery*, 127–34.
60. The third Gungtang, Konchok Tenpai Drome, *Kun mkhyen 'jam dbangs bzha pa sku 'phreng gnyis pa rje 'jigs med dbang po'I rnma thar*, 181–91.
61. Nietupski, *Labrang Monastery*, 132.
62. The third Gungtang Konchok Tenpai Drome, *Kun mkhyen 'jam dbangs bzha pa sku 'phreng gnyis pa rje 'jigs med dbang po'I rnma thar*, 192.
63. The third Detri, Jamyang Tubten Nyima, *'jam dbyangs thub bstan nyi ma'i gsung 'bum* [Collected works of Jamyang Tubten Nyima], vol. kha (Labrang Monastery: blab rang bkra shis 'khyil par khang, [1999?]), 613–22 (BDRC W22204).
64. Sonam Dorje, "The Sixth Detri, Kelzang Khyenrab Gyatso," The Treasury of Lives, http://treasuryoflives.org/biographies/view/Sixth-Detri-Kelzang-Khyenrab-Gyatso/7876.
65. I thank Isabelle Charleux for directing me to this monastery. For a concise introduction to the monastery, its history, and a sketch, see Charleux, *Catalogue of the Main Monasteries of Inner Mongolia*, 322–25.
66. Isabelle Charleux, personal communication with author, May 30, 2021.
67. Brenton Sullivan, *Building a Religious Empire: Tibetan Buddhism, Bureaucracy, and the Rise of the Gelukpa*, Encounters with Asia (Philadelphia: University of Pennsylvania Press, 2021), 130.
68. Sullivan, *Building a Religious Empire*.
69. Nietupski, *Labrang Monastery*, 110.
70. Schwieger, *The Dalai Lama and the Emperor of China*, 192–93.

3. ASSEMBLIES

71. Patricia Ann Berger, *Empire of Emptiness: Buddhist Art and Political Authority in Qing China* (Honolulu: University of Hawai'i Press, 2003); and Wenhua Luo, *Longpao yu jiasha: Qinggong zangchuan Fojiao wenhua kachao* [The emperor's court dress and robes: Tibetan Buddhist culture in the Qing court] (Beijing: Zijincheng chubanshe, 2005).
72. Terese Tse Bartholomew, "Introduction to the Art of Mongolia," September 7, 1995, https://www.asianart.com/mongolia/introduct.html; Uranchimeg Tsultemin, *A Monastery on the Move: Art and Politics in Later Buddhist Mongolia* (Honolulu: University of Hawai'i Press, 2021).
73. I thank Isabelle Charleux for the reference on the circulation of Dolonnuur products, especially beyond Inner Asia and into Europe; Charleux, personal communication with author, July 12, 2021. For more on Buddhist art production in southern Mongolia, see Bartholomew, "Introduction"; Yulia Elikhina and Victoria Demenova, "A Study of Stylistic Features and Metal Composition of the Buddhist Sculpture from Inner Mongolia (Dolonnor)," *Artibus Asiae* 80, no. 2 (2020): 145–66.
74. Bartholomew calls arts produced in Dolonnuur "Dolonnuur or Inner Mongolian style." See Bartholomew, "Introduction."
75. I speculate that the lost-wax casting technique was still in use in Dolonnuur in the eighteenth century; see Lan Wu, "Crafting Buddhist Art in Qing China's Contact Zones During the Eighteenth Century," in "East-Southeast," special issue, *Journal 18: A Journal of Eighteenth-Century Art and Culture* 4 (Fall 2017), http://www.journal18.org/issue4/crafting-buddhist-art-in-qing-chinas-contact-zones-during-the-eighteenth-century/. Elikhina and Demenova's publication in 2020 and Charleux's earlier publication point out that the prevailing metalworking hammering technique was repoussé. I thank Isabelle Charleux for sharing her publication and for directing me to the other source. See Charluex, "The Making of Mongol Buddhist Art and Architecture"; Elikhina and Demenova, "A Study of Stylistic Features," 145.
76. Bartholomew, "Introduction."
77. Huc's observations were quoted in Ren Yuehai, *Duolun wenshi ziliao* [Duolun literary and historical sources] (Hohhot: Neimenggu Daxue chubanshe, 2008), 3:20–21.
78. Ren, *Duolun wenshi ziliao*, 3:20–21.
79. The third Detri, Jamyang Tubten Nyima, '*jam dbyangs thub bstan nyi ma'i gsun 'bum.*
80. The third Detri, Jamyang Tubten Nyima, '*jam dbyangs thub bstan nyi ma'i gsun 'bum.*
81. Berger, *Empire of Emptiness*, 23–27; Uranchimeg Tsultem, "Ikh Khuree: A Nomadic Monastery and the Later Buddhist Art of Mongolia" (PhD diss., University of California, Berkeley, 2009), xi.
82. Luo, *Longpao yu jiasha*, 347; Wang Jiapeng, "Zhongzhengdian yu Qinggong zangchuan Fojiao" [Zhongzheng Hall and Tibetan Buddhism in the Qing imperial palace], *Gugong Bowuyuan yuankan* [Bulletin of the National Palace Museum] 3 (1991): 58–71.
83. Tsultemin, *A Monastery on the Move*, 74.

84. Valrae Reynolds, *From the Sacred Realm: Treasures of Tibetan Art from the Newark Museum* (Munich: Prestel Publishing, 1999), 226–27.
85. Reynolds, *From the Sacred Realm*.
86. Jacques Marchais Museum of Tibetan Art, with Barbara Lipton and Nima Dorjee Ragnubs, *Treasures of Tibetan Art: Collections of the Jacques Marchais Museum of Tibetan Art* (New York: Oxford University Press, 1995), 171.
87. On the Khalkha style, see Tsultermin, *A Monastery on the Move*; Bartholomew, "Introduction"; Luo, *Longpao yu jiasha*, 298, 355–56.
88. Elikhina and Demenova, "A Study of Stylistic Features," 146.
89. Claus Deimel, Wolf-Dietrich Freiherr Speck von Sternburg, and Grassimuseum, *Buddhas Leuchten und Kaisers Pracht: die Pekinger Sammlung Hermann Speck von Sternburg* [Buddha's radiance and emperors: The Sammlung Hermann Speck von Sternburg's Peking collections] (Leipzig: Staatliche Ethnographische Sammlungen Sachsen, Grassi Museum für Völkerkunde, 2008), 62–65.
90. Tsultemin, *A Monastery on the Move*, 183, fig. 6.3; 249nn20,21. Tsultemin identifies the Mongolian rendering of the chief Chinese artist's name as Ayush-tunjan. It could be a phonetic transliteration of Ayushi (one of the major foundries in Dolonnuur) and *tongjiang*, meaning "copper artisan," a more generic term referring to metalwork professionals at the time.
91. For more on this topic, see Wu, "Crafting Buddhist Art."
92. Tsultemin, *A Monastery on the Move*, esp. chaps. 3 and 6.
93. Huc, *Travels in Tartary*, 32.
94. Huc, *Travels in Tartary*, 36.
95. Isabelle Charleux, "The Inner Mongol City of Hohhot/Guihuacheng in the Eyes of Western Travellers," in "Traveling to the Heart of Asia: A History of Western Encounters with Mongolia," special issue, *Mongolica Pragensia' 17* 10, no. 1 (2020): 37–88, https://halshs.archives-ouvertes.fr/halshs-02984229/document
96. Huc, *Travels in Tartary*, 32.
97. Huc, *Travels in Tartary*, 35.
98. Huc, *Travels in Tartary*, 35.
99. Jianhongsheng, "Duolun nuo'er ji" [A survey of Dolonnuur], *Dongfang Zazhi* [Eastern miscellany] 5, no. 10 (October 1908): 128–34, https://babel.hathitrust.org/cgi/pt?id=pst.000066964766&view=1up&seq=1&skin=2021. The content of this survey was reproduced in Ren Yuehai, *Duolun wenshi ziliao* [Duolun literary and historical sources] (Hohhot: Neimenggu Daxue chubanshe, 2006), 1:1–8.
100. Jianhongsheng, "Duolun nuo'er ji," 37.
101. Joseph Fletcher, "Ch'ing Inner Asia c. 1800," in *The Cambridge History of China*, vol. 10, *Late Ch'ing 1800–1911*, ed. John K. Fairbank (Cambridge: Cambridge University Press, 1978), 48–53.
102. Wei-chieh Tsai, "Mongolization of Han Chinese and Manchu Settlers in Qing Mongolia, 1700–1911" (PhD diss, Indiana University, 2017), 40–41; Dear, "Holy Rollers."
103. On merchants active in the Qing's Mongolia, see Yi Wang, "Irrigation, Commercialization, and Social Change in Nineteenth-Century Inner Mongolia," *International Review of Social History* 59, no. 2 (August 2014): 215–46; Dear, "Holy Rollers," 73n10.
104. Ren, *Duolun wenshi* ziliao, 1:6. For Mongols' pilgrimage to Mount Wutai, see Isabelle Charleux, "Mongol Pilgrimages to Wutai Shan in the Late Qing Dynasty,"

Journal of the International Association of Tibetan Studies 6 (December 2011): 275–326.
105. Shigeru, *shindai ni okeru Mōko no shakai seido*, 333.
106. For more on the changing economic patterns in southern Mongolia during the Qing, see Bello, "Relieving Mongols of Their Pastoral Identity"; Jonathan Schlesinger, *A World Trimmed with Fur: Wild Things, Pristine Places, and the Natural Fringes of Qing* (Stanford, CA: Stanford University Press, 2017), 93–128.
107. Zhao, *Qianlongchao neifu chaoben "Lifanyuan zeli,"* 162.
108. Tsai, "Mongolization," 68n53, 69n59.
109. Tsai, "Mongolization," 32.
110. M. Sanjdorj, *Manchu Chinese Colonial Rule in Northern Mongolia*, trans. Urgunge Onon (New York: St. Martin's Press, 1980), 27–28.
111. For Shanxi merchants, see Luman Wang, "Money and Trade, Hinterland and Coast, Empire and Nation-state: An Unusual History of Shanxi Piaohao, 1820–1930" (PhD diss., University of Southern California, 2014.); Wang, "Irrigation, Commercialization, and Social Change."
112. Chia Ning, "The Lifanyuan and the Inner Asian Rituals in the Early Qing (1644–1795)," *Late Imperial China* 14, no. 1 (1993): 64–66, 70–75.
113. Chia, "The Lifanyuan," 64–65.
114. Ren, *Duolun wenshi ziliao*, 45. Chia separates "tribute" trips (*chaogong*) from "pilgrimages" (*chaojin*), though in actuality the two seemed to be interrelated in many ways. Chia, "The Lifanyuan"; see also Zhang Shuangzhi, "Qingchao waifan tizhi nei de chaojin nianban yu chaogong zhidu" [Systems of Chaojin nianban and Chaogong in the Qing's outlying regions in the Qing], *Qingshi yanjiu* [Qing history journal] 3 (2010).
115. For more on this case, see Lai Hui-min, "From Religious Centers to Temple Fairs: Tibetan Buddhist Temples and Tributary Trade with Khalkha Mongolian Royalty During the Qing Dynasty," *Bulletin of the Institute of Modern History, Academia Sinica* 72 (2011): 17.

4. GOVERNANCE

1. One exemplary scholarship is Patricia Berger, *Empire of Emptiness: Buddhist Art and Political Authority in Qing China* (Honolulu: University of Hawai'i Press, 2003).
2. For Gombjab's biographical sketch, see Coyiji, preface to *Tangy-a-yin urusqal* [The current of Gangga] (Kökeqota: Öbör Mongyol-un arad-un keblel-ün qoriya, 1984). On Gombjab's manuscript, see Sh. Bira, *Mongolian Historical Literature of the XVII–XIX Centuries Written in Tibetan*, trans. S. Frye (Bloomington, IN: Mongolia Society, 1970), 32–40.
3. Jiayi Du, *Qingchao Man Meng lianyin yanjiu* [Studies of marriage alliances between the Mongols and Manchus in the Qing] (Beijing: Renmin Chubanshe, 2003), 128. On Gombjab's ranking and title, see entry 2986, Charles O. Hucker, *A Dictionary of Official Titles in Imperial China* (Stanford, CA: Stanford University Press, 1985), 268.

4. Evelyn Rawski, *The Last Emperors: A Social History of Qing Imperial Institutions* (Berkeley: University of California Press, 1998), 126.
5. Willard Sunderland, "Imperial Space: Territorial Thought and Practice in the Eighteenth Century," in *Russian Empire: Space, People, Power, 1700–1930*, ed. Jane Burbank, Mark von Hagen, and Anatolyi Remnev (Bloomington: Indiana University Press, 2007), 33–66; Gwenn A. Miller, *Kodiak Kreol: Communities of Empire in Early Russian America* (Ithaca, NY: Cornell University Press, 2010).
6. Matthew W. Mosca, *From Frontier Policy to Foreign Policy: The Question of India and the Transformation of Geopolitics in Qing China* (Stanford, CA: Stanford University Press, 2015).
7. Christine Philliou, "Preface," in *Biography of an Empire: Governing Ottomans in an Age of Revolution* (Berkeley: University of California Press, 2010), 13–24.
8. Joanna Waley-Cohen, *The Culture of War in China* (London: I. B. Tauris, 2006).
9. Peter C. Perdue, *China Marches West: The Qing Conquest of Central Eurasia* (Cambridge, MA: Belknap Press of Harvard University Press, 2005).
10. For the leading scholarship on the Qing ruler's identity and how they upheld it, see Pamela Kyle Crossley, *A Translucent Mirror: History and Identity in Qing Imperial Ideology* (Berkeley: University of California Press, 2002); Mark Elliot, *The Manchu Way: The Eight Banners and Ethnic Identity in Late Imperial China* (Stanford, CA: Stanford University Press, 2001). For the Qing's imperial institution, see Rawski, *The Last Emperors*; Beatrice S. Bartlett, *Monarchs and Ministers: The Grand Council in Mid-Ch'ing China, 1723–1820* (Berkeley: University of California Press, 1991).
11. Qi Meiqin, *Qingdai Neiwufu* [Department of the Imperial Household in the Qing] (Shenyang: Liaoning minzu chubanshe, 2009); Preston M. Torbert, *The Ch'ing Imperial Household Department: A Study of Its Organization and Principal Functions, 1662–1796*, Harvard East Asian Monographs 71 (Cambridge, MA: Council on East Asian Studies, Harvard University, 1977).
12. Bartlett, *Monarchs and Ministers*.
13. The original title in the Tibetan language is *rgya nag yul du dam pa'i chos dart shul gtso bor bshad pa blo gsal kun tu dga' ba'i rna rgyan ces bya ba bzhugs so* [The enchanting earring of the omniscient minds: An explanation for the spread of the Dharma in the land of China]. Several modern editions of the text exist: mgon po skyabs, *rgya nag yul du dam pa'i chos dart shul gtso bor bshad pa blo gsal kun tu dga' ba'i rna rgyan ces bya ba bzhugs so* [The enchanting earring of the omniscient minds: An explanation for the spread of the Dharma in the land of China], transl. blo bzang bstan 'dzin (Luosang Danzeng) (Beijing: krung go'i bod rig pa dpe skrun khang, 2005); Gung mGon-po skyabs-mchog, *lyul-du dam-pa'i chos dar-tshul gtso-bor bshad-pa blo-gsal kun-tu dga'-ba'i rna-rgyan zhes-bya-ba bzhugs* [The penetration and the spread of Buddhism in China] (Berkeley, CA: Namgyal Dorje Dalama, 1969). Thanks to Cynthia Col for providing information on the other editions.
14. mgon-po-skyabs, *rgya nag chos 'byungs*, 173.
15. mgon-po-skyabs, *rgya nag chos 'byungs*.
16. Gray Tuttle and Johan Elverskog, eds., "Wutaishan and Qing Culture," special issue, *Journal of the International Association of Tibetan Studies* 6 (December 2011).
17. Wen-Shing Chou, *Mount Wutai: Visions of a Sacred Buddhist Mountain* (Princeton, NJ: Princeton University Press, 2018), 72.

4. GOVERNANCE

18. Johan Elverskog, "Wutai Shan, Qing Cosmopolitanism, and the Mongols," *Journal of the International Association of Tibetan Studies* 6 (December 2011): 243–74; Isabelle Charleux, "Mongol Pilgrimages to Wutai Shan in the Late Qing Dynasty," *Journal of the International Association of Tibetan Studies* 6 (December 2011): 275–326.
19. Peter Schwieger, "History as Myth: On the Appropriation of the Past in Tibetan Culture, an Essay in Cultural Studies," in *The Tibetan History Reader*, ed. Gray Tuttle and Kurtis R. Schaeffer (New York: Columbia University Press, 2013), 74.
20. Leonard W. J. van der Kuijp, "Tibetan Historiography," in *Tibetan Literature: Studies in Genre*, ed. José Cabezón and Roger Jackson (Ithaca, NY: Snow Lion Publications, 1996), 39–57.
21. See Bira, *Mongolian Historical Literature*, n. 8. Bira dates Gombjab's text to 1736. mgon po skyabs, *rgya nag yul du dam pa'i chos dart shul gtso bor bshad pa blo gsal kun tu dga' ba'i rna rgyan ces bya ba bzhugs so*. The 2005 translation refers to the text as *Hanqu Fojiao yuanliu ji* (History of Buddhism in China). For a discussion of this particular edition, see Françoise Wang-Toutain, "Circulation Du Savoir Entre La Chine, La Mongolie et Le Tibet Au XVIIIe Siècle : Le Prince MGon-Po Skyabs" [Circulation of knowledge between China, Mongolia, and Tibet in the 18th century: Prince mGon-po Skyabs], *Études Chinoises* 24 (2005): 57–111; Fan Zhang, "Reorienting the Sacred and Accommodating the Secular: The History of Buddhism in China (rGya Nag Chos 'Byung)," *Revue d'Études Tibétaines* 37 (2016): 569–91. Thanks to the anonymous reader for pointing out other texts in the genre.
22. Johan Elverskog, *Our Great Qing: The Mongols, Buddhism and the State in Late Imperial China* (Honolulu: University of Hawai'i Press, 2006), 136. On the genre of *chos 'byung* (roughly translated as "history of Buddhism" or "origin of Buddhism"), see van der Kuijp, "Tibetan Historiography," 46.
23. Elverskog, *Our Great Qing*, 136.
24. Elverskog, *Our Great Qing*.
25. mgon-po-skyabs, *rgya nag chos 'byungs*, 193.
26. Elverskog, *Our Great Qing*, 127–65.
27. Schwieger, "History as Myth," 69.
28. Dominique Townsend explains that Geluk monasteries in Central Tibet, especially the three great seats, did not encourage monks to write extensively, for fear that writing would mobilize them to engage in politics, but writing among Geluk monks in eastern Tibet seemed central to their Buddhist studies. For more, see Dominique Townsend, *A Buddhist Sensibility: Aesthetic Education at Tibet's Mindröling Monastery*, Studies of the Weatherhead East Asian Institute, Columbia University (New York: Columbia University Press, 2021), 141.
29. For a concise introduction to this figure, see Ron Garry, "Rigdzin Tsewang Norbu," The Treasury of Lives, https://treasuryoflives.org/biographies/view/Rigdzin-Tsewang-Norbu/9372 (BDRC P676). For his political career, see Michael Monhart, "Seeing All as One, Mediating Between Gods, Humans, and Demons: The Travels of Katok Tsewang Norbu, 1749–1751" (master's thesis, Columbia University, 2011). For his home monastery and Kham religiopolitical practice, see Jann Michael Ronis, "Celibacy, Revelations, and Reincarnated Lamas: Contestation and Synthesis in the Growth of Monasticism at Katok Monastery from the 17th Through 19th Centuries" (PhD diss., University of Virginia, 2009).

4. GOVERNANCE

30. Rigzin Tsewang Norbu, *gsung 'bum/_tshe dbang nor bu* [Rigzin Tsewang Norbu's collected works], 4 vols. (Darjeeling: Kargyud sungrab nyamso khang, 1973), ff. 724 (BDRC W23176).
31. Bira, *Mongolian Historical Literature*, 32–40.
32. Kurtis R. Schaeffer, *The Culture of the Book in Tibet* (New York: Columbia University Press, 2009); Joseph Scheier-Dolberg, "Treasure House of Tibetan Culture: Canonization, Printing, and Power in the Derge Printing House" (master's thesis, Harvard University, 2005).
33. I use the modern typeset edition: mgon po skyabs, *rgya nag chos 'byungs* [History of Buddhism in China] (1983; repr., Chengdu: si khron mi rigs dpe skrunkhang, 1998), 265–66 (BDRC W21925). Many thanks to Lauran Hartley and Sonam Tsering Ngulphu for helping me identify the sources listed in Gombjab's colophon.
34. Benjamin Nourse, "Politics and Printing in Eighteenth-Century Co ne" (paper presented at the Twelfth Seminar of the International Association of Tibetan Studies, August 17, 2010); Sonam Dorje and Catherine Tsuji, "The Eleventh Ruler of Chone, Makzor Gonpo," The Treasury of Lives, http://treasuryoflives.org/biographies/view/Eleventh-Chone-Sakyong-Makzor-Gonpo/6346.
35. Yudru Tsomu, *The Rise of Gönpo Namgyel in Kham: The Blind Warrior of Nyarong* (Lanham, MD: Lexington Books, 2014), 214n55. For the Dergé Printery, see Kurtis R. Schaeffer, "Si tu paṇ chen on Scholarship," *Journal of the International Association of Tibetan Studies* 7 (August 2013): 302–15, http://www.thlib.org?tid=T5752. Large print houses in Amdo include Labrang Tashikyil print house and co ne dgon chen print house, both of which are in southern Gansu Province. See "co ne dgon chen," Buddhist Digital Resource Center, BDRC G435, http://tbrc.org/link?RID=G435.
36. For more on Dergé, see Lauran Hartley, "The Kingdom of Dergé," in Tuttle and Schaeffer, *The Tibetan History Reader*, 525–48, esp. 541n7; Ronis, "Celibacy, Revelations, and Reincarnated Lamas," 33–42; Evelyn S. Rawski, "Qing Publishing in Non-Han Languages," in *Printing and Book Culture in Late Imperial China*, ed. Cynthia Brokaw and Kai-wing Chou (Berkeley: University of California Press, 2005), 304–31.
37. Paul Harrison, "A Brief History of the Tibetan bKa' 'gyur," in Cabezón and Jackson, *Tibetan Literature*, 86.
38. Harrison, "A Brief History"; Walther Heissig, *Die Pekinger Lamaistischen Blockdrucke in Mongolischer Sprache; Materialien Zur Mongolischen Literaturgeschichte* [Tibetan Buddhist block prints in the Mongolian language in Beijing and Mongolian literary history], Göttinger Asiatische Forschungen; Monographienriehe Zur Geschichte, Sprache Und Literatur der Völker Süd-, Ost- Und Zentraiasiens (Wiesbaden: O. Harrassowitz, 1954). For a list of monastic printing houses (Tib.: *Par khang*) in Central Tibet, see Gene Smith, *dbus gtsang khul du shing par ji bzhugs kyi dkar chag phan bde'i pad tshal 'byed pa'i nyin byed* / [Printeries in Central Tibet], BDRC W1KG9262, http://tbrc.org/link?RID=W1KG9262. For Labrang Tashikhyil, see Paul Nietupski, *Labrang Monastery: A Tibetan Buddhist Community on the Inner Asian Borderlands, 1709–1958* (Lanham, MD: Lexington Books, 2010), 26, 84, 130, 140, 207. For a map of historical printing houses in the Himalayas, see http://worldmap.harvard.edu/maps/tibet.
39. Rawski, "Qing Publishing in Non-Han Languages," 304–25.

4. GOVERNANCE

40. mgon po skyabs, *Rgya nag chos 'byungs*, 265–66.
41. Oidtmann, *Forging the Golden Urn*, 258n129.
42. Guilaine Mala identifies this figure differently. The trülku line to which Lobzang Tenpai Nyima belonged remains underexplored. His predecessor went to Mongolia, and Tibetan sources indicate that he returned to northeastern Tibet and his reincarnate was found in Amdo, in Lobzang Tenpai Nyima. But the honorific title Sertri appeared in names found in Mongolia. Further research may yield a conclusive understanding of the reincarnation lineage. For Mala's identification of the text's commissioner, see Guilaine Mala, "A Mahayanist Rewriting of the History of China by Mgon Po Skyabs in the Rgya Nag Chos 'Byung," in *Power, Politics, and the Reinvention of Tradition: Tibet in the Seventeenth and Eighteenth Centuries*, ed. Brian Cuevas and Kurtis Schaeffer (Leiden: Brill, 2006), 145–69.
43. David Jackson, "Lineages and Structure in Tibetan Buddhist Painting: Principles and Practice of an Ancient Sacred Choreography," *Journal of the International Association of Tibetan Studies* 1 (October 2005): 5.
44. Gombjab, Preface to the *Canon of Buddhist Iconometry*, Rare Books and Manuscripts Collection, Tsinghua University, Beijing.
45. Terese Tse Bartholomew, "Introduction to the Art of Mongolia," September 7, 1995, https://www.asianart.com/mongolia/introduct.html, nn. 4–6.
46. Bryan J. Cuevas and Kurtis R. Schaeffer, eds., *Power, Politics, and the Reinvention of Tradition: Tibet in the Seventeenth and Eighteenth Centuries* (Leiden: Brill, 2006).
47. Janet Gyatso, "Experience, Empiricism, and the Fortunes of Authority: Tibetan Medicine and Buddhism on the Eve of Modernity," in *Forms of Knowledge in Early Modern Asia: Explorations in the Intellectual History of India and Tibet, 1500–1800*, ed. Sheldon Pollock (Durham, NC: Duke University Press, 2011): 311–35.
48. Sonam Dorje, "Ngawang Trinle Gyatso," The Treasury of Lives, https://treasuryoflives.org/zh/biographies/view/Ngawang-Trinle-Gyatso/13547; Shihong Yang, *Zhuoni Tusi Lishi Wenhua* [History and culture of the Co Ne chieftains] (Lanzhou: Gansu minzu chubanshe, 2007).
49. BDRC G435; Tib.: co ne dga' ldan bshad sgrub gling.
50. Luo Wenhua, *Longpao yu jiaosha: Qinggong Zangchuan Fojiao wenhua kachao* [The emperor's court dress and robes: Tibetan Buddhist culture in the Qing court] (Beijing: Zijincheng Chubanshe, 2005), 90. Luo identified the commissioner as a monk from Taozhou, modern-day Shaanxi Province. I have yet to locate a Chandi Si in the Shaanxi region since the Qing period, and the region of Taozhou fell outside of Shaanxi in the Qing.
51. grags pa bshad sgrub, *co ne bstan 'gyur* [Catalogue of the co ne bstan 'gyur] (co ne dgon chen: co ne par khang, 1926), 209 vols (BDRC W1GS66030).
52. Vladimir Uspensky, "Gombjab: A Tibetan Buddhist in the Capital of the Qing Empire," in *Biographies of Eminent Mongol Buddhists*, ed. Johan Elverskog (Halle: International Institute for Tibetan and Buddhist Studies, 2008), 59–60.
53. Chen Qingying, *Zhongguo xibei wenxian congshu, Xibei shaoshuminzu yuyan wenxian* [Collections of bibliographical materials in minority languages in northwestern China] (Lanzhou: Lanzhou guji chubanshe, 1990), vol. 154; Danqu, *Zhuoni Zangchuan Fojiao lishi wenhua* [History and culture of Cho ne Tibetan Buddhism] (Lanzhou: Gansu minzu chubanshe, 2007), 189.

4. GOVERNANCE

54. For a concise biographical account of Prince Guo, Vladimir L. Uspensky, *Prince Yunli (1697–1738): Manchu Statesman and Tibetan Buddhist* (Tokyo: Institute for the Study of Languages and Cultures of Asia and Africa, 1997), 2–5.
55. Luciano Petech, "Administration of Tibet During the First Half-Century of Chinese Protectorate," in Tuttle and Schaeffer, *The Tibetan History Reader*, 389–410.
56. Peter Schwieger, *The Dalai Lama and the Emperor of China: A Political History of the Tibetan Institution of Reincarnation* (New York: Columbia University Press, 2015), 112–45.
57. The third Tukwan, Lobzang Chokyi Nyima, *khyab bdag rdo rje sems dpa'i ngo bo dpal ldan bla ma dam pa ye shes bstan pa'i sgron me dpal bzang po'i rnam par thar pa mdo tsam brjod pa dge ldan bstan pa'i mdzes rgyan* [The major biography of the third Changkya, Rolpai Dorje] (Lanzhou: Kan-suu mi rigs dpe skrun khan, 1989), 140. For the second Tukwan, Ngawang Chokyi Gyatso, see Samten Chhosphel, "The Second Tukwan, Ngawang Chokyi Gyatso," The Treasury of Lives, http://treasuryoflives.org/biographies/view/Tukwan-02-Ngawang-Chokyi-Gyatso/3225.
58. The seventh Dalai Lama, Kelzang Gyatso, *khri chen sprul sku blo bzang bstan pa'i nyi ma dpal bzang po'i rnam par thar pa dpyod ldan yid dbang 'gugs pa'i pho nya* [The biography of the second Sertri, Lobzang Tenpai Nyima], in *gsung 'bum/_bskal bzang rgya mtsho* [Collected works of skal bzang rgya mtsho] (gangtok: dodrup sangye, 1975–1983), 10:345–448 (BDRC W2623). For the role of imperial women in Buddhist activities in the imperial core families, see Rawski, *The Last Emperors*, 128–60.
59. Nara Chuuktu, "Guo qinwang Yunli yiji Mengyi Fuzangjing" [Prince Guo and the treasure texts in Mongolian translation], *Qingshi yanjiu* [Qing history research] 3 (2002): 99–105.
60. Janet Gyatso, "Drawn from the Tibetan Treasury: The gTer ma Literature," in *Tibetan Literature: Studies in Genre*, ed. José Cabezón and Roger Jackson (Ithaca, NY: Snow Lion, 1996), 147; Ronald M. Davidson, *Tibetan Renaissance: Tantric Buddhism in the Rebirth of Tibetan Culture* (New York: Columbia University Press, 2005); Anya Bernstein, *Religious Bodies Politic: Rituals of Sovereignty in Buryat Buddhism* (Chicago: University of Chicago Press, 2013), 96–98.
61. Hanung Kim, "Renaissance Man from Amdo: The Life and Scholarship of the Eighteenth-Century Amdo Scholar Sum Pa Mkhan Po Ye Shes Dpal 'Byor (1704–1788)" (PhD diss., Harvard University, 2018), 57.
62. Rawski, *The Last Emperors*, 96–126.
63. Yael Bentor, "Literature on Consecration (Rab Gnas)," *Tibetan Literature: Studies in Genre*, ed. José Cabezón and Roger Jackson (Ithaca, NY: Snow Lion Publications, 1996), 298.
64. Uspensky, *Prince Yunli*, 22.
65. Bentor, "Literature on Consecration," 299–300.
66. Prince Guo Yunli, *Xizang riji* [Diary to Tibet] (repr., Beijing: Quanguo tushuguan wenxian suowei fuzhi zhongxin, 1992), 1.
67. Yunli, *Diary to Tibet*, 11. The title of dusi was ranked 4a in the Qing, a subordinate to a brigade commander in the Green Standards, a Chinese military force. See entry 7285, Hucker, *A Dictionary of Official Titles*, 542.
68. Yunli, *Diary to Tibet*.

4. GOVERNANCE

69. Prince Guo's *Diary to Tibet* was not the first travelogue documenting Qing's functionaries making their way to Tibet. In 1721, Jiao Yingqi wrote *Report on an Expedition to Tibet* (*Zang cheng jilüe*) on his mission to Tibet, deployed by the Kangxi emperor. See Nicole Willock, "An Analysis of Jiao Yingqi's 'Report on an Expedition to Tibet (Zangcheng jilüe)' Written in 1721 and the Historical Significance of this Source Material" (master's thesis, University of Hamburg, 2001).
70. Rawski, *The Last Emperors*, 125. Uspensky, *Prince Yunli*, 1997.
71. Prince Zhuang previously oversaw the Department of the Imperial Household in 1722.
72. It seemed that he was involved in networking with other close imperial clansmen and was removed for possible conspiracy against the emperor. See Mark P. McNicholas, *Forgery and Impersonation in Imperial China: Popular Deceptions and the High Qing State* (Seattle: University of Washington Press, 2015), 41.
73. Chen Jiahua, "Manzu kexuejia Yunlu jiqi zhushu" [The Manchu scientist Yunlu and his writings], *Minzu yanjiu* [Research on ethnicities] 4 (1992): 40–47.
74. Elverskog, *Our Great Qing*, 256.
75. Wen Ming and Wenhua Luo, "Xianruoguan gongcang cacafo zhengli yanjiu-qian ji yu Zhu fo Pusa shengxiang zan zhi bijiao" [Tsa-tsa statues in the Xianruo Hall and their comparisons with the Tibetan Buddhist pantheon), *Gugong Bowuyuan yuankan* [Journal of the National Palace Museum] 5 (2009): 49.
76. Wen and Luo, "Xianruoguan gongcang."
77. Bartlett, *Monarchs and Ministers*, 181–84.
78. Elverskog, *Our Great Qing*, 256.
79. Rawski, *The Last Emperors*, 96–126.
80. Rebecca Nedostup, *Superstitious Regimes: Religion and the Politics of Chinese Modernity* (Cambridge, MA: Harvard University Asia Center, 2010), 3.
81. Benjamin A. Elman, *On Their Own Terms: Science in China, 1550–1900* (Cambridge, MA: Harvard University Press, 2005).
82. Stacey van Vleet, "Medicine, Monasteries and Empire: Tibetan Buddhism and the Politics of Learning in Qing China" (PhD diss., Columbia University, 2015).
83. Berger, *Empire of Emptiness*; David Farquhar, "Emperor as Bodhisattva in the Governance of the Ch'ing Empire," *Harvard Journal of Asiatic Studies* 38, no. 1 (1978).
84. Kim Sung Soo [Jin Chengxiu], *Ming Qing zhiji zangchuan fojiao zai Menggu diqu chuanbo* [Tibetan Buddhism in Mongolia during the Ming and Qing] (Beijing: Shehui kexue wenxian chubanshe, 2006).
85. On trülkus residing in Beijing, see Chen Xiaomin, *Qingdai zhujing Lama Yanjiu* [A study of Lamas in Beiing in the Qing period] (Beijing: Beijing yan shan Chubanshe, 2011).
86. The full title in Wylie is '*dzam gling chen po'i rgyas bshad snod bcud kun gsal me long* (BDRC W00KG03991).
87. Serkhok Monastery is also known as Tsenpo Gon or Dga' ldan dam chos gling (BDRC G294). Lobsang Yongdan, "Tibet Charts the World: Btsan Po No Mon Han's 'The Detailed Description of the World,' an Early Major Scientific Work in Tibet," in *Mapping the Modern in Tibet*, ed. Gray Tuttle (Andiast: International Institute for Tibetan and Buddhist Studies, 2011).
88. Yongdan, "Tibet Charts the World," 115.

4. GOVERNANCE

89. Toni Huber, *The Holy Land Reborn: Pilgrimage and the Tibetan Reinvention of Buddhist India* (Chicago: University of Chicago Press, 2008), 193–232.
90. *Zhongguo wenshi ziliao jicui* [Collection of Chinese literary and historical documents] (Beijing: Beijing Superstar International Technology, 2006), 113. For information on a later reincarnate of the Kagyurwa lineage, see Paul Hyer, *A Mongolian Living Buddha: Biography of the Kanjurwa Khutughtu* (Bloomington: Indiana University Press, 1984). Thanks to Gray Tuttle for recommending this publication. The other Buddhist named in the colophon was Tsendrok nomönhen Jampel Tenba Rapgyé; information about him is currently insufficient for a positive identification.
91. Benjamin Nourse, email communication with author, December 10, 2018.
92. The fourth Tsenpo Mindrol Nominhan, Jampel Chokyi Tendzin Trinle, *'dzam glingchen po'i rgyas bshad snod bcud kun gsal me long* [Geography of the world] (1830, woodblock prints found in the palace library, gagtok, Sikkim; repr. 1980), 408 (BDRC P4994).
93. For the aspect of knowledge transmission, see Helen Watson-Verran and David Turnbull, "Science and Other Indigenous Knowledge Systems," in *Handbook of Science and Technology Studies*, ed. Sheila Jasanoff et al. (Thousand Oaks, CA: Sage Publications, 1995), 115–39.
94. The "new schools" (Tib.: Sarmapa) was an umbrella term including the Sakya, Kagyü, and Kadam schools, which were introduced into Tibet between the tenth and twelfth centuries. They were "new" in comparison to the ancient Nyingma School that was introduced to Tibet in the seventh to ninth centuries. The Kadam School ceased to exist as a school by the end of the sixteenth century, but its teachings were found in all the four major schools of Tibetan Buddhism, especially the Gelug School. For more, see Geoffrey Samuel, "The Subtle Body in India and Beyond," in *Religion and the Subtle Body in Asia and the West: Between Mind and Body*, ed. Geoffrey Samuel and Jay Johnston (London: Routledge, 2013), 47. Many thanks to Cynthia Col for pointing out the source.
95. Tadeusz Skorupski, "The Canonical Tantras of the New School," in *Tibetan Literature: Studies in Genre*, ed. José Cabezón and Roger Jackson (Ithaca, NY: Snow Lion Publications, 1996), 95.
96. I thank one of the anonymous reviewers for pointing out this distinction.
97. Oidtmann, *Forging the Golden Urn*; Matthew W. King, *Ocean of Milk, Ocean of Blood: A Mongolian Monk in the Ruins of the Qing empire* (New York: Columbia University Press, 2019).
98. Laura Hostetler, *Qing Colonial Enterprise: Ethnography and Cartography in Early Modern China* (Chicago: University of Chicago Press, 2005); Waley-Cohen, *The Culture of War in China*; Elman, *On Their Own Terms*.
99. For Faššan and this project, see Michele Matteini, "Fashishan as Patron and Antiquarian in Jiaqing-Period Beijing" (presentation at the Annual Conference of the Association for Asian Studies, Chicago, March 28, 2015).
100. Mi Yanqing, "Qingdai zhongqi Mengguzu jiazu wenxue yu wenxue jiazu" [An overview of Mongolian family literature and literary families in mid-Qing Dynasty], *Neimenggu daxue xuebao: Zhexue yu shehui kexue ban* [Journal of Inner Mongolian University: Philosophy and social sciences] 43, no. 2 (March 2011): 5–8.

101. Mosca, *From Frontier Policy to Foreign Policy*.
102. Stephen Roddy, "Toward Buddhist Cosmopolitanism: The Pan-Asian Vision of Gong Zizhen," in *Cosmopolitanism in China, 1600–1950*, ed. Minghui Hu and Johan Elverskog (Amherst, NY: Cambria Press, 2016), 146.
103. Karl Debreczeny, "The Art Historical Context of Antwerp's Vairocana Album," in *The All-Knowing Buddha: A Secret Guide*, ed. Karl Debreczeny et al. (Seattle: University of Washington Press, 2014), 26.
104. Chou, *Mount Wutai*; Wen-Shing Chou, "Maps of Wutai Shan: Individuating the Sacred Landscape through Color," *Journal of the International Association of Tibetan Studies* 6 (2011): 372–88; Wen-Shing Chou, "Ineffable Paths: Mapping Wutaishan in Qing-Dynasty China," *Art Bulletin* 89, no. 1 (March 2007): 108–29.
105. Kurtis Schaeffer, "Tibetan Poetry on Wutai Shan," *Journal of the International Association of Tibetan Studies* 6 (2011): 215–42.
106. Johan Elverskog, "Wutai Shan, Qing Cosmopolitanism, and the Mongols," *Journal of the International Association of Tibetan Studies* 6 (2011): 243–74; Gray Tuttle, "Tibetan Buddhism at Wutai Shan in the Qing," *Journal of the International Association of Tibetan Studies* 6 (2011): 163–214.

EPILOGUE

1. Fernanda Pirie, "The Limits of the State: Coercion and Consent in Chinese Tibet," *Journal of Asian Studies* 72, no. 1 (February 2013): 69–89; see especially the first case introduced in the study, 81–83.
2. Ben Hillman, "Monastic Politics and the Local State in China: Authority and Autonomy in an Ethnically Tibetan Prefecture," *China Journal* 54 (July 2005): 29–51.
3. David Germano, "Re-membering the Dismembered Body of Tibet: The Contemporary Ter Movement in the PRC," in *Buddhism in Contemporary Tibet: Religious Revival and Cultural Identity*, ed. Melvyn Goldstein and Matthew Kapstein (Berkeley: University of California Press, 1998), 64.
4. Thomas Borchert, "The Abbot's New House: Thinking About How Religion Works Among Buddhists and Ethnic Minorities in Southwest China," *Journal of Church and State* 52, no. 1 (December 2010): 112–37.
5. Nicole Willock, *Lineages of the Literary: Tibetan Buddhist Polymaths of Socialist China* (New York: Columbia University Press, 2021), 7.
6. Jonathan Spence, *The Search for Modern China* (New York: Norton, 1991), 202.
7. Benno Weiner, *The Chinese Revolution on the Tibetan Frontier*, Studies of the Weatherhead East Asian Institute, Columbia University (Ithaca, NY: Cornell University Press, 2020), 13.
8. Quoted in Spence, *The Search for Modern China*, 200.
9. Gray Tuttle, *Tibetan Buddhists in the Making of Modern China* (New York: Columbia University Press, 2005).
10. C. Patterson Giersch, "'Grieving for Tibet': Conceiving the Modern State in Late-Qing Inner Asia," *China Perspectives* 3 (July 2008): 4–18.

BIBLIOGRAPHY

PRIMARY SOURCES IN TIBETAN, CHINESE, MONGOLIAN, AND MANCHU

blo bzang tshe 'phel. *chen po Hor gyi yul du dam pa'i chos ji ltar byuṅ ba'i bśad pa rgyal ba'i bstan pa rin po che gsal bar byed pa'i sgron me* [History of Buddhism in Mongolia]. Xining: mtsho snong mi rigs dpe skrun khang, 1993.

brag dgon dkon mchog bstan pa rab rgyas. *yul mdo smad kyi ljongs su thub bstan rin po che ji ltar dar ba'i tshul gsal bar brjod pa Deb ther rgya mtsho* [The ocean annals of Amdo]. Lanzhou: Kan su'u mi rigs dpe skrun khang, 1982.

"co ne dgon chen." Buddhist Digital Resource Center, BDRC G435, http://tbrc.org/link?RID=G435.

Desi, Sangye Gyatso. *dga'-ldan chos 'byung Baiḍūrya ser po* [Yellow Beryl: The history of Dge-lugs-pa sect and its monasteries in Tibet]. Beijing: Kruṅ-go Bod kyi śes rig dpe skrun khang, 1991.

dkon mchog 'jigs med dbang po. "'jam dbyangs bzhad pa'i rnam thar." Lanzhou: Kan su'u mi rigs dpe skrun khang, 1989.

dkon mchog rgyal mtshan. *bla brang bkra shis 'khyil gyi gdan rabs lha'i rnga chen* [History of Bla brang Bkra shis 'khyil]. Vol 1. Lanzhou: Kan su'u mi rigs dpe skrun khang, 1987.

"Dolonnuur ting diaocha ji" [Survey of Duolun Nuo'er]. *Dongfang zazhi* [Oriental magazine] 10, no. 11.

First Historical Archives of China and Yonghegong Administration Office. *Qingdai Yonghegong Dang'an shiliao* [Yonghegong archival documents in the Qing dynasty]. Beijing: Zhongguo minzu sheying chubanshe, 2004.

BIBLIOGRAPHY

The fourth Tsenpo Nominhan, Jampel Chokyi Tendzin Trinle. *'dzam glingchen po'i rgyas bshad snod bcud kun gsal me long* [Geography of the world]. 1830, woodblock prints found in the palace library, gagtok, Sikkim. Reprint, 1980.

Gansu Library Reference Cataloguing Department, ed. *Xibei minzu zongjiao shiliao wenzhai* [Selected essays on the religious history of the northwestern ethnicity]. Lanzhou: Gansu tushuguan, 1984.

Gongzhongdang Qianlong chao zouzhe [Memorials of the Qianlong reign]. Taipei: Guoli Gugong bowuyuan, 1982.

grags pa bshad sgrub. *co ne bstan 'gyur* [Catalogue of the co ne bstan 'gyur]. 209 vols. co ne dgon chen: co ne par khang, 1926.

The Grand Council's Correspondences in Manchu Language, First Historical Archives of China, Beijing, China. Archival identification number: 03-133-5-038.

gser tog Blo bzang tshul khrims rgya mtsho. *sku 'bum byams pa gling gi gdan rabs don ldan tshaṅs pa'i dbyangs snyan* [Monastic chronicle of the Kumbum Monastery]. Xining: mtsho sgnon mi rigs dpe skrun khang, 1983.

The first Jamyang Zhepa, ngagwang tsondru. *gsung 'bum/_'jam dbyangs bzhad pa'i rdo rje* [Collected works of bgangwang tsondru]. Vol. 1. South India: Gomang College, 1997.

mgon po skyabs. *The Canon of Buddhist Iconometry*. Rare Books and Manuscripts Collections, Tshinghua University, Beijing, China.

——. [Gung mGon-po skyabs-mchog]. *lyul-du dam-pa'i chos dar-tshul gtso-bor bshad-pa blo-gsal kun-tu dga'-ba'i rna-rgyan zhes-bya-ba bzhugs* [The penetration and the spread of Buddhism in China]. Berkeley, CA: Namgyal Dorje Dalama, 1969.

——. *rgya nag chos 'byungs* [History of Buddhism in China]. 1983. Reprint, Chengdu: si khron mi rigs dpe skrunkhang, 1998.

——. *rgya nag yul du dam pa'i chos dart shul gtso bor bshad pa blo gsal kun tu dga' ba'i rna rgyan ces bya ba bzhugs so* [The enchanting earring of the omniscient minds: An explanation for the spread of the Dharma in the land of China], trans. blo bzang bstan 'dzin (Luosang Danzeng). Beijing: krung go'i bod rig pa dpe skrun khang, 2005.

mgon-po-skyabs, Jingfeng Cai, and Michael Henss, eds. *The Buddhist Canon of Iconometry: With Supplement*. Ulm: Fabri Verlag, 2000.

mi rigs dpe mdzod khang gi dpe tho las gsung 'bum skor gyi dkar chag shes bya'i gter mdzod [Catalogues of Tibetan collected works in Minzu Library]. 3 vols. khreng tu'u: si khron mi rigs dpe skrun khang, 1984–1997.

Mkhas grub dpal bzang po. *rgyud sde spyiḥi rnam par gźag pa rgyas par brjod* [mkhas grub rje's fundamentals of the Buddhist tantras]. Indo-Iranian Monographs. The Hague: Mouton: n.d.

National Archives of Mongolia, Ulaanbaatar, Mongolia. Catalog nos. series M 166-1, M166-2, and M166-3.

Nayancheng. *Nayancheng Qinghai zou yi* [Nayancheng's memorials on Qinghai affairs]. Xining: Qinghai renmin chubanshe, 1997.

Neige daku dang'an [Archive of the grand secretariat of the Qing dynasty]. Institute of History and Philosophy, Academia Sinica, Taipei.

Nian Gengyao. *Nian Gengyao Man Han zouzhe yi bian* [The annotated palace memorials of Nian Gengyao in Manchu and Chinese], ed. Ji Yonghai et al. Tianjin: Tianjin guji chubanshe, 1995.

BIBLIOGRAPHY

Qinghai Archive. Qingshi gongcheng [Qing history project]. Renmin University of China, Beijing.

The second Changkya, Ngawang Lobzang Choden. *ngag dbang blo bzang chos ldan'i gsung 'bum* [Collected works of the second Changkya, Ngawang Lobzang Choden]. 5 vols. Lhasa: zhol par khang chen mo, n.d.

The second 'jam dbyangs bzhad pa, dkon mchog 'jigs med dbang po. "le'u bcu gsum pa/ zhe hor dang pe cin du phebs nas gong ma chen lung rgyal po'i thugs bzhed bskangs pa'i skor/" [Section on the Sixth Panchen Lama's visit to Beijing]. In *rje bla ma srid zhi'i gtsug rgyan paN chen thams cad mkhyen pa blo bzang dpal ldan ye shes dpal bzang po'i zhal snga nas kyi rnam par thar pa nyi ma'i 'od zer* [The biography of the sixth Panchen Lama, Lobzang Pelden Yeshe], vol. 2, 924–1076. Beijing: krung go'i bod rig pa dpe skrun khang, 2002.

The second Jamyang Zhepa, Konchok Jigme Wangpo. *dkon mchog 'jigs med dbang po'i gsung 'bum* [Collected works of the second Jamyang Zhepa, Konchok Jigme Wangpo]. South India: Goman College, 1997.

Sertok Lobzang Tsültrim Gyatso. *sku 'bum byams pa gling gig dan rabs don ldan tshangs pa'i dbyangs snyan* [The monastic chronicle of Kumbum Monastery]. Xining: mtsho sngon mi rigs dpe skrun khang, 1982.

The seventh Dalai Lama, Kelzang Gyatso. *gsung 'bum/_bskal bzang rgya mtsho* [Collected works of skal bzang rgya mtsho]. gangtok: dodrup sangye, 1975–1983.

———. *khri chen sprul sku blo bzang bstan pa'i nyi ma dpal bzang po'i rnam par thar pa dpyod ldan yid dbang 'gugs pa'i pho nya* [The biography of the second Sertri, Lobzang Tenpai Nyima]. In *gsung 'bum/_bskal bzang rgya mtsho* [Collected works of skal bzang rgya mtsho]. gangtok: dodrup sangye, 1975–1983.

Sum pa mkhan po ye shes dpal 'byor.*'dzam gling spyi bshad* [Geography of the world]. 1777. Reprint, Delhi: International Academy of Indian Culture, 1975.

Thebo-Trinlé Ozer (Chenlie Aosai). "Introduction to the Zhabdrung Karpo Lineages." Unpublished manuscript.

The third Changkya, Rolpai Dorje. *skal bzang rgya mtsho'i rnam thar* [The biography of the seventh Dalai Lama, Kelzang Gyatso]. 2 vols. Lhasa: bod ljongs mi dmangs dpe skrun khang, 1990.

The third Detri, Jamyang Tubten Nyima. *'jam dbyangs thub bstan nyi ma'I gsung 'bum* [Collected works of Jamyang Tubten Nyima]. 6 vols. Labrang Monastery: blab rang bkra shis 'khyil par khang, [1999?].

The third Gungtang, Konchok Tenpai Drome. *Kun mkhyen 'jam dbyangs bzhad pa sku 'phreng gnyis pa rje 'jigs med dbang po'i rnam thar* [The biography of the second Jamyang Zhepa, Konchok Jigme Wangpo]. Lanzhou: kan su'u mi rigs dpe skrun khang, 1990.

The third Tukwan, Lobzang Chokyi Nyima. *gling bśad sgrub bstan pa'i 'byung gnas chos sde chen po dgon-lung-byams-pa-gling gi dkar chag dpyod ldan yid dbang 'gugs pa'i pho nya* [The monastic chronicle of Gönlung Jampa Ling]. Xining: mtsho sgnon mi rigs dpe skrun khang, 1988.

———. *khyab bdag rdo rje sems dpa'Io dpal ldan bla ma dam pa ye shes bstan pa'i sgron me dpal bzang po'i rnam par thar pa mdo tsam brjod pa dge ldan bstan pa'i mdzes rgyan* [The major biography of the third Changkya, Rolpai Dorje]. Lanzhou: Kan su'u mi rigs dpe skrun khang, 1989.

———. *Zhangjia Guoshi Ruobiduojie zhuan* [The biography of the imperial preceptor Changkya Rolpai Dorje], trans. Lianlong Ma and Qingying Chen. Beijing: Zhongguo Zangxue yanjiu zhongxin, 2007.

Thub bstan legs bśad rgya mtsho. *Gateway to the Temple: Manual of Tibetan Monastic Customs, Art, Building, and Celebrations: Originally Entitled a Requisite Manual for Faith and Adherence to the Buddhist Teaching, Including the Way of Entering the Door of Religion, the Root of the Teaching, the Method for Erecting Temples, the Resting Place of the Teaching, and Cycle of Religious Duties, the Performance of the Teaching.* Bibliotheca Himalayica, series 3, vol. 1. Kathmandu: Ratna Pustak Bhandar, 1979.

tshe 'phel. *chen po hor gyi yul du dam pa'i chos ji ltar byung ba'i bshad pa rgyal ba'i bstan pa rin po che gsal bar byed pa'i sgron me* [History of Buddhism in Mongolia]. Xining: mtsho sngon mi rigs dpe skrun khang, 1993.

Wen Da, Palace Museum, ed. Qinzheng pingding shuomo fanglue [General plans for imperial pacification of the north]. 1708; Hathi Trust Digital Library, 1970.

Wenfu. *Qinghai shiyi jielue* [Concise reports on Qinghai affairs]. Xining: Qinghai Renmin Chubanshe, 1993.

Zhabs drung 'jam pa'i dbyangs rim byon gyi 'khrungs rabs rnam par thar pa gsal bar byed pa'i rin po che baidurya'i me long [Biographies of the successive Stong 'khor reincarnates]. Beijing: Krung go'i Bod rig pa dpe skrun khang, 2005.

Zhongguo di 1 li shi dang an guan. *Qingdai Junjichu Manwen Aocha Dang* [Tea offering archives in the Manchu language of the grand council during the Qing]. Shanghai: Shanghai guji chubanshe, 2010.

SECONDARY SOURCES

Ágoston, Gábor. "A Flexible Empire: Authority and Its Limits on the Ottoman Frontiers." *International Journal of Turkish Studies* 9 (2003): 15–31.

Ahmad, Zahiruddin. *Sino-Tibetan Relations in the Seventeenth Century*. Serie Orientale Roma. Rome: Istituto italiano per il Medio ed Estremo Oriente, 1970.

Armitage, David. "Three Concepts of Altantic History." In *The British Atlantic World, 1500–1800*, ed. David Armitage and Michael J. Braddick, 11–29. Basingstoke: Palgrave Macmillan, 2002.

Aslanian, Sebouh David. *From the Indian Ocean to the Mediterranean: The Global Trade Networks of Armenian Merchants from New Julfa*. Berkeley: University of California Press, 2011.

Ates, Sabri. "Empires at the Margin: Towards a History of the Ottoman-Iranian Borderland and the Borderland Peoples, 1843–1881." PhD diss., New York University, 2006.

Bai Wengu and Xie Zhanlu. "Qingdai Lama yidanliang zhidu tantao" [A survey on the Lama's stipend practice of the Qing]. *Zhongguo zangxue* [China Tibetology] 3 (2006).

Balden, Charles, trans. and ed. *The Jebtsundamba Khutukhtus of Urga*. Asiatische Forschungen 9. Wiesbaden: O. Harrassowitz, 1961.

Barfield, Thomas J. *The Perilous Frontier: Nomadic Empires and China*. Studies in Social Discontinuity. Cambridge, MA: Basil Blackwell, 1989.

BIBLIOGRAPHY

Barkey, Karen. *Bandits and Bureaucrats: The Ottoman Route to State Centralization*. Ithaca, NY: Cornell University Press, 1996.
———. *Empire of Difference: The Ottomans in Comparative Perspective*. Cambridge: Cambridge University Press, 2008.
Bartholomew, Terese Tse. "Introduction to the Art of Mongolia." September 7, 1995. https://www.asianart.com/mongolia/introduct.html.
Bartlett, Beatrice S. *Monarchs and Ministers: The Grand Council in Mid-Ch'ing China, 1723–1820*. Berkeley: University of California Press, 1991.
Baud, Michiel, and Willem Van Schendel. "Toward a Comparative History of Borderlands." *Journal of World History* 8, no. 2 (October 1997): 211–42.
Baxter, Denise. "Introduction: Constructing Space and Identity in the Eighteenth-Century Interior." In *Architectural Space in Eighteenth-Century Europe: Constructing Identities and Interiors*, ed. Denise Baxter and Meredith Martin, 1–12. London: Routledge, 2016.
Bayly, C. A. *Empire and Information: Intelligence Gathering and Social Communication in India, 1780–1870*. Cambridge, Cambridge University Press, 1999.
Bayly, C. A., Sven Beckert, Matthew Connelly, Isabel Hofmeyr, Wendy Kozol, and Patricia Seed. "AHR Conversation: On Transnational History." *American Historical Review* 111, no. 5. (December 2006): 1441–64.
Bello, David A. *Across Forest, Steppe and Mountain: Environment, Identity and Empire in Qing China's Borderlands*. New York: Cambridge University Press, 2015.
———. "Relieving Mongols of Their Pastoral Identity: Disaster Management on the Eighteenth-Century Qing China Steppe." *Environmental History* 19, no. 3 (July 2014): 480–504.
Belsky, Richard. *Localities at the Center: Native Place, Space, and Power in Late Imperial Beijing*. Cambridge, MA: Harvard University Asia Center, 2006.
Bentor, Yael. "Literature on Consecration (Rab Gnas)." In *Tibetan Literature: Studies in Genre*, ed., José Ignocio Cabezón and Roger Jackson, 290–311. Ithaca, NY: Snow Lion Publications, 1996.
Berger, Patricia Ann. "After Xanadu: The Mongol Renaissance of the Sixteenth to the Eighteenth Centuries." In *Mongolia: The Legacy of Chinggis Khan*, ed. Patricia Berger and Terese Tse Bartholomew, 50–75. London: Thames and Hudson, 1996.
———. *Empire of Emptiness: Buddhist Art and Political Authority in Qing China*. Honululu: University of Hawai'i Press, 2003.
Bernstein, Anya. *Religious Bodies Politic: Rituals of Sovereignty in Buryat Buddhism*. Chicago: University of Chicago Press, 2013.
Bira, Sh. *Mongolian Historical Literature of the XVII–XIX Centuries Written in Tibetan*, trans. S. Frye. Bloomington, IN: Mongolia Society, 1970.
Bogin, Benjamin. *The Illuminated Life of the Great Yolmowa*. Chicago: Serindia Publications, 2013.
Borchert, Thomas. "The Abbot's New House: Thinking About How Religion Works Among Buddhists and Ethnic Minorities in Southwest China." *Journal of Church and State* 52, no. 1 (December 2010): 112–37.
Borjigidai, Uyunbilig. "The Hoshuud Polity in Khökhnuur (Kokonor)." *Inner Asia* 4 (2002): 181–96.
Bredon, Juliet. *Peking: A Historical and Intimate Description of Its Chief Places of Interest*. Shanghai: Kelly and Walsh, 1922.

BIBLIOGRAPHY

Brook, Timothy. "At the Margin of Public Authority: The Ming State and Buddhism." In *Culture and State in Chinese Society: Conventions, Accommodations, and Critiques*, ed. Theodore Huters, R. Bin Wong, and Pauline Yu, 161–81. Stanford, CA: Stanford University Press, 1997.

———. *Praying for Power: Buddhism and the Formation of Gentry Society in Late-Ming China*. Cambridge, MA: Harvard University Press, 1994.

Brophy, David. "The Junghar Mongol Legacy and the Language of Loyalty in Qing Xinjiang." *Harvard Journal of Asiatic Studies* 73, no. 2 (2013): 231–58.

Cabezón, José. "Firm Feet and Long Lives: The Zhabs brtan literature of Tibetan Buddhism." In *Tibetan Literature: Studies in Genre*, 344–57. Ithaca, NY: Snow Lion Publications, 1998.

Cabezón, José, and Penpa Dorjee. *Sera Monastery*. Somerville, MA: Wisdom Publications, 2019.

Cai Jiayi and Zhu Guangmei. "Xining banshi dachen de shezhi jiqi dui Qinghai diqu de guanzhi" [Establishment of the Xining banshi dachen and its management of Qinghai]. *Qinghai minzu yanjiu, shehui kexue ban* [Qinghai nationality research: Social science edition] 1 (1990): 30–35.

Caiwujiapu. "Qingchao shiqi de Xinjiang Zhunga'er hanguo zangchuan Fojiao" [Tibetan Buddhism in Zungharia in Xinjiang under the Qing]. *Xinjiang shifan daxue xuebao: Zhexue shehui kexue ban* [Bulletin of Xinjiang Normal University: Social science edition] 3 (2005): 66–73.

Campbell, Ian. *Knowledge and the Ends of Empire: Kazak Intermediaries and Russian Rule on the Steppe, 1731–1917*. Ithaca, NY: Cornell University Press, 2017.

Charleux, Isabelle. "Buddhist Monasteries in Southern Mongolia." In *The Buddhist Monastery: A Cross-cultural Survey*, ed. Pierre Pichard and Francois Lagirarde, 351–90. Paris: École Francaise d'Extrême-Orient, 2003. https://halshs.archives-ouvertes.fr/halshs-00409747/document.

———. *Catalogue of the Main Monasteries of Inner Mongolia*. 2006. https://halshs.archives-ouvertes.fr/halshs-01788006/document.

———. "From North India to Buryatia: The Sandalwood Buddha from the Mongols' Perspective." *Palace Museum Journal* 154, no. 2 (2011): 81–100.

———. "The Inner Mongol City of Hohhot/Guihuacheng in the Eyes of Western Travellers." In "Traveling to the Heart of Asia: A History of Western Encounters with Mongolia." Special issue, *Mongolica Pragensia'17* 10, no. 1 (2020): 37–88. https://halshs.archives-ouvertes.fr/halshs-02984229/document.

———. "The Making of Mongol Buddhist Art and Architecture: Artisans in Mongolia from the Sixteenth to the Twentieth Centuries." In *Meditation: The Art of Zanabazar and His School, Catalogue trilingue (polonaise, anglaise, mongol) de exposition éponyme organisée au Asia and Pacific Museum*, ed. Elvira Eevr Djaltchinova-Malets, 59–105. Warsow: Państwowe Muzeum Etnograficzne w Warszawie, 2010. https://halshs.archives-ouvertes.fr/halshs-00702140/document.

———. "Mongol Pilgrimages to Wutai Shan in the Late Qing Dynasty." *Journal of the International Association of Tibetan Studies* 6 (December 2011): 275–326.

———. *Nomads on Pilgrimage: Mongols on Wutaishan (China), 1800–1940*. Brill's Inner Asian Library 33. Leiden: Brill, 2015.

———. "Object #84: Vajrapani, Dolonnor (Dolonnnur), Mid-eighteenth Century." In *Himalayan Art in 108 Objects*. New York: Rubin Museum of Art, forthcoming.

BIBLIOGRAPHY

———. "Qing Imperial Mandalic Architecture for Gelugpa Pontiffs Between Beijing, Inner Mongolia and Amdo." In *Along the Great Wall: Architecture and Identity in China and Mongolia*, ed. Eric Lehner, Alexandra Harrer, and Hildegard Sint, 107–18. Vienna: IVER-ICRA, 2010.
Chatterjee, Indrani. *Forgotten Friends: Monks, Marriages, and Memories of Northeast India*. Oxford: Oxford University Press, 2013.
Chayet, Anne. "Architectural Wonderland: An Empire of Fictions." In *New Qing Imperial History: The Making of the Inner Asian Empire at Qing Chengde*, ed. James Millward, 33–53. London: Routledge Curzon, 2004.
———. *Les Temples de Jehol et leurs modèles tibétains* [The Jehol temples and their Tibetan models]. Paris: Editions Recherche sur les civilisations, 1985.
Chen Jiahua. "Manzhu kexuejia Yunlu jiqi zhushu" [The Manchu scientist Yunlu and his writings]. *Minzu yanjiu* [Research on ethnicities] 4 (1992): 40–47.
Chen Qingying. *Chen Qingying zangxue lunwen ji* [Chen Qingying's essays on Tibetan studies]. Vol. 2. Beijing: Zhongguo zangxue yanjiu zhongxin chubanshe, 2006.
———. *Zhongguo xibei wenxian congshu, Xibei shaoshuminzu yuyan wenxian* [Collections of bibliographical materials in minority languages in northwestern China]. Vol. 154. Lanzhou: Lanzhou guji chubanshe, 1990.
Chen Xiaomin. *Qingdai zhujing Lama Yanjiu* [A study of Lamas in Beijing in the Qing period]. Beijing: Beijing yan shan Chubanshe, 2011.
Chhosphel, Samten. "The Fifty-Fourth Ganden Tripa, Ngawang Chokden." The Treasury of Lives. https://treasuryoflives.org/biographies/view/Trichen-54-Ngawang-Chokden/6526.
———. "The Second Jamyang Zhepa, Konchok Jigme Wangpo." The Treasury of Lives. http://www.treasuryoflives.org/biographies/view/Jamyang-Zhepa-02-Konchok-Jigme-Wangpo/2996.
———. "The Second Tukwan, Ngawang Chokyi Gyatso." The Treasury of Lives. http://treasuryoflives.org/biographies/view/Tukwan-02-Ngawang-Chokyi-Gyatso/3225.
———. "The Sixty-First Ganden Tripa, Ngawang Tsultrim." The Treasury of Lives. http://treasuryoflives.org/biographies/view/Trichen-61-Ngawang-Tsultrim/5652.
———. "Sumpa Khenpo Yeshe Peljor." The Treasury of Lives. https://treasuryoflives.org/biographies/view/Sumpa-Khenpo-Yeshe-Peljor/5729.
Chou, Wen-Shing. "Ineffable Paths: Mapping Wutaishan in Qing-Dynasty China." In *Art Bulletin* 89, no. 1 (March 2007): 108–29.
———. "Maps of Wutai Shan: Individuating the Sacred Landscape through Color." *Journal of the International Association of Tibetan Studies* 6 (2011): 372–88.
———. *Mount Wutai: Visions of a Sacred Buddhist Mountain*. Princeton, NJ: Princeton University Press, 2018.
Clancy-Smith, Julia A. *Mediterraneans: North Africa and Europe in an Age of Migration, c. 1800–1900*. Berkeley: University of California Press, 2012.
Coleman, William M. "Making the State on the Sino-Tibetan Frontier: Chinese Expansion and Local Power in Batang, 1842–1939." PhD diss., Columbia University, 2014.
Coyiji. *Neimengu Lamajiao* [Lamaism in Inner Mongolia]. 2 vols. Unpublished private manuscripts.

——. *Neimenggu Zangchuan fojiao siyuan* [Tibetan Buddhist monasteries in Inner Mongolia]. Lanzhou: Gansu minzu chubanshe, 2014.
——. *Tangy-a-yin urusqal* [The current of Gangga]. Kökeqota: Öbör Mongyol-un arad-un keblel-ün qoriy-a, 1984.
Crossley, Pamela. *A Translucent Mirror: History and Identity in Qing Imperial Ideology*. Berkeley: University of California Press, 2002.
Crossley, Pamela, Helen Sui, and Donald Sutton, eds. *Empire at the Margins: Culture, Ethnicity, and Frontier in Early Modern China*. Berkeley: University of California Press, 2006.
Cuevas, Bryan J., and Kurtis R. Schaeffer, eds. *Power, Politics, and the Reinvention of Tradition: Tibet in the Seventeenth and Eighteenth Centuries*. Leiden: Brill, 2006.
Dai, Yingcong. *The Sichuan Frontier and Tibet: Imperial Strategy in the Early Qing*. Seattle: University of Washington Press, 2009.
Danqu. *Zhuoni Zangchuan Fojiao lishi wenhua* [History and culture of Cho ne Tibetan Buddhism]. Lanzhou: Gansu minzu chubanshe, 2007.
Davidson, Ronald M. *Tibetan Renaissance: Tantric Buddhism in the Rebirth of Tibetan Culture*. New York: Columbia University Press, 2005.
Dear, Devon. "Holy Rollers: Monasteries, Lamas, and the Unseen Transport of Chinese–Russian Trade, 1850–1911." *International Review of Social History* 59, no. S22 (December 2014): 69–88.
Debreczeny, Karl. "The Art Historical Context of Antwerp's Vairocana Album." In *The All-Knowing Buddha: A Secret Guide*, ed. Karl Debreczeny, Elena Pakhoutova, Christian Luczanits, and Jan van Alphen, 25–37. Seattle: University of Washington Press, 2014.
——. "Ethnicity and Esoteric Power: Negotiating the Sino-Tibetan Synthesis in Ming Buddhist Painting." PhD diss., University of Chicago, 2007.
Deimel, Claus and Freiherr Wolf-Dietrich Speck von Sternburg, and Grassimuseum. *Buddhas Leuchten und Kaisers Pracht: Die Pekinger Sammlung Hermann Speck von Sternburg* [Buddha's radiance and emperors: The Sammlung Hermann Speck von Sternburg's Peking collections]. Leipzig: Staatliche Ethnographische Sammlungen Sachsen, Grassi Museum für Völkerkunde, 2008.
Di Cosmo, Nicola. *Ancient China and Its Enemies: The Rise of Nomadic Power in East Asian History*. Cambridge: Cambridge University Press, 2004.
——. "Qing Colonial Administration in Inner Asia." *International History Review* 20, no. 2 (1998): 287–309.
——. "State Formation and Periodization in Inner Asian History." *Journal of World History* 10, no. 1 (1999): 1–40.
Di Cosmo, Nicola, and Dalizhabu Bao. *Manchu-Mongol Relations on the Eve of the Qing Conquest: A Documentary History*. Leiden: Brill, 2003.
Dorje, Sonam. "The Fifth Tongkhor, Ngawang Sonam Gyatso." The Treasury of Lives. https://treasuryoflives.org/biographies/view/Fifth-Tongkhor-Sonam-Gyatso/2755.
——. "Ngawang Trinle Gyatso." The Treasury of Lives. https://treasuryoflives.org/zh/biographies/view/Ngawang-Trinle-Gyatso/13547.
——. "The Second Tongkhor, Yonten Gyatso." The Treasury of Lives. https://treasuryoflives.org/biographies/view/Second-Tongkhor-Yonten-Gyatso/3708.

BIBLIOGRAPHY

———. "The Seventh Tatsak Jedrung, Lobzang Pelden Gyeltsen." The Treasury of Lives. http://treasuryoflives.org/biographies/view/Seventh-Tatsak-Jedrung-Lobzang-Pelden-Gyeltsen/9693.

———. "The Sixth Detri, Kelzang Khyenrab Gyatso." The Treasury of Lives. http://treasuryoflives.org/biographies/view/Sixth-Detri-Kelzang-Khyenrab-Gyatso/7876.

Dreyfus, Georges B. J. "An Introduction to Drepung's Colleges." The Tibetan and Himalayan Library. http://www.thlib.org/places/monasteries/drepung/essays/#essay=/dreyfus/drepung/colleges/s/b1.

———. "Law, State, and Political Ideology in Tibet." *Journal of the International Association of Buddhist Studies* 18, no. 1 (July 1995): 117–38.

———. "The Shuk-Den Affair: History and Nature of a Quarrel." *Journal of the International Association of Buddhist Studies* 21, no. 2 (1998): 227–70.

———. *The Sound of Two Hands Clapping: The Education of a Tibetan Buddhist Monk.* Berkeley: University of California Press, 2003.

Du, Jiayi. *Qingchao Man Meng lianyin yanjiu* [Studies of marriage alliances between the Mongols and Manchus in the Qing]. Beijing: Renmin Chubanshe, 2003.

Dung dkar blo bzang 'phrin las. *Dung Dkar Tshig Mdzod Chen Mo* [Dungkar Tibetological great dictionary]. Beijing: Zhongguo zangxue yanjiu chubanshe, 2002.

Dunnell, Ruth W., Mark C. Elliott, Philippe Forêt, and James A. Millward, eds. *New Qing Imperial History: The Making of the Inner Asian Empire at Qing Chengde.* London: Routledge, 2004.

Duolun xian wenshi weiyuanhui ed. *Duolun wenshi ziliao* [Duolun literary historical sources]. Hohhot: Neimenggu daxue chubanse: 2006.

———. *Duolun Xianzhi* [Duolun county gazetteer]. Haila'er: Neimenggu wenhua chubashe, 2000.

Eimer, Helmut. "Preliminary Remarks on the Second A-Kya." In *Tibetan Studies in Honor of Hugh Richardson: Proceedings of the International Seminar on Tibetan Studies, Oxford, 1979*, ed. Michael Aris and Aung San Suu Kyi, 97–103. Warminster: Aris and Phillips, 1979.

Elikhina, Yulia, and Victoria Demenova. "A Study of Stylistic Features and Metal Composition of Buddhist Scripture from Inner Mongolia (Dolonnor)." *Artibus Asiae* 80, no. 2 (2020): 145–66.

Elliot, Mark. "The Limits of Tartary: Manchuria in Imperial and National Geographies." *Journal of Asian Studies* 59, no. 3 (August, 2000): 603–46.

———. *The Manchu Way: The Eight Banners and Ethnic Identity in Late Imperial China.* Stanford, CA: Stanford University Press, 2001.

Elman, Benjamin A. *A Cultural History of Civil Examinations in Late Imperial China.* Berkeley: University of California Press, 2000.

———. *On Their Own Terms: Science in China, 1550–1900.* Cambridge, MA: Harvard University Press, 2005.

Elman, Benjamin, and A. Woodside, eds. *Education and Society in Late Imperial China, 1600–1900.* Berkeley: University of California Press, 1994.

Elverskog, Johan. *Our Great Qing: The Mongols, Buddhism and the State in Late Imperial China.* Honolulu: University of Hawai'i Press, 2006.

———. "The Tumu Incident and the Chinggisid Legacy in Inner Asia." *Silk Road* 15 (2017):142–52.

———. "Wutai Shan, Qing Cosmopolitanism, and the Mongols." *Journal of the International Association of Tibetan Studies* 6 (December 2011): 243–74.
Fang Jianchang. "Zangwen 'Shijie guanglun' duiyu Zhongguo dilixueshi de gongxian" [Cntribution of "Geography of the World" to the history of geography in China]. *Zhongguo lishi dili luncong* [Bulletin of history and geography of China] 4, no. 4 (1995): 221–27.
Farquhar, David. "Emperor as Bodhisattva in the Governance of the Ch'ing Empire." *Harvard Journal of Asiatic Studies* 38, no. 1 (1978): 5–34.
Faure, David. *Emperor and Ancestor: State and Lineage in South China.* Stanford, CA: Stanford University Press, 2007.
Fedotov, Alexander. "Some Aspects of the Influence of Tibetan Literature Over Mongolian Literary Tradition." In *Tibetan Studies: Proceedings of the 4th Seminar of the International Association for Tibetan Studies, Schloss Hohenkammer, Munich, 1985*, ed. Helga Uebach and Jampa L. Panglung, 157–61. Munich: Kommission für Zentralasiatische Studien, Bayerische Akademie der Wissenschaften, 1988.
Fletcher, Joseph. "Ch'ing Inner Asia c. 1800." In *The Cambridge History of China*. Vol. 10, *Late Ch'ing 1800–1911*, ed. John K. Fairbank, 35–106. Cambridge: Cambridge University Press, 1978.
Flood, Finbarr B. *Objects of Translation: Material Culture and Medieval "Hindu-Muslim" Encounter.* Princeton, NJ: Princeton University Press, 2009.
Flora, Liz. "The Eighth Tatsak Jedrung, Yeshe Lobzang Tenpai Gongpo." The Treasury of Lives. https://treasuryoflives.org/biographies/view/Eighth-Tatsak-Yeshe-Lobzang-Tenpai-Gonpo/5328.
Forêt, Philippe. *Mapping Chengde: The Qing Landscape Enterprise.* Honolulu: University of Hawai'i Press, 2000.
Franke, Wolfgang. *The Reform and Abolition of the Traditional Chinese Examination System.* Literary Licensing, LLC, 2011.
French, Rebecca. "The Cosmology of Law in Buddhist Tibet." *Journal of the International Association of Buddhist Studies* 18, no. 1 (July 1995): 97–116.
Games, Alison. "Atlantic History: Definitions, Challenges, and Opportunities." *American Historical Review* 111, no. 3 (2006): 741–57.
Gardner, Alexander. "The Twenty-Five Great Sites of Khams: Religious Geography, Revelation, and Non-sectarianism in Nineteenth-Century Eastern Tibet." PhD diss., University of Michigan, 2006.
Gell, Alfred. *Art and Agency: An Anthropological Theory.* Oxford: Clarendon Press, 1998.
Germano, David. "Re-Membering the Dismembered Body of Tibet: The Contemporary Ter Movement in the PRC." In *Buddhism in Contemporary Tibet: Religious Revival and Cultural Identity*, ed. Melvyn Goldstein and Matthew Kapstein, 53–94. Berkeley: University of California Press, 1998.
Giersch, C. Patterson. *Asian Borderlands: The Transformation of Qing China's Yunnan Frontier.* Cambridge, MA: Harvard University Press, 2006.
———. "'Grieving for Tibet': Conceiving the Modern State in Late-Qing Inner Asia." *China Perspectives* 3 (July 2008): 4–18.
Goldstein, Melvyn. "Tibetan Buddhism and Mass Monasticism." In *Des moines et des moniales dans le monde: La vie monastique dans le miroir de la parenté*, ed. Adeline Herrou and Gisele Krauskopff. Press Universitaires de Toulouse le Mirail, 2010.

BIBLIOGRAPHY

https://case.edu/affil/tibet/tibetanMonks/documents/Tibetan_Buddhism_and_Mass_Monasticism.pdf.

Gordanier, Amy. "The (Male) Divas of Beijing: Trade Networks, Professional Ties, and the Road to Stardom in Eighteenth-Century China." Paper abstract, American Historical Association Annual Meeting 2016. https://aha.confex.com/aha/2016/webprogram/Paper19382.html.

Greenwood, Kevin R. E. "Yonghegong: Imperial Universalism and the Art and Architecture of Beijing's 'Lama Temple.'" PhD diss., University of Kansas, 2013.

Grousset, René. *The Empire of the Steppes:A History of Central Asia*. New Brunswick, NJ: Rutgers University Press, 1970.

Gyatso, Janet. "Drawn from the Tibetan Treasury: The gTer ma Literature." In *Tibetan Literature: Studies in Genre*, ed. José Cabezón and Roger Jackson, 147-69. Ithaca, NY: Snow Lion, 1996.

———. "Experience, Empiricism, and the Fortunes of Authority: Tibetan Medicine and Buddhism on the Eve of Modernity." In *Forms of Knowledge in Early Modern Asia: Explorations in the Intellectual History of India and Tibet, 1500-1800*, ed. Sheldon Pollock, 311-35. Durham, NC: Duke University Press, 2011.

———. "Image as Presence: The Place of the Work of Art in Tibetan Religious Thinking." In *The Newark Museum Tibetan Collection*. Vol. 3, *Sculpture and Painting*, ed. Valrae Reynolds, Amy Heller, and Janet Gyatso, 171-75. Newark, NJ: Newark Museum, 1986.

Guy, R. Kent. *Qing Governors and Their Provinces: The Evolution of Territorial Administration in China, 1644-1796*. Seattle: University of Washington Press, 2013.

———. "Who Were the Manchus? A Review Essay." *Journal of Asian Studies* 61, no. 1 (February 2002): 151-64.

Hämäläinen, Pekka. *The Comanche Empire*. New Haven, CT: Yale University Press, 2009.

———. *Lakota America: A New History of Indigenous Power*. New Haven, CT: Yale University Press, 2019.

Harrison, Paul. "A Brief History of the Tibetan bKa' 'gyur." In *Tibetan Literature: Studies in Genre*, ed. José Cabezón and Roger Jackson, 70-94. Ithaca, NY: Snow Lion Publications, 1998.

Haskett, Christian P. B. Review of *Identity, Ritual and State in Tibetan Buddhism: The Foundations of Authority in Gelukpa Monasticism*, by Martin A. Mills. *Buddhist—Christian Studies* 27 (2007): 187-93.

Hay, John. "The Body Invisible in Chinese Art?" In *Body, Subject, and Power in China*, ed. Angela Zito and Tani E. Barlow, 42-77. Chicago: University of Chicago Press, 1994.

He Bin, Yanghui Xie, and Huocheng xianzhi bianzuan weiyuanhui, eds. *Huocheng Xianzhi* [Huocheng county gazetteer]. Urumuqi: Xinjiang renmin chubanshe, 1998.

He Feng. "Cong 'Fan Li' kan Qing wangchao dui Qinghai Zangqu de guanli cuoshi" [The Qing management of Qinghai Tibetan region: A study of Tibetan injunctions]. *Qinghai shehui kexue* [Qinghai social science Bulletin] 6 (1996): 72-76.

Heilong. "Kulunboleqi huimeng Mengguwen dang'an yijie" [Annotation and translation of Mongolian archives on the Khüree assembly]. *Manzu yanjiu* [Manchu minority research] 1 (2017): 43-52.

Heissig, Walther. *Die Pekinger Lamaistischen Blockdrucke in Mongolischer Sprache; Materialien Zur Mongolischen Literaturgeschichte* [Tibetan Buddhist block prints in the Mongolian language in Beijing and Mongolian literary history]. Göttinger Asiatische Forschungen; Monographienriehe Zur Geschichte, Sprache Und Literatur Der Völker Süd-, Ost- Und Zentraiasiens. Wiesbaden: O. Harrassowitz, 1954.

———. *A Lost Civilization: The Mongols Rediscovered*. New York: Basic Books, 1966

Herman, John E. "The Cant of Conquest: Tusi Offices and China's Political Incorporation of the Southwest Frontier." In *Empire at the Margins: Culture, Ethnicity, and Frontier in Early Modern China*, ed. Pamela Crossley, Helen Siu, and Donald Sutton, 135–70. Berkeley: University of California Press, 2006.

———. "From Land Reclamation to Land Grab: Settler Colonialism in Southwest China, 1680–1735." *Harvard Journal of Asiatic Studies* 78, no. 1 (2018): 91–123.

Hidehiro, Okada. *Kōkitei no tegami* [Emperor Kangxi's letters]. Tokyo: Fujiwarashoten, 2013.

Hillman, Ben. "Monastic Politics and the Local State in China: Authority and Autonomy in an Ethnically Tibetan Prefecture." *China Journal* 54 (July 2005): 29–51.

Hirano, Satoshi. *Shin teikoku to Chibetto mondai: tanminzoku tōgō no seiritsu to gakai* [The Qing Empire and the Tibetan question: The rise and fall of national unification]. Nagoya: Nagoya Daigaku Shuppankai, 2004.

Ho, Engseng. *The Graves of Tarim: Genealogy and Mobility across the Indian Ocean*. Berkeley: University of California Press, 2006.

———. "Inter-Asian Concepts for Mobile Societies." *Journal of Asian Studies* 76, no. 4 (2017): 907–28.

Ho, Hsiang-Ling. "Qianlong huangdi dui Beijing simiao zhi zanzhu" [The Qianlong emperor's patronage of religious establishments in Beijing]. Master's thesis, Soochow University, 2005.

Ho, Pingti. *The Ladder of Success in Imperial China: Aspects of Social Mobility, 1368–1911*. New York: Columbia University Press, 2008.

Horden, Peregrine, and Nicholas Purcell. "The Mediterranean and 'the New Thalassology.'" *American Historical Review* 111, no. 3 (2006): 722–40.

Hostetler, Laura. *Qing Colonial Enterprise: Ethnography and Cartography in Early Modern China*. Chicago: University of Chicago Press, 2005.

Huber, Toni. *The Holy Land Reborn: Pilgrimage and the Tibetan Reinvention of Buddhist India*. Chicago: University of Chicago Press, 2008.

Huc, Évariste Régis. *Travels in Tartary, Thibet and China During the Years 1844-5-6*, trans. W. Hazlitt. London: Vizetelly, 1852; Project Gutenberg, 2010.

Hucker, Charles O. *A Dictionary of Official Titles in Imperial China*. Stanford, CA: Stanford University Press, 1985.

Hurcha, Coyiji, and Wuyun. *Zangchuan Fojiao zai Menggu diqu chuanbo yanjiu* [Research on the dissemination of Tibetan Buddhism in Mongolia]. Beijing: Minzu chubanshe, 2012.

Hyer, Paul. *A Mongolian Living Buddha: Biography of the Kanjurwa Khutughtu*. Bloomington: Indiana University Press, 1984.

Ikejiri, Yōko. *Shinchō zenki no Chibetto Bukkyō seisaku: Jasaku-rama seido no seiritsu to tenkai* [Tibetan Buddhist policies in the early Qing: The establishment and development of the institution of Jasak Lama]. Tokyo: Kyūko shoin, 2013.

Illich, Marina. "Selections from the Life of a Tibetan Buddhist Polymath: Chankya Rolpai Dorje (Lcang Skya Rol Pa'i Rdo Rje), 1717–1786." PhD diss., Columbia University, 2006.

BIBLIOGRAPHY

Ishihama Yumiko. *Shinchō to chibetto bukkyō: Bosatsuō to natta kenryūtei* [Qing China and the Tibetan Buddhist world: The Qianlong emperor who had become a Buddhist king]. Waseda Daigaku Gakujutsu Sosho 20. Tokyo: Wasedadaigakushuppanbu, 2011.

Jackson, David. "Lineages and Structure in Tibetan Buddhist Painting: Principles and Practice of an Ancient Sacred Choreography." *Journal of the International Association of Tibetan Studies* 1 (October, 2005): 1–40.

Jacobs, Justin. *Xinjiang and the Modern Chinese State*. Seattle: University of Washington Press, 2016.

Jacoby, Sarah H. *Love and Liberation: Autobiographical Writings of the Tibetan Buddhist Visionary Sera Khandro*. New York: Columbia University Press, 2014.

Jacques Marchais Museum of Tibetan Art, with Barbara Lipton and Nima Dorjee Ragnubs. *Treasures of Tibetan Art: Collections of the Jacques Marchais Museum of Tibetan Art*. New York: Oxford University Press, 1995.

Jansen, Berthe. *The Monastery Rules: Buddhist Monastic Organization in Pre-Modern Tibet*. Berkeley: University of California Press, 2018.

Jasanoff, Maya. *Edge of Empire: Lives, Culture, and Conquest in the East, 1750–1850*. New York: Vintage Books, 2006.

Jianhongsheng. "Duolun nuo'er ji" [A survey of Dolonnuur]. *Dongfang Zazhi* [Eastern miscellany] 5, no. 10 (October 1908): 134. https://babel.hathitrust.org/cgi/pt?id=pst.000066964766&view=1up&seq=1&skin=2021.

Jin, Liang. *Yonghegong zhi lue* [A concise history of Yonghegong]. Beijing: Zhongguo zangxue yanjiu zhongxin chubanshe, 1994.

Joan-Pau, Rubies. "Instructions for Travelers: Teaching the Eye to See." *History and Anthropology* 9 (1996): 139–90.

Kam, Tak-Sing. "The DGe-Lugs-Pa Breakthrough: The Uluk Darxan Nangsu Lama's Mission to the Manchus." *Central Asiatic Journal* 44, no. 2 (2000): 161–76.

Kapstein, Matthew, ed. *Buddhism Between Tibet and China*. Boston: Wisdom Publications, 2009.

———. *The Tibetans*. Malden, MA: Wiley-Blackwell, 2006.

Kasaba, Resat. *A Moveable Empire: Ottoman Nomads, Migrants, and Refugees*. Seattle: University of Washington Press, 2009.

Khazeni, Arash. *Sky Blue Stone: The Turquoise Trade in World History*. Berkeley: University of California Press, 2014.

Kim, Hanung. "Renaissance Man from Amdo: The Life and Scholarship of the Eighteenth-Century Amdo Scholar Sum Pa Mkhan Po Ye Shes Dpal 'Byor (1704–1788)." PhD diss., Harvard University, 2018.

Kim, Kwangmin. *Borderland Capitalism: Turkestan Produce, Qing Silver, and the Birth of an Eastern Market*. Stanford, CA: Stanford University Press, 2016.

Kim Sung Soo [Jin Chengxiu]. *Ming Qing zhiji zangchuan fojiao zai Menggu diqu chuanbo* [Tibetan Buddhism in Mongolia during the Ming and Qing]. Beijing: Shehui kexue wenxian chubanshe, 2006.

King, Matthew W. "'Miscellaneous Writings' of Čaqar Gebši Luvsančültem." In *Sources of Mongolian Buddhism*, ed. Vesna Wallace, 155–66. Oxford: Oxford University Press, 2020.

———. *Ocean of Milk, Ocean of Blood: A Mongolian Monk in the Ruins of the Qing Empire*. New York: Columbia University Press, 2019.

Köhle, Natalie. "Why Did the Kangxi Emperor Go to Wutai Shan? Patronage, Pilgrimage and the Place of Tibetan Buddhism at the Early Qing Court." *Late Imperial China* 29, no. 1 (2008): 73–119.
Kollmann, Nancy. *The Russian Empire 1450–1801*. Oxford: Oxford University Press, 2017.
Koss, Daniel. "Political Geography of Empire: Chinese Varieties of Local Government." *Journal of Asian Studies* 76, no. 1 (February 2017): 159–84.
ko źul grags pa 'byung gnas. *Gangs Can Mkhas Grub Rim Byon Ming Mdzod* [Biographical dictionary of prominent Tibetans in Tibet]. Lan chou: Mtsho sgnon Żing chen Żin hwa dpe khang gis bkrams, 1992.
Kuhn, Philip A. *Soul Stealers: The Chinese Sorcery Scare of 1768*. Cambridge, MA: Harvard University Press, 2006.
Kung, Ling-Wei. "The Transformation of the Qing's Geopolitics: Power Transitions Between Tibetan Buddhist Monasteries in Amdo, 1644–1795." *Revue d'Etudes Tibétaines* 45 (April 2018): 110–44.
Lai Hui-min. "From Religious Centers to Temple Fairs: Tibetan Buddhist Temples and Tributary Trade with Khalkha Mongolian Royalty During the Qing Dynasty." *Bulletin of the Institute of Modern History, Academia Sinica* 72 (2011): 1–54.
——. "Qingdai Guihuacheng de zangchuan fosi yu jingji" [Tibetan Buddhist monasteries and their economy in Guihua City in the Qing]. *Neimenggu shifan daxue xuebao: Zhexue shehui kexue ban* [Journal of Inner Mongolia Normal University: Philosophy and social science] 39, no. 3 (May 2010): 88–101.
——. *Tian huang gui zhou: Qing huangzu de jieceng jiegou yu jingji shenghuo* [Qing imperial lineage: Its hierarchical structure and economic life]. Taipei: Zhongyang yanjiuyuan jindaishi yanjiusuo, 1997.
Lai Hui-min and Chang Su-ya. "Qing Qianlong shidai de Yonghegong—yige jingji wenhua cengmian de kaocha" [Yonghegong under the Qing Qianlong reign: A culture and economic perspective]. *National Palace Museum Research Quarterly* 23, no. 4 (June 2006): 131–64.
Lama Sherab, Rhaldi. "India in 'dZam gling rgyas bshad." *Sikkim: Bulletin of Tibetology* 2 (1984): 21–34.
Lawrence, Lok, and Cheung Zhang. "Power for a Price: Office Purchase, Elite Families, and Status Maintenance in Qing China." PhD diss., Harvard University, 2010.
Lessing, Ferdinand. *Yung-Ho-Kung, an Iconography of the Lamaist Cathedral in Peking: With Notes on Lamaist Mythology and Cult, Volume One*. Sino-Swedish Expedition, 1942.
Li Delong and Yu Bing, eds. *Lidai Riji Congchao* [Anthology of diaries in Chinese history]. Beijing: Xueyuan chubanshe, 2006.
Lin, Wei-Cheng. *Building a Sacred Mountain: The Buddhist Architecture of China's Mount Wutai*. Seattle: University of Washington Press, 2014.
Liu Fengyun and Liu Wenpeng, eds. *Qingchao de guojia rentong: Xin Qingshi yanjiu yu zhengming* [The identity of the Qing state: Research and debates on the new Qing history]. Beijing: Zhongguo renmin daxue chubanshe, 2010.
Liu, Gary. "Archive of Power: The Qing Dynasty Imperial Garden-Palace in Rehe." *Meishu shi yanjiu jikan* [Journal of art history] 28 (2010): 43–82.
Liu Hainian, and Yang Y., eds. "Regulations of Qinghai Tibetans, Xining." *Collections of Rare Chinese Legal Codes*, vol. 2, section 3. Beijing: Kexue chubanshe, 1994.

BIBLIOGRAPHY

Liu, Xiaomeng. *Qingdai Beijing qiren shehui* [Social life of Qing bannermen in Beijing]. Beijing: Zhongguo shehui kexue chubanshe, 2016.
Luo, Weiwei. "Land, Lineage and the Laity: Transactions of a Qing Monastery." *Late Imperial China* 36, no. 1 (2015): 88–123.
Luo Wenhua. *Longpao yu jiasha: Qinggong Zangchuan Fojiao wenhua kachao* [The emperor's court dress and robes: Tibetan Buddhist culture in the Qing court]. Beijing: Zijincheng chubanshe, 2005.
Maher, Derek. "The Lives and Time of 'Jam Dbyangs Bzhad Pa." In *Proceedings of the Tenth Seminar of the IATS, 2003*. Vol. 3, *Power, Politics, and the Reinvention of Tradition: Tibet in the Seventeenth and Eighteenth Centuries*, ed. Bryan J. Cuevas and Kurtis R. Schaeffer, 129–44. Leiden: Brill, 2006.
Mala, Guilaine. "A Mahayanist Rewriting of the History of China by Mgon Po Skyabs in the Rgya Nag Chos 'Byung." In *Power, Politics, and the Reinvention of Tradition: Tibet in the Seventeenth and Eighteenth Centuries*, ed. Brian Cuevas and Kurtis Schaeffer, 145–69. Leiden: Brill, 2006.
Man-Cheong, I. D. *The Class of 1761: Examinations, State and Elite in Eighteenth Century China*. Stanford, CA: Stanford University Press, 2004.
Mann, Susan. *Precious Records: Women in China's Long Eighteenth Century*. Stanford, CA: Stanford University Press, 1997.
Masters, Bruce. *The Arabs of the Ottoman Empire, 1516–1918: A Social and Cultural History*. New York: Cambridge University Press, 2013.
Matteini, Michele. "Fashishan as Patron and Antiquarian in Jiaqing-Period Beijing." Presentation at the Annual Conference of the Association for Asian Studies, Chicago, March 28, 2015.
McCleary, Rachel M., and Leonard W. J. van der Kuijp. "The Market Approach to the Rise of the Geluk School, 1419–1642." *Journal of Asian Studies* 69, no. 1 (2010): 149–80.
McKeown, Adam. *Chinese Migrant Networks and Cultural Change: Peru, Chicago, and Hawaii 1900–1936*. Chicago: University of Chicago Press, 2001.
McNicholas, Mark P. *Forgery and Impersonation in Imperial China: Popular Deceptions and the High Qing State*. Seattle: University of Washington Press, 2015.
Meng Xiaoying and Meng Xiaoyan. "Jiexi dangdai Gannan muqu minjian jiufen tiaojie zhongde Zangzu buluo xiguanfa" [A study of the customary laws in civil conflicts in nomadic Tibetan communities in the southern Gansu region]. *Zhongguo Zangxue* [China's Tibetan studies] 1 (2010): 89–92.
Metcalf, Alida C. *Go-Betweens and the Colonization of Brazil: 1500–1600*. Austin: University of Texas Press, 2005.
Metcalf, Thomas R. *Imperial Connections: India in the Indian Ocean Arena, 1860–1920*. Berkeley: University of California Press, 2008.
Mgon-po, Mi-nyag. *Gangs-Can Mkhas Dbang Rim Byon Gyi Rnam Thar Mdor Bsdus Bdud Rtsi'i Thigs Phreng* [Concise biographies of historical Tibetan scholars]. Beijing: Mtsho-sngon Zhin-chen Zhin-hwa dpe tshong khang gis bkram, 1996.
mi 'gyur rdo rje ed. *bod kyi gal che'i lo rgyus yig cha bdams bsgrigs* [Selections of historical documents on Tibetan Buddhism of Tibet]. Lhasa: bod ljongs bod yig dpe rñiṅ dpe skrun khang, 1991.
mi nyag mgon po, ye shes rdo rje, thub bstan nyi ma, dpal rdor, lha mo skyabs. *gangs can mkhas dbang rim byon gyi rnam thar mdor bsdus* [Biographical dictionary of

eminent Tibetans in Tibet]. 2 vols. Beijing: krung go'i bod kyi shes rig dpe skrun khang, 1996–2000.

Mi Yanqing. "Qingdai zhongqi Mengguzu jiazu wenxue yu wenxue jiazu" [An overview of Mongolian family literature and literary families in mid-Qing dynasty]. *Neimenggu daxue xuekan: Zhexue yu shehui kexue ban* [Journal of Inner Mongolian University: Philosophy and social sciences] 43, no. 2 (March 2011): 5–8.

Michie, Alexander. *The Siberian Overland Route from Peking to Petersburg, Through the Deserts and Steppes of Mongolia, Tartary.* 1864; Project Gutenberg, 2014.

Miller, Gwenn A. *Kodiak Kreol: Communities of Empire in Early Russian America.* Ithaca, NY: Cornell University Press, 2010.

Miller, Robert James. *Monasteries and Culture Change in Inner Mongolia.* Asiatische Forschungen 2. Wiesbaden: O. Harrassowitz, 1959.

Mills, Martin. *Identity, Ritual and State in Tibetan Buddhism: The Foundations of Authority in Gelukpa Monasticism.* London: Routledge Curzon, 2003.

Millward, James. *Beyond the Pass: Economy, Ethnicity, and Empire in Qing Central Asia, 1759–1864.* Stanford, CA: Stanford University Press, 1998.

Miyanqing. "Qingdai zhongqi Mengguzu jiazu wenxue yu wenxue jiazu" [Mongolian lineage literature and literary lineages in the High Qing era]. *Neimenggu daxue xuebao: Zhexue shehui kexue ban* [Journal of Inner Mongolia University: Philosophy and social sciences] 43, no. 2 (March 2011): 5–8.

Miyawaki, Junko. "The Qalqa Mongols and the Oyirad in the Seventeenth Century." *Journal of Asian History* 18, no. 2 (1984): 136–73.

mkhas grub dpal bzany po. *rgyud sde spyiḥi rnam par gźag pa rgyas par brjod* [mkhas grub rje's fundamentals of the Buddhist tantras]. Indo-Iranian Monographs. The Hague: Mouton, n.d.

Monhart, Michael. "Seeing All as One, Mediating Between Gods, Humans, and Demons: The Travels of Katok Tsewang Norbu, 1749–1751." Master's thesis, Columbia University, 2011.

Mosca, Matthew W. *From Frontier Policy to Foreign Policy: The Question of India and the Transformation of Geopolitics in Qing China.* Stanford, CA: Stanford University Press, 2015.

Munkh-Erdene, Lhamsuren. "The 1640 Great Code: An Inner Asian Parallel to the Treaty of Westphalia." *Central Asian Survey* 29, no. 3 (September 2010): 269–88.

Namgyal, Tsering. "The Second Changkya, Ngawang Lobzang Choden." The Treasury of Lives. http://www.treasuryoflives.org/biographies/view/Second-Changkya-Ngawang-Lobzang-Choden/3758.

———. "The Third Rongpo Drubchen, Gendun Trinle Rabgye." The Treasury of Lives. http://treasuryoflives.org/biographies/view/Rongwo-Drubchen-03-Gendun-Trinle-Rabgye/5436.

Naquin, Susan. *Chinese Society in the Eighteenth Century.* New Haven, CT: Yale University Press, 1987.

———. *Peking: Temples and City Life, 1400–1900.* Berkeley: University of California Press, 2000.

Nara Chuuktu. "Guo Qinwang Yunli yiji Mengyi Fuzangjing" [Prince Guo and the treasure texts in Mongolian translation]. *Qingshi yanjiu* [Qing history research] 3 (2002): 99–105.

BIBLIOGRAPHY

———. "Shishu Qingdai dui Qinghai mengzang minzu difang de lifa" [A preliminary discussion of Qing China's legislation in the Mongolian and Tibetan areas of Qinghai]. *Neimenggu shehui kexue: Hanwen ban* [Social science of Inner Mongolia, Chinese edition] 1 (2008): 67–71.
Natasgdorj, Sh. *Khalkhyn tüükh* [History of Khalkha]. Ulaanbaatar: Ulsyn khebleliin khereg erkhlekh khoroo, 1963.
Nebesky-Wojkowitz, René de. *Tibetan Religious Dances: Tibetan Text and Annotated Translation of the 'Chams Yig*. The Hague: Mouton, 1976.
Nedostup, Rebecca. *Superstitious Regimes: Religion and the Politics of Chinese Modernity*. Cambridge, MA: Harvard University Asia Center, 2010.
Newby, L. J. "China: Pax Manjurica." *Journal for Eighteenth-Century Studies* 34. no. 4 (2011): 557–63.
Nietupski, Paul. *Labrang: A Tibetan Buddhist Monastery at the Crossroads of Four Civilizations*. Ithaca, NY: Snow Lion Publications, 1999.
———. *Labrang Monastery: A Tibetan Buddhist Community on the Inner Asian Borderlands, 1709–1958*. Lanham, MD: Lexington Books, 2010.
Ning, Chia. "The Lifanyuan and the Inner Asian Rituals in the Early Qing (1644–1795)." *Late Imperial China* 14, no. 1 (1993): 60–92.
———. "The Li-Fan Yuan in the Early Ch'Ing Dynasty." PhD diss., Johns Hopkins University, 1992.
Nourse, Benjamin. "Politics and Printing in Eighteenth-Century Co ne." Paper presented at the Twelfth Seminar of the International Association of Tibetan Studies, August 17, 2010.
Oidtmann, Max. "Between Patron and Priest: Amdo Tibet Under Qing Rule, 1792–1911." PhD diss., Harvard University, 2014.
———. "A 'Dog-Eat-Dog' World: Qing Jurispractices and the Legal Inscription of Piety in Amdo." *Extrême-Orient Extrême-Occident* 40 (2016): 151–82.
———. *Forging the Golden Urn: The Qing Empire and the Politics of Reincarnation in Tibet*. New York: Columbia University Press, 2018.
Oyuncimeg. *Monggol sudulul-un nebterkei toli, Siasin surtaqun* [Encyclopedia of Mongolian studies: Volume on religion]. Hohhot: Oiboir Mongγol-un Arad-un Keblel-uin Qoriy-a, 2007.
The Palace Museum. *Zangchuan Fojiao zaoxiang* [Tibetan Buddhist sculptures]. Beijing: Zi jin cheng chubanshe, 2009.
Payne, Richard. "Ritual." In *Encyclopaedia of Buddhism*, ed. Robert E. Buswell. New York: MacMillan Reference, 2004.
Perdue, Peter C. *China Marches West: The Qing Conquest of Central Eurasia*. Cambridge, MA: Belknap Press of Harvard University Press, 2005.
———. "Nature and Nurture on Imperial China's Frontiers." *Modern Asian Studies* 43, no. 1 (2009): 245–67.
Petech, Luciano. "Administration of Tibet during the First Half-Century of Chinese Protectorate." In *The Tibetan History Reader*, ed. Gray Tuttle and Kurtis Schaeffer, 389–410. New York: Columbia University Press, 2013.
———. *China and Tibet in the Early 18th Century: History of the Establishment of Chinese Protectorate in Tibet*. Leiden: Brill Archive, 1950.
———. "Notes on Tibetan History of the 18th Century." *T'oung Pao* 52, no. 4–5 (1966): 276–92.

BIBLIOGRAPHY

Philliou, Christine M. *Biography of an Empire: Governing Ottomans in an Age of Revolution*. Berkeley: University of California Press, 2010.

Pirie, Fernanda. "The Limits of the State: Coercion and Consent in Chinese Tibet." *Journal of Asian Studies* 72, no. 1 (February 2013): 69–89.

Prince Guo Yunli. *Xizang riji* [Diary to Tibet]. Beijing: Quanguo tushu guanwen xiansuo weifuzhi zhongxin, 1992.

Qi Meiqin. *Qingdai Neiwufu* [Department of the Imperial Household in the Qing dynasty]. Shenyang: Liaoning minzu chubanshe, 2009.

Qiguang. *Daqing diguo shiji Menggu de zhengzhi yu shehui: Yi Alashan Heshuotebu yanjiu wei zhongxin* [Politics and society of the Mongols in the Qing empire: Research centered on the Alashan Qoshoot Mongols]. Shanghai: Fudan daxue chubanshe, 2013.

Raffles, Hugh. "The Uses of Butterflies." *American Ethnologist* 28, no. 3 (2001): 513–48.

Rawski, Evelyn. *Early Modern China and Northeast Asia: Cross-Border Perspectives*. Asian Connections. Cambridge: Cambridge University Press, 2015.

———. "The Imperial Way of Death: Ming and Ch'ing Emperors and Death Ritual." In *Death Ritual in Late Imperial and Modern China*, ed. James Watson and Evelyn Rawski, 228–53. Berkeley: University California Press, 1990.

———. *The Last Emperors: A Social History of Qing Imperial Institutions*. Berkeley: University of California Press, 1998.

———. "Presidential Address: Re-envisioning the Qing: The Significance of the Qing Period in Chinese History." *Journal of Asian Studies* 55, no. 4 (November 1996): 829–50.

———. "The Qing in Historiographical Dialogue." *Late Imperial China* 37, no. 1 (2016): 1–4.

———. "Qing Publishing in Non-Han Languages." In *Printing and Book Culture in Late Imperial China*, ed. Cynthia Brokaw and Kai-wing Chou, 304–25. Berkeley: University of California Press, 2005.

Ren Yuehai. *Duolun wenshi ziliao* [Duolun literary and historical sources]. 3 vols. Hohhot: Neimenggu Daxue chubanshe, 2006–2008.

Reynolds, Elizabeth. "Tibet Incorporated: Institutional Power and Economic Practice on the Sino-Tibetan Borderland, 1930–1950." PhD diss., Columbia University, 2020.

Reynolds, Valrae. *From the Sacred Realm: Treasures of Tibetan Art from the Newark Museum*. Munich: Prestel Publishing, 1999.

Rhoads, Edward J. *Manchus and Han: Ethnic Relations and Political Power in Late Qing and Early Republican China, 1861–1928*. Seattle: University of Washington Press, 2000.

Roddy, Stephen. "Toward Buddhist Cosmopolitanism: The Pan-Asian Vision of Gong Zizhen." In *Cosmopolitanism in China, 1600–1950*, ed. Minghui Hu and Johan Elverskog, 121–58. Amherst, NY: Cambria Press, 2016.

Ronis, Jann Michael. "Celibacy, Revelations, and Reincarnated Lamas: Contestation and Synthesis in the Growth of Monasticism at Katok Monastery from the 17th Through 19th Centuries." PhD diss., University of Virginia, 2009.

Rothman, E. Natalie. *Brokering Empire: Trans-Imperial Subjects Between Venice and Istanbul*. Cornell University Press, 2011.

BIBLIOGRAPHY

Rowe, William T. *Saving the World: Chen Hongmou and Elite Consciousness in Eighteenth-Century China*. Stanford, CA: Stanford University Press, 2002.
Ruegg David. "Mchod, yon, yon mchod and mchod gnas/yon gnas: On the Historiography and Semantics of a Tibetan Religio-social and Religio-political Concept." In *Tibetan History and Language: Studies Dedicated to Uray Géza on his Seventieth Birthday*, ed. Ernst Steinkeller, 441–53. Vienna: Arbeitskreis für Tibetische und Buddhistische Studien Universität Wien, 1991.
———. "The Preceptor-Donor (yon mchod) Relation in Thirteenth-Century Tibetan Society and Polity, Its Inner Asian Precursors and Indian Models." In *Tibetan Studies: Proceedings of the 7th Seminar of the International Association of Tibetan Studies, Graz 1995*, ed. H. Krasser, M. T. Much, E. Steinkellner, and H. Tauscher, 857–72. Vienna: Österreichische Akademie der Wissenschaft, 1997.
Ryavec, Karl E. *A Historical Atlas of Tibet*. Chicago: University of Chicago Press, 2015.
Samten Chhosphel. "The Fifty-Fourth Ganden Tripa, Ngawang Chokden." The Treasury of Lives. https://treasuryoflives.org/biographies/view/Trichen-54-Ngawang-Chokden/6526.
———. "The Forty-Fourth Ganden Tripa, Lodro Gyatso." The Treasury of Lives. http://www.treasuryoflives.org/biographies/view/Trichen-44-Lodro-Gyatso/2872.
———. "The Second 'jam dbyangs bzhad pa, Konchok Jigme Wangpo." The Treasury of Lives. http://www.treasuryoflives.org/biographies/view/Jamyang-Zhepa-02-Konchok-Jigme-Wangpo/2996.
———. "The Second Tukwan, Ngawang Chokyi Gyatso." The Treasury of Lives. http://www.treasuryoflives.org/biographies/view/Tukwan-02-Ngawang-Chokyi-Gyatso/3225.
———. "The Sixty-First Ganden Tripa, Ngawang Tsultrim." The Treasury of Lives. http://www.treasuryoflives.org/biographies/view/Trichen-61-Ngawang-Tsultrim/5652.
Samuel, Geoffrey. "The Subtle Body in India and Beyond." In *Religion and the Subtle Body in Asia and the West: Between Mind and Body*, ed. Geoffrey Samuel and Jay Johnston, 33–47. London: Routledge, 2013.
Sangs rgyas, rin chen. "Lhamo Dechen'i sku phyag gser khri rin po che'i sku phreng rim byon gyi lo rgyus mdo bsdus ngo sprod" [A concise introduction to the successive reincarnations of the Ser Khri lineage in the Lhamo Dechen Monastery]. In *Research on Amdo Mdo Smad Zhib 'Jug* (1999): 108–18.
Sanjdorj, M. *Manchu Chinese Colonial Rule in Northern Mongolia*, trans. Urgunge Onon. New York: St. Matin's Press, 1980.
Schaeffer, Kurtis R. *The Culture of the Book in Tibet*. New York: Columbia University Press, 2009.
———. "Si tu paṇ chen on Scholarship." *Journal of the International Association of Tibetan Studies* 7 (August 2013): 302–15. http://www.thlib.org?tid=T5752.
———. "Tibetan Poetry on Wutai Shan." *Journal of the International Association for Tibetan Studies* 6 (2011): 215–42.
Schaeffer, Kurtis R., Matthew Kapstein, and Gray Tuttle. *Sources of Tibetan Tradition*. New York: Columbia University Press, 2013.
Schäfer, Dagmar. *The Crafting of the 10,000 Things: Knowledge and Technology in Seventeenth-Century China*. Chicago: University of Chicago Press, 2011.

BIBLIOGRAPHY

Scheier-Dolberg, Joseph. "Treasure House of Tibetan Culture: Canonization, Printing, and Power in the Derge Printing House." Master's thesis., Harvard University, 2005.

Schlesinger, Jonathan. *A World Trimmed with Fur: Wild Things, Pristine Places, and the Natural Fringes of Qing.* Stanford, CA: Stanford University Press, 2017.

Schwieger, Peter. *The Dalai Lama and the Emperor of China: A Political History of the Tibetan Institution of Reincarnation.* New York: Columbia University Press, 2015.

Scott, James C. *The Art of Not Being Governed: An Anarchist History of Upland Southeast Asia.* Yale Agrarian Studies Series. New Haven, CT: Yale University Press, 2010.

Serruys, Henry. "A Study of Chinese Penetration Into Chahar Territory in the Eighteenth Century." *Monumenta Serica* 35 (1981–1983): 485–544.

Seuberlich, Wolfgang. *Zur Verwaltungsgeschichte der Mandschurei (1644–1930)* [History of administration in Manchuria, 1644–1930]. Asien- Und Afrika-Studien Der Humboldt-Universität Zu Berlin 7. Wiesbaden: Harrassowitz, 2001.

Shepherd, John Robert. *Statecraft and Political Economy on the Taiwan Frontier, 1600–1800.* Stanford, CA: Stanford University Press, 1993.

Shi Miaozhou. *Mengzang Fojiao shi* [History of Buddhism in Mongolia and Tibet]. Yangzhou: Guangli shushe, 2009.

Shijie tuhua sheying [Images and photography of the world] 1, no. 1 (1924).

Shim, Hosung. "The Zunghar Conquest of Central Tibet and Its Influence on Tibetan Military Institutions in the 18th Century." *Revue d'Etudes Tibétaines* 53 (March 2020): 56–113.

Sihlé, Nicolas. "Quasi-generalized, Mostly Temporary, Monasticism Among Boys: An Uncommon Form of Tibetan 'Mass Monasticism.' " *The Himalayas and Beyond: The Center for Himalayan Studies Blog*, July 10, 2011. https://himalayas.hypotheses.org/85#footnote_1_85.

Skorupski, Tadeusz. "The Canonical Tantras of the New School." In *Tibetan Literature: Studies in Genre*, ed. José Cabezón and Roger Jackson, 95–110. Ithaca, NY: Snow Lion Publications, 1996.

Smith, Gene. *dbus gtsang khul du shing par ji bzhugs kyi dkar chag phan bde'i pad tshal 'byed pa'i nyin byed/* [Printeries in Central Tibet]. BDRC W1KG9262. http://tbrc.org/link?RID=W1KG9262.

Sneath, David. *The Headless State: Aristocratic Orders, Kinship Society, and Misrepresentations of Nomadic Inner Asia.* New York: Columbia University Press, 2007.

Snellgrove, David, and Hugh Richardson. *A Cultural History of Tibet.* Boston: Shambala, 1995.

Sonam Dorje. "The Sixth Detri, Kelzang Khyenrab Gyatso." The Treasury of Lives. http://treasuryoflives.org/biographies/view/Sixth-Detri-Kelzang-Khyenrab-Gyatso/7876.

Sonam Dorje and Catherine Tsuji. "The Eleventh Ruler of Chone, Makzor Gonpo." The Treasury of Lives. http://treasuryoflives.org/biographies/view/Eleventh-Chone-Sakyong-Makzor-Gonpo/6346.

Song, Nianshen. *Making Borders in Modern East Asia: The Tumen River Demarcation, 1881–1919.* Cambridge: Cambridge University Press, 2019.

BIBLIOGRAPHY

Spence, Jonathan. *The Search for Modern China*. New York: Norton, 1991.
Sperling, Elliot. "Tibetan Buddhism, Perceived and Imagined, Along the Ming-Era Sino-Tibetan Frontier." In *Buddhism Between Tibet and China*, ed. Matthew Kapstein, 155–80. Somerville, MA: Wisdom Publications, 2009.
———. *The Tibet-China Conflict: History and Polemics*. Policy Studies 7. Washington, DC: East-West Center, 2004.
Sullivan, Brenton. *Building a Religious Empire: Tibetan Buddhism, Bureaucracy, and the Rise of the Gelukpa*. Encounters with Asia. Philadelphia: University of Pennsylvania Press, 2021.
———. "Monastic Customaries and the Promotion of Dge lugs Scholasticism in Amdo and Beyond." *Asian Highlands Perspectives* 36 (2015): 84–105.
———. "The Mother of All Monasteries: Gönlung Jampa Ling and the Rise of Mega Monasteries in Northeastern Tibet." PhD diss., University of Virginia, 2013.
Sunderland, Willard. "Imperial Space: Territorial Thought and Practice in the Eighteenth Century." In *Russian Empire: Space, People, Power, 1700–1930*, ed. Jan Burbank, Mark von Hagen, and Anatolyi Remnev, 33–66. Bloomington: Indiana University Press, 2007.
Suny Grigor, Ronald, and Terry Martin, eds. *A State of Nations: Empire and Nation-Making in the Age of Lenin and Stalin*. Oxford: Oxford University Press, 2001.
Szonyi, Michael. *Practicing Kinship: Lineage and Descent in Late Imperial China*. Stanford, CA: Stanford University Press, 2002.
Tambiah, Stanley. "The Galactic Polity in Southeast Asia." *HAU: Journal of Ethnographic Theory* 3 (2013): 503–34.
———. *World Conqueror and World Renouncer: A Study of Buddhism and Polity in Thailand against a Historical Background*. Cambridge: Cambridge University Press, 1977.
Tarab Trülku. *A Brief History of Tibetan Academic Degrees in Buddhist Philosophy*. NIAS Report Series, no. 43. Copenhagen: NIAS, in association with the Royal Library, 2000.
Taupier, Richard. "The Rise of the Jöüngars Based on Primary Oyirod Sources." *Inner Asia* 21, no. 2 (October 2019): 140–61.
Tayama, Shigeru. *shindai ni okeru Mōko no shakai seido* [The Mongolian social system in Qing dynasty]. Tokyo: Tōkyō Bunkyō Shoin, 1954.
Teng, Emma Jinhua. *Taiwan's Imagined Geography: Chinese Colonial Travel Writing 1683–1895*. Cambridge, MA: Harvard University Asia Center, 2006.
Thum, Rian. *The Sacred Routes of Uyghur History*. Cambridge, MA: Harvard University Press, 2014.
Torbert, Preston M. *The Ch'ing Imperial Household Department: A Study of Its Organization and Principal Functions, 1662–1796*. Harvard East Asian Monographs 71. Cambridge, MA: Council on East Asian Studies, Harvard University, 1977.
Townsend, Dominique. *A Buddhist Sensibility: Aesthetic Education at Tibet's Mindröling Monastery*. Studies of the Weatherhead East Asian Institute, Columbia University. New York: Columbia University Press, 2021.
———. "The Third Changkya, Rolpai Dorje." The Treasury of Lives. http://treasuryoflives.org/biographies/view/Chankya-Rolpai-Dorje/3141.
Tsai, Wei-chieh. "Mongolization of Han Chinese and Manchu Settlers in Qing Mongolia, 1700–1911." PhD diss., Indiana University, 2017.

Tsehua. "The Fifth Zhabdrung Karpo, Khetsun Gyatso." The Treasury of Lives. http://treasuryoflives.org/biographies/view/Fifth-Zhabdrung-Karpo-Khetsun-Gyatso/8860.

Tsering, Sonam. "The Role of Texts in the Formation of the Geluk School in Tibet During the Mid-fourteenth and Fifteenth Centuries." PhD diss., Columbia University, 2020.

Tsewang Norbu, Rigzin. *gsung 'bum/_tshe dbang nor bu* [Rigzin Tsewang Norbu's collected works]. 4 vols. Darjeeling: Kargyud sungrab nyamso khang, 1973.

Tsomu, Yudru. "Local Aspirations and National Constraints: A Case Study of Nyarong Gonpo Namgyel and His Rise to Power in Kham (1836–1865)." PhD diss., Harvard University, 2006.

———. *The Rise of Gönpo Namgyel in Kham: The Blind Warrior of Nyarong*. Lanham, MD: Lexington Books, 2014.

Tsultemin, Uranchimeg. "Ikh Khuree: A Nomadic Monastery and the Later Buddhist Art of Mongolia." PhD diss., University of California, Berkeley, 2009.

———. *A Monastery on the Move: Art and Politics in Later Buddhist Mongolia*. Honolulu: University of Hawai'i Press, 2021.

Tucci, Giuseppe. *mc'od rten ets'a ts'a nel Tibet Indiano ed Occidentale: Contributo allo studio dell'arte religiosa tibetana e del suo sigificato* [Stupas and tsa-tsa in Indian and Western Tibet: Contributions to the study of Tibetan religious art and its significance]. Indo-Tibetica 1. Roma: Reale Accademia d'Italia, 1932.

Tuttle, Gray. "Challenging Central Tibet's Dominance of History: The Oceanic Book, a 19th-Century Politico-Religious Geographic History." In *Mapping the Modern in Tibet*, ed. Gray Tuttle, 135–72. Andiast: International Institute for Tibetan and Buddhist Studies, 2011.

———, ed. *Mapping the Modern in Tibet*. Andiast: International Institute for Tibetan and Buddhist Studies, 2011.

———. "An Overview of Amdo (Northeastern Tibet) Historical Polities." The Tibetan and Himalayan Library. http://www.thlib.org/tools/about/wiki/An%20Overview%20of%20Amdo%20%28Northeastern%20Tibet%29%20Historical%20Polities.html.

———. "The Role of Mongol Elite and Educational Degrees in the Advent of Reincarnation Lineages in Seventeenth Century Amdo." In *Tibet's Turbulent Seventeenth Century and the Tenth Karmapa*, ed. Karl Debreczeny and Gray Tuttle, 235–62. Chicago: Serindia Publications, 2016.

———. "Tibetan Buddhism Among the Mongol and Manchu Noble Families Before the Rise of Dge-Lugs Hegemony (1576–1651)." Master's thesis, Harvard University, 1996.

———. "Tibetan Buddhism at Wutai Shan in the Qing: The Chinese-language Register." *Journal of the International Association of Tibetan Studies* 6 (December 2011): 163–214.

———. "A Tibetan Buddhist Mission to the East: The Fifth Dalai Lama's Journey to Beijing, 1652–1653." In *Tibetan Society and Religion: The Seventeenth and Eighteenth Centuries*, ed. Bryan Cuevas and Kurtis Schaeffer, 65–87. Leiden: Brill, 2006.

———. *Tibetan Buddhists in the Making of Modern China*. New York: Columbia University Press, 2005.

BIBLIOGRAPHY

Tuttle, Gray, and Johan Elverskog, eds. "Wutaishan and Qing Culture." Special issue, *Journal of the International Association of Tibetan Studies* 6 (December 2011).
Tuttle, Gray, and Kurtis R. Schaeffer, eds. *The Tibetan History Reader*. New York: Columbia University Press, 2013.
Tuttle, Gray, and Lan Wu. "Tibetan Buddhist Vanguards in Mongolia, 1576–1644." Forthcoming.
Ü (Ünenci-yin) Tuyaġ-a. *Mongġol Keblel-Ün Teüke* [History of Mongolian-language printing]. Hohhot: Öbör Mongġol-un Surġan Kümüjil-ün Keblel-ün Qoriy-a, 2010.
Uspensky (Uspenskii), Vladimir L. "The 'Beijing Lamaist Centre' and Tibet in the 17th to early 20th Centuries." In *Tibet and Her Neighbors: A History*, ed. Alex McKay, 107–15. London: Thames and Hudson, 2004.
———. "Gombjab: A Tibetan Buddhist in the Capital of the Qing Empire." In *Biographies of Eminent Mongol Buddhists*, ed. Johan Elverskog, 59–69. Halle: International Institute for Tibetan and Buddhist Studies, 2008.
———. *Prince Yunli (1697–1738): Manchu Statesman and Tibetan Buddhist*. Tokyo: Institute for the Study of Languages and Cultures of Asia and Africa, 1997.
van der Kuijp, Leonard W. J. "The Dalai Lamas and the Origins of Reincarnate Lamas." In *The Tibetan History Reader*, ed. Gray Tuttle and Kurtis R. Schaeffer, 335–47. New York: Columbia University Press, 2013.
———. "Tibetan Historiography." In *Tibetan Literature: Studies in Genre*, ed. José Cabezón and Roger Jackson, 39–56. Ithaca: Snow Lion Publication, 1996.
Van Schaik, Sam. *Tibet: A History*. New Haven, CT: Yale University Press, 2011.
van Vleet, Stacey. "Medicine, Monasteries and Empire: Tibetan Buddhism and the Politics of Learning in Qing China." PhD diss., Columbia University, 2015.
Venturi, Federica. "To Protect and to Serve: The Military in Tibet as Described by the Fifth Dalai Lama." *Cahiers d'Extrême-Asie* 27, no. 1 (2018): 23–47.
Vink, Markuts P. M. "Indian Ocean Studies and the 'New Thalassology.'" *Journal of Global History* 2, no. 1 (May 2007): 41–62.
Waldron, Arthur. *The Great Wall of China: From History to Myth*. Cambridge Paperbacks: Oriental Studies, History. Cambridge: Cambridge University Press, 1998.
Waley-Cohen, Joanna. *The Culture of War in China*. London: I. B. Tauris, 2006.
———. "The New Qing History." *Radical History Review* 88, no. 1 (2004): 193–206.
Wallace, Vesna, ed. *Buddhism in Mongolian History, Culture, and Society*. Oxford: Oxford University Press, 2015.
Walsh, Michael J. "The Economics of Salvation: Toward a Theory of Exchange in Chinese Buddhism." *Journal of the American Academy of Religion* 75, no. 2 (2007): 353–82.
———. *Sacred Economics: Buddhist Monasticism and Territoriality in Medieval China*. Sheng Yen Series in Chinese Buddhist Studies. New York: Columbia University Press, 2010.
Wang Jiapeng. "Zhongzhengdian yu Qinggong zangchuan Fojiao" [Zhongzheng Hall and Tibetan Buddhism in the Qing Imperial Palace]. *Gugong Bowuyuan yuankan* [Bulletin of the National Palace Museum] 3 (1991): 58–71.
Wang Li. *Mingmo Qingchu Dalai Lama xitong yu Menggu zhubu hudong guanxi yanjiu* [Interactions between the Dalai Lama line and Mongol communities in the Ming-Qing transitional period]. Beijing: Minzu chubanshe, 2011.

Wang, Luman. "Money and Trade, Hinterland and Coast, Empire and Nation-State: An Unusual History of Shanxi Piaohao, 1820–1930." PhD diss., University of Southern California, 2014.

Wang, Xiangyun. "The Qing Court's Tibet Connection: Lcang Skya Rol Pa'i Rdo Rje and the Qianlong Emperor." *Harvard Journal of Asiatic Studies* 60, no. 1 (2000): 125–63.

———. "Tibetan Buddhism at the Court of Qing: The Life and Work of lCang-Skya Rol-Pa'i-Rdo-Rje (1717–1786)." PhD diss., Harvard University, 1995.

Wang, Xiuyu. *China's Last Imperial Frontier: Late Qing Expansion in Sichuan's Tibetan Borderlands*. Lanham, MD: Lexington Books, 2011.

Wang, Yi. "Irrigation, Commercialization, and Social Change in Nineteenth-Century Inner Mongolia." *International Review of Social History* 59, no. 2 (August 2014): 215–46.

Wang-Toutain, Françoise. "Circulation Du Savoir Entre La Chine, La Mongolie et Le Tibet Au XVIIIe Siècle: Le Prince MGon-Po Skyabs" [Circulation of knowledge between China, Mongolia, and Tibet in the 18th century: Prince mGon-Po Skyabs]. *Études Chinoises* 24 (2005): 57–111.

Watson-Verran, Helen, and David Turnbull. "Science and Other Indigenous Knowledge Systems." In *Handbook of Science and Technology Studies*, ed. Sheila Jasanoff, Gerald E. Markle, James C. Peterson, and Trevor Pinch, 115–39. Thousand Oaks, CA: Sage Publications, 1995.

Wei Kaizhao. *Yonghegong manlu* [Leisurely collections of Yonghegong]. Zhengzhou: Henan renmin chubanshe, 1985.

Weidner, Martha. Review of *Empire of Emptiness: Buddhist Art and Political Authority in Qing China*, by Patricia Berger. *Journal of Asian Studies* 62, no. 4 (November 2003): 1215–18.

Weiner, Benno. *The Chinese Revolution on the Tibetan Frontier*. Studies of the Weatherhead East Asian Institute, Columbia University. Ithaca, NY: Cornell University Press, 2020.

Weinstein, Jodi L. *Empire and Identity in Guizhou: Local Resistance to Qing Expansion*. Seattle: University of Washington Press, 2013.

Wen Ming and Luo Wenhua. "Xianruoguan gongcang cacafo zhengli yanjiu-jianjiyu 'Zhufo Pusa shengxiang zan' zhi bijiao" [Tsa-tsa statues in the Xianruo Hall and their comparisons with the Tibetan Buddhist pantheon]. *Gugong Bowuyuan yuankan* [Journal of the National Palace Museum] 5 (2009): 26–55.

Whiteman, Stephen H. "From Upper Camp to Mountain Estate: Recovering Historical Narratives in Qing Imperial Landscapes." *Studies in the History of Gardens and Designed Landscapes: An Internationally Quarterly* 33, no. 4 (October 2013): 249–79.

———. *Where Dragon Veins Meet: The Kangxi Emperor and His Estate at Rehe*. Seattle: University of Washington Press, 2020.

Willock, Nicole. "An Analysis of Jiao Yingqi's 'Report on an Expedition to Tibet (Zangcheng jilüe)' Written in 1721 and the Historical Significance of this Source Material." Master's thesis, University of Hamburg, 2001.

———. *Lineages of the Literary: Tibetan Buddhist Polymaths of Socialist China*. New York: Columbia University Press, 2021.

Wu Hung. "Emperor's Masquerade: 'Costume Portraits' of Yongzheng and Qianlong." *Orientations* 26, no. 7 (July/August 1995): 25–41.

BIBLIOGRAPHY

Wu, Jiang. *Enlightenment in Dispute: The Reinvention of Chan Buddhism in Seventeenth-Century China*. Oxford: Oxford University Press, 2008.
Wu, Lan. "Crafting Buddhist Art in Qing China's Contact Zones During the Eighteenth Century." "East-Southeast," special issue, *Journal 18: A Journal of Eighteenth-Century Art and Culture* 4 (Fall 2017). http://www.journal18.org/issue4/crafting-buddhist-art-in-qing-chinas-contact-zones-during-the-eighteenth-century/.
Wu, Shuhui. *Die Eroberung von Qinghai unter Berücksichtigung von Tibet und Khams, 1717–1727: Anhand der Throneingaben des Grossfeldherrn Nian Gengyao* [The conquest of Qinghai under the consideration of Tibet and Kham, 1717–1727: Based upon the imperial memorials of General Nian Gengyao]. Otto Harrassowitz Verlag, 1995.
Wuritu. "A Research Study on the Political Activities of the First Jebtsundamba Khutuktu." PhD diss., University of Inner Mongolia, 2010.
Wylie, Turrell V. *The Geography of Tibet According to the 'dZam-Gling-rGyas-bShad*. Roma: Istituto italiano per il Medio ed Estremo Oriente, 1962.
———. "Was Christopher Columbus from Shambhala?" *Bulletin of the Institute of China Border Area Studies* 1 (1970): 24–34.
Xu Ke. *Qing bai lei chao* [Qing petty matters anthology]. Vol. 1. 1916; repr., Beijing: Zhonghuashuju, 1984.
Yamamoto, Carl S. *Vision and Violence: Lama Zhang and the Politics of Charisma in Twelfth-Century Tibet*. Brill's Tibetan Studies Library 29. Leiden: Brill, 2012.
Yang, Shihong. *Zhuoni Tusi Lishi Wenhua* [History and culture of the Co Ne chieftains]. Lanzhou: Gansu minzu chubanshe, 2007.
Yang Ying. *Xiningfu xinzhi* [New chronicle of Xining]. Vol. 15. Xining: Qinghai renmin chubanshe, 1988.
"yi guan Yonghegong dagui" [Memory of watching the ghost festival at Yonghegong]. *Liyuan huakan* [Li Yan pictorial journal] 282 (1944): 15.
Yongdan, Lobsang. "Tibet Charts the World: Btsan Po No Mon Han's 'The Detailed Description of the World,' an Early Major Scientific Work in Tibet." In *Mapping the Modern in Tibet*, ed. Gray Tuttle, 73–134. Andiast: International Institute for Tibetan and Buddhist Studies, 2011.
Yonghegong Tangka guibao [Yonghegong Tangkha treasures]. Beijing: Zhongguo minzu sheying chubanshe, 1998.
Zelin, Madeleine. *The Magistrate's Tael: Rationalizing Fiscal Reform in Eighteenth Century Ch'ing China*. Berkeley: University of California Press, 1992.
Zha Zha. "Lidai Jiamuyang hutuketu jiating Beijing yanjiu" [A primary research on the family backgrounds of each Jamyang Zhepa]. *Zangxue yanjiu zhongxin qikan: Zhexue yu shehui kexu ban* [Journal of Tibet Nationalities Institute: Philosophy and social sciences] 27, no. 5 (September 2006): 19–25.
Zhang, Fan. "Reorienting the Sacred and Accommodating the Secular: The History of Buddhism in China (RGya Nag Chos 'byung)." *Revue d'Etudes Tibétaines* 37 (2016): 569–91.
Zhang, Shuangzhi. "Qingchao waifan tizhi nei de chaojin nianban yu chaogong zhidu" [Systems of Chaojin nianban and Chaogong in the Qing's outlying regions in the Qing]. *Qingshi yanjiu* [Qing history journal] 3 (2010).
Zhang Yuxin. *Qing zhengfu yu Lamajiao* [Qing government and Tibetan Buddhism]. Lhasa: Xizang renmin chubanshe, 1988.

——. *Qingdai Lamajiao beiwen* [Tibetan Buddhist stelae of the Qing dynasty]. Tianjin: Tianjin guji chubanshe, 1987.

Zhao, Yuntian ed. *Qianlongchao neifu chaoben "Lifanyuan zeli"* [Lifanyuan regulations in the Qing's Qianlong reign]. Beijing: Zhongguo Zangxue yanjiu zhongxin chubanshe, 2006.

——. *Qingding Daqing huidian shili: Lifanyuan* [Collected statutes of the Great Qing: Lifanyuan]. Beijing: Zhongguo Zangxue chubanshe, 2006.

Zhou Runnian. "Beijing Yonghegong yuzhi 'Lama shuo' beiwen jiaolu kaquan" [Studies of the *Proclamation on Lamas* at Beijing's Yonghegong]. *Xizang yanjiu* 3 (1991): 87–98.

Zito, Angela. *Of Body and Brush: Grand Sacrifice as Text/Performance in Eighteenth-Century China*. Chicago: University of Chicago Press, 1997.

Zhongguo wenshi ziliao jicui [Collection of Chinese literary and historical documents]. Beijing: Beijing Superstar International Technology, 2006.

INDEX

Page numbers in *italics* refer to figures and tables.

Ahmad, Zahiruddin, 181n50
Aisin Gioro: bureaucratic posts held by, 122, 141; Chongde emperor (Huang Taiji), 126; clansmen. *See* Gombjab; Yunli (Prince Guo); Yunlu (Prince Zhuang); Daoguang emperor, 72; engagement with Tibetan Buddhist social-textual communities, 118, 124–25, 140–41; Shunzhi emperor, 113. *See also* Jiaqing emperor; Kangxi emperor; Qianlong emperor; Yongzheng emperor
Akyä trülkus: appeal to certify Kumbung Jampa Ling's property, 54; second Akyä, Lobzang Tenpai Gyeltsen, 82–83
Amdo: independence of Buddhist trülkus from Amdo's official administrative operation, 57–58; Lobzang Danjin Uprising (1723), 2, 35–37, 49, 59, 105, 114; monasteries as a social force in, 55–56; monasteries in. *See* Gönlung Jampa Ling; Kumbum Jampa Ling; Labrang Monastery; Serkhok Monastery; Tongkhor Ganden Chokhor Ling; multilayered social dynamics of the area, 34–35; Qinghai (Mon. Kokonuur; Tib. tso ngön) prefecture established by the Qing, 35. *See also* Akyä trülkus; Chone principality; Zhabdrung Karpo trülku line

Barfield, Thomas J., 4
Bartholomew, Terese Tse, 107
Bartlett, Beatrice S., 122, 140
Bayly, C. A., 40
Bentor, Yael, 138
Berger, Patricia, 106, 108, 173n28
Bredon, Juliet, 69
British Empire and the British, 114, 145; advances in Central Eurasia, 153; lack of local knowledge affecting its governance, 39–40
Buddhist images: as Buddhist infrastructural mechanisms, 18, 60; cartographical references reinforcing the historical memory of Buddhist

Buddhist images (*continued*)
pilgrims, 146; convergent vision of Buddhist and secular power articulated by, 67, 109–10; as embodiments of the Buddha, 65, 67; employeed by seventh Dalai Lama to articulate Geluk presence in an imperial space, 67, 75; Gombjab's *Canon of Buddhist Iconometry*, 130–32, 132t4.1, 145–46; of Maitreya, 67; visualization of Buddhist practices facilitated by paintings, 146

Buddhist Inner Asia: followers of Tibetan Buddhism. *See* Tibetan Buddhism; "Inner Asian Buddhists" as collective term for the Qing's Inner Asian Buddhist world, 22; interconnectivity of regions, 2–3, 26–27; location of, 2

Buddhist Inner Asia–as a common ground between Qing Beijing and Lhasa: Buddhist art production as a locus of, 67, 109–10; Buddhist images used to articulate Geluk presence in an imperial space, 67, 75; cross-cultural Buddhist spaces. *See* Mount Wutai; Yonghegong; link between Beijing's Ganden Jinchak Link (Yonghegong) and Lhasa's Ganden Monastery, 76; and mandalic expansion of the Ganden Podrang, 30, 33, 115–17; Mongolian monks living alongside Tibetan Buddhist iconography and Chinese architecture in Beijing, 63; negotiated nature of, 1–4, 27–29, 50–53, 72–74, 77, 87–88, 147–49; role of the trülku practice, 35; Tibetan Buddhist knowledge network as key to, 2–3, 5, 18–26; trading network established by sojourning merchants (Ch. *lümeng shang*) in Mongolia, 113–15; Yonghegong as institutional hub, 79. *See also* Tibetan Buddhism

Buddhist knowledge network: circulation of knowledge about Buddhist sites and practices, 145–46; common ground between Qing Beijing and Lhasa established in, 2–3, 5–6, 109–10; facilitation by Geluk School's emphasis on writing and literary production, 3, 58, 127, 133, 146; Gombjab's facilitation of. *See under* Gombjab; and mandalic expansion of the Ganden Podrang, 30, 33, 115–17; Tibetan Buddhism understood as a knowledge system, 2–3, 3, 5, 18–26, 120–21, 142, 145

Buddhist material production: in Dolonnuur. *See* Dolonnuur–Art Production; interdependent nature of the Tibetan Buddhist knowledge network reflected in, 109–10; Qianlong emperor's employment of, 142, 147; as a Qing imperial enterprise, 106, 108–9; the Qing's imperial landscape as part of, 63. *See also* Buddhist images

Changkya trülku line, Gönlung Jampa Ling residence of, 48, 49n.2

Changkya trülku line–second Changkya, Ngawang Lobzang Choden, 103; monastery established in Dolonnuur, 59

Changkya trülku line–third Changkya, Rolpai Dorje: conferral of imperial tablets on Amdo monasteries requested by, 50; as an eight-year-old during Qing attack on monasteries in Amdo, 48; meeting with seventh Dalai Lama in Kham, 80; Qianlong emperor's Buddhist enterprise led by, 9, 11; second Sertri, Lobzang Tenpai Nyima as his principal teacher, 130, 136

Charleux, Isabelle, 19, 94, 183n75

Chatterjee, Indrani, 24

Chone Gönchen (Ganden Shedrub Ling in Gansu Province; Ch. Chanding Si), Ngawang Trinlé Gyatso as abbot of, 133–34

Chone Ngawang Tsultrim: abbacy of Yonghegong, 79; as a high-profile

INDEX

Buddhist trülku at Qianlong court, 95; and Lobzang Tsultrim, 95; political career in both Lhasa and Beijing, 79–80; Tsemonling trülku lineage established by, 80

Chone principality: Buddhist canon production supported by, 129, 134, 136; Makzor Gonpo as head of, 133

Chou, Wen-Shing, 5, 19

Comanche empire, 14

common ground: defined in terms of process, 1; and the dynamics of cross-cultural Buddhist Inner Asia. *See* Buddhist Inner Asia–common ground between Qing Beijing and Lhasa

cross-cultural Buddhist sphere. *See* Buddhist Inner Asia–as a common ground between Qing Beijing and Lhasa

Dalai Lama–third, Altan Khan's meeting with, 100, 101

Dalai Lama–fourth, enthronement as abbot of the Drepung Monastery, 99

Dalai Lama–fifth: Ganden Podrang government founded by, 12–13, 36; Geluk learning institutionalized by, 23, 81, 131; meeting at Khüree (modern-day Ulaanbaatar) attended by a representative of, 90

Dalai Lama–sixth, selection of, 36

Dalai Lama–seventh: forty-one tapestries commissioned to commemorate Yonghegong's transformation, 66–67; Maitreya Bodhisattva of sandalwood gifted to Yonghegong, 67; meeting with Rolpai Dorje in Kham, 80; and seventh Tatsak Jedrung, Lobzang Pelden Gyeltsen, 77, 79; yellow hats provided for monks at Yonghegong's four monastic colleges, 66

Dalai Lama–eighth: reluctance to take control of the Ganden Podrang government, 79

Dalai Lama–fourteenth, exile to India, 6

Dear, Devon, 112

Debreczeny, Karl, 146

Dergé, 128–29

Detri trülku line: third Detri, Jamyang Tubten Nyima's visit to Dolonnuur, 104, 107–8; ties to eastern Mongolian region, 104

Di Cosmo, Nicola, 159n29

discursive space: individual cross-cultural Buddhist spaces. *See* Mount Wutai; Yonghegong; interactions and negotiations between Beijing and Lhasa revealed in, 2; of the location of the Ganden Podrang government, 15–16; Mongolia as, 22; Yonghegong as, 28, 63–68, 75–76, 173n28

Dolonnuur (Tib. tso bdun): as node of convergence transcending spatial and administrative boundaries, 101; economic activity in, 111–15; Kangxi emperor's assembly of Khalkha Mongols (1691), 28, 86, 88, 93, 114; population of, 111, 113; Qing's flexible governing practices reflected in, 115–17; sixth Panchen Lama's visit to, 96–97

Dolonnuur–art production: Ayushi foundry, 108, 110, 184n90; foundries in, 104; Mañjuśri statue and other Buddhist figures produced at, 104; and Inner Asian Buddhists' demand for Buddhist artifacts, 107–8, 110–11; sculpture identified as the "Dolonnuur school," 107

Drepung Monastery: fourth Dalai Lama as abbot of, 99; Gomang Monastic College, 24, 77; as one of the "three great seats," 23

Dreyfus, Georges B. J., 15, 72

Elikhina, Yulia, and Victoria Demenova, 107

Elverskog, Johan, on Mongolian historical literature, 125

Fletcher, Joseph, on Mongolia in the nineteenth century, 112

INDEX

French, Rebecca, 15
frontiers and frontier space: as an analytical category, 4–5; as dynamic spaces, 6–7

Ganden Monastery: founding by Je Tsongkhapa, 13; as one of the "three great seats," 23
Ganden Podrang government: failure to achieve statehood in the twentieth century, 14; founding by fifth Dalai Lama, 12–13, 36; knowledge-making enterprises of, 147–48; location within a discursive space of, 15–16
Ganden Podrang government–mandalic structure: as a concept, 15–16; Geluk monastic clusters as infrastructural elements of, 22–24, 76–77, 82, 148; and interpenetration of Buddhist Inner Asia and Qing Inner Asia, 30, 33, 116–17; intertwining of mobile trülkus moored to immobile monasteries, 31, 90–91, 155–56
Geluk School: Buddhist knowledge network of, 3, 58, 146–47; dominance in Tibetan politics of, 20; "mass monasticism" system, 22–23, 76, 100–101, 148; monasteries. *See* Drepung Monastery; Ganden Monastery; Kumbum Jampa Ling; Labrang Monastery; Serkhok Monastery; Yonghegong; Qianlong emperor's support of, 7–8; textuality as a Buddhist hallmark facilitated by, 127, 133, 144, 146; "three great seats" (Sera, Ganden, and Drepung), 23; yellow hats associated with, 66. *See also* Dalai Lama; Ganden Podrang government; Gönlung Jampa Ling; Labrang Monastery; Panchen Lama
golden urn practice: institutionalization by Qianlong emperor, 8, 156; local practice exemplified by Zhabdrung Karpo trülku line's use of, 43–44
Goldstein, Melvyn, on "mass monasticism" by the Geluk, 22

Gombjab (Tib.: mGon po skyabs, 1690?–1750): Aisin Gioro clan relations of, 119; *Canon of Buddhist Iconometry*, 130–32, 132t4.1, 145–46; circulation of Tibetan Buddhist knowledge facilitated by, 118–19; *History of Buddhism in China*, 123–24, 126–27, 130, 136; intellectual genealogy defining his religious belonging established by, 126–27; Katok Ridzin Tsewang Norbu's letter to, 127–28
Gönlung Jampa Ling Monastery: cultivation of patrons from Inner Mongolia, 105; destruction during Nian Gengyao's pacification campaign, 48; location of, 61map 2
Gungtang lineage: second Gungtang, 176n67; sixth Gungtang, Jingme Tenpai Wangchuk, 168n51
Gyatso, Janet, 65, 131

Hämäläinen, Pekka, 14
Ho, Engseng, 4
Huc, Évariste Régis: on Buddhist Mongolia, 101; on Chinese craftsmen in Mongolia, 108; on Dolonnuur, 93, 111–12

Ili: Puhua Temple (formerly Lama Si) relocated to, 79; Qing conquest of, 43, 77–78, 159n30
Inner Asia: border regions. *See* frontiers and frontier space; common ground sought in. *See* Buddhist Inner Asia–common ground between Qing Beijing and Lhasa; as dynamic space open to structural and social change, 4, 18–19, 25; Oirat Zunghars as influence on. *See* Zunghars and Zungharia; rise of the Jurchen Jin polity, 148; as a term, 4, 159n29. *See also* Buddhist Inner Asia; Dolonnuur; Mongolia
Inner Asian Buddhists. *See* Buddhist Inner Asia
Inner Asia–Qing Inner Asia: cross-cultural Buddhist knowledge

INDEX

network in, 2–3, 5–6; flexible governing practices reflected in Dolonnuur, 115–17; "high territoriality" as a hallmark of Qianlong's reign, 120; impact of power brokers on regional politics within, 25, 40, 46; Kangxi emperor's conferral of titles as a means to consolidate his power in, 134; multinodal network of monasteries in, 20; nodes of convergence transcending spatial and administrative boundaries employed by, 20, 77, 147–48, 181n54; Qing patronage of selective monasteries in, 21–22; and the Qing's drive to expand as a conquest regime, 121

Ishihama Yumiko, 76

Jamyang Zhepa reincarnation line: education of successive trülku at Drepung's Gomang Monastic College, 24; first Jamyang Zhepa's construction of Labrang Tashikhyil, 21, 41, 55; Labrang Tashikhyil base of, 104; second Jamyang Zhepa, 41–42, 100; third Jamyang Zhepa, 42

Jansen, Berthe, 21

Jehol, 21; location of, 61map 2

Jiaqing emperor: golden urn practice used during his reign, 44; uncollected revenue from Yonghegong's endowed land as a problem for, 71

Kagyü School: Katok Ridzin Tsewang Norbu's letter to Gombjab, 127–28; as one of the "new schools" (Tib. Sarmapa), 192n94; Situ Panchen Chökyi Jungné, 128; tenth Zhamarpa, Chodrub Gyatso, 10

Kangxi emperor: assertion of Manchu power, 92–93; conferral of titles as a means to consolidate his power in Inner Asia, 134; meeting with the Khalkha Mongols at Dolonnuur (1691), 28, 86, 88, 93, 114; Tibetan Buddhist art appropriated by, 108–9

Khalkha and the Khalkha Mongols, 67; Bogdo Gegen Zanabazar, 106–7, 109, 110; Buddhist art produced in the "Khalkha style," 109–10; the Great Code (Mon. Yeke cayaja) formed with the Oirat confederation (1640), 89; meeting with the Kangxi emperor at Dolonnuur (1691), 28, 86, 88, 93, 114; patronage of monasteries in Dolonnuur, 99

King, Matthew W., 5, 180–81n54

Kublai Khan: Nepalese-style Tibetan Buddhist art associated with Mongol imperial authority, 108; Pakpa Lodro Gyeltsen appointed as imperial preceptor by, 11–12; Yuan state established by, 89

Kumbum Jampa Ling, 170n76; conferral of imperial tablets on (requested by Rolpai Dorje), 50; destruction by Qing troops, 49–50; main assembly hall of, 45f1.1; reclamation of its land, 53–54

Labrang Monastery (Labrang Tashikhyil): first Jamyang Zhepa's construction of, 21, 41, 55; political common ground for power negotiations facilitated at, 21

Lhasa: common ground sought with Qing Beijing. See Buddhist Inner Asia–as a common ground between Qing Beijing and Lhasa; Great Prayer Festival (Tib. Monlam Chenmo), 82; link between Beijing's Ganden Jinchak Ling (Yonghegong) and Lhasa's Ganden Monastery, 76; location of, 61map 2. See also Drepung Monastery; Ganden Podrang government

Lifanyuan: land purchased by Ayuxi for Yonghegong, 70; management of Yonghegong, 174n40

Lobzang Tsultrim: as the "Geshe from Chahar," 83; as mediator in Buddhist Inner Asia, 96; studies in Dolonnuur, 86; translation of collected works of sixth Panchen Lama, 97

INDEX

Mala, Guilaine, 189n42
monasteries: monasteries—Qing administration of, Nian Gengyao's memorial directed at restricting their power, 36–38, 43, 50–51, 155; as nodes of convergence helping transcend spatial and administrative boundaries, 20, 77, 84–85
monasteries as Buddhist infrastructural mechanisms, 18, 20–24; immobility of as a feature of, 20; monastic constitutions (Tib. *bca' yig*), 20–21; power derived from the institutional capacity of, 20–21. *See also* Yonghegong
monasteries—Qing administration of: multimodal network in Qing Buddhist Inner Asia formed by, 20; by the Office of Lama Seals and Affairs (Ch. Lama yinwu chu), 94, 179–80n23; ordination permits (Ch. *dudie*), 51–52, 169n70
Mongolia and Mongolians: Altan Khan's meeting with future third Dalai Lama, 100, 101; damage to society inflicted by monastic institutions (in the nineteenth century), 112; as a discursive space, 22, 115–17; Gombjab's Mongolian aristocratic upbringing, 126; "origin of Buddhism" (Tib. *chos 'byung*) genre of literature in, 124–5; power enabled by the institution of trülku, 99; trading network established by sojourning merchants (Ch. *lümeng shang*), 113–15. *See also* Dolonnuur; Khalkha and the Khalkha Mongols; Kublai Khan; Oirat confederation; Qoshots; Zunghars and Zungharia
Mongolia and Mongolians-banners and bannermen: Faššan (Fashishan), 145; patronage of monasteries in Dolonnuur, 99; payments to support monk disciples at Yonghegong, 72–73; and the Qoshots in Amdo, 43
Mongolia and Mongolians-Chahar: Ligdan Kahn's venture to produce a Buddhist canon, 129; Ligdan Khan as the last ruler of, 90; Lobzang Tsultrim remembered as the "Geshe from Chahar," 83; marriage of Ligdan Kahn's widows to Manchu imperial family, 126
Mongol Yuan (1279–1368), Tibetan Buddhism during, 3, 12
Mount Wutai: as a discursive space, 5, 19; as a node of convergence helping transcend spatial and administrative boundaries for the Qing, 181n54

Naquin, Susan, 175n54
Nationalist government: concept of ethnicity deployed by, 153; monastic landholding rights and economic resources enabled by, 53–54, 56
Nayancheng, on issues faced by the Qing's imperial rule in Amdo, 44–47
Nian Gengyao: court memorial to the Yongzheng emperor proposing restrictions on Buddhist institutions, 36–38, 43, 50–51, 155; pacification campaign to defeat the Oirat Qoshot in Amdo (1723), 10, 49
Nietupski, Paul, 43, 105–6
Ning, Chia, 174n40
Nyingma School: Mindröling Monastery, 24; tantric texts considered treasures by, 144

Oidtmann, Max, 19, 168n50, 179–80n23
Oirat confederation: as a driving force in shaping Inner Asian history, 16–18; the Great Code (Mon. Yeke cayaja) formed with the Khalkha Mongols (1640), 89; Oirat Zunghars. *See* Zunghars and Zungharia
Ottoman empire, local intermediaries employed by, 25, 53

Panchen Lama, golden urn practice presided over, 8
Panchen Lama-fifth, Oirat Zunghars offerings to pay respect to, 50

INDEX

Panchen Lama-sixth: and Tenth Zhamarpa, 10; translation of his collected works by Lobzang Tsultrim, 97; travels to Dolonnuur en route to Beijing, 95, 96–97
Panchen Lama-seventh: Jampel Chokyi Tendzin Trinle referred to European sources by, 143; Kentsun Gyatso's selection as the fifth Zhabdrung Karpo confirmed by, 44
Perdue, Peter C., 16, 17, 162n57
Prince Guo. *See* Yunli
Prince Zhuang. *See* Yunlu
Puhua Monastery in Zungharia, location of, 61map 2

Qianlong emperor: Buddhist material production employed by, 142, 147; Buddhist notions of belonging to Buddhist Inner Asia transformed during, 63; campaigns against the Zunghar state, 16–17; golden urn practice institutionalized by, 8, 156; "high territoriality" as a hallmark of his reign, 120; imperial territorial expansions completed by, 6, 7, 9; legitimation of his right to rule, 121
Qianlong emperor-*Proclamation on Lamas*: Geluk School called the Yellow Hat School in, 66; "to propitiate the Mongols" as a rhetorical device in, 9; stele engraved with its text erected at Yonghegong, 7, 60, 82; trülku practice disparaged in, 8–9, 11–12, 79
Qing dynasty: administration of monasteries. *See* monasteries—Qing administration of; anti-Qing and anti-Manchu movements of Nationalist revolutionaries, 153; emperors. *See* Jiaqing emperor; Kangxi emperor; Qianlong emperor; Yongzheng emperor; impact of Tibetan Buddhism on Qing imperial governance, 122–23, 128, 130; Inner Asia governed by. *See* Inner Asia-Qing Inner Asia; ministry of minority affairs. *See* Lifanyuan; ruling class. *See* Aisin Gioro; territorial expansions and power consolidation, 6, 7, 17, 120–22
Qoshots: banner led by the Zhabdrung Karpo trülku, 43–44; defeat of the Zunghars, 36; Güshri Khan, 36; Lobzang Danjin Uprising (1723), 2, 35–37, 49, 59, 105, 114; Qing defeat of, 10, 27, 32–33, 35, 59, 87

Rawski, Evelyn S., 4
Reynolds, Valrae, 109
Rolpai Dorje. *See* Changkya trülku line-third Changkya, Rolpai Dorje

Sakya School: disunion of, 12; as one of the "new schools" (Tib. Sarmapa), 192n94; Pakpa Lodro Gyeltsen appointed as imperial preceptor by Kublai Khan, 11–12
Schwieger, Peter, on the institutional history of Tibetan trülku, 19, 106
Serkhok Monastery (also Tsenpo Gon or Dga' ldan dam chos gling, Ch. Guanghui Si), 48, 50; Jampel Chokyi Tendzin Trinle as abbot of, 143
Sertri reincarnation lineage, second Sertri, Lobzang Tenpai Nyima, 95, 103, 129–30, 136, 137, 189n42
Sullivan, Brenton, 20, 105

Tambiah, Stanley, galactic scheme of political structures, 14–16
Tatsak Jedrung lineage, seventh Tatsak Jedrung, Lobzang Pelden Gyeltsan, 77, 78, 79
Tibetan Buddhism: in Inner Asia. *See* Buddhist Inner Asia; as a knowledge system, 2–3, 3, 5, 18–26, 120–21, 142, 145; limitations caused by categorizing it as a religion, 141–42; during the Mongol Yuan, 3; Qing imperial patronage and appropriation of, 3, 108–9, 115–18, 124–25, 140–41; schools. *See* Geluk School; Kagyü School; Nyingma

INDEX

Tibetan Buddhism (*continued*) School; Sakya School. *See also* Mount Wutai
Tongkhor Ganden Chokhor Ling, 42–43, 52, 181n50
Tongkhor reincarnation line: Ngawang Sonam Gyatso (fifth trülku of), 41, 42, 54, 100; Yonten Gyatso (second trülku of), 100
Townsend, Dominique, 24, 197n28
transregional studies: binary metropole-periphery model eschewed by, 5; frontier zones reconsidered as dynamic spaces, 6–7
trülku lineages: Chahan nomonhan lineage (also transcribed as Čagan Nomunhan), 45–46; independence of Buddhist trülkus from Amdo's official administrative operation, 57–58; influence in Qing handling of Tibet, 80; institutional history of, 19, 106; Mongol power over monastic and political contestations in Tibet enabled by, 96, 99; practice of drawing lots. *See* golden urn practice; Qianlong's disparagement of, 8–9, 11–12, 79; Tibetan agency in the selection of, 19; and wealth and religious economy of monasteries, 54–55. *See also* Changkya trülku line; Dalai Lama; Detri trülku line; Gungtang lineage; Jamyang Zhepa reincarnation line; Panchen Lama; Sertri trülkus; Tatsak Jedrung lineage; Tongkhor reincarnation line; Tsemonling; Zhabdrung Karpo trülku line
Tsai, Wei-chieh, 112
Tsemonling, trülku lineage established by Ngawang Tsultrim, 80
Tsenpo Mindrol Nominhan, Jampel Chokyi Tenzin Trinle: world geography text by, 143, 144; writing process of, 143
Tsultemin, Uranchimeg, 67, 109, 110, 168n50, 184n90

Tukwan lineage: second Tukwan, Ngawang Chökyi Gyatso, 136; third Tukwan, Lobzang Chokyi Nyima, 50

Venturi, Federica, 13

Wallace, Vesna, 163n71
Weiner, Benno, 153
Whiteman, Stephen H., 85

Yonghegong (Ganden Jinchak Ling): as a node of convergence transcending spatial and administrative boundaries, 82, 84–85; architectural design of, 64f2.1, 68; the Buddhist knowledge network facilitated by, 75–76; as a discursive space, 28, 63–68, 75–76, 173n28; as a Geluk institution, 60, 76; incorporation under the Department of the Imperial Household, 62; land acquired as "incense-lamp land," 70–71, 174n38; land acquisition practices, 70–71, 174n40; main assembly hall, 73f2.2; monastic support from the Mongolian banners, 72–73; monastic wealth of, 68–75; monk population and monastic life at, 69, 73–74, 175n54; as part of the Qing's imperial landscape, 63; as princely residence of Yinzhen (future Yongzheng emperor), 62; Qing-Tibet relations influenced by Buddhist dignitaries at, 79; seventh Tatsak Jedrung as abbot of, 78; stele bearing Qianlong's *Proclamation on Lamas. See* Qianlong emperor–*Proclamation on Lamas*; uncollected revenue from its endowed land as problematic, 71
Yongzheng emperor: Nian Gengyao's court memorial proposing restrictions on Buddhist institutions, 36–38, 43, 50–51, 155; Nian Gengyao's pacification

INDEX

campaign to defeat the Qoshot in Amdo (1723), 10; Yonghegong as his former residence, 62

Yuan dynasty. *See* Mongol Yuan

Yunli (Prince Guo, 1797–1738): administrative posts held by, 62, 134–35; Aisin Gioro clan relations of, 29, 119–20; circulation of Tibetan Buddhist knowledge facilitated by, 118–20, 137–38; embrace of multiple Buddhist traditions, 137; shaping of the Qing imperial agenda, 138

Yunlu (Prince Zhuang, 1695–1767): multilingual texts on Buddhist art production by, 140; political posts held by, 140, 191n71; preface to the *Canon of Buddhist Iconometry*, 132

Zhabdrung Karpo trülku line, 43–44; Lhamo Dechen Monastery as the seat of, 43, 51f1.3

Zunghars and Zungharia: defeat of Khalkha Mongols, 93; offerings made at Kumbum Jampa Ling on their way to Central Tibet, 50; Oirat confederation as a driving force in shaping Inner Asia, 16–18; Qing campaign in Ili, 43, 77–78, 159n30; Qing-Zunghar wars, 16, 17, 78, 159n30. *See also* Ili; Puhua Monastery

STUDIES OF THE WEATHERHEAD EAST ASIAN INSTITUTE
COLUMBIA UNIVERSITY

Selected Titles

(Complete list at: weai.columbia.edu/content/publications)

Policing China: Street-Level Cops in the Shadow of Protest, by Suzanne Scoggins. Cornell University Press, 2021.

Mobilizing Japanese Youth: The Cold War and the Making of the Sixties Generation, by Christopher Gerteis. Cornell University Press, 2021.

Middlemen of Modernity: Local Elites and Agricultural Development in Modern Japan, by Christopher Craig. University of Hawai'i Press, 2021.

Isolating the Enemy: Diplomatic Strategy in China and the United States, 1953–1956, by Tao Wang. Columbia University Press, 2021.

A Medicated Empire: The Pharmaceutical Industry and Modern Japan, by Timothy M. Yang. Cornell University Press, 2021.

Dwelling in the World: Family, House, and Home in Tianjin, China, 1860–1960, by Elizabeth LaCouture. Columbia University Press, 2021.

Disunion: Anticommunist Nationalism and the Making of the Republic of Vietnam, by Nu-Anh Tran. University of Hawai'i Press, 2021.

Made in Hong Kong: Transpacific Networks and a New History of Globalization, by Peter Hamilton. Columbia University Press, 2021.

China's influence and the Center-periphery Tug of War in Hong Kong, Taiwan and Indo-Pacific, by Brian C.H. Fong, Wu Jieh-min, and Andrew J. Nathan. Routledge, 2020.

The Power of the Brush: Epistolary Practices in Chosŏn Korea, by Hwisang Cho. University of Washington Press, 2020.

On Our Own Strength: The Self-Reliant Literary Group and Cosmopolitan Nationalism in Late Colonial Vietnam, by Martina Thucnhi Nguyen. University of Hawai'i Press, 2020.

A Third Way: The Origins of China's Current Economic Development Strategy, by Lawrence Chris Reardon. Harvard University Asia Center, 2020.

Disruptions of Daily Life: Japanese Literary Modernism in the World, by Arthur M. Mitchell. Cornell University Press, 2020.

Recovering Histories: Life and Labor after Heroin in Reform-Era China, by Nicholas Bartlett. University of California Press, 2020.

Figures of the World: The Naturalist Novel and Transnational Form, by Christopher Laing Hill. Northwestern University Press, 2020.

Arbiters of Patriotism: Right Wing Scholars in Imperial Japan, by John Person. University of Hawai'i Press, 2020.

The Chinese Revolution on the Tibetan Frontier, by Benno Weiner.
Cornell University Press, 2020.

Making It Count: Statistics and Statecraft in the Early People's Republic of China,
by Arunabh Ghosh. Princeton University Press, 2020.

Tea War: A History of Capitalism in China and India, by Andrew B. Liu.
Yale University Press, 2020.

Revolution Goes East: Imperial Japan and Soviet Communism, by Tatiana Linkhoeva.
Cornell University Press, 2020.

*Vernacular Industrialism in China: Local Innovation and Translated
Technologies in the Making of a Cosmetics Empire, 1900-1940*, by Eugenia Lean.
Columbia University Press, 2020.

Fighting for Virtue: Justice and Politics in Thailand, by Duncan McCargo.
Cornell University Press, 2020.

Beyond the Steppe Frontier: A History of the Sino-Russian Border, by Sören Urbansky.
Princeton University Press, 2020.

GPSR Authorized Representative: Easy Access System Europe, Mustamäe tee 50, 10621 Tallinn, Estonia, gpsr.requests@easproject.com

www.ingramcontent.com/pod-product-compliance
Lightning Source LLC
Chambersburg PA
CBHW022050290426
44109CB00014B/1042